"WHAT WENT ON
INSIDE THE GERMAN WAR MACHINE
DURING WORLD WAR II...
AUTHENTIC AND DRAMATIC"

"The author gathered material for this valuable book from the files of the German general staff and from the letters, diaries and memoirs of generals and diplomats, common soldiers and commercial travelers who saw events behind the scenes and on three war fronts.

"The Fall of Fortress Europe is the story of madness and megalomania taking flight on the wings of Valkyrie. The madness, of course, is Adolf Hitler's."
—*Indianapolis Star*

The Crossroads of World History Series
Edited by Orville Prescott

THE
FALL
OF
FORTRESS
EUROPE

BY FRED MAJDALANY

CURTIS
BOOKS

MODERN LITERARY EDITIONS PUBLISHING COMPANY
NEW YORK, N.Y.

For Sheila and Emma

CONTENTS

Part One

MOSCOW: THE FIRST CRACK

(November 1941-August 1942)

Chapter 1

THE SPECTER OF NAPOLEON—
AND THE U.S.A.

☐ The strip of sometimes turbulent water, three hundred miles long, which passes between England and France from the Atlantic Ocean to the North Sea—funnelling from a width of one hundred miles at the Atlantic end to a mere twenty at the other—is called the English Channel by the British, by the French simply La Manche.

The choice of name is not, as Frenchmen sometimes teasingly suggest, yet another example of characteristic British arrogance but reflects with precision the relative importance of the Channel in the history, the psychology and the consciousness of the two nations.

To the people of France, historically a land power, the the Channel is simply the way to England. To the British, immemorially a sea power, it is more than the simple converse of that. It is their way to the whole world, both a threshold and a barrier. Above all it is the protective, almost mystical, moat that has spared their islands from foreign invasion since 1066.

Three times has this narrow waterway saved Britain from an all-powerful ruler determined to complete the subjugation of Europe by the addition of this last reluctant prize to his conquests. In 1588 it was Philip II and his Armada, in 1805 Napoleon and his Grande Armée, in 1940 it was Adolf Hitler and the most powerful army the world had yet seen.

In June 1940 Hitler, whose invasion of Poland on September 1, 1939, had precipitated the Second World War, could look back with satisfaction on what his armies had achieved for him in only nine months. Poland, Norway, Denmark, Holland, Belgium and France had all been conquered (Austria and Czechoslovakia had been annexed by blackmail the year before the war): the British Army had been "driven from the shores of Europe forever": Hitler's irresistible panzer divisions now commanded the Channel coast.

The climactic phase of this stupendous victory in the west had been a fifty-six-day *blitzkrieg* that had culminated in the surrender of France and her great army; in the retreat of the

British Expeditionary Force back to England in anything that would float, ranging from large warships to tiny weekend yachts; and Hitler, like Napoleon before him, gazing across the Channel after them.

Never, it seemed, had "This fortress built by Nature for herself Against infection and the hand of war" been so wide open: Nor England been so completely at the mercy of a conqueror whom nothing had yet stopped. Yet nothing had fundamentally changed. Even in the age of the tank and the airplane and unprecedented mechanization of all the weapons of war the English Channel was still a formidable moat. In 1940 it was enough to deter Hitler as it had deterred Napoleon. For Britain had command of the sea and Hitler's Luftwaffe failed (in the Battle of Britain) to gain him the command of the air that might have offset his weakness on the water. Without sea or air supremacy he saw that an invasion was not feasible and by the summer's end had abandoned the project. The Channel had won again. But from now on there was a difference.

The moat was still good but it was no longer a private moat behind which the British could make faces at the world. For the first time in history it was a German moat protecting the mainland of occupied Europe—conquered in less than a year —from those who might one day wish to liberate it. In less than a twelvemonth the mechanized legions of Adolph Hitler had driven the Western frontier of the Third Reich to the Channel coast and the Channel ports were now German frontier stations. Until further notice it was the German Channel and this was where the final reckoning would eventually have to come; in this no-man's water between armed camps; between Great Britain and what was now, in all respects that mattered, Germany. It was from the British side that invasion would at some time or other have to be launched if Hitler's dream of a thousand-year reich was not to become an iron reality.

The quite irrational certainty that they would one day go back was at once a tribute to the deep faith and stubborn character of the British people and the aggressive and inspiring leadership of Winston Churchill. Almost before the last British soldiers were back from Dunkirk plans were being considered for a programme of raids on the now-occupied French coast. Within three weeks of Dunkirk the first of these raids took place. It was a well-meant but amateur improvisation that achieved nothing.

The intention was to send a raiding force of two hundred

to land at four points on a twenty-mile stretch of coast west of Bologne to bring back information about German defences and, if possible, prisoners. But only enough suitable boats were available to take half the intended number and each of the four landing parties eventually set off in two motor launches manned by civilians. Near the French coast the four pairs of boats dispersed and made for their allotted landing beaches.

One party landed without difficulty on a deserted stretch of sand dunes where they were able to wander at will for some time without hearing anyone or anything, after which they returned to their boats and came home. Another found that the place where they had to come ashore was an enemy seaplane anchorage. They were quickly spotted and withdrew without attempting to land. The third group landed and made a brief reconnaissance but while re-embarking were detected by a sentry who fired and managed to wound one of them slightly—the raid's only casualty. The fourth group came nearest to achieving anything. They surprised two sentries and killed them both but were so carried away by this success that no one remembered to take a uniform identification or to search the bodies for documents.

The four parties safely made their separate ways back to England but the seal was set on a somewhat naive performance when one group, trying to make a triumphant landing at Folkestone, was detained by naval police outside the harbour for more than an hour because they could not establish their identity. For all its innocent absurdity the action was nonetheless a symbolic gesture. It not only reaffirmed the British conviction that they would one day go back but also defined cross-Channel invasion as the inevitable climactic theme of the war. To win this war somebody would eventually have to successfully invade somebody across the English Channel. In June 1940 the odds seemed to be on Germany. The British "symbolic gesture" on the night of June 24 was a reminder that this would not always be so. It was the prototype of the Commando raids that in the next two years were to harass Hitler's long European coastline and keep the Führer in a constant state of awareness of its vulnerability even when this could not matter.

Even in 1941, when the invasion of England had finally been shelved and he had made the momentous and fatal decision to redirect his armies eastwards in a gigantic onslaught on Russia, Hitler was still keeping a wary eye on the English Channel. At the beginning of December of that year the sweeping successes of the German armies in Russia had

14

brought Field-Marshal Ritter von Leeb's Army Group North to the outskirts of Leningrad; Field-Marshal Fedor von Bock's Army Group Centre to the outer suburbs of Moscow; and Field-Marshal Gerd von Rundstedt's Army Group South to the Don and the threshold of the Caucasus, with most of the rich and fertile Ukraine behind it. Marshal Georgi Zhukov's counteroffensive, which was to save Moscow and inflict on the Germans their first reverse after six months of seemingly irresistible success, had not yet opened. Yet Hitler was anxiously concerning himself with his back door in the West—a back door that had become increasingly remote.

In October he had ordered [1] the "build-up and defence of the English Channel Islands": appending to this órder the comment that "large-scale English operations against the Western occupied areas remain unlikely . . . [but] . . . account must be taken of the possibility that the English may at any time carry out isolated attacks as the result of pressure from their eastern allies and for political and propaganda reasons; in particular they may attempt to recapture the Channel Islands which are of considerable importance for our escort traffic."

Then, on December 14, the Führer made another personal policy decision without consultation or discussion with his staff. The Operations Staff of OKW (Oberkommando der Wehrmacht) were told to prepare an order[2] "for the construction of a 'new West Wall' to assure the protection of the Arctic, North Sea and Atlantic coasts." Its strategic object was "to assure protection against any landing operation even of very considerable strength with the employment of the smallest number of static forces." In priority of construction Norway was to come first followed by the coast of France and Belgium which was divided into the following three sectors: first, the area between the mouths of the Scheldt and the Seine, the area south of Brest and the area from Quiberon to the Gironde; secondly, the Normandy and Brittany peninsulars; thirdly, the coast of Holland and the west and north coasts of Jutland; and finally, the German Bight. Only the Baltic coasts were excluded from this comprehensive coverage and Hitler felt confident enough to direct that the existing fortifications there should be dismantled.

This order, according to General Walter Warlimont who as assistant to Chief of Operations at Supreme Headquarters had to contribute to its working out in detail, was the first appearance in broad terms of Hitler's subsequent "Fortress Europe." The most curious feature of it was that the first outline plans worked out were, according to Warlimont, based on the assumption that Russia would shortly have been defeated. Hitler had not yet been shaken in his belief that a rapid defeat of Russia was the essential preliminary to a final reckoning with Britain.

This renewal of concern for the Western Front came in the midst of a succession of dramatic developments that were to transform the whole prospect of the war which, till then, had gone entirely Hitler's way.

On the eve of Operation Barbarossa, the invasion of Russia, Hitler had made his much-quoted prediction *The world will hold its breath!* and no doubt most of the world did. But the Western world at any rate and Britain in particular, so far from holding their breath exhaled it in the most cosmic sigh of deep relief that was ever heard: though this as it were strategic relief was shadowed for the next five months by considerable tactical anxiety as one overwhelming German victory followed another and it looked as though Hitler's boasts might be made good. Then in November the Russian winter, striking earlier than usual, gave the now fully extended German armies their first taste of fighting in temperatures that rapidly sank to thirty degrees below zero. Oil froze in the vehicles. Tractors and tanks, trying to drag heavy guns out of frozen mud, failed to shift them or pulled them apart broken. No winter equipment had been provided for a campaign that had not been expected to last this long. German casualties in six months were more than 750,000.

As the offensives on the Eastern Front in turn froze to a halt, with appalling hardship and misery to the invaders who were unprepared for it, the German soldiers suddenly began to remember with chilling clarity all the half-forgotten horrors they had ever heard or read or been told at school about Napoleon's retreat from Moscow. In the officers' messes books containing descriptive accounts of what happened to the Grande Armée in 1812 were passed round and devoured with a kind of avid sickly dread. The generals pressed for a tactical withdrawal to a tenable line a little way back where they could consolidate their gains and dig in for the winter. They were sharply snubbed for even mentioning the idea.

With Leningrad and Moscow still untaken, von Rundstedt's Southern Army Group made a desperate last attempt to reach Rostov, so-called gateway to the Caucasus, at the mouth of the Don. A few tanks of General Field-Marshal Paul von Kleist's Seventh Panzer Army (von Rundstedt's armoured spearhead) managed to reach the town but had to withdraw.

This withdrawal from Rostov on November 29 by von Rundstedt's Army Group South was the first the Germans had so far had to make on the Eastern Front and it started the dramatic sequence of events that transformed the prospect of the war. It brought an angry intervention from Hitler who ordered von Rundstedt to stand firm. The Field-Marshal signaled back that he would resign rather than pass on this order. He was curtly told that his resignation was accepted.

One week later, on December 6, Marshal Zhukov counter-attacked with a hundred fresh divisions of whose existence the Germans had been unaware, took von Bock by surprise, saved Moscow and even threatened for a time to force a general German retreat all along the front. Hitler's reaction was a ruthless reaffirmation that there was to be no retreat: "The army is not to retire a single step. Every man must fight where he stands." Two more generals went the way of von Rundstedt for authorizing local withdrawals: the most brilliant and renowned of the panzer generals, Heinz Guderian, and another panzer general, Erich Hoeppner, who was not merely relieved, like the other two, of his command but also dismissed from the service, stripped of his rank and decorations and forbidden even to wear uniform. Some German military historians (e.g. General von Tippelskirch) have maintained that Hitler's "no withdrawal" order saved the German army in a moral crisis that might have deteriorated into panic retreat. Others (e.g. Rudolf Hofmann) that it merely caused the troops heavier casualties and greater suffering as, from a position only a short distance back, they could have defended themselves against a numerically superior enemy more economically and easily. The new Russian army and the Russian winter caused grievous casualties and suffering but the Germans held on. Moscow had been saved. But there was no Russian breakthrough.

The day after Zhukov launched his December counteroffensive, the Japanese made their crippling attack on the United States Navy at Pearl Harbor. Hitler had gained a formidable new ally in Southeast Asia. He took the earliest opportunity to ensure that he had also acquired an even more formidable new enemy. Undaunted by the implications of what he was doing, he hastened off to Berlin and on December 11 personally declared war on the U.S.A. and celebrated this event with a violent speech in the Reichstag. It was the second of the two colossal aberrations in Hitler's thinking that it never seemed to occur to him that America's entry into the war alongside Britain placed its final issue beyond any possible

17

doubt. (The first had been the sublime effrontery of imagining that Russia could be polished off in six to eight weeks as a preliminary step to forcing Britain to come to terms.)

The curious underestimation of America was based on a classically Hitlerian blend of paranoia, megalomania, manic racial and social prejudices, and the sheer ignorance of a man without breeding or education who had never travelled. He was intoxicated by the thought that the conflict, *his* conflict, now embraced the whole world. In the course of the December 11 speech he said [3]: "I can only be grateful to Providence that it entrusted me with the leadership in this historic struggle which for the next five hundred or a thousand years, will be described as decisive not only for the history of Germany but for the whole of Europe and indeed the whole world . . . A historical revision on a unique scale has been imposed on us by the Creator."

To his staff he sneered at the soldiers of the United States, declaring them to be a "bunch of rowdies" lacking the ideals to carry them through a crisis.[4] A few days before in a conversation with Mussolini he had spoken of the "Jewish clique which surrounds Roosevelt and exploits the American people." He easily convinced himself that America, with its racial mixture, was not to be taken seriously as a military proposition. It was a Jewish-dominated decadent democracy and Roosevelt was a tool of the Jews.

The speech gave him a chance to air all his American prejudices to the point of frenzy but not overlooking the bogus sob of the persecution complex:[5]

> I understand only too well that a world-wide distance separates Roosevelt's ideas and mine. Roosevelt comes from a rich family and belongs to the class whose path is smoothed in the democracies. I was only the child of a small poor family and had to fight my way by work and industry.

Blinded by his own masturbatory rhetoric Hitler, normally no fool in the realities of war, could ignore for the moment such considerations as America's huge availability of manpower and her pre-eminent industrial and technological know-how. Thus it happened that Hitler actually welcomed the United States as an enemy at the very time when his previously triumphant Russian offensive was meeting its first setback. Paranoia could scarcely do better than that.

Three days later—on December 14—the manic-depressive

pendulum swung to the other extreme; to sober and realistic reflection on the significance of what had happened in the previous few days.

It was then that he began to worry about his Atlantic coast-line and told his Operations Chief at OKW to prepare an order for "a new West Wall."

Chapter 2

THE WOLF'S LAIR

□ It could be said that this first fortnight in December 1941 —when the Russians administered to the hitherto victorious German armies their first reverse in the East, and in the West the great weight of the U.S.A. was for the first time overtly ranged alongside Great Britain—was for Hitler's Germany the very beginning of the end, albeit an end that would still be long deferred. The chips were down. There had not after all been the speedy conquest of Russia prior to a final settlement with Britain. Germany was now wholly and irrevocably involved in the war on two fronts that had long been the night-mare of her leaders. And to those among his highly able generals and staff officers who had seen it coming, it merely underlined and italicized the writing on the wall when, on December 21, General Field-Marshal Walther von Brauchitsch, the Commander-in-Chief of the Army, was dismissed and Hitler himself took his place. Nor did it afford them any comfort at all when the Army's new C-in-C made the early pronouncement, recorded by General Franz von Halder in his diary:

> Anyone can do the little job of directing operations in war. The task of the Commander-in-Chief is to educate the Army to be a National Socialist. I do not know any Army general who can do this as I want it done. I have therefore decided to take over command of the Army myself.[1]

It was one of the few compliments, even if it was unintentional, ever paid by the Führer to the General Staff. In fact

19

von Brauchitsch had never been an effective C-in-C as he could not stand up to Hitler and had been utterly worn out by his faltering attempts through the years to do so. When the campaign had begun to run into trouble the strain had proved too much for him and after a heart attack he had asked to be relieved. But it was a month before his request had been granted.

At this point it will be of interest to give some idea of the location and set-up from which Hitler's war was being guided through its first organic check.

Supreme Headquarters of the Armed Forces (Oberkommando der Wehrmacht—OKW) had moved thirty-six hours after the invasion of Russia on June 22, 1941, to a prepared camp in the forest of Görlich a few miles east of the small town of Rastenburg in East Prussia. It was one of those damp northern forests which belong in the symphonies of Sibelius and the mysticism of Nordic folklore. The silence and the remoteness of OKW from the fighting contrasted eerily with the thunder and lightning of the events, several hundred miles to the east, over which it exercised control in formal orders and directives. General Walter Warlimont, Assistant Chief of the Operations Staff, has described his early impressions of the headquarters.[2]

The journey from Berlin by special train took thirteen hours before depositing its complement at the humble wayside halt that was now for the time being the most exalted rail terminal in the Greater Reich.

The headquarters consisted of two compounds half a mile apart and separated by the road. Each compound was entirely sealed off by high barbed-wire and in the cover of the forest all buildings and installations were wholly invisible from the road. HQ Compound One housed Hitler and his immediate entourage of State and Party officials and the highest officers of the Wehrmacht—notably Field-Marshal Wilhelm Keitel, the Chief of Staff, and General Alfred Jodl, the Chief of Operations. The military complement also included Colonel Schmundt, Hitler's personal military aide, and a newly appointed resident historian, Colonel Scherff. Hitler's own hut and bunker were at the northernmost end of the area. All the windows faced north. This was usual with the Führer who, true to his Nordic self, disliked the sun.

In HQ Compound Two, where the less eminent had to live and work, most of the offices were in wooden huts ranged round a country inn which in peacetime had been a popular rendezvous for the Sunday outings of the people of Rastenburg. Warlimont was disconcerted by the completeness of the furnishings and fittings which did not accord with his idea of a Field headquarters.

> He thought it looked as if the regulations governing the Berlin Ministries had been followed as regards size of rooms, number of windows and furnishings. Even more remarkable was a semiunderground construction looking like a long railway sleeping car with a row of doors side by side; this proved to contain additional offices and sleeping accommodation for the officers; I even had a double room. The concrete walls were covered with wooden panelling painted in cheerful colours; there were built-in cupboards, glazed basins and baths with water laid on, central heating and every type of electrical gadget.

Warlimont was the first, a few nights later, "to get out of this catacomb" and install himself in the special train which had brought him and his party from Berlin and was still in the station. Later he moved into the Inn where he set up a "simple type of mess" for the officers of his section who worked in the office huts nearby. He does not mention who eventually used the bathrooms which initially offended his sense of what is proper to a field headquarters. It may be presumed, however, that Warlimont and his fellow members of Section L must have overcome their purist scruples and from time to time used them. Unless they left them for the Party officials they claimed to despise.

Army High Command (OKH—Oberkommando des Heeres) was an hour's journey along the road and a little farther along still was Air Force High Command (OKL—Oberkommando der Luftwaffe) presided over by Reichsmarschall Hermann Goering. Navy High Command (OKM—Oberkommando der Kriegsmarine) were in Berlin.

Hitler himself chose the schoolboyish codename by which the headquarters was known—the Wolf's Lair (*Wolfschanze*). Others besides General Warlimont found the headquarters in the lonely detachment of the forest depressing. It was altogether too much for Count Galeazzo Ciano, the Italian Foreign Minister as well as the son-in-law of Hitler's ally and friend Mussolini. After a visit to the Wolf's Lair to see his German opposite number Ribbentrop Ciano recorded the following entry in his diary:[3]

The atmosphere is heavy. To the bad news there should perhaps be added the sadness of that damp forest and the boredom of collective living in the Command barracks. There isn't a spot of colour, not one vivid note. Waiting-rooms filled with people smoking, eating, chatting. Kitchen odour, smell of uniforms, of boots. All this is in great measure unnecessary, at least for a mass of people who have no reason to be here. First among them is Ribbentrop, who compels the greater number of his employees to live a senseless troglodite life which in fact impedes his normal work as Foreign Minister.

But that was written a year later in December 1942, by which time the painted panels on the concrete walls that had offended General Warlimont must have endured a good deal of wear and tear and, moreover, the news from the Front was gloomier. In any case the gloom and damp of a northern forest are never calculated to bring out the best in a volatile Roman temperament.

It was one of the difficulties of the German generals that they were beholden not only to their own immediate Army bosses at OKH but also to the all-highest at OKW who frequently held conflicting views. With Hitler now actively running both headquarters there was less chance for the Army to get on with running its own business while OKW's back was turned or temporarily distracted by news from other fronts.

To begin with, the theory was that OKH was concerned with the direction of the Eastern Front while OKW handled all the other fronts and co-ordinated their planning with the main front in Russia. But as time went on Hitler tended more and more to interfere with the actual conduct of operations, issuing orders direct from OKW and by-passing his "own" Army HQ, OKH, altogether. The chief sufferer from this schizophrenic exercise of command was General Franz Halder, the Chief of Staff of the Army at OKH. Unlike any other Army Chief of Staff, who is normally the Army's top man and chief military adviser of the Head of State, Halder was further responsible to the higher Armed Forces Headquarters OKW, with its own Chief of Staff, Field-Marshal Keitel, who owed his position to his talent for agreeing with Hitler. The fact that after December 29 Hitler was common to both OKW and OKH increased rather than relieved the confusion as there was constant tension between the two staffs and Hitler himself frequently communicated direct with commanders in the field behind OKH's back.

Halder was in the opinion of his professional peers "The personification of the highest tradition of the German General Staff, both in knowledge and judgment, in style and approach"—the highest mark of approval which a German officer can achieve, yet when he attended the Hitler conferences at OKW it was almost as a stranger of little account that he had to face what the fighting generals now called "the military bureau of Corporal Hitler." Halder would come over from OKH for the morning conference but would not appear until Hitler and the OKW senior staff had run over the ground in the light of Jodl's general report.

Halder would now present a more detailed situation report which would be considered with a larger scale map (but still only 1:300,000) and he would find that Hitler's mind was already made up on most of the relevant issues.

In the evenings there would be a further conference when Hitler would hold forth at tedious length, breaking off occasionally to have long telephone conversations with commanders at the Front. Another difficulty of the evening conferences was the number of hangers-on of all sorts, party officials and suchlike—who had no responsibility for the conduct of operations but who regarded the conferences as a sort of free-for-all in which they could chip in with comments or merely exclamations of warm agreement with what the Führer was saying.

Warlimont has written[4] that these "other personalities also present" were one of the worst features of the conduct of business at the evening conferences. But the worst of all the crosses that Halder and the others had to bear, he suggests was "Hitler's flow of speech."

> The urgent concrete questions and proposals under discussion would be drowned in the ceaseless repetitive torrent of words in which matters old and new, important and unimportant were jumbled up together.

Occasionally, when tricky problems came up Jodl would support Halder, but more often than not he would stay silent in his characteristic attitude of lounging with one hand in his trouser pocket.

The long telephone conversations with the Front were a feature of the evenings. Sometimes Hitler made the calls when he was in a bad mood hoping that someone could give him better news. Sometimes commanders called, knowing they could be certain of catching him at this time, in the hope of wresting an urgent decision from him.

Goering often dropped over from OKL and would take every opportunity to vent his spite on the Army and disparage the efforts of the generals.

It was no way to run the most ambitious land campaign of modern times. That it succeeded as well as it did for so long was a tribute to the inborn efficiency of German organizational genius and its dogged, almost masochistic, compulsion to be industrious. The sufferer was the German soldier, now dying of exposure as well as Russian bullets in the snows before Moscow, and deprived of that winter clothing which a rapid victory had been expected to render unnecessary.

Yet even at the beginning of the Russian winter misery the mass of the soldiery retained their faith in the capacity of their Führer to see them through their present difficulties as men must believe in something when they are hurt and it is 40° below zero. After all, were they not the finest army there had ever been? Look at what they had accomplished in two years. The whole of Europe conquered except for the two southern extremities, Spain and Turkey, and Switzerland in the middle. And now they were six hundred miles into Russia and in the Ukraine they had been welcomed by many of the wretched inhabitants as liberators from the Bolshevik tyranny. That's what they were, liberators! Bringing German enlightenment and efficiency to these poor wretched peasants who were no better off now under their new Czar, Stalin, than they had been before the Revolution.

One had to admit that they fought quite hard. And there were a lot of them. But they were, after all, an Asiatic rabble: a stupid mass of ill-equipped, ill-led subhumans. You couldn't take them or their equipment seriously in a military sense. And yet, and yet there was that nagging thought of what had happened to Napoleon. His army had been good, too. It would be fine (thought the soldiers) if the Staff could provide them with some winter equipment instead of just sitting on their backsides in comfort miles to the rear while they themselves froze to death at the front. It was perhaps just as well, now that the "Asiatic rabble" was just beginning to hit back, that the soldiers could not know that their casualties to date exceeded half a million killed, wounded and missing. The Führer would see them through.

In Berlin the Propaganda Minister Dr. Joseph Goebbels

had tried to angle his bulletins to make people conclude that von Brauchitsch's dismissal meant that the recent setbacks in Russia had been blamed on him and that things would improve now that the Führer had personally taken over as Army C-in-C. But though many people were prepared to accept this, by no means everybody did. On January 24 Goebbels was noting in his diary that [5] "There is still a lot of talk about the dismissal of Brauchitsch. People haven't quite made up their minds whether he left because he wanted to or not. It certainly isn't true that this incident has already dropped out completely in public discussions."

Meanwhile Berliners rummaged in their clothes closets and chests for unwanted furs they could hand in for the soldiers on the Eastern Front, in response to the urgent appeals from which there was no escape.

It is hardly surprising that amid these portentous happenings of December it passed almost without notice at OKW that General Erwin Rommel, who had been sent with a small armoured force to Libya in March to stiffen the wilting Italian ally, had just been forced to withdraw in the face of a new British offensive, the most powerful yet, under General Sir Claude Auchinleck who during the year had replaced General Sir Archibald Wavell as British C-in-C in the Middle East. Libya was a long way away. At the Wolf's Lair they had much more pressing matters to attend to.

Chapter 3

GENERALS NOVEMBER
AND DECEMBER

☐ Before passing to the new impulses that emerged from the crisis of December 1941 when a turn in the flood-tide of German success seemed for the first time within the realm of possibility, it may be pertinent to summarize briefly what had gone wrong in Russia. First, why did Hitler undertake the final gamble of an invasion of Russia?

The articulate General Warlimont,[1] who as deputy chief of operations at OKW had close contact with the Führer before as well as after Barbarossa, considered Hitler's motivation identical with Napoleon's.

Both men looked upon Britain as their strongest and most dangerous adversary. Both could not persuade themselves to attempt the overthrow of England by invading the British Isles. Both believed however that Great Britain could be forced to come to terms with the dominating continental power, if the prospect vanished for the British to gain an armoured arm as an ally on the Continent. Both of them suspected Russia of becoming this ally of Britain's.

Hitler, therefore, like Napoleon before him, considered that the answer was to get in his blow first. In this connection it has to be realized that ever since the Nazi-Soviet Non-aggression Pact of 1939 the relationship between Hitler and Stalin had prickled with mutual distrust beneath the thin skin of the Pact. Both dictators were only buying time. The Pact had been accurately assessed by a London newspaper cartoonist who had depicted a confrontation between Hitler and Stalin, bowing to each other and smiling broadly, but each with a pistol concealed behind his back.

During the early months of 1941 there had been a considerable build-up of Russian military strength—a German Intelligence report of February estimated Russian strength in West Russia at 150 divisions. There was some justification, therefore, for Hitler thinking that Stalin was about to attack him.

Even so three senior Army chiefs, Field-Marshal von Brauchitsch (Commander-in-Chief), General Halder (Chief of Staff), and Field-Marshal von Rundstedt (scheduled to command one of the three Army groups carrying out the operation) were strongly opposed to it and told Hitler so. They had vivid memories of service in Russia during the First World War and knew from experience what that vast country and its brutal climate could do to an army—especially to its logistics and its power of movement.

"Have you weighed up what you are undertaking in an attack on Russia?" demanded the forthright von Rundstedt.[2] Hitler apparently had. He merely stressed that the Russian army must be destroyed on the west side of the Dnieper before it could withdraw into Russia's limitless interior and prolong the war into the winter. It must be won by autumn.

Another forthright critic of the Barbarossa plan was General Heinz Guderian, the brilliant panzer commander who

26

had covered himself with glory in the earlier blitzkriegs in Poland and France.

Earlier that year Guderian had been ordered to send his two senior staff officers to OKH for a conference and they had brought back with them the Barbarossa plan.

> When they spread out a map of Russia before me I could scarcely believe my eyes. Was something which I had held to be utterly impossible now to become a fact? Hitler had criticised the leaders of German policy of 1914 in the strongest possible words for their failure to avoid a war on two fronts; was he now, on his own initiative and before the war with England had been decided, to open this second-front against the Russians? His soldiers had warned him repeatedly and urgently against this very error and he had agreed with them.[3]

Guderian had made no attempt to hide his "disappointment and disgust." The vehemence of his language had surprised the two staff officers who had returned from OKH "entirely convinced" by the Russian invasion plan as it had been presented to them. And if (as General Guenther Blumentritt later alleged to Liddell Hart) Halder did in fact support von Brauchitsch and von Rundstedt in advising Hitler against the invasion,[4] he was certainly confident enough at the briefing attended by these staff officers; for their enthusiastic account of it to their chief included the information[5] that "Chief of Army General Staff, Halder, had calculated that Russia would be defeated in a campaign of eight to ten weeks' duration."

German Intelligence assessments grossly underestimated the Russian strength. An estimated strength of 155 Russian divisions were at hand to oppose the 121 German divisions carrying out the opening phase of Barbarossa. But numerical inferiority can be offset by superior training and equipment. At OKW it was easy for Hitler's entourage, including its military members, to gloss over the disparity or make light of it. Was not one determined well-armed German worth ten Asiatic subhumans? Hitler disliked the Army General Staff anyway and it was not difficult for the military courtiers (Keitel and Jodl) at OKW to keep from the Führer, or to minimize, any more realistic qualms about the operation that might emanate from OKH. To this must be added the Russian genius for secrecy. So that even the fact of having a German military attaché in Moscow right up to the time of invasion was of little help in the face of the professional secret-keepers of the Kremlin. Churchill once said "Russia is a riddle wrapped in a mystery inside an enigma." So Hitler attacked Russia without any realistic idea of the potential strength opposing him and in any case in the certainty that to begin with he was pitting 121 divisions against 155. Right from the beginning he would be outnumbered locally.

Of the three Army groups that projected the invasion, only the centre group under Field-Marshal Fedor von Bock, advancing in the direction of Moscow, had local superiority with fifty-one divisions (including nine armoured and seven motorized). Field-Marshal von Leeb's northern army directed on Leningrad and the Baltic (thirty divisions including three armoured and three motorized) was about the same as the Russian strength opposing it. Field-Marshal von Rundstedt's southern army group headed for the Ukraine and lower Dnieper with a total of thirty-seven divisions including a panzer group of five armoured, three motorized divisions was markedly inferior to the forces opposing it. The commander of that panzer army General Field-Marshal Paul von Kleist had only six hundred tanks ("all we could assemble after the return of the divisions from Greece") whereas Marshal Semyon Budenny whose army group was facing von Rundstedt had 2400. It was the Russian tank strength that Hitler most seriously underestimated.

In spite of the forebodings of more orthodox military minds, the German attack was at first brilliantly successful. Achieving complete surprise the three German Army groups tore into the western flank of Russia on June 22, 1941, and in a series of giant pincer movements mangled such opposition as an unprepared and inexperienced enemy could hurriedly improvise in its first shock and bewilderment.

The advance of von Bock's centre group of armies was the most spectacular. Spearheaded by the two panzer armies of Generals Heinz Guderian and Hermann von Hoth its progress in another series of giant encircling pincer movements was exhilarating and deadly. Within a week Guderian and Hoth had closed their pincers beyond Minsk two hundred miles into Russia and had captured 300,000 prisoners. At the end of another three weeks the pincers had again closed east of Smolensk, another two hundred miles on, and this time the number of prisoners captured was 600,000.

With Moscow only two hundred miles ahead von Bock wanted to be allowed to make straight for it, his two panzer generals Guderian and Hoth both believing they could reach the capital if no time was wasted. But Hitler ruled otherwise. Leningrad and the Ukraine were in his view more important: Leningrad, not only for its symbolic importance as the "cradle of the Revolution," but to secure the Baltic flank and to effect a link-up with the Finns; the Ukraine for its economic value and as a step to the Crimean airfields from which the Russians could threaten the Rumanian oilfields.

So the Moscow drive was halted and instead von Bock was ordered to divert forces north to help von Leeb and south to assist von Rundstedt. The southerly switch was extremely successful and resulted in a crushing of the large Russian forces that had been holding up von Rundstedt in the Kiev area. Once again there was a huge bag of prisoners— 600,000. The diversion of forces from the centre group to the Leningrad front was not carried out. The armies of the centre were by this time too heavily engaged to be easily extricated, and Hitler changed his mind. Fearing a direct assault on Leningrad because of the heavy cost in casualties it would entail, he had now decided on a blockade to starve it into submission prior to having it razed to the ground by the Luftwaffe.

By the end of September, when the Kiev annihilation battle had been finished off, the Germans claimed that Russian losses in the first three months of the campaign were 2,500,000 men, 22,000 guns, 18,000 tanks, and 14,000 aircraft.[6] Of the initial objectives, Leningrad, though unconquered, had been isolated and a crippling blockade established; the Ukraine, with its agricultural wealth and the industrial complex along the Donetz, had been sucked into the German economy. Field-Marshal von Bock, having discharged his diversionary duties in support of Field-Marshal von Rundstedt in the south, was now free and authorized to pursue his advance to Moscow, the great prize, and Hitler ordered a new offensive to this end. Unfortunately instead of reinforcing von Bock and throwing everything into the drive on Moscow the Führer insisted that at the same time von Rundstedt should resume his offensive to the southeast with the task of reaching the Caucasus, having cleared the Black Sea coast on the way. The simultaneous pursuit of both these formidable objectives at the same time as Army Group Centre was trying for Moscow was to result in failure to achieve either.

The new offensive on Moscow began with a tremendous new encirclement battle around Vyasma and Bryansk which netted another 600,000 prisoners and seemingly opened the way to the capital. But ominously the first snow of the year fell on the night October 6-7. It did not lie on the ground but wet it sufficiently to turn the roads into "canals of bottomless mud, along which our vehicles could only advance at snail's pace and with great wear to the engines." [7] As further snow showers between heavy rains dramatically slowed down the hitherto irresistible panzers and immobilized the Germans' wheeled transport, Guderian put in a request for winter clothing. He was told that he would receive it "in due course" and that he was not to make "further unnecessary requests of this type." No winter equipment reached him that year. In fact no provision had been made for a campaign prolonging itself into the winter—it had been supposed to be finished long before.

About this time the Russians sent into action a new tank, the T.34, which was superior to the German Mark IV. The German short-barreled 75-mm tank gun was only effective against the T.34 if it attacked it from the rear and even then had to hit it on the grating above the engine. It required great skill to manoeuvre into a position to do this. In addition to its thick armour and squat shape—which resulted in the panzer crews seeing most of their shells bounce off—the T.34 had extra-broad tracks which enabled it to traverse the increasingly muddy terrain when the German tanks were bogged down and helpless. The Russians were now fighting back with a new tactical skill as well as with the courage they had always shown even in their earlier outclassing by a more skilful, better-equipped opponent.

By early in December von Bock had been stopped when almost in sight of the Kremlin. The other half of the double offensive, von Rundstedt's drive to the Caucasus, had been stopped short, even, of its first objective: the line of the Don between Voronezh and Rostov. Hitler's gamble, so nearly successful, had failed. The story of its failure seems to be enshrined in two remarks by General Halder.[8]

At the end of the second week of the campaign: "It is probably not an exaggeration when I contend that the campaign against Russia has been won in fourteen days." At the end of the second month: "We underestimated Russia; we reckoned with 200 divisions, but now we have already identified 360."

To which may be added the following observations by generals[9] who had to do the fighting.

General Field-Marshal von Kleist: "The main cause of

30

our failure was that winter came early that year." To which Field-Marshal von Rundstedt added: "But long before winter came the chances had been diminished owing to the repeated delays in the advance caused by bad roads, and mud. The 'black earth' of the Ukraine could be turned into mud by ten minutes' rain stopping all movement until it dried . . . a heavy handicap . . . increased by the lack of railways . . ." General Blumentritt agreed: "The badness of the roads was the worst handicap but next to that the inadequacy of the railways."

It was eighty-eight years since Czar Nicholas I had said at the outbreak of the Crimean War that Russia had two generals in which she could confide—Generals January and February. In 1941 it seemed that to this pair could be added Generals November and December.

Chapter 4

ANXIETY ABOUT THE WEST

□ The hard handsome face of Field-Marshal Gerd von Rundstedt, with its clipped moustache and steel-blue eyes, could have belonged to almost any senior professional soldier of any West European army. It was the quintessential Nordic officer face of its time, as its owner was the archetypal Prussian officer of the best kind among those who, having survived the First World War and its aftermath, found themselves forced to compromise their inherited sense of honour and integrity to a regime they despised in a second conflagration that was to be even more disastrous for their country.

Born in 1875 into an aristocratic family that could trace its origins back to the twelfth century, his upbringing was the classically severe one of the Prussian eldest son dedicated from birth to continuing the family tradition of military service. He was undergoing the spartan rigours of junior cadet school at twelve, senior cadet school two years later, an ensign in the Royal Prussian Infantry two years after that and second lieutenant in two more years. At all stages he did well and showed himself to be an outstanding student of his pre-

31

destined profession. But there was also a human side to him too. On his mother's side there was Huguenot blood and from her he inherited a taste and aptitude for drawing and, in a small way, for acting; though, after his cadet days, this was confined to mimicry at which he excelled. It was said that he could reproduce on demand every German dialect with convulsive accuracy. And, on nights when the senior officer in him could be prevailed upon to unbend, deadly imitations of military and political personalities. But, understandably, these performances were not lightly or too freely given and his wit, inclined to be caustic, was probably what members of his staff most remembered about him.

His methodical, almost goosestepping, climb to the top of his profession, taking the First World War in his stride, only faltered when the Old Guard of the Army found itself at odds with "the Austrian Corporal" and "that brown scum" as von Rundstedt was known to refer to Hitler and his Nazi Brownshirts. Like others of his kind he found it impossible to resist the revolutionary tide and he preferred to turn his back on them in disgust. In 1938 he applied for and obtained his retirement on the grounds of age. One year later he was recalled to take charge of Army Group South for the invasion of Poland. Like the rest of the Old Guard who in the late 1930s had been professing the view that another war with England would be fatal for Germany, von Rundstedt had been forced to come to terms with the inescapable fact that Hitler's actual run of successes had confounded all cautious military counsels; that sixty percent of Germany's adult population and the country's entire youth were solidly behind Hitler; finally, and placing opposition further out of reach, he, Rundstedt, German officer and gentleman in accordance with the highest precepts of Prussian honour, had sworn a sacred oath of personal allegiance to the Führer. As a German officer he had to obey when the Fatherland (albeit in the person of Adolf Hitler) called.

This was the man—this ageing General in his sixty-fourth year—who found himself leading the legions of the Austrian corporal to the swift conquest of Poland, the Low Countries, and France: found himself emerging as a father-figure of the German Army. Once again the Führer's intuition had been right and the military experts (including von Rundstedt) wrong.

By the time the invasion of Russia was being proposed by an insatiable conqueror, the Field-Marshal's natural scepticism and caustic tongue had reasserted their habitual hold.

With the brusqueness which only a Field-Marshal going to be sixty-seven next birthday can perhaps afford, von Rundstedt told Hitler that the Russian operation would be a madness to undertake.

He had fought in Russia in the first war. It was a terrible country in which to campaign. No roads to speak of: Once the summer weather ended the country became impossible for supply, transport, movement. He knew too how ferociously the Russian peasant would fight to the death however inferior his equipment and training might be to begin with. He knew what prodigal expenditure of life the Russian leaders could afford to accept with their unlimited reserves of manpower. The Russian Army had only to withdraw, pulling the invader deeper and deeper in behind it and then hit back with untouched reserves when the Russian winter had done its deadly work. After all, no one had to remind anyone what had happened to Napoleon, who had had the same idea.

Nevertheless the invasion had been launched and once again the counsels of prudence and caution had been proved wrong. The gamble had nearly succeeded and von Rundstedt had claimed his usual lion's share of the credit. But now, in the tightening grip of winter—with Army Group North still short of Leningrad, Army Group Centre stopped short of Moscow, and his own Army Group South pawing with weakening blows at the outer approaches to the Caucasus—he saw that the limit had been reached.

During the month he had persistently urged Hitler to modify the overambitious southern objectives that had been assigned him and this running battle with OKW was probably more responsible than the other battle for the heart attack he had early in November when he collapsed in the street at Poltava where he had his headquarters. But these almost daily representations by telephone, telegraph, and memorandum had made no impression on OKW. Rastenburg was a thousand miles from the realities of the southeast front. In the remote and tranquil isolation of the Wolf's Lair it was not difficult for the yes-men of Hitler's entourage to keep courageously calm in the face of difficulties so distant and to encourage the Führer in his customary belief that the generals at the Front were as usual exaggerating their difficulties to cover up their incompetence.

The breaking-point had been reached when the panzers of his subordinate, General Field-Marshal von Kleist, had managed to force their way into Rostov but in so doing had created a weak salient which there was no hope of their holding and where they were almost certain to be cut off by a strong counterattack in the flank. It was now that he sent his strongly worded request for permission to withdraw the forces in Rostov to the line of the Mius thirty-five miles back, adding in his own handwriting that last sanction of the commander in the field, an offer to resign, if confidence in his leadership had been lost. As we saw, brusque intimation that his resignation had been accepted came through within a few hours.

Four days later Hitler flew to the Front and at last heard at first hand what had been going on. Von Rundstedt's chief of staff von Soderstern made full use of his opportunity to describe the existing situation with no punches pulled and also to stress the number of warnings that he had passed on to OKW without being able to make the slightest impression. Hitler for once listened in silence until he had finished.

The members of Hitler's party who were present listened to the recital with growing nervousness and braced themselves for the expected explosion when it ended. Instead Hitler said quietly:

"You will understand, General, that I am angry because no one reported any of these occurrences to me."

Hitler then sent for von Rundstedt—who was waiting in an anteroom as ordered—and in a private interview apologized and excused himself for what had happened on the grounds that it had "all been a misunderstanding." He expressed deep concern for the Field-Marshal's health after his recent heart attack and ended by ordering him to go straight home to Germany on sick leave and not to offer himself for re-posting until he was fully recovered and rested. So it happened that Field-Marshal Gerd von Rundstedt, in disgrace since November 30, on December 5 left the Eastern front forever—in a special train, with flags flying, bands playing, and attended by a guard of honour and a parade of the entire officer strength of Army Group South HQ. By the time Hitler—his eyes newly opened to the reality of this situation —had authorized the order directing that the German armies should go on to the defensive along the entire Russian Front, von Rundstedt was safely back in his home at Cassel preparing to spend Christmas and his sixty-seventh birthday with his wife. He was actually still on the way there when the news of Pearl Harbor broke.[1]

Even before he had been forced to accept the failure of

his blitzkrieg to complete the conquest of Russia before winter brought operations to a standstill, Hitler, as we have seen, never lost sight of the vulnerability of his rear and had issued precautionary instructions about "a new West Wall" in mid-December. In the early weeks of 1942 he had good reason to address himself more precisely and in greater detail to the defence of Fortress Europe's western seaboard.

All was not well in Norway. The Norwegian people, few in number (4,000,000) but as hardy and rugged as their thousand-mile mountainous fjord-scarred seaboard, did not take kindly to occupation. Like their Viking forebears they had taken to their boats in some numbers and had made their way across the bleak North Sea to Britain, where a sizeable (and constantly increasing) number of them were training with all the branches of the British Armed Forces. While the younger men were making their way to Britain, those they left behind were by no means accepting their situation compliantly. They found their own ways of resisting the occupying power and at the turn of the year 1941-42 German intelligence had to report such an increase in incidents that OKW had to issue orders for new penal and repressive measures to cope with them. Nor was it only in Norway that the Germans were having trouble. Resistance movements in the Balkans were beginning to take recognizable shape and on a scale that necessitated the transfer to the Mediterranean of an air corps. There were also the earliest hints of organized resistance in France.

These first faint rumblings within the European Fortress were as yet no more than portents of what was to come later when the Resistance movements in France and elsewhere had become organized, and were being armed, co-ordinated, and largely directed from London. But they reinforced Hitler's new concern for the Fortress's western ramparts. For though he had no doubts about completing in 1942 the Russian victory that had just eluded him in 1941, he could not in the early weeks of that year ignore the possibility that the British and their new allies the Americans might attack in the west. By March his qualms had stiffened into fears: precautionary instructions that had started in December were now superseded by one of the special Führer Directives which retrospectively can be seen as milestones in Hitler's strategic thinking.

As this Directive No. 40 was the Führer's own blueprint for the defence of Fortress Europe in the west, it is worth quoting the greater part of it in full.[2] The italics are Hitler's.

The Führer and Supreme
Commander of the
Armed Forces.

Führer Headquarters,
23rd March 1942
25 copies

Directive No. 40
*Ref. Competence of Commanders
in coastal areas*

I. *General Considerations:*

*The coastline of Europe will, in the coming
months, be exposed to the danger of an enemy
landing in force.*

The time and place of the landing operations
will not be dictated to the enemy by operational
considerations alone. Failure in other theatres of
war, obligations to allies, and political considerations may persuade him to take decisions which
appear unlikely from a purely military point of
view.

Even enemy *landings with limited objectives*
can interfere seriously with our own plans if
they result in the enemy gaining any kind of
foothold on the coast. They can interrupt our
coastal sea traffic, and pin down strong forces
of our Army and Air Force, which will therefore have to be withdrawn from areas of crucial
importance. It would be particularly dangerous
should the enemy succeed in capturing our airfields or in establishing his own in areas which
he has occupied.

The many important military and industrial
establishments on the coast or in its neighbour-
hood, some of them equipped with particularly
valuable plant, may moreover tempt the *enemy
to undertake surprise attacks of a local nature.*

Particular attention must be paid to English
preparations for landings on the open coast, for
which they have at their disposal many armoured
landing craft, built to carry armoured fighting
vehicles and heavy weapons. The possibility of
parachute and airborne attacks on a large scale
must also be envisaged.

II. *General operational instructions for coastal defence:*

1. *Coastal defence is a task for all Armed Forces,* calling for particularly close and complete cooperation by all units.

2. The intelligence service, as well as the day-to-day reconnaissance by the *Navy* and *Air Force,* must strive to obtain early information of *enemy readiness and approach* preparations for a landing operation.

All suitable sea and air forces will then concentrate on enemy points of embarkation and convoys, with the aim of destroying the enemy as far from the coast as possible.

It is however possible that the enemy, by skilful camouflage and by taking advantage of unpredictable weather conditions, may achieve a completely surprise attack. *All troops* who may be exposed to such surprise attacks must be in *a state of permanent readiness.*

One of the most important duties of Commanding Officers will be to overcome the lack of vigilance among the troops which, as experience has shown, increases with the passage of time.

3. *In defending the coast*—and this includes *coastal waters* within range of medium coastal artillery—*responsibility for the planning and implementation of defensive measures must,* as recent battle experience dictates, lie unequivocally and unreservedly in the hands of a single Commander.

The Commander responsible must make use of all available forces and weapons of the branches of the Armed Forces, and of our civil headquarters in the area, for the destruction of enemy transports and landing forces. He will use them so that the attack collapses *if possible before it can reach the coast, or at the latest on the coast itself.*

Enemy forces which have landed must be destroyed or thrown back into the sea by immediate counterattack. All personnel bearing arms—irrespective to which branch of the Armed Forces or to which non-service organisation they may belong—will be employed for this. Moreover, the required working capacity of the naval shore supply establishments must be guaranteed, in so far as they are not involved in the land fighting themselves. The same applies to the readiness for action of the Air Force ground staff and the anti-aircraft defence of airfields.

No headquarters or formation is to initiate withdrawal in such circumstances. All German troops stationed on or near the coast must be armed and trained for battle.

The enemy must be prevented from securing a foothold on all islands which could present a threat to the mainland or coastal shipping.

4. The distribution of forces and the extension of defensive works must be so carried out that our strongest defence points are situated in those sectors most likely to be chosen by the enemy for landings (fortified areas).

Other coastal sectors which may be threatened by small-scale surprise attacks will be defended by a series of strong-points, supported if possible by coastal batteries. All military and industrial plant of importance to the war effort will be included within these strong-points.

The same principles will apply to off-shore islands.

Less threatened sectors will be kept under observation.

5. *The division of the coast into sectors* will be decided by the three services in mutual agreement, or, should the situation demand it, by the responsible Commander (referred to here in paragraph III, 1), whose decision will be final.

6. *The fortified areas and strong-points* must be able, by proper distribution of forces, by completion of all-round defence, and by their supply situation, to hold out for some time even against superior enemy forces.

Fortified areas and strong-points will be defended to the last man. They must never be forced to surrender from lack of ammunition, rations or water.

7. The responsible Commander (referred to here in paragraph III, 1) will issue orders for keeping the coast under constant observation, and ensure that reconnaissance reports from all services are quickly evaluated, co-ordinated, and transmitted to the headquarters and civilian authorities concerned.

As soon as there is any evidence that an operation by the enemy is imminent, the Commander is authorised to issue the necessary instructions for co-ordinated and complementary reconnaissance on sea and land.

8. There can be no question of peace-time privileges for any headquarters or formation of the Armed Forces in coastal areas, or for non-military organisations and units. Their accommodation, and the use they make of the terrain, will be entirely dependent upon the necessity of meeting any enemy attack as swiftly and in as great strength as possible. Where the military situation requires it, the civilian population will be immediately evacuated.

III. *Competence of Commanders.*

1. The following are responsible for the preparation and execution of coastal defence in the *areas under German command:*

- (a) In the Eastern area of operations (excluding Finland):
  The Army Commanders appointed by High Command of the Army.
- (b) In the coastal area of Army High Command Lapland:
  Commander-in-Chief Army High Command Lapland.
- (c) In Norway:
  Commander Armed Forces Norway.
- (d) In Denmark:
  The Commander of German troops Denmark.

(e) In the occupied Western territories (including the Netherlands):
Commander-in-Chief West.

For coastal defence the responsible Commanders in (d) and (e) will be directly subordinate to the High Command of the Armed Forces (OKW).

(f) In the Balkans (including the occupied islands):
Commander Armed Forces South-east.

(g) In the Baltic territories and the Ukraine:
Commander Armed Forces Baltic Territories and Ukraine.

(h) In the Home theatre of war: the Commanding Admirals.

2. The Commanders named in paragraph III (1) will have for these tasks *full powers of command* over staffs commanding all Armed Forces, the German civil authorities, and the non-military units and organisations in their area.

In exercising their authority they will issue the necessary tactical, administrative, and supply instructions, and will ensure that they are complied with. In all matters relating to land fighting, training of units will follow their ruling, and all necessary information will be put at their disposal.

3. Among the orders to be given and measures to be taken, the following must be *given first place*.

(a) The inclusion within fortified areas or strong-points of all military and industrial establishments connected with defence, particularly those of the Navy (submarine bases) and the Air Force.

(b) The co-ordination of coastal reconnaissance.

(c) The defence of fortified areas and strong-points by infantry.

(d) The defence by infantry of all isolated positions outside the fortified areas and strong-points—e.g. coastal look-out points and air-attack warning-posts.

- (e) Artillery defence against land targets. (The Navy has priority in the installation of new batteries, or the conversion of existing batteries.)
- (f) The defensive readiness, development, and supply facilities of installations, as well as of isolated positions away from these installations. (This includes being equipped with all weapons needed for defence: mines, hand-grenades, flame-throwers, barbed-wire, etc.)
- (g) The signals network.
- (h) Methods for ensuring that troops are always on the alert, and that infantry and gunnery training is being carried out in accordance with the special defence requirements.

4. *The same authority is conferred upon local commanders up to sector commanders,* in so far as they are responsible for the defence of a part of the coast.

The Commanders designated in paragraph III, (1) will, in general, appoint Commanders of *Army Divisions* employed in coastal defence as local Commanders with full powers. In Crete the "Fortress Commandant Crete" will appoint them.

As far as their other duties allow, local Commandants or Commanders of the Air Force and Navy will be made responsible for the general defence of individual sectors or sub-sectors, particularly Air and Naval strong-points.

5. *All naval and air units employed in strategic warfare* are subordinate to the Navy or Air Force. In the event of enemy attacks on the coast, however, they are required to comply, in so far as tactical considerations allow, with the orders of the Commanders responsible for defence. They must therefore be included in the distribution of such information as they require for their duties, and close liaison will be maintained with their headquarters.

IV. *Special duties of the branches of the Armed Forces in the field of coastal defence.*

1. *Navy.*
   (a) Organisation and protection of coastal traffic.
   (b) Training and employment of all coastal artillery against targets at sea.
   (c) Employment of naval forces.

2. *Air Force.*
   (a) Air defence of coastal areas. The use against enemy landings of suitable and available anti-aircraft guns, under the orders of the commander responsible for local defence, will not be affected.
   (b) The completion of ground organisations and their protection against air attack and surprise by land; the latter in cases where airfields are not included in the coastal defences and are therefore insufficiently protected.
   (c) Operational employment of air forces. Attention will be paid to the duplication of command implied by these special duties.

V. Orders and instructions which run contrary to this directive are cancelled from 1st April 1942.
New Operation orders, which will be issued by Commanders on the basis of my directive, are to be submitted to me through the High Command of the Armed Forces.

signed: Adolf Hitler.[8]

By any standards Führer Directive 40 is a military document of the highest historical interest. Behind the formal military language—yet in terms comprehensible to any layman—it enshrined a breath-taking concept. It was a design for the defence of almost the entire continental landmass of German-held Europe against the encircling alliance of the United States, Russia, and Great Britain. It was a proposition that military staff college students might have played around with as an end-of-term fantasy; a frivolous exercise of in-

42

genuity to liven the last days of study before the course dispersed and officers returned to their regiments.

Yet this was no fantasy, no military classroom test of mental agility. It was real. It was serious. This was the logical end to the inescapable and inevitable brink to which Hubris in Siegfried's armour, and Megalomania, soaring on Valkyrie wings, had brought Adolf Hitler and the German people at the end of 1941. It is not clear precisely when the name Fortress Europe (*Festung Europa*) was first used though later It caught the imagination and obsessively fascinated both sides: Hitler and his propagandists as an angry yell of defiance, the Allies, when they first began to penetrate the "fortress" as a sneering crow of triumph. Whatever the origin of the name, after the issue of the twenty-five copies of the Top Secret Directive 40 Fortress Europe was a fact even if it was not yet a registered name and slogan. Directive 40 had conferred upon it an identity.

Two weeks before one of the twenty-five copies of the Directive duly found its way into the possession of Commander-in-Chief West, this key post in the defence of the West had changed hands, so that the new incumbent who received Directive 40 was Field-Marshal von Rundstedt. Thoroughly refreshed by two months of sick leave and home comforts, the Field-Marshal had written to Hitler at the beginning of March to say that he was now fully recovered and would welcome the opportunity to resume serving his Führer and the Fatherland. His request to return to duty coincided therefore with Hitler's decision to overhaul his western defences, and he was accordingly ordered to take over as Commander-in-Chief West from General Field-Marshal Erwin von Witzleben, an elderly man whom illness had rendered increasingly feeble and ineffective.

The first reaction of von Rundstedt when he arrived to take up his new appointment was one of personal pleasure at finding himself once again in France[4] after the Eastern Front that he had left just before Christmas. By contrast Occupied France seemed almost a country at peace. The troops were in comfortable billets. There was every kind of recreation available. The climate was pleasant and seemed particularly so after Russia. It was good, too, to be back in his old headquarters in the historic Paris riverside resort of Saint-Germain-en-Laye with its centuries-old links with France's kings, especially Louis XIV: to be able to walk again along its celebrated mile-and-a-half terrace designed by that monarch's redoubtable architect Le Notre: to walk in the Jardin

Anglais: to enjoy the panoramic view of the capital only twenty-one kilometres away across the bends of the Seine. It was here that von Rundstedt had spent the first euphoric months after the great victory over France in 1940 and here that he had prepared for Operation Sealion, the invasion of England that he had never quite believed in and that in the end had never come off. For a Francophile there could be no more gratifying posting.

The attitude of this austere aristocratic professional to the more congenial aspects of soldiering in Paris was not perhaps that of the majority of his staff. But though he never attended public entertainments when he was there in 1940 and would not do so now (except for a very occasional chamber concert or recital in a private house) he was sufficiently urbane as well as human to appreciate how helpful to morale being stationed near Paris could be: and he was no spoilsport as far as his HQ staff were concerned so long as they behaved themselves and conducted themselves like German officers and gentlemen. After all Paris was Paris whichever side you were on! There was an anecdote of this time that was very revealing of Field-Marshal von Rundstedt. For a time, it appears, there hung in the Orderly Officer's duty room two identical street maps of Paris, one covered with blue markers, the other with red. The blue markers denoted good eating places, the red indicated where accommodating female company was to be found. Every overnight visitor to the Mess was expected before leaving to contribute to the maps the products of any original research carried out during his stay. For a long time von Rundstedt showed no awareness of the existence of these maps. Then, one day when he was in the duty room, he suddenly walked across to the wall and stared at them for a long time in straight-faced silence while the two or three officers present blushed and fidgeted. Then without a flicker of a smile he said, "I see your red map isn't nearly full enough yet!"

Apart from the satisfaction of knowing that his troops were comfortably billeted and had ample facilities for recreation and entertainment, von Rundstedt had a warm personal regard for France which no doubt derived from his Huguenot blood. He liked the country and its people and felt at home among them and he championed Marshal Henri Pétain whose influence alone, he considered, had restrained Hitler from completing the occupation of the southern half of the country after the armistice of June 1940. He went out of his way to help Pétain and constantly (though in vain) urged

Hitler to make some declaration that after the war France would be restored to her proper place in Europe as an independent power. He even tried to organize a French Defence Force but was forced to admit that "for various reasons beyond my control this unfortunately was unsuccessful." One reason, of course, was a man called Charles de Gaulle—who was temporarily taking care of the French national soul in London—and the fifty percent of the French people who believed in what he was doing. There was evidently a well-meaning if unimaginative streak of idealism in von Rundstedt. As one marshal to another he thought he saw what Pétain was trying to do and thought it was right. But like all the German military hierarchy he had been meticulously shielded from politics, knew nothing about them and would have been the first to say so.

From his new staff von Rundstedt soon learned of some of the difficulties of Western Command; difficulties which they hoped their new commander would be more successful in solving than his predecessor had been. The biggest problem was the indeterminate division of command responsibility as between Army and Navy. Another was how to prepare for service on the Eastern Front. All divisions in France had to be prepared to move to Russia at short notice. But how to prepare them properly? You could not lay on a Russian winter to order near Nice. Nevertheless von Rundstedt issued new orders for rigorous training designed to offset a little the violent shock of being switched within a few days from the "soft" soldiering in France to the full horror of the Russian campaign in winter.

Such were the matters and the personal attitudes which informed the background to von Rundstedt's thinking on his return to Saint-Germain and his early discussions with his new staff. Nor did he neglect to tell some scarifying tales of the Eastern Front with its bitter fighting in temperatures as low as 40 below; stubborn Russian fighters who never gave up; the psychotic effect on the German soldiers of the awful limitlessness of that vast daunting space without end.

Meanwhile it was good to be back at Saint-Germain in the comfortable villa close to the Pavillon Henri IV, the hotel named after one of the five royal pavilions built by Louis XIV, where the bulk of his headquarters staff were located. It was a pleasant villa with a large garden and the Field-Marshal took a keen interest in its upkeep and enjoyed his daily talks with the gardener. Each day he went for a two-hour walk in the Jardin Anglais and along the splendid terrace, the showpiece of Saint-Germain. He always went un-armed and unaccompanied though this led to trouble with OKW who were always trying to make him take a body-guard, and on one occasion even arranged for him to be shadowed secretly by detectives, because he declined to do so.

Führer Directive 40, though undeniably grandiose in con-ception and on the face of it seemingly comprehensive in scope and detail, did not look so good when subjected to the critical scrutiny of a commander brought up in the exacting school of von Moltke and von Schlieffen. This was especially so when the Navy and Air Force had followed it up with their Führer-authorized amendments. Instead of clarifying beyond doubt the command set-up it perpetuated its ambiguities and dichotomies of responsibility to which von Rundstedt's staff had been drawing his attention since his arrival. The cause of the trouble was at the very top. Hitler did not like delegat-ing too much authority to any one subordinate.

The Navy and Air Force in the persons of Grand Admiral Erich Raeder and Reichsmarschall Hermann Goering had influential heads at Court. Spending most of their time at OKW they could "get at" Hitler and wring concessions out of him for their own services. The Army had no such champion to fight for its interests as its C-in-C was now Hit-ler himself. So far from favouring his own "family," Hitler as Supreme Commander of all the Armed Forces was con-stantly making concessions in command matters to the Navy and Air Force chiefs at the expense of Hitler in his other capacity of Commander-in-Chief Army. It was a prepos-terous irony and its effect was keenly apparent when C-in-C West set about implementing Directive 40 and the naval amendments that followed. The division of responsibility as between Army and Navy was one that might understandably worry an Army commander charged with repelling an in-vasion.

The principle laid down was that everything that happened on the water was *naval warfare* and the Army only came into action after the enemy had landed. The Navy there-fore was in charge of the siting and control of all coastal ar-tillery even though some of these batteries were manned by Army personnel. This arrangement had some curious effects. The Navy tended to regard the headlands of the French coast as just another kind of ship. They sited their batteries in far too forward and exposed a position as if in a battleship gun turret, so that most of them could not fire directly on the shore but only out to sea. Von Rundstedt pointed out the folly of this to Hitler but could make no headway against the Navy "lobby" and Grand Admiral Raeder who had the ear of the Führer at OKW. It was in vain that von Rundstedt protested that an invasion of the approaches to the coast was "just the same thing as when in the east, Russian tanks rolled over the Steppes directly against my position." That it was not a naval but a land war when enemy ships approached the coast with the obvious intention of landing and that he it was who should be in charge of repelling them. The Navy "lobby" beat him every time.

At the root of the trouble was the number of different commands involved. In this critical western sector of Fortress Europe upon which renewed interest had just focussed there were:

1. The Commander-in-Chief West, Field-Marshal von Rundstedt.
2. The Commander-in-Chief 3rd Air Fleet, Field-Marshal Sperrle.
3. The Commander-in-Chief Western Naval Group, Admiral Krancke.
4. The Military Commander France, General von Stülpnagel.
5. The Military Commander Belgium-Northern France, General von Falkenhausen.

In addition to these services commands there were the civil authorities: the German Embassy in Paris, the Vichy French Government, and the Organization Todt, the para-military corps of civilian contractors responsible for the building of the extensive and massive fortifications that were now to be top priority in the west.

Within this top-heavy command structure, additionally confused by the interference of the Nazi party organizations, there was almost limitless scope for inter-service conflict and personal jealousies and frustrations. Directive 40 which should have resolved the conflict in fact perpetuated it.

It laid down for instance that von Rundstedt, though Commander-in-Chief was only the top strategic and tactical authority in the defence of the *coast*—but not the *approaches* —against invasion. Only within these terms of reference could he give orders to the Navy and Air Force. He was not in charge, in fact, until an invasion had actually happened. Sperrle, C-in-C 3rd Air Fleet, ranked equally with von Rundstedt and had only to carry out those of his orders that related to the *strategic* defence of the coast. In all other spheres of activity—the air war against England, for instance, and

47

all reconnaissance operations over the Atlantic and Mediterranean—Sperrle was quite independent and he alone could give orders to the Luftwaffe.

The position with the Navy was the same. The C-in-C Western Naval Group (Admiral Krancke) ranked equally with the land and air commanders and one of the anomalies to which this led—as we have seen—was the involved matter of the siting of the coastal batteries. The Navy wanted complete charge of this; the Army resisted strongly; Hitler was appealed to but dodged giving a decision and an unsatisfactory compromise was arrived at which resulted in there being three kinds of coastal artillery.

First, heavy medium and long-range naval batteries, sited as if in battleship turrets to fire out to sea but unable to fire on the beaches. These gun positions were mostly so exposed that the Navy demanded, and were provided by the Todt Organization with, immense concrete emplacements as much as twenty or thirty feet thick for their protection from air or sea bombardment.

Second, there were Army coastal batteries with a certain amount of concrete cover sited to fire on beaches and foreshore and manned by the Army—but under Navy orders.

Finally, there were the Army's own batteries, sited as normal land artillery and remaining under Army command; but forced to make do with natural cover and camouflage as by this time there was no more concrete available for them to be afforded the same protective treatment as the others.

Needless to say this compromise over the artillery was not arrived at without a great deal of argument and inter-services feeling. In the allocation of protective steel and concrete for defences the Army always came last. It usually worked out that after the Navy (for their U-boat pens and coastal guns) and the Luftwaffe (for their various installations) had been provided for there was little left for the Army. It was in this kind of respect that the Navy and Air Force scored heavily through having their own powerful chiefs, Raeder and Goering, at OKW to speak up for them.

The designation Commander-in-Chief West was in fact delusory. Field-Marshal von Rundstedt was in reality a member of a triumvirate and in some ways its least powerful member. It was a glaring weakness of the German command set-up for this crucially important assignment of the defence of Fortress Europe against cross-Channel invasion that the man in charge of it, its supreme commander, was not in fact supreme. In a dictatorship there is room for only one commander-in-chief.

There were other constricting factors in von Rundstedt's situation. The sizeable forces disposed by the Military Governors of France and Belgium were beyond his jurisdiction except in the narrow context of coastal defence. It was the same with Holland, which had no Military Governor but a so-called Reich-Deputy, responsible directly to Hitler (with all that this implied) and a Commander of the Wehrmacht in the Netherlands who was an air general.

The SS divisions, directly answerable to Heinrich Himmler who often sent them orders without reference to the military commanders, came under C-in-C West's orders only for strictly tactical employment authorized from above. Even the Todt Organization took its orders from OKW.

The command structure for the crucial defence of Fortress Europe against attack from the West approximated therefore to what Field-Marshal Lord Montgomery used to call "an absolute dog's breakfast." It was a tribute to the innate German flair for organization and passion for order that, in spite of everything, for a long time it worked tolerably well.

Chapter 5

THE FÜHRER FEELS THE COLD

☐ The exceptionally hard winter, which was scourging the German armies in Russia with the extremest agonies of frostbite and exposure, was reflected, with only proportionately less severity, in East Prussia and indeed the whole of eastern Europe during the winter of 1941-42. At the Wolf's Lair it prolonged itself remorselessly into March and no one was more miserable than the Wolf himself. Despite his bizarre preference for sunless northern aspects, Adolf Hitler could not stand the cold.

For the logical realists among the staff of OKW it was an appalling time in which to have to brood on the inescapable implications of what had happened in early December: to begin to adjust to the probability that the war had reached the beginning of a potential turning-point: to continue to address

49

themselves as keenly as ever to the daily business of running the present and planning the future of a war in which their secret hearts could now no longer wholly believe. It was hard enough anyway to initiate the process of mental reorientation required to swing their basic thinking from the unquestioned offensive to the defensive after two-and-a-half years. The paralysing cold of an interminable winter made the task infinitely harder.

The effect of an extreme winter in human terms as a moral and psychological factor of war cannot be overestimated. During these timeless few weeks of crisis in the Russian snows, more than one less-than-dedicated Nazi, blowing through his aching hands in the petrified forest at Rastenburg, must have thought to himself, "All this—and Hitler too!" Nevertheless the hysterically confident briefings continued with the same certainty, and their essence, distilled and as far as possible rationalized, flooded unabated through the IN trays and the OUT trays to the field commands; preparing for a resumption of the onslaught on Russia when the winter ended; preparing for the western defence of Fortress Europe that had now become something to be taken seriously.

In the evenings the Führer held forth as before with his cronies and those of his staff chiefs who obliged by agreeing with whatever he thought, felt, or suggested and who could cheer him up by telling him what he wanted to hear: cronies like Admiral Raeder and Reichsmarschall Goering (who constantly dropped in from OKL in his private diesel train, as flamboyant and gaudy as his dress): staff yes-men like Field-Marshal Keitel and General Jodl.

There was no more dedicated crony than the egregious little club-footed Minister of Propaganda Dr. Joseph Goebbels who periodically dropped over from Berlin. A copious diarist, Goebbels had a long account of a visit to Rastenburg in March 1942 which is in more senses than one revealing:

> Will this winter never end? Is a new ice age in the offing? Judging by these constant, repeated attacks of freezing weather, one might almost think so.

After this opening wail, Goebbels[1] goes on to observe that the Führer is "really to be pitied," having to take the "entire burden of the war on his own shoulders."

"Added to this," continues the doctor, "the Führer practically lives in a concentration camp. Whether the guards before his HQ are furnished by the SS or by some prisoner-of-war camp, the effect is the same." The headquarters itself the method of working and the amount of work Hitler has to get through in solitude are bound to have a depressing effect on him, Goebbels thinks. That he managed to survive the winter and still look reasonably healthy showed that he must have "a constitution as strong as a bear's." This makes a convenient cue for a snide remark about the decline in the reputation of the generals and their failure to stand up to the demands made on them. That the front had been saved during the winter was entirely due to the Führer and the fact that he would not yield and gave no sign of weakness whatever.

It was because he realized what his poor Führer must be going through during these weeks that Goebbels had considered it "all the more my duty to let the Führer now and then have reports, news and information which will to some extent distract him from his immediate war tasks." So he had constantly sent material to OKW that "interested the Führer from the purely human side, especially items about art and cultural life from which he is completely cut off, although in normal times they are one of his main preoccupations."

After describing how deeply touched he has been by his two long intimate talks with Hitler—"one cannot fail to notice how happy the Führer is to welcome one of his old collaborators and especially to be able to say in complete privacy all those things that he can't tell a larger circle"—Goebbels turns to the Führer's health. Superficially he seemed to be in the best of shape but actually this was not the case, and to Goebbels he had confided that he had lately been fighting off attacks of giddiness.

> The long winter has affected his spiritual condition
> . . . The Führer, I recall, never cared very much for
> winter. In the old days we sometimes used to laugh at
> his physical revulsion against frost and snow. For in-
> stance he could never understand how some people
> in spring could look for altitudes where there was still
> snow for skiing! Now his aversion to winter has
> been cruelly and terribly justified!

Warming to his task the little doctor now sees the winter as a malevolent act of nature deliberately directed at his beloved master who

> certainly never imagined that a time would come when winter would so unrelentingly take advantage of his instinctive antipathy and inflict such suffering upon German troops . . . This long hard cruel winter be damned! . . . This winter put not only the German Wehrmacht but especially its Supreme Commander under a cruel strain. It is nothing short of a miracle that we stood it!

At least the unfortunate German soldiers get a mention— but how dare the winter do this to our beloved Führer!
With a reverent sob Goebbels continues:

> It is still too early to appreciate fully what the Führer suffered during these months . . . What worries and torments the Führer most is the fact that frost and cold are still stalking through field and forest . . . one can feel how unhappy he is about the long duration of the winter—a winter that came so suddenly and is departing so unwillingly.

At last they talk of other things than the weather. Food rations will again have to be reduced in Berlin. They are confident the people will endure this with good grace if the reasons are properly explained and they are properly led. Hitler thinks that before long they will start getting reasonable supplies out of the Ukraine. Goebbels does not share this optimism: he thinks they lack the necessary manpower, organization and (especially) the transport. This question of food supplies brings Goebbels back to the subject of the weather. "This damnably long winter" is preventing the authorities from opening up the large supplies of potatoes buried underground.

> Here we are at the beginning of spring, and still we are struggling with problems of the winter as though it were only the turn of the year!

The Führer authorizes top transport priority for a rapid distribution of the potatoes as soon as the ground thaws sufficiently for the underground storage dumps to be opened. But this provokes an outburst by Goebbels against the Ministry of Transport which has "failed again." The Ministry has failed to build up the reserve of locomotives that will soon be needed. "The old fogeys in the Ministry" (he tells Hitler) "fumbled the ball so criminally that an example ought to be made of them." It is clear that Goebbels only brought up the food question in order to cue in his denunciation of the Ministry of Transport. Hitler shares his rage and plunges into a general threat of severer measures against ministers and officials who fail—imprisonment or in extreme cases death.

Goebbels skilfully fans Hitler's rising temper by smearing other German leaders and services chiefs and reports with satisfaction that the Führer "does not think as much of the generals as he did. For many of them he has nothing but contempt." Dr. Robert Ley is attacked by Goebbels for an inopportune publicity campaign for greater production at a time when rations have been reduced and Goebbels is authorized to "talk to him personally" about this.

Goebbels next gives a graphic account of "the disgusting incidents at German railway stations and in express trains" where the wealthier citizens, it seems, were monopolizing the first-class seat and sleeper reservations and soldiers were being forced to stand in crowded discomfort or elbowed off the trains altogether. "The wealthier people simply will not heed our advice and requests," said Goebbels. Hitler authorized him "to invoke concentration-camp punishment to put an end to this nuisance."

After some political discussion Goebbels returns to the weather:

> Then the Führer spoke about himself. It is really touching to hear him complain about the winter that has caused him such terrific worries and difficulties. I noted that he has already become quite grey and that merely talking about the cares of the winter makes him seem to have aged very much . . .
>
> The Führer described to me how close we were during the past months to a Napoleonic winter. Had he weakened for only one moment, the front would have caved in and a catastrophe ensued that would have put the Napoleonic disaster far into the shade.

Field-Marshal Walther von Brauchitsch ("a coward and

a nincompoop") was to blame and Goebbels quotes at length from a long diatribe by the Führer against the wretched von Brauchitsch. Turning now to the future, he discloses that the Führer again has a "perfectly clear plan" for the coming summer. He does not intend to overextend the war. His aims are the Caucasus, Leningrad, and Moscow. If these objectives are achieved he will build a "gigantic line of defence" and let the eastern campaign stop there: even if it means "a hundred years' war in the east" he won't mind. "Our position towards what remains of Russia would then be like that of England towards India." The proposed offensive would probably not be able to get launched before the end of May.

> I can only hope (says Goebbels fervently) that when spring comes the Führer will soon be at the peak of health again. What he needs now is air, sunshine, spring and the prospect of good weather. The whole atmosphere at OKW is most depressing. Always surrounded by snow, ice, and frost, no man can live there happily, not even a superman.

So they talked on and on for several hours, master and disciple. Before they went in to supper—served early so that Goebbels could share it before leaving—Hitler asked tenderly after each member of the Goebbels family. How were Helga, Hilde, and Holge and the other children and what were they doing? Goebbels was touched and "decided that my family and I must look after him more after the war."

> Finally we talked about the Jewish question. Here the Führer is as uncompromising as ever. The Jews must be got out of Europe, if necessary by applying the most brutal methods.
> For the present he does not want to become very active in the church question. He would like to save that up until after the war. . . .

The doctor is nearing the end of the long account of the two meetings and he is suffused with emotion at the recollection of them.

> Our whole conversation was most cordial and intimate. I was happy to be with the Führer again. The Führer was glad to be able to talk in so personal a

manner in absolute privacy. His devotion and meticulous care are touching . . .

It is almost a declaration of love. By a viper for a crocodile. But Goebbels is not quite finished. There is a coda to the Te Deum.

> A little dog which he has been given now plays about in his room. His whole heart belongs to that dog. It can do anything it wants in his bunker. At present it is nearer the Führer's heart than anything else.

Nearer, apparently, than the gangrenous wounded, dying in their frostbitten thousands in Russia. Nearer, apparently, than the women and children in the German cities, beginning to learn now what it was like to spend the night in air raid shelters. Certainly nearer than the Jews dying in Himmler's gas chambers.

For one little dog it was a good war and there was nothing to complain of.

When describing to Goebbels his "perfectly clear plan" for the summer campaign in Russia—with Leningrad, Moscow, and the Caucasus as its three objectives—Hitler must have been infected by something of his Propaganda Minister's own zeal for exaggeration. In a conversation with the Japanese Ambassador two months before, the Führer had indicated his intentions for the summer in terms much closer to the truth as it turned out in the event. What he told the ambassador was that his object was "to resume the offensive towards the Caucasus as soon as the weather allows."

> This is the most important direction for an offensive; we must reach the oil fields there and also in Iran and Iraq. Once we have got there we hope that we can assist the rise of the freedom movement in the Arab world.[2]

He had added—but it was more of an afterthought—that he would naturally do all he could to "obliterate Moscow and Leningrad" but he had made it clear that oil was now the point. The oil of the Caucasus was to be the real objective of the new offensive which was to be the northern arm of a huge pincer movement. The southern arm was to be a drive on Egypt and Britain's Middle East oilfields by the German-Italian army of General Erwin Rommel that had been fighting the British Eighth Army in Libya for the past year.

This was one of the few recorded occasions when Hitler credited the North African campaign with any importance. As the frustrated Rommel was constantly pointing out, Hitler more usually regarded it as a peripheral campaign of only secondary importance into which he had been drawn, largely by accident, to help out a weak and incompetent ally; and to which he had been reluctant to commit more than the minimal forces that could be spared from the gigantic conflict in Russia and the defence requirements of conquered Europe. What had upset the reckoning and forced the Führer to take notice, if only temporarily, of the African front was that the general he had sent to Africa, Erwin Rommel, was a brilliant tactical opportunist and battle commander who had achieved results with his small Afrika Korps (two armoured divisions and a force of infantry) beyond anyone's expectations. North Africa remained in Hitler's view an Italian responsibility and the campaign was fought under Italian supreme command, but the mercurial Rommel, idolized by the Italian as well as the German troops and admired even by his British opponents, had taken over and established a personal ascendancy over the campaign by sheer force of personality. As this "secondary" front—outside Fortress Europe but strategically more related to it than Hitler as yet realized—was to provide, later in the year, the first of the two great body blows against Germany that together would comprise the fulfilment of the ominous rumblings of December 1941, some account of the position in Africa must now be given.

Mussolini, whom Churchill used to call "Hitler's jackal," had deferred Italy's reluctant entry into the war until the mid-summer of 1940 when France had been defeated and England seemed almost certain to be. Italy's role in the Axis strategy had of course been first to wrest control of the Mediterranean from Britain by closing it to British convoys, and by threatening her three air and naval bases of Gibraltar, Malta, and Alexandria; and secondly, to attack Egypt (key to the Middle East area from which Britain received most of her oil) and the Suez Canal, the vital link in the imperial lifeline from Britain through India to Australia and New Zealand. The effect of the Italian declaration of war was that the British garrison of 55,000 (nearly half of them base troops) then in Egypt were confronted by an Italian army of 250,000 across the desert border in the then Italian colony of Libya. But the Italian Navy showed no disposition to seize control of the Mediterranean, though by its mere presence it forced Britain to route its Middle East convoys round the Cape of Good Hope and the Red Sea adding forty-two days to the journey. The Italian army showed as little inclination to attack Egypt. So when, in November, the British Commander-in-Chief General Sir Archibald (later Field Marshal Earl) Wavell ordered his tiny field force of one armoured, one infantry division, and a brigade of tanks to launch a surprise offensive against its considerable but hesitant opponent, his boldness succeeded beyond his wildest hopes.

In ten weeks the task force advanced five hundred miles to Benghazi destroying, in a series of bold encircling actions mainly executed at night, the bulk of the ten Italian divisions, and capturing 130,000 prisoners, 400 tanks and 1290 guns. With other divisions now available to reinforce the task force there seemed every chance of continuing the advance to Tripoli, but just as they were poised to do so, General Wavell received orders from London to divert part of his force to Greece, and the weakened Western Desert Force (as it was named) was forced to go on the defensive. It was just at this time that the deflated Mussolini decided to appeal to Hitler for help, and the latter, scarcely able to spare any troops from Russia or Europe, rather grudgingly sent a small armoured force to Tripoli, the nucleus of what was soon to turn into the German Afrika Korps: an iron spearhead for Mussolini's frail wooden shaft. In charge of it he sent one of his younger panzer generals, not yet fifty, who had greatly distinguished himself in the blitzkrieg against France. His name was Erwin Rommel and he was given strictly limited orders. In the first place he came under the Italian Supreme Command in Rome. Secondly, he was to attempt no more than to dislodge the British in the spring from their present positions and, if successful, he might try to recapture Benghazi. But that was all. He was to take no risks.

Rommel, however, had other ideas. Bold, ambitious, above all an opportunist he decided to try a surprise attack at the end of March. It succeeded as brilliantly as the British offensive had done in the previous autumn. Having defeated the weakened British forces at El Agheila and Marsa el Brega, he decided to disregard his orders and, subordinating everything to speed, boldness, and improvisation, he raced on to the Egyptian frontier, recapturing in a few weeks all the ground (except for Tobruk which he bypassed and invested) lost by the Italians before Christmas.

The score, as it were, was one-all and it was not until November that the British Eighth Army (as the Western Desert Force was now called) had opened a new offensive under a new Commander-in-Chief, General Sir Claude Auchinleck. After some extremely tough fighting Rommel's German-Italian army had been driven back to El Agheila to make the score two-one to Britain; and as this reverse coincided with the German army's first real reverses on the Russian front it did not excite much attention or interest at Rastenburg, where Hitler and his OKW staff had infinitely bigger worries to occupy them. Nor could they summon up much interest in the fact that Rommel in the end managed to knock some of the shine off the British victory by counterattacking and recapturing the western half of Cyrenaica including the airfields that had been one of the main British objectives because of their value for the protection of Malta. Rastenburg was a long way from Benghazi.

By early in 1942 the two desert armies faced one another across a line south of Gazala some two hundred miles east of Benghazi, and a supply race began to see who would be ready first to open a new offensive. It was at this stage that Hitler, miserably cold, mentally reeling under the disasters of December, and no doubt anxious to impress the Japanese Ambassador chose for once to upgrade the forthcoming North African offensive to the status of southern jaw of a pincer whose northern jaw would be the tremendous assault planned for the Caucasus in the summer. But—as we shall see—when the summer offensive in Africa came within sight of victory and Rommel was pleading for the extra support that might have made the vital difference, it was not forthcoming: Africa was back where it belonged—a secondary front that Hitler and OKW were too busy to bother about.

If Hitler, who had no clear understanding of sea power, failed at this time to see what a chance he was missing to damage Britain in the Mediterranean, there were those about him who saw more clearly. Foremost among them, not unexpectedly, was Grand Admiral Raeder, the naval Commander-in-Chief who, early in 1942, had reinforced the Axis Mediterranean fleets with thirty-six U-boats. Raeder and the German Naval Staff thought that the time had never been so propitious for a major stroke against Britain in the Mediterranean. On February 13 he strongly urged Hitler to mount an attack on Egypt and the Suez Canal. He could point out, with truth, that the British had not one heavy ship in the Mediterranean that was fully seaworthy. The Axis controlled the air and the sea in the Central Mediterranean. Now, insisted Raeder, was the time to strike at Egypt and "the main artery of the British Empire." In support of this operation, Raeder continued, an attempt must be made to seize Malta which had managed to survive months of aerial bombardment but which was being supplied with increasingly sacrificial losses of shipping.

The little island, ten miles long, only sixty miles from Sicily, lying athwart the short sea crossing from Sicily to North Africa was the hub of the whole British Mediterranean position. It was from Malta, so long as it could be maintained, that British submarines and aircraft maintained their assault on Axis convoys supplying Rommel. Malta was an essential staging point for British bombers headed for the Middle East and beyond. But conversely it was at the mercy of the Sicily-based Axis air fleet that had recently been reinforced by squadrons withdrawn for the time-being from the Russian front. To Raeder and the naval staff it seemed obvious that this was the moment to initiate a more positive strategy in the Mediterranean. But the Army thought otherwise, and it was the Army's opinion that prevailed with Hitler.

General Halder considered that the attack on Suez was out of the question until it could be co-ordinated with a simultaneous German advance from the Caucasus. This was not likely to be possible in 1942 as there still remained the little matter of actually conquering the Caucasus. To the proposed invasion of Malta Hitler agreed but half-heartedly. He did not trust the Italians to go through with it, though Count Ugo Cavallero, their Chief of Staff, professed great enthusiasm for the idea. Hitler also feared the cost of an invasion of the island fortress which would have to be mainly carried out by airborne troops. He had never got over the cost of the Pyrrhic victory the cream of his paratroopers had won for him in Crete. This haunting recollection coupled with his distrust of his allies and his conviction, more than once confided to members of his entourage, that they would let him down, made it seem unlikely that Operation Hercules (as the Malta project was called) would ever come off. He would bear it in mind, he said, and discuss it again with Mussolini when they met at the end of April.

There was further vacillation over the timing and precise objectives of Rommel's summer offensive against the Eighth

Army. As late as March 18 Hitler was specifying Tobruk as the objective and an advance beyond it to the Libyan-Egyptian border as the extreme limit. The timing was also subject to changes of mind. At one time, with Rommel's agreement, it was not to be until late summer. Though Hitler readily agreed when Rommel told him in April that he would like to attack at the end of May or early in June so as to race the British to the draw.

The truth is that Hitler was not very interested in the Mediterranean. It was not important. Russia was what mattered, and in his rear the long coastlines of Norway and Europe at some point of which the Anglo-Americans might at any time attempt a landing. Hence the orders he had issued in March for the tightening up of the defences of the West and of Norway, a second European theatre in its own right.

It is an oddity worth remarking in passing that an obsession about Norway haunted both Adolf Hitler and Winston Churchill. Hitler (though not his staff) was convinced that Norway would be invaded. The daring exploit of the capital ships *Gneisenau, Scharnhorst*, and *Prinz Eugen* in February in dashing up the English Channel under the guns of the British Navy and Air Force to take up station in Norwegian waters was a measure for the defence of Norway. Not, as the British thought, so that the ships could reinforce Germany's surface raiders in the North Atlantic.

But Hitler's appreciation would not have been so wrong if Churchill could have had his way. A project for a landing in northern Norway to join up with the Russians was a pet notion of his which his Chief of Staff General Sir Alan Brooke described as a "recurrent nightmare" in a diary note quoted by Sir Arthur Bryant: [3]

> Why he wanted to go back and what he was going to do there . . . we never found out. The only reason he ever gave was that Hitler had unrolled the map of Europe starting with Norway and he would start rolling it up again with Norway . . . Heaven knows what we should have done in Norway had we landed there!

Against the background of what was to come in Russia and what it was feared might come in the west there is a certain charm about the two war leaders, each in his own way implacable, scowling away at each other across an imaginary

Norwegian battlefield while their stone-faced pragmatical staff advisers in effect told both of them not to be silly.

Diaries, as we have noted, often say less but tell more than logs and chronicles. This chapter opened with a diarist's impression of a visit to Hitler at the height of the Germans' first winter of discontent. Let it end with another diarist's impressions of a meeting between Hitler and Mussolini at the end of that same long winter when spring was in the air and with it renewed hope—but hope that on the German side was too automatic, as if reissued by order; and on the Italian side increasingly tinged with disillusion and resentment of the new patronizing attitude of the senior Axis partner.

Count Galeazzo Ciano, the Italian Foreign Minister, was as reprehensible as anyone else in the Axis hierarchies but he did have—something unusual to the point of uniqueness in a fascist—the saving grace of humour. It was a bitchy humour, Roman and treacherous but undeniably droll, and his *Diary* does give a human as well as a mordantly humorous inside view of personalities and events that cannot be found anywhere else in the bibliography of the Nazi-Fascist era.

The spring meeting of the two dictators and their advisers took place at the Schloss Klessheim in Salzburg on April 29 and 30, "a meeting," Ciano comments "that was desired by the Germans, and for which, as usual,[4] they have given us no indication of an agenda."

> We are staying at Klessheim Castle. This is a grandiose building, once owned by the prince-bishops of Salzburg, which has now become a guest-house for the Führer. It is very luxurious and well arranged: furniture, hangings, carpets, all having been brought from France. Probably they did not pay very much for them.
>
> There is much cordiality, which puts me on my guard. The courtesy of the Germans is always in inverse ratio to their good fortune. Hitler looks tired. The winter months in Russia have weighed heavily upon him. I see for the first time that he has many grey hairs.

Hitler and Mussolini talk in one room, their Foreign Ministers in another, "and the same record is played in both." Ribbentrop "plays his usual record" which Ciano finds boring—the one about Napoleon, the Beresina and the drama of 1812 and how "the ice of Russia has been conquered by the genius of Hitler."

Ciano who has heard it all before wants to know what is to happen next and what the future holds. When it comes to answering these questions "Ribbentrop is less explicit."

An offensive against the Russians in the south with the oil wells as a politico-military objective? When Russia's sources of oil are exhausted she will be brought to her knees. Then the British Conservatives, and even Churchill himself, who, after all, is a sensible man, will bow in order to save what remains of their mauled empire. Thus spoke Ribbentrop.

"But what," asked Ciano, "if all this doesn't happen? What if the British, who are stubborn, decided to continue? How are they to be made to change their minds?" By tanks and airplanes, says Ribbentrop. So it is back to 1940, Ciano comments. It did not work then, why should it work now? Ciano is not convinced and tells Ribbentrop so—to the dismay of a more timorous colleague from the Foreign Ministry.

The name of America can scarcely be kept out of the talks for long and Ciano has this significant note.

America is a big bluff. This slogan is repeated by everyone, big and little, in the conference rooms and in the antechambers. In my opinion the thought of what the Americans can and will do disturbs them all, and the Germans shut their eyes to it. But this does not keep the more intelligent and the more honest from thinking about what America can do, and they feel shivers running down their spines.

A subject that prompts an observation in Ciano's long diary entry is the German casualty toll in Russia. The Germans give the number of killed to date as 270,000 but the Italian military leaders at Salzburg estimate that the true figure is probably nearer 700,000. To which Ciano adds the comment that with amputations, frostbite and the permanently disabled "the figure rises to three million."

One of his notes concerns the growing power of the British air offensive, another of the talking points at the conference.

The British Air Force is striking hard . . . The Germans strike back at the English cities but with less violence. Which only partly consoles the German population, accustomed as it has always been to hit but never to be hit back. Which leads many Germans, who have devastated half Europe, to weep about "The brutality of the British" . . . The worst of it is that they really feel this way.

Most revealing of all, perhaps, is Ciano's account of the second afternoon of the Salzburg meeting. For two days it had been a question of "Hitler talks, talks, talks, talks. Mussolini suffers—he, who is in the habit of talking himself, and who, instead, has to remain practically silent." But by now everything has been said and said again and after lunch on the second day the time has come for the final meeting between the two dictators: one the fanatic, baleful and dominant; the other the braggart who desperately tried to emulate him but, when they were together, was only his pale copy.

In the ancient Austrian castle with its sumptuous French furnishings, probably looted, it has been a sort of eve-of-Waterloo Ball with talking instead of dancing. A new campaigning season is about to begin. Like swimmers on the high diving board of destiny, the two dictators who control the Axis will shortly plunge into a twelvemonth that must decide, one way or the other, whether Hitler's black dream of world conquest can succeed, or whether even now, though he may not know it, the chance has gone forever.

All the more fascinating, therefore, is Ciano's account of the anticlimax of that last afternoon when Hitler had the stage to himself:

> Hitler talked uninterruptedly for an hour and forty minutes. He omitted absolutely no argument: war and peace, religion and philosophy, art and history. Mussolini automatically looked at his wristwatch, I had my mind on my own business, and only Cavallero, who is a phenomenon of servility, pretended he was listening in ecstasy, continually nodding his head in approval. The Germans, however, dreaded the ordeal less than we did. Poor people. They have to endure it every day, and I am certain there isn't a gesture, a word, or a pause which they don't know by heart. General Jodl, after an epic

struggle, finally went to sleep on the divan. Keitel was yawning, but he succeeded in keeping his head up. He was too close to Hitler to let himself go as he would have liked to do.

It seems Mussolini was quite satisfied with the Salzburg meeting and with his talks with Hitler. "This always happens," Ciano comments tartly. And then he adds a somewhat enigmatic footnote.

> But although he doesn't say it openly, this time he is led to think deeply about many things which are not yet apparent, but which one can feel in the air.

No explanation or amplification is offered. What did Ciano mean? Was it that the more subtle intelligence and volatile instinct of the Italian dictator had received a tiny but unmistakable intuition—too remote and too appalling to say out loud—that, despite the well-drilled enthusiasm of the Germans and the burning eloquence of the Führer, the prospect was not quite so perfect as they made out? That difficulties were on the way?

At least there seemed to be one firm outcome of the Salzburg talks, Hitler's final agreement that the Malta invasion should take place: but (so as not to interfere with Rommel's coming offensive in Libya) not until mid-July or at the latest mid-August. But even in this there was still a doubt, still a feeling that Operation Hercules would never happen: that its only enthusiastic champion was General Cavallero who (says Ciano contemptuously) "does not conceal the fact that he hopes to derive a great deal of personal glory" from it.

Chapter 6

NEW PLANS FOR THE EAST: CONTINUING FEARS FOR THE WEST

☐ Throughout the winter there was endless worried appraisal and reappraisal of the plan for the summer campaign in Russia. Franz Halder, the Army Chief of the German General Staff of the Army, was at one time considering the advisability of going over to the defensive along the entire Eastern front but did not dare mention this to Hitler. Intelligence reports that between six and seven hundred tanks were being turned out each month by Russian factories caused acute concern at OKW—but Hitler refused to believe them.

Most important of all there was heavy pressure on Hitler from his economic advisers who were insisting that without wheat from the Ukraine and oil from the Caucasus before the summer's end Germany would not be able to continue fighting.

So in its final form the plan was less ambitious than the grandiloquent outline Hitler had given to Goebbels earlier in the year with its three objectives, Leningrad, Moscow, and the Caucasus. There was now but one objective, the Caucasus, while the Northern and Central Army Groups would remain on the defensive, except that Army Group North was to make one final attempt to capture Leningrad in the late summer after victory had been achieved in the Caucasus.

Before the offensive proper opened in the middle of June, preliminary operations were to be put in hand to clear and occupy the Crimea and to establish a firm base in the Kharkov-Izium area from which the main attack could be launched east and southeast.

These preliminary operations, which began on May 8 and extended over nearly two months, were extremely successful. By June 28, when the main offensive was scheduled to open, all objectives had been attained except that Sebastopol, the last bastion in the Crimea, managed to hold out until July 4. The line-up for the new phase was formidable for South East Army Group, who were to carry it out, now included the following forces: First Panzer Army, Seventeenth Army, Second Army, Fourth Panzer Army, and General Friedrich Paulus's highly esteemed Sixth Army of eleven infantry and three panzer or motorized divisions—an army of which much was to be heard. In addition there were in reserve a division each from Italy and Hungary and two from Rumania. On top of this encouraging Crimean prelude to the summer campaign in Russia, there was good news from North Africa. Rommel had opened his offensive against the British on May 26, decisively defeated them at Gazala and had captured Tobruk on June 21. Tobruk was his specified objective and he was under orders to continue no farther than the Egyptian border. But Rommel, who was mercifully a long way from Supreme Headquarters, and who made a specialty of disobeying orders when he was going well and knew he could get away with it, was now exuberantly chasing the beaten Eighth Army back to the Nile.

In those sunny last days of June fortune seemed once more to be smiling on Hitler. Was he after all going to be able to make good the boast he had made in March to the German people during a Memorial Day speech in Berlin? That day he had shouted:

> During the coming summer the Soviets will be completely destroyed. There is no longer any escape for them. So this summer will be the decisive phase of this war. The Bolshevists will be thrown back so far that they will never again touch the cultured soil of Europe.[1]

During those days of 1942 when the sun was beating down alike on Egypt, the Crimea and Kharkov the prospect was brighter than it had been for many months. But for those with eyes to see there was another side to the briefly flashing coin of resurrected success. It was contained in a a paper[2] headed *War Potential 1942* signed and issued by the granite-faced Assistant Chief of Operations General Warlimont. It disclosed among other things that the army on the Eastern Front was 625,000 below strength as a result of the previous twelve months' operations, and that this deficit could not be made up. That armoured divisions in Army Groups Centre and North—the two not immediately concerned in the forthcoming offensive—would have to be reduced to one tank battalion (forty to fifty tanks) each. That serious ammunition shortages could be expected as early as August. That the vehicle deficiency was such that many formations would have to convert to horse transport. The Air Force was on average 50 to 60 percent below its establishment of serviceable aircraft.

Warlimont thinks that Hitler probably never saw this paper—that Keitel was probably afraid to show it to him. But many of those who were helping to carry the war into a new and critical phase saw it. It cannot have made comforting reading.

The deficiency in manpower on the Eastern Front had not been helped by Hitler's obsession with Norway which had been one of the running refrains of the winter. He had repeatedly insisted on having this theatre reinforced against invasion. A first-class mountain division had been brought

66

up to full strength and sent there: twenty "fortress battalions" and innumerable coastal batteries had been formed—measures which had deprived the Eastern Front of thousands of badly needed high quality soldiers.

Hitler's other recurrent anxiety concerned the Atlantic coast. The daring British commando raids on the French seaboard must have had something to do with this jumpiness. It was as if he who had imposed upon so many the haunting fear of the policeman's knock was now beginning to learn just what it was like to fear that knock himself. Long since beyond the nagging reach of conscience, he would increasingly experience the sensations of the criminal who feels the retributive net closing in on him. The master of the "nerve war" was about to become increasingly its victim.

About the middle of June—when everything was going so well in Libya and the Crimea—Hitler became particularly uneasy about the possibility of landing attempts in the West, issuing a flurry of warning orders and instructions to his commanders in Norway and France, and constantly haranguing his entourage with speculations about probable Anglo-American landing operations supported by "thousands of airborne troops."

On June 26 however there was something more tangible on which Hitler could base his fears. It was reported that concentrations of small shipping were forming off the south coast of England.

At this point, with the main German striking force looming over the Volga like an iron cloud and Rommel's Panzer-Armée Afrika chasing a beaten British army back to the Nile which nothing, it now seemed, could prevent his reaching, it is time to turn for a moment to the other side. During that first Russian winter while Hitler had been comforting his cheated legions with crowns of thorns when what they were begging for was winter clothing, Britain and the United States, like a newly married couple, had been taking the first shy tentative steps towards the consummation of that most difficult of marriages, a military alliance: an alliance, moreover, complicated by a third party of alien political and moral philosophy that would add its own enigmatic nuances to one of the strangest *ménages a trois* in history.

Even before the Japanese surprise attack on Pearl Harbor had precipitated America into the war in December 1941, a measure of Anglo-American alliance had existed for a long time unofficially. During the time she was fighting Hitler alone, Britain had been sustained and encouraged by more than one "decisive act of non-belligerence" in Churchill's felicitous phrase; notably the Lend-Lease act of 1941 by which America became (in President Franklin D. Roosevelt's equally happy phrase) "The arsenal of democracy" by undertaking to supply essential war material to countries resisting Hitler and to lend them the money with which to pay for it.

So natural and spontaneous was the alliance between the United States and the British Commonwealth in this war that long before it existed openly and, so to speak, on paper, the Services chiefs of the two nations had been in close touch with each other and there had been secret staff discussions about the joint strategy to be adopted when America came into the war—it being accepted by both that it was a case of *when* rather than *if*. It was at one of these secret discussions, nine months before Pearl Harbor, that the cardinal principle of "Europe first" had been agreed: to be more explicit, that as Germany was the major enemy the main Anglo-American effort—when America was in the war—would be directed first at defeating Hitler in Europe. At the Roosevelt-Churchill conference held in Washington a month after the United States was at war, the "Europe first" principle was reaffirmed —though then as later there were voices, mainly U. S. Navy voices, arguing that for the United States the Pacific war should come first.

For the next six months the joint planners wrestled with the problem of how they could strike at Hitler in Europe in 1942 and so take some of the weight off the Russians. Both the American and the British military chiefs took a pessimistic view of Russia's chances of surviving another summer. Though the air offensive against Germany was increasing all the time and would continue to do so during the year, it was agreed that an invasion of Europe and the opening of a second front was the best way of helping the Russians, and indeed the only way of drawing off some of the strength of the German assault.

But Britain was almost fully extended fighting the Axis in the Libyan-Egyptian Desert and the Japanese in the Far East: and it would be some time before America could raise and train enough divisions of high enough quality to tackle battle-hardened Germans in that trickiest of military operations, an opposed landing. Nevertheless the proposition was studied and discussed at length and it received an extra impetus when Vyacheslav Molotov, the Soviet Foreign Minister, came to London and then Washington in the spring to present what was virtually a demand by Stalin for a "Second Front now." A plan that was hardening in favour (though endlessly revised, amended, and hedged with qualifying *ifs* and *buts*) envisaged a full-scale Anglo-American invasion of Northwest Europe in spring 1943 (codename: Roundup). As an act of desperation, if this were necessary to keep Russia in the war, Roundup would be preceded in the late summer of 1942 by Sledgehammer, a smaller-scale operation by some six to eight divisions, and designed to gain a foothold on the continent of Europe and to hold a bridgehead in readiness for the larger operation of the following spring.

The British chiefs, with considerable experience of fighting the Germans in this war, considered an invasion in 1943 to be highly dubious and the Sledgehammer landing proposed for 1942 plain silly. No one, American or British, was happy about the idea of a landing in 1942 and the only reason so much time was spent on it was the very real fear at that time that something extreme might have to be done to stave off a Russian collapse, even to the point of a sacrifice landing. There was more British than American relief when President Roosevelt, determined that a new front should be opened *somewhere* that year, reverted to another project that had been considered for 1942, a landing in northwest Africa. Churchill could not agree fast enough for, though he had played along with the American plans for an invasion of the continent in 1943, his belief was that the way back to Europe was in the first place through the Mediterranean. The northwest Africa proposal was naturally pleasing to the Prime Minister as it meant that Rommel would now have an Anglo-American army behind him as well as the British Eighth Army to his front. This must place beyond doubt the total clearance of the North African coast and the reopening of the Mediterranean as a sea route and as a base for further operations as well.

It was pleasing to the President who was determined that American troops should face the German Army *somewhere* that year. It was displeasing to elements in the American High Command who favored a direct attack on Germany by the shortest route, across the English Channel, and feared the indirect strategy which came naturally to the British through history, habit, and a traditional reliance on sea power to offset the superiority on land of more powerful enemies. The American fear was that the Mediterranean operations would escalate and suck more and more American forces and resources into what they regarded as a secondary theatre—as indeed Hitler did.

This difference in the strategic attitudes[3] of the Americans and the British, which will long be debated by the historians of the Second World War, was to be a constant nag though never an open breach. Essentially it was a reflection of each nation's character, temperament, history, and wealth at that time in terms of manpower, money, and industrial productivity. Whatever the pros and cons—and in the complex patchwork of the Second World War no strategic issue could ever be considered in simple isolation—the decision[4] was made by the two leaders on July 25: North Africa it was to be, codename Torch.

This, they well knew, was not what Stalin would agree to consider a "second front" and, with the German offensive in the Caucasus already under way, it was strongly felt that some kind of a gesture must be made across the Channel. It was with timely relief that Churchill was able to reply, with some conviction, to another peremptory demand from Stalin for a second front, received on July 23, that a policy of heavy raids on the European coast would be carried out in the near future. For a plan for the largest raid yet had just been resurrected by Combined Operations Command after being planned, rehearsed twice and finally abandoned on July 7. The project was for a raid by two brigades of infantry and a regiment of tanks on the German-occupied French port of Dieppe, ostensibly to destroy military and dock installations but in reality to test the German defences; to test the British equipment currently available for amphibious operations; to find out whether a port could be captured and held for a few hours and to discover whether tanks could be effectively used to assist an assault landing. Churchill defined the operation as a "reconnaissance in force"—a military euphemism for a process less formally describable as "try it and see what happens": a process sometimes unavoidable in war especially when new techniques are being developed.

The Dieppe raid had been first conceived in April and the Canadian Army was delighted to hear that it was to provide the two infantry brigades and the regiment of Churchill tanks that were to comprise its main force. After two frustrating years of training in the United Kingdom the Canadians had that eagerness for action common to all soldiers who have yet to experience it—eagerness in this case sharpened by the knowledge that they were the only Dominion troops in this situation; Australians, New Zealanders, South Africans, and

70

Indians had all been heavily involved for many months in the desert war in North Africa.

The raid was provisionally scheduled for the night June 20-21, the first of a sequence of nights when tide and moon would be right. At a full-scale rehearsal on the night June 11-12, everything went so hopelessly wrong—as only an amphibious operation can—that the raid was postponed to allow time for further intensive training. A second full trial was held ten days after the first and as it was much more satisfactory the raid was now scheduled for the night of July 4, first of the next sequence of nights when moon and tide would be right. The troops were embarked on July 2. Then the weather broke and the operation had to be postponed from night to night until July 8 the last night of the current period of tide-moon suitability, so the operation was cancelled and the disappointed troops dispersed. On security grounds alone it seemed sensible to consider the operation finally cancelled.

To Admiral Lord Louis Mountbatten's Combined Operations HQ, however, this operation was more than a gesture in lieu of a seriously intended second front. It was a vital step in a process of planned research on the way to the eventual true second front. Combined Operations HQ were determined to bring up Dieppe again if they could. It so happened that as a result of Russia's plight a vociferous section of public opinion (especially of the extreme political Left) in America and Britain was maintaining an ill-informed near-hysterical clamour for a second front and it was convenient for Churchill to be able to reply to Stalin's note of July 25 with an assurance that a major raid was now contemplated. Everything seemed to conspire to restore the Dieppe raid to the agenda and within a week of its final cancellation it was once again scheduled, this time for the morning of August 19.

It was realized that the stand-down must have created a security risk and to mitigate this it was decided not to muster the raiding force off the Isle of Wight as before, but to disperse it among five south of England ports where it would embark into its assault boats immediately before the operation. The plan remained basically the same but two commandos took over from airborne troops the task of silencing key batteries on the heights flanking Dieppe.

Meanwhile in July the situation in Egypt had been stabilized. The British had succeeded in stopping Rommel at El Alamein only sixty miles from Alexandria and Churchill, on

71

his way to Moscow for a meeting with Stalin, was touching down at Cairo to make a clean sweep of the British Middle East Command with a view to giving a new lease of life to the Eighth Army. The great U.S. naval victory of Midway in June had done much to restore American morale after its early shocks.

The centre of the stage would now be held briefly and, as it turned out, tragically by the Canadian soldier and the port and holiday resort of Dieppe for an occasion invested with the quality of sick glamour associated at that time with a direct assault on Hitler's Fortress Europe.

It was a perfect summer's evening with a clear sky, smooth sea and a gentle breeze. The small armada heading across the English Channel for the French coast soon after dusk on August 18 numbered 237 with its naval escort headed by eight destroyers and it included a variety of invasion craft that were being tried out under battle conditions for the first time. The raiding force being carried in these ships numbered approximately 6100 of whom 4963 were Canadian and 1075 United Kingdom troops. In addition fifty U.S. Rangers accompanied various of the units as observers.

The final plan provided for a main frontal attack on Dieppe by three Canadian battalions supported by tanks. This attack was to be supported by two inner flank attacks on Puys and Pourville (respectively two miles east and west of the town) each to be carried out by two Canadian battalions. In addition British Commandos were to make two outer flank attacks at Berneval and Varengeville, five miles east and west of Dieppe, for the purpose of silencing the two heavy coastal batteries which commanded the main assault beaches from the heights near these places.

There was to be no preliminary bombardment from the air or the sea partly to maintain surprise and partly to spare the civilian population: but the attendant destroyers and fighters of the Royal Air Force would give close fire support as required once the assaults had gone in at dawn. A subsidiary purpose of the operation was to provoke the Luftwaffe to a major air battle in the hope of inflicting upon it sufficiently crippling losses to affect the German air effort on the Eastern Front. To this end seventy-four air squadrons were on hand.

As the assault ships and their escort lapped quietly through lanes cleared for them by mine-sweepers the soldiers had the whole of the long calm night in which to think about what lay ahead. Had the security of this on-off-on operation really survived the postponements and the cancellations? Why had it been so suddenly revived? Was there something they had not been told? Was Russia in a bad way? Was there an emergency of some kind? A long night at sea in an open boat moving to the invasion of a hostile strongly defended coast "concentrates a man's mind wonderfully" as Dr. Johnson said in a context not dissimilar. The Canadians were still enthusiastic and pleased that two weeks before the war was three years old they were at last going to meet the enemy in battle. But for most of them it was bound to be a thoughtful as well as an interminable night. When, at 0347, the night was abruptly pierced by streams of red tracer and the stutter and boom of distant gunfire far over on the left, it momentarily relieved the tension: then created a new more urgent tension. This was not on the programme. They were still seven or eight miles from Dieppe. The group of boats on the far left must have run into something.

Chapter 7

RECONNAISSANCE IN FORCE: FORTRESS EUROPE RAIDED

☐ We have seen that in June the successes of his armies in North Africa and the Crimea could not stem the rising tide of Hitler's nervousness about an Anglo-American assault in the west. On June 25, despite the imminence of his main Russian offensive, he ordered a significant strengthening of von Rudstedt's Western Command, personally nominating certain powerful armoured or elite formations that were to be earmarked as reserves for France "Until further notice." These were the 10th Panzer Division, the SS Division *Das Reich,* 7th (Airborne) Division, and the Hermann Goering Motorized Regiment which was to be enlarged to divisional strength. Air and naval forces covering the English Channel were also to be appropriately strengthened.

These precautions seemed dramatically justified when on the very next day June 26 German Air Reconnaissance reported a "gathering of small vessels" off the south coast of England. (This was of course the shipping assembling in the Solent in readiness for the Dieppe raid first scheduled as we saw for early July.) To this Hitler reacted by giving orders that the SS Division *Das Reich* was to move to France as soon as it had reorganized and to issue a warning order that he would probably send two further divisions the *Liebstandarte* Adolf Hitler and the SS Division *Totenkopf* (Death's Head) if the Russian offensive, now due to start in only forty-eight hours, went well enough for them to be spared from the Eastern front.

On July 9 Hitler issued a further directive emphasizing his anxiety about impending danger in the West. He said that the British were faced with a choice between establishing a second front immediately or seeing Russia eliminated from the war. He warned that there was mounting evidence from agents' reports that a major landing was being planned and he named, as the areas most likely to be the target of a landing, the sectors of the Channel coast between Le Havre and Dieppe and also the coast of Normandy: his reason being that these areas were within range of fighter aircraft and the types of invasion craft that had been identified by his Reconnaissance.

In view of this the *Das Reich* and the *Liebstandarte* Divisions were not to wait until they had completed reorganization but were to move as many units as possible to the West at once and in fact sent a reinforced regimental group equivalent to about half a division. Headquarters SS Panzer Corps was also to move to France immediately to take command of all SS Divisions, which in the end proved to be only one, *Das Reich*. The other formations earmarked for France never in fact left the Eastern Front.

In Mid-August therefore von Rundstedt had thirty-six divisions in France and the Low Countries of which three and a half were armoured and one and a half motorized and one the elite 7th Airborne which had distinguished itself in Crete. The rest were coast defence divisions of medium to low category much called upon to provide reinforcements for the Eastern Front, but recently brought up to strength; in some cases with half-trained soldiers; but soldiers who, under good regular officers and NCOs, could shoot well enough from well-sited heavily protected emplacements.

Periods when tide and moon would be particularly favourable for a landing had been categorized as periods of "Threatened Danger" and maximum alertness was ordered for these times. One such period extended from August 10 to August 19. With ample infantry reserves at hand; the nearest panzer division only a few hours march away at Amiens; and Hitler's constant nagging about the certainty that the British must attempt a landing; the Dieppe garrison—the far from elite 302nd Division and its attendant artillery—could scarcely have been better prepared if the British had sent them a formal invitation to be ready to receive a British landing party in the early hours of August 19.

In spite of this, through faulty radar interpretation and slow communications, one hour and eleven minutes elapsed between the raid force's clash with the coastal convoy and the full alerting of the Dieppe garrison. This was about the only thing that went wrong for the Germans that day and it was a lesson which they were able to study and profit by for the future. Almost everything went wrong for the British raiders.

The one thing that went absolutely according to plan was the outer flank landing by 4th Commando at Varengeville on the extreme west of the landing. Achieving complete surprise the 250-strong commando successfully scaled the heights and destroyed the six-gun heavy coastal battery and its garrison as ordered. The complementary mission of 3rd Commando on the extreme east flank went awry because their boats were the ones that had the unlucky collision with the German coastal convoy on its way from Bologne to Dieppe. The group became disorganized and only seven out of twenty-three assault craft managed to land. The best this fraction of the force could do was to engage with fire the battery they were expected to destroy, and to some extent neutralize its effectiveness.

Of the two inner flank landings two miles west and east of Dieppe the westerly one at Pourville achieved a limited success. The landing was smooth and on time and a limited penetration succeeded in surprising the defenders. But, the expected follow-up tanks not materializing, the landing force was unable to follow through to any conclusive objectives. But the complementary landing on the eastern side of the town at Puys was a total disaster. Confusion between Army and Navy led to the assault party reaching their beach a vital seventeen minutes late to be confronted by a sea wall and a murderous curtain of fire from a fully alerted defence. The Royal Regiment of Canada, who were assigned this landing, died in their scores on the beach. Ross Munro, Canadian war correspondent, was with them:

> I was near the stern and to one side. Looking out the open bow over the bodies on the ramp, I saw the slope leading a short way up to a stone wall littered

with Royals casualties. There must have been sixty
or seventy of them . . . They had been cut down
before they had a chance to fire a shot . . .

I don't know how long we were nosed down on
that beach. It may have been five minutes it may
have been twenty. On no other front have I wit-
nessed such a carnage. It was brutal and terrible
and shocked you almost to insensibility to see the
piles of dead and feel the hopelessness of the attack
at this point.[1]

Of the twenty-six officers and 528 other ranks of this battalion who took part all the officers and 496 other ranks
were killed, wounded or captured. Only two officers and
sixty-five other ranks returned to England with the remnants
of the expedition later in the day and half of these were
wounded. The final death roll was 227 of all ranks out of
554.

Such was the price in August 1942 of being seventeen
minutes late for an invasion: such the cost of imperfect understanding between soldiers carrying it out and sailors
taking them to it.

The failure at Puys and the consequent failure to capture
the dominating headland which was its final objective meant
that the main landing on the Dieppe sea front was now exposed to a withering cross fire from the open left flank. Small
parties of infantry did manage to scale the sea wall and penetrate into the town but the tanks, which were to have been
the trump card of the operation achieved very little. Of the
thirty Churchills (a new British heavy tank making its battle
debut) that were brought twenty-seven managed to disem-
bark but because of the formidable sea wall could get no farther than the beach from which they had to content themselves with giving supporting fire to the infantry. Not one
tank succeeded in forcing its way into the town. When the
remnants of the expedition re-embarked the tanks had to be
abandoned for the Germans to examine at their leisure.

The final casualty list was grievously heavy.

Of the 6100 soldiers taking part 3642 of all ranks were
killed, wounded, or taken prisoner. Navy casualties totalled
550 of all ranks and ship losses were one destroyer, five
tank landing craft, and twenty-eight small assault landing
craft. The Royal Air Force and their attached Allied squadrons lost 106 aircraft: German losses were forty-eight aircraft destroyed, twenty-four damaged. The German person-

nel casualties for all three services totalled no more than 591.

So ended disastrously the first assault on Hitler's Fortress Europe.[2] In nine terrible hours the Allies had learned more about the implications and techniques of amphibious warfare than they could have learned in nine months of theorizing and experiment. They had learned the hard way which in war is sometimes the only way. Two years later the lessons were to be put to good use. It was tragic, however, that the price in blood fell so disproportionately on the young eager and untried army of Canada.

Apart from anything else, Dieppe was a stark indication of the disaster that must have resulted had the Allied leadership allowed itself to be stampeded into an attempt to establish a second front in 1942 for which a senseless agitation was being conducted by left wing elements in the U.S.A. and Britain—a clamour to which even the British right wing cabinet minister and newspaper proprietor Canadian-born Lord Beaverbrook—a notorious espouser of doomed causes—was lending the shrill voice of his mass circulation newspapers. At least, from an Allied point of view, *that* particular catastrophe had been avoided.

From the German point of view the Dieppe raid had been a highly successful operation. In the first place it had relieved the tension that had been building up all summer over Allied intentions and current capability. It had proved reassuring on both counts. The sigh of relief was almost audible.

For the defenders of Dieppe there were congratulations and thanks from Division, Corps, Army, and Commander-in-Chief West ending with the usual admonitory soldierly reminders that there must be no relocation, vigilance must be keener than ever. Finally a signal to von Rundstedt from the Führer himself to be passed on to the troops:

> Thanks to the careful foresight of the Command and of the troops, a strong attempt at a British landing was crushed with the shortest possible delay. You are requested, Herr Feldmarschall, to convey my thanks and my gratitude to the three arms of the Wehrmacht. I know that I can rely in future on the Command and the soldiers of the Wehrmacht.
> Adolf Hitler

Even the official OKW communiqué from Vinnitsa had no need in the circumstances to resort to omission or exaggeration. It could permit itself the luxury of sober objectivity:

An important landing carried out by British, American, Canadian and Gaullist troops, the first wave of which was equivalent to approximately a division, took place on the French coast near Dieppe.

In the early morning, protected by powerful naval and air formations and supported by a tank landing, this attempt crumbled in the face of the reaction by German forces entrusted with the defence of the coast. . . .

In its estimates of the British casualties the communiqué was creditably near the truth—naval losses being somewhat overestimated, Royal Air Force losses considerably underestimated. Only once did it deviate slightly from report into comment; it could not resist an uncomplimentary reflection on the competence of the raiders:

In the course of this attempted invasion, carried out contrary to all good military sense and which served only political ends, the enemy suffered a crushing defeat. The German army guarding the west has given the necessary reply to this undertaking.

It was left to the newspapers, guided by Dr. Goebbels and his shrill underlings in the Ministry of Propaganda, to let imagination play on the events of August 19. CATASTROPHIC DEFEAT . . . A SETBACK TO INVASION . . . WHAT DOES STALIN SAY ABOUT THIS DISASTER TO CHURCHILL'S INVASION? were some of the headings to news stories in the German press. Most of the reports made merry with the suggestion that the raid was a bungled act of desperation carried out solely to please Stalin: they pointed out that it had given the Germans a valuable opportunity to test their defences: they crowed with triumph at the resounding success with which the defences had come through the test. Churchill's second front had been smashed on the teeth of the Atlantic Wall. The same or worse would be the fate of any other Allied soldier presumptuous enough to try to set foot on Fortress Europe . . . Dieppe was a gift to the German propagandists and they made the most of it.

The German military assessment of Dieppe was analytical and practical and in some of its conclusions unflattering to the Canadian and British planners as well as to the executants of the operation. The headquarters of the two Canadian infantry brigades had been authorized to take ashore two copies each of the main operation order. Inevitably one of these found itself among the many trophies garnered that day from the Canadian dead. Field-Marshal von Rundstedt had it translated and distributed through his command for study by officers. The covering letter which the Field-Marshal sent with it was less than flattering to his British enemies.

He began by stating contemptuously that according to German ideas the order was not even an order, but an aide-memoire or a scheme worked out for a map exercise. Nevertheless, he conceded, it did contain "many points of value to us."

> First, how much the enemy knows about us.
> Second, the peculiarities of his method of landing and fighting.
> For that reason, this order is to be thoroughly studied by all staffs, to collect lessons for our coastal defence and for the training and education of our troops.

But (he concluded) it would be an error to believe that the enemy would mount his next operation in the same manner. He would learn lessons from his mistakes in planning and from his failure, and next time he would do things differently.

Other German comments agreed that the raiding force had been too small to take on the defending force it had to tackle; and that the naval and air bombardment at the beginning had been woefully insufficient to neutralize the defences during the landings.

One German higher formation report criticized the plan for being "too detailed" to allow scope for initiative on the part of subordinate commanders. Another thought the time-table in the withdrawal plan had been drawn up "in a theoretical manner reflecting inexperience of battle."

It must be said that over at Admiral Mountbatten's Combined Operations Headquarters in England they were all busy coming to much the same conclusions.

Compared with the great offensive hammering away towards the Caucasus or even the critical Battle of the Atlantic—in the three months June, July, August Allied shipping losses in the North Atlantic had reached the staggering total of 1,618,936 tons—Dieppe was a small affair. But for Hitler its implications were far from small. For it was reasonable to suppose now that a serious Anglo-American invasion across the Channel was off for that year. The German defences had been usefully tested under battle conditions and such weaknesses as had been exposed could now be put right. Next time the Allies tried anything they would find that Fortress Europe had grown a thicker and harder crust. After the anxiety of the summer it was good for Adolf Hitler to be able to feel this.

Dieppe, in fact, was an occasion for celebration and it is to be hoped that the Führer made the most of it. For it was going to be an unconscionable long time before he would again have anything to celebrate. The war, Hitler's war, was grinding inexorably towards two traumatic turning points after which the rage of conquest would be gone forever. The once irresistible force, soon to be compelled to assume the defensive, would have to learn the less rewarding role of the immovable object.

Fortress Europe was going to need that extra crust. There were difficult days ahead.

Part Two

SUMMER OF CRISIS
THE SCORCHING STEPPE AND SAND

(*May-November 1942*)

Chapter 8

VICTORY—SO NEAR, SO FAR

☐ In the blistering heat of August the men of recently promoted Field-Marshal Erwin Rommel's German Afrika Korps fought without success their ceaseless daily battle with the flies and the choking white dust that are the particular torment of those who choose to make war in the Egyptian desert. Stripped to the waist, their hands and arms black with grease as they dismantled and reassembled portions of their tanks, they resembled dirty mechanics rather than *élite* soldiers. The motorcyclists who sped endlessly between units bearing messages resembled nothing so much as surrealist clowns with their red-rimmed eyes peering like open wounds out of dust-caked white faces. There was little joy in tending panzers and armoured cars hot enough to cook on, machines that scorched the flesh and started off those desert sores that were so difficult to heal and were another specialty of this parched and punishing battlefield. At least the thrice-blessed sea was not far away and, except for those tied to strictly front-line alertness, most of them managed to take advantage of the fact. A cool swim was just about the most desirable experience open to a man soldiering in the Egyptian desert in high summer. The Afrika Korps (German element of the German-Italian Panzer Army Afrika) had certainly earned any sea-bathing that came their way that August.

There had been no let-up since the end of May when Field-Marshal Rommel's panzers had dazed and shattered the British Eighth Army at Gazala. It had been another of Rommel's characteristic turning movements round the open southern flank of the desert: an armoured outflanking drive unloosed with the force and speed of a hurricane. Rommel had swept round the British left and raced headlong for the coast —cutting off the bulk of the British forces and pressing on to capture the key fortress and naval base of Tobruk. From Tobruk he had continued the pursuit of the Eighth Army to Egypt, the final conquest of which now seemed so imminently at hand that Mussolini flew to Libya and stood by ready to make a triumphal entry into Alexandria on a white charger.

But Mussolini and his charger had waited in vain. Near El Alamein, a whistle stop on the Alexandria-Tobruk railway, General Auchinleck had managed to rally the retreating British Eighth Army. The Panzer Army Afrika—tired, very short of gasoline, and now severely handicapped by its over-extended communications—was effectively stopped by Auchinleck only sixty miles from Alexandria. There the two armies wore themselves to a final stand-still by thrust and counter-thrust until both were too tired to do any more. The desert campaign had come to a halt at El Alamein in an area the British had partially prepared for just such a last-ditch defence of Egypt against attack from the west.

The uniqueness of the El Alamein position was that it was the only one, in 450 miles of desert, that provided two secure flanks. Everywhere else the only secure flank was provided by the sea. A classic pattern of desert warfare had accordingly developed whereby the attacker opened his offensive with a rapid wheel round his opponent's open southern (i.e. inland) flank prior to cutting northward across his rear to the sea. Both sides had practised this gambit in previous offensives. If Rommel had used it more successfully to date (at Gazala, for example, two months before) this reflected the superior quality till then of his tanks and the greater skill of his tank crews—in addition to the greater flair for this kind of warfare that Rommel himself had displayed as compared with his previous British opponents. Only at El Alamein was this outflanking manoeuvre not possible. For instead of the usual open south flank of the desert nature had provided, only thirty-eight miles south of the secure sea flank, a great sunken salt marsh impassable to vehicles. Realizing the unique value of this comparative bottleneck of thirty-eight miles with two secure flanks, the British had partly developed it as a defensive zone quite early in the campaign, recognizing that if ever it ever came to a last-ditch defence of Egypt, this was where it would have to be made: as indeed it had been in July. It was not, therefore, by accident that the summer fighting came to its final halt at El Alamein.

For Rommel and the Panzer Army it was infuriating to have come so close to complete victory and then to have been cheated of it by so few miles. Supplies, of course, were the trouble. The Italian Navy just could not get their convoys through the British blockade. British submarines and the torpedoes of Royal Navy pilots were sinking more than half the cargoes that made the perilous journey across the Sicilian narrows. Nor was it only gasoline that was running short. Some of the Axis vehicles were by this time held together only by rust and string, more or less, but if units indented for replacements they were told there were none to spare; everything was needed for the Eastern front; they must make do with what they had. Rommel's army in North Africa could lay claim to the ancient and bitter title of "forgotten army."

At least a few infantry reinforcements were beginning to come through to replace the heavy losses in the summer fighting. A parachute and an infantry division had joined the Italian element of the Panzer Army. The German 164th Division had arrived from Crete, but without its transport which would have to be made up on the spot, largely with captured British vehicles. Another useful addition was the Ramcke Parachute Brigade, an *élite* German formation to be employed as ordinary infantry. There were four tough battalions of them and they had a big reputation as fighters.

Meanwhile there were constant reports of shiploads of men and equipment and material of all kinds arriving at Suez for the British, having made their way by the laborious forty-two-day route round the Cape of Good Hope and the Red Sea. Moreover the British were more active in the air than ever before and a number of American squadrons were now flying with the Royal Air Force. More than one veteran of the Panzer Army found himself sighing for the good old days when the Luftwaffe had the air to itself. However—these veterans were reassuring themselves—it could not be long now before Rommel, *their* Rommel, the incomparable Rommel mounted a new attack to polish off those last maddening few miles to the Nile. And that was going to be a reward worth having after eighteen gruelling months of desert fighting: eighteen months of flies, dust, dysentery, and above all the crucifying heat of every single day, winter and summer. By all accounts the British had organized life well in Cairo and Alexandria. One heard that the country clubs, hotels, shops, cafes, and apartment houses were on a European scale of luxury. After the desert one could do with a little luxury. Once they had secured Egypt the whole of the Middle East would be wide open, including the precious oilfields on which the British depended. Without that oil they would soon be finished, even with the Americans to come to their rescue: for American oil could hardly run the gauntlet of the Atlantic U-boat packs in sufficient quantity to replace what Britain drew from the Middle East. Surely it couldn't be long before they were on the move again—towards those hotels and night clubs and swimming pools.

While the officers and men of the Panzer Army, sweating to keep their weapons and vehicles in good order, distracted themselves with these mirage thoughts of rewards that lay just around the corner, their commander Rommel, in addition to sharing their discomforts and the intestinal illness that was plaguing the whole army, had also to contend with the fretfulness and frustration of being constantly let down by the Italian Comando Supremo under whose command he nominally remained and who were responsible for supplying him with all his administrative needs. This, coupled with the galling disappointment of having come so close to total victory before his offensive gave out at El Alamein, had taken some of the shine out of the exhilarating successes of the summer. Between May 26 and July 20 Rommel's men had captured 60,000 British and Commonwealth troops and destroyed some 2000 armoured vehicles.[1] Vast quantities of stores of all kinds had been taken, especially at Tobruk which the British had built up as a forward base for their own offensive that had been forestalled by Rommel's. Captured British vehicles and gasoline had been a great help in mitigating Rommel's shortage of these essentials. All this had been achieved by Rommel for a German loss of 12,500 of all ranks killed, wounded and captured: while the more numerous Italian element of the Panzer Army had lost 16,000. It was an achievement to be proud of. But still there remained the El Alamein defences and a now stabilized British army between him and the so-near so-far prize of Egypt. Meanwhile the British were being heavily reinforced. His Intelligence brought daily news of ships unloading men, tanks, guns at Suez. Churchill had replaced the Eighth Army commander with a new man, General Bernard L. Montgomery; a new theatre commander, General Sir Harold Alexander, had taken over as Commander-in-Chief Middle East. The great numbers of tanks reaching Suez for the British were known to include many American Shermans, a new tank better than anything the British had previously had and one that was going to be a serious challenge to the hitherto triumphant German Mark IVs.

It was all very depressing and complaints to Comando Supremo in Rome produced little more than flowery and meaningless Italian promises that were never kept. Gasoline was promised—but either never left Italy or was sunk by Brit-

ish submarines on the way. The Italian Navy seemed power-
less to provide adequate protection for these supply convoys.
Complaints to OKW were no more effective, for the view persisted that Africa was very much a secondary front and even
the one division more that might have made a difference
could not be spared from the Eastern Front. Whereas to the
British this was their main front and they were putting everything into it.

His sickness, his supply problems and the mounting aggression of the British (especially in the air) were the themes
that dominated Rommel's diary notes at this time and even
his letters to his wife.

On August 2, he wrote her:[2]

> Dearest Lu,
>   All quiet, except for intense air activity against
> my supply lines. I'm thankful for every day's respite
> we get. A lot of sickness. Unfortunately many of the
> older officers are going down now . . .
>   Holding on to our Alamein position has given us
> the severest fighting we've yet seen in Africa. We've
> all got heat diarrhoea now, but it's bearable. A year
> ago I had jaundice and that was much worse.

The German military attaché in Rome was General Emil
von Rintelen who was also OKW's representative attached
to the Italian High Command. As such he should have worked
assiduously on Rommel's behalf to iron out the eternal and
recurrent supply problems created by British naval and air
vigilance. But this was not so. He was no match for the
more nimble-witted Italians. On August 5 Rommel's diary
note was again concerned with the subject of supplies.[3]

> Trouble with supplies. Rintelen does little in Rome
> and constantly lets himself be done in the eye, for
> the Italian supplies are working excellently.

It was a source of friction between the Axis allies that the
Italians always seemed better off for transport than the Germans. For instance the Pistoia Division, which had just arrived with a full complement of vehicles, was intended only
for garrison duties, not for front-line combat. Yet the German 164th Division, which was destined for immediate combat duty, had had to come from Crete without transport and
had to make do with what could be found for them from the

86

scratch assortment of spares and captured vehicles available on the spot.

In spite of the scorching heat of every single day, the desert is basically a healthy and by no means unpleasant place, for the heat is clean and dry and the nights as refreshingly cool as they are beautiful. Soldiers who have become acclimatized actually thrive on it in spite of the dust (mostly man-made, except for the periodical paralysing sand storms) and the flies. Men become physically hard and deeply tanned and, when they have mastered how to look after themselves, they feel wonderfully fit. Some even fall a little in love with the emptiness, the tranquillity, the solitude. But there are difficulties. The merest scratch can turn quickly into a septic sore; one sore into a suppurating patchwork of them. There is the constant imminence of that intestinal disorder familiar to everyone who has ever visited the Mediterranean area and, in particular, the Near and Middle East. The British Army, with its long imperial experience of military service east and south of Suez, was well practised in the medical disciplines essential to the health and well-being of soldiers in these circumstances. The British health record was superior to that of the Axis armies—especially the Germans, who were least accustomed to a Mediterranean climate. This had an important bearing on morale and general well-being, including Rommel's.

There is nothing more debilitating to an active and normally ebullient commander—faced with critical decisions in the face of practical difficulties—than diarrhoea. There was every reason why Erwin Rommel, a restless emotional man of action with little aptitude for bearing frustration gracefully, should feel dejected that August.

Rommel was a short strongly built Swabian from the wine-growing southwest of Germany. The cold blue-grey eyes, deep-set behind high pug-dog cheekbones, were softened by strongly etched wrinkles that betrayed the humour that is a characteristic of Swabians who are otherwise noted for their broad regional accent and strong local pride, their hard commonsense, and a sense of fun that both amuses other Germans and is amused by them. The son and grandson of middle-class schoolmasters, he had inherited no intellectual pretensions but had dedicated himself to soldiering, his chosen profession, with such zeal that he had climbed swiftly to the top in spite of lacking the aristocratic background and social connections of most of the Prussian officer class who dominated the German military hierarchy. It was probably this background, as well as his spectacular success when war gave him his opportunity, that made him a special favourite of the class-conscious Hitler. Dedicated to his profession (like Montgomery, the man who had just become his chief opponent) Rommel did not smoke, drank hardly at all, ate frugally, and imposed on himself a spartan personal regime. He was a one-woman man who married his first youthful love and remained devotedly married to her for the rest of his life. But in August 1942 there was little laughter in the creases around the eyes, and the deep slow speaking voice was in its other manifestation when it had the crack of an antitank gun. It was no time then for even a fellow Swabian to make jokes carelessly in his presence.

This was Field-Marshal Erwin Rommel, the "Desert Fox," leader and idol of the Afrika Korps and their Italian allies, the man whose dazzling exploits had captured the imagination not only of the German-speaking world but of the English-speaking world too. The British General, Auchinleck, had found it necessary to check what he called the "Rommel-complex" of his troops virtually ordering them to stop admiring Rommel so much. Winston Churchill had paid his tribute in the House of Commons when he said (and was strongly criticized for saying): "We have a very daring and skilful opponent against us, and, may I say across the havoc of war, a great general."

But it was not the shortage of gasoline, the shortcomings of the Italian General Staff, the lack of reinforcements or even the diarrhoea that was responsible for Rommel's dejection: it was something more fundamental. It was the dawning realization that time was running out. The growing awareness that the supreme opportunity was beginning to glide from the quayside of events like a great ship just missed. That the golden moment was passing had perhaps already passed and that this was a symptom of what was about to happen to Germany everywhere.

The enemy was getting visibly stronger. Very soon it would be too late. Perhaps very soon it was going to be too late everywhere. Above everything Rommel was a tactical opportunist. He of all men did not have to be told by Shakespeare that there was a tide in the affairs of men that had to be taken at the flood. The flood, *his* flood, was now abating. He would have to try again very soon if he were not to find himself vainly chasing the ebb. Without fail he would have to catch the August moon: September would be too late, the way the British were going ahead with their build-up. In the flat featureless desert, where there were no landmarks of any kind and vehicles, especially tanks, thickened up the very darkness itself with an impenetrable dust fog, moonlight was essential to a night attack if it was not to break down in total confusion.

On August 10 he had a meeting with Field-Marshal Albert Kesselring, Commander-in-Chief South, and settled on the night of August 30-31 for the start of his last effort to break through to the Nile. It was leaving it a little late—it would be five nights past full moon—but he was allowing the maximum possible time for Comando Supremo to deliver the extra gasoline stocks which he needed for the new offensive. He had new assurances from Rome that the gasoline would reach North Africa in time but he was sceptical about it and as collateral he had a promise from Kesselring that if it did not, he, Kesselring, would arrange for the Luftwaffe to fly Rommel five hundred tons daily for the duration of the battle.

Rommel's plan for the new attack followed the usual desert pattern that has been described—that is to say a wheeling armoured thrust from the south aimed across the enemy rear towards the coast—but with one vital difference. At the southern end of the El Alamein line there was no open flank but the impassable Qattara depression. This time the Panzer Army would have to break through the British line before making its left wheel to cut off the main defending force. Which meant of course that unlike the earlier offensives this one could not hope to achieve the same degree of surprise. Rommel decided to make three penetrations towards the south of the line where his Intelligence assured him that an eight-mile stretch was held by only light defences and a minefield.

The main penetration was to be made on the right near the extreme south of the line and it was to be made by the two panzer divisions the 15th and 21st of the Afrika Korps. On their left would be the Italian armoured corps (Ariete and Littorio Armoured and Trieste Motorized Divisions); further left still, a third division of the Afrika Korps, the 90th Light Division. The panzer divisions were given a difficult schedule. By dawn they were to be through and thirty miles beyond the British minefield, ready to make their encircling sweep to the coast. There the Afrika Korps would reorganize and then go all-out for the Nile, one panzer division heading for Alexandria, the other for Cairo.

Having made the decision and given the necessary orders there was nothing for Rommel but to wait fretfully for news

89

of the promised supply convoys, an anguish not made easier by the almost certain feeling in his heart that he would again be let down. This feeling, and the gnawing bitterness that went with it, doubtless contributed to the deterioration in his health which took place about a week before the offensive was due to open. He was extremely sick for a day or two with bouts of fainting, and only his iron will enabled him to keep going. His doctor—Professor Horster, one of the leading German abdominal specialists—gave him a thorough examination as a result of which a signal—signed by Horster and General Gause, the Chief of Staff—was sent to OKW informing them that Rommel was suffering from "chronic stomach and intestinal catarrh, nasal diphtheria and considerable vasculatory trouble" and adding the opinion[4] that he was "not in a fit condition to command the forthcoming offensive." Rommel was ill enough to agree to the dispatch of this report, but clear-headed enough to insist on their adding to it his personal recommendation that General Guderian be sent to Africa as Acting Commander of the Panzer Army to handle the offensive. This produced within hours the negative reply: "Guderian unacceptable."

This rebuff stung the Field-Marshal into a defiant and fighting effort of will which pulled him out of his despondency and helped him to recovery. Within a few days, and with D-day for the offensive only a day or two ahead, he instructed Professor Horster to send another signal to OKW stating roundly that the Commander-in-Chief's condition was "so far improved that he can command the battle, but under constant medical attention. Nevertheless, essential to have a replacement on the spot." But no replacement appeared: at OKW, which had moved forward from East Prussia to Vinnitsa in the Ukraine, they had too many troubles of their own to be able to spare time to worry about the Commander-in-Chief in distant Egypt and his wretched health and his eternal grumbling about his supply problems. In the blazing heat of southern Ukraine it was as hot and as trying as it was in Egypt. The opening phase of the German summer offensive in the East was running into its first difficulties. Frayed tempers and irritability, exacerbated by the extreme heat, were constantly near flashpoint. Hitler was at his most difficult and on August 24—the day that Rommel, after a few days of being too ill even to write home—wrote to his wife:[5] "I'm now well enough to get up occasionally"—there was a furious argument between Hitler and General Halder in which the long-suffering Army Chief of Staff, goaded beyond endurance, raged back at the Führer in terms that made absolutely certain his early removal from his post. It was hardly surprising that Rommel's request for a deputy went unanswered.

By the morning of August 30—the offensive was to open that night—he was sufficiently recovered to be able to make the effort to write quite cheerfully to his wife:[6]

> Dearest Lu,
>
> Today has dawned at last. It's been such a long wait worrying all the time whether I should get everything I needed together to enable me to take the brakes off again. Many of my worries have been by no means satisfactorily settled and we have some very grave shortages. But I've taken the risk. . . .
>
> As for my health I'm feeling quite on top of my form. There are such big things at stake. If our blow succeeds, it might go some way towards deciding the whole course of the war. If it fails, at least I hope to give the enemy a pretty thorough beating. . . .

For his wife a soldier puts the best face on things. The real truth about Rommel's feelings on that fateful morning are to be found in a note subsequently made by General Fritz Bayerlein[7] (now Chief of Staff of the Afrika Korps) after talking to Professor Horster who, as Rommel's doctor, was seeing more of him than anyone at this time. Horster told Bayerlein that Rommel had left his caravan that morning "with a very troubled face."

"Professor," the Field-Marshal had said, "the decision to attack today is the hardest I have ever taken. Either the army in Russia succeeds in getting through to Grozny [the oil town in the Eastern Caucasus] and we in Africa manage to reach the Suez Canal, or . . ." He completed the aposiopesis with a gesture of defeat.

Rommel's forebodings were not, as it turned out, misplaced. In the six-day battle of Alam Halfa—named after the long low ridge, five miles behind the El Alamein line, which proved to be the key ground feature in the engagement—nothing went right for him. The chief reason was that the British Eighth Army and their new commander, the unknown General Montgomery, had accurately appreciated when Rommel would attack, where he would attack, and how.

The British had reasoned that he was bound to make one last desperate effort to break through to the Nile; that he would attack during the August full-moon period for fear that September would be too late; that he would attack the southern sector of their line and, following the usual pattern of his offensives, would attempt a wide outflanking armoured sweep to the coast across their rear. As a counter to this Montgomery decided that the key piece of ground in their defence plan was the Alam Halfa ridge five miles long and running from west to east, i.e. at right angles to the main El Alamein front and some five miles east of it; the ridge was a sort of backstop to the main front. Montgomery proposed to garrison this ridge with a brigade of tanks dug in to fight a purely defensive battle, and also a division of infantry. Two further tank brigades would be at hand in positions from which they could readily close on Alam Halfa as required. It would be out of the question for any outflanking force to leave on its flank a dominating piece of ground so formidably defended: it would have to attack Alam Halfa and clear it first. It was the defending army that would then seize the initiative.

So the first thing that went wrong was that for once Rommel failed to achieve his usual whirlwind surprise and found instead an alerted British defence that had correctly appreciated both where and when he was going to attack. Led by infantry and engineers his assault groups duly went to work on the British minefield soon after dark on the night of August 30, the armour following close behind. The next blow to Rommel's plan was the discovery that his Intelligence estimates had misled him: the "weakly held" British minefield had been thickened and deepened and was covered not only by a great weight of artillery but also by mobile covering parties provided by a British light armoured division.

This formation had orders to use its motorized infantry and armoured cars to harass the passage of the Afrika Korps through the minefield; and thereafter to fight delaying actions without letting itself be drawn into a major battle; and eventually to draw the panzers towards the ambush on Alam Halfa ridge, where the main British tank force was waiting in prepared defensive positions.

The success of Rommel's plan depended entirely on the speed with which his spearhead—the veteran 15th and 21st Panzer Divisions of the Afrika Korps—could traverse the British minefield and start their wide sweep to the coast. For this reason he had imposed a difficult schedule requiring them to be thirty miles east of the minefield by dawn, preparatory to their drive north to the coast. But when dawn came they were still struggling through the minefield which had proved wider and better defended than they had been led to expect. It was 0930 before the bulk of the tanks were through and they had suffered many casualties including the commander of the 21st Panzer Division, Major General Georg von Bismarck, who had been killed by mortar fire.

With the arrival of daylight the Royal Air Force began a nonstop series of carpet-bombing attacks by tight formations of medium bombers flying in groups of twelve or eighteen and concentrating on the follow-up echelons of the panzer divisions, destroying large numbers of vehicles as well as disrupting headquarters and assembly areas where troop concentrations could be seen forming. An early victim of one of these bombing attacks was another senior commander, Lieutenant General Walther Nehring, commander of the Afrika Korps. With the plan now hopelessly behind schedule, the British defences very much stronger than expected and nothing to oppose to the new British tactic of tactical carpet-bombing by what was virtually a shuttle-service of bomber formations, Rommel considered abandoning the operation there and then. For it had really been defeated in the British minefield the night before. But after a mid-morning conference with his Chief of Staff, Major General Fritz Bayerlein, who had temporarily taken command of the Afrika Korps in place of the wounded Nehring, he decided that the attack should continue; but with a closer wheel than the wide encirclement originally planned; a wheel, in fact, to assault and capture the Alam Halfa ridge. This was his undoing. It was for precisely this contingency that the British defence plan had been prepared, the Alam Halfa ridge having been correctly assessed as the key piece of ground in a defence in depth of the El Alamein position. Montgomery's tanks were waiting for him in hull-down positions behind what cover was available or could be contrived by digging. The ridge had been turned into a prickly ambush, a death trap. For three days the Afrika Korps tried to breach the powerful British ground defences which were supported by continuous air attacks that inflicted crippling losses on men and machines. When it was clear that no progress was being made Rommel gave up. The Panzer Army spent the next three days conducting an orderly fighting withdrawal through the minefield they had so recently and so painfully breached, so that they finished almost, though not quite, back where they had come from. The dream of Egyptian conquest was now as remote as Cleopatra. A skilfully planned and resolutely executed defensive action by a revitalized British Eighth Army had ended it forever.

The German troops afterwards referred always to Alam Halfa[8] as the *Sechstagerennen* or "Six Day Race"—a pre-war national bicycle race with nostalgic associations for them. They had a nickname too for the British bombing attacks by squadrons flying in tight formation and bombing from as low as three thousand feet: "party rallies" they called them because they could only connect such close formation-flying with the sort of performance the Luftwaffe used to provide for Nazi rallies.

Rommel had started the battle with 443 tanks of which two hundred were German, the remainder obsolescent Italian types which had little value in the battle: fifty-one were left on the battlefield, though many of those damaged were later recovered. The British lost rather more tanks but as they had started the engagement with more than seven hundred and had more in reserve, they could afford it. Rommel's combined losses of German and Italian personnel was three thousand compared with a British loss of half that number. The loss of four hundred German and Italian trucks told its own tale of the effectiveness of the new British bombing tactics.

In its scale—ten Axis, some under strength, were engaging eleven British and Commonwealth divisions—Alam Halfa seems a small affair compared with the operations on the Russian front. Its significance, however, was greater than the bare statistics suggest. For by failing to win it Rommel lost not a battle but a front—a front where a total defeat of the British could have been (and earlier that summer nearly was) achieved. In the wider context it was Hitler's last chance to defeat the British decisively on land—and with untold economic advantage to Germany through Middle East oil—before American participation became sufficiently substantial to place the possibility of a British defeat right out of the question.

Alam Halfa therefore, not a large battle in itself, had large implications. It was in fact a microcosm of what was to be the story of the Wehrmacht everywhere at this time and in the near future. Ascendancy was inexorably changing hands, the initiative changing the colour of its uniform. The Wehrmacht's opponent—hitherto dominated in Africa as in Russia—had painfully learned the lessons and was now beginning to apply them. The situation of Rommel was a symbol of all this. With defeat, illness, and the neglect of his superiors closing in on him his volatile gambler's temperament was discovering that when a man's luck begins to run out it keeps running.

For Rommel, Hitler and Germany, Alam Halfa was Game and Set. The next few months would disclose whether the formidable new opponent Montgomery was destined also to make it Match.

Chapter 9

"NO MORE THAN A NAME
ON THE MAP"

☐ "At the start," General Field-Marshal Paul Ludwig von Kleist was to remark long afterwards,[1] "Stalingrad was no more than a name on the map to us." It was a name that had been mentioned in Hitler's Directive 41 of April, the one that had laid down the pattern of the great summer offensive of 1942 on the Eastern front. But there was nothing either then, or in the orders and counterorders which followed, to give the slightest hint that there was anything special about Stalingrad.

We have seen that, as the strategic objectives of the offensive, Hitler had opted for the cereal, industrial and mineral wealth of the Ukraine and the oil of the Caucasus. The drive into the vast and mountainous Caucasus area was to be the climax to the summer programme and it would call for the shelter of a secure northern flank before it could safely be undertaken. Stalingrad was the name on the map which indicated the area that Hitler thought should mark the eastern extremity of the proposed defensive north flank. There was nothing which military logic, intuition, or even inspired guesswork could have caused anyone to think that this was where the campaign, the war, the entire Hitlerian dream was destined to crash in flames—figuratively and literally. Even the Russians attached no particular importance to Stalingrad. They considered that the Germans were almost certain to make Moscow their main target again and their best formations had been positioned to this end in the centre. When the attack came in the south the forces available to meet it were of a lower category and in many cases as helpless in the face of

the German armoured spearheads as they and others like
them had been the year before. And when Stalingrad eventually came into the picture it was far from prepared and its
defence had to be hurriedly improvised.

In the closing days of June, when Field-Marshal Rommel's
Panzer Army Africa, sweltering in the white-hot dust of
Egypt, was preparing its last efforts to break through the
rallying British desert army to the Nile, in southern Russia,
Field-Marshal von Bock's Army Group South was crouching
in readiness along some four hundred miles of parched and
scorching steppe from Kursk southwards to the Sea of Azov.
This huge army of 1,500,000 men included the German Second, Sixth, Eleventh, and Seventeenth Armies, the First and
Fourth Panzer Armies with, in addition, the satellite armies
provided by Hungary, Rumania, and Italy. So that von Bock
had under his command in Army Group South as many armies as Rommel had divisions in Africa.

The preliminary conquest of the Crimea had been completed by Field-Marshal Erich von Mannstein's Eleventh
Army; its climax, the capture of Sebastopol, was now so certain that it was going to be possible to start the main attack
without waiting for that event. Von Bock's huge army group,
less the Eleventh Army which would remain in the Crimea
and along the two-hundred-mile north shore of the Sea of
Azov as a protective right flank, was the force chosen to renew the blitzkrieg and complete the conquest of Russia.

All along this line, stretching southwards from Kursk
through Kharkov and Stalino to Taganrog, the German soldiers went about their preparations cursing the heat and the
flies and the great dust clouds that swirled in the wake of
every vehicle that moved but most especially the tanks: for in
summer the steppe here becomes almost as parched and fur-
nace-hot as the Egyptian desert. Even the greatest of the
south Russian rivers—the Dnieper, Donets, and Don—dry
up in places or shrink to a small muddy stream. To many of
the newly arrived reinforcements the dusty heat and the flies
came as an unpleasant surprise for they associated the Russian steppe with snow and ice and piercing cold winds and it
was as disconcerting as it was unexpected to find themselves
bathed in sweat and gasping for breath in the midday sun
and tantalized by the dried up beds of the rivers and streams
in which they might have bathed and refreshed themselves.

In spite of the great heat von Bock's armies were in good
heart. The operations designed to prepare the way for the

main offensive had all been successful. The Crimea had been conquered and possessed: the fall of the great fortress of Sebastopol would be announced any day now. More important still, a great Russian counterattack on Kharkov, designed to disrupt the German offensive preparations, had been smashed with losses to the Russians that they would feel for the rest of the summer. The orders from the German Army High Command were that the Russians were to be allowed to come close to Kharkov before von Bock made his counterattack. Accordingly Marshal Semyon Timoshenko was overextended when at last Army Group South tore into his long flank with Paulus's Sixth Army and von Kleist's First Panzer Army. In a series of swift and drastic encirclements the Germans wrecked Timoshenko's offensive and inflicted crippling losses on the Russians. OKW claimed the destruction of twenty infantry and seven cavalry divisions and fourteen armoured brigades and a total of 240,000 prisoners. The Russians said nothing about their Kharkov losses for three weeks: then somewhat guardedly referred to a loss of 5000 killed and 70,000 missing.[2] But in his famous "Dethronement of Stalin" speech in 1956, Nikita Krushchev blamed Stalin for the Soviet disaster at the Second Battle of Kharkov, and spoke of a loss of "hundreds of thousands of our soldiers." Whatever the true figures it is clear that the Russian losses were enormous, and the Germans were naturally heartened by so huge a victory before their main offensive opened. Second Kharkov was additionally interesting in owing its master-plan to General Halder, the Army Chief of Staff. It was Halder at OKH who laid down that the German counterattack was to be withheld until the very last moment, until Timoshenko was practically in Kharkov. The Army Group commander Field-Marshal von Bock and General Paulus, who was to be the counterattack's main executant, both pressed to be allowed to counterattack as early in the offensive as possible. In the event the vindication of Halder's insistence on it being as late as possible—to ensure an overextended flank to bite into—made a profound impression on Paulus[3] who later admitted that the higher command sometimes was in a position to know best: and we shall see the influence of this later in the story.

Coupled with the successes of von Mannstein in the Crimea shortly to be crowned by the fall of Sebastopol after a nine-month siege, the great victory of Kharkov was a marvellous preoffensive tonic not only to the German soldiers who would soon be enmeshed in its execution but also to their Supreme Commander and Führer, commuting exultantly between Rastenburg, Berchtesgaden, and Berlin. But the euphoria and high elation of the early summer victories carried within them the seeds of a future less congenial. For Hitler made from them the unwise deduction that the Russians were as helpless and incompetent as they had been the year before; that his highly professional armies, with another year's experience behind them, were as irresistible as ever; that the Red Army was already defeated and would be polished off very quickly; no matter what tasks he piled on his generals they would carry them out successfully. Hubris was in the ascendant again.

The German offensive, due to open on June 28, was to be in four phases which seemed a lot clearer on paper and on a small-scale map than they were to prove when translated to an army of 1,500,000 men operating on a front of some 750 miles.[4]

First, an advance by Fourth Panzer and Second Armies (supported by Second Hungarian Army) to capture Voronezh, the key river, road and rail junction on the Don 150 miles east of the jumping-off area.

Second, this force would turn and drive southeast with the task of destroying all Russian forces west of the Don in conjunction with Sixth Army one hundred miles to the south who would advance eastwards to complete the cut-off and encirclement of the retreating Russians.

Third, a double thrust on Stalingrad would be made by the northern force sweeping down the Don in conjunction with First Panzer and Seventeenth Armies pushing eastwards from Taganrog two hundred miles south of Sixth Army.

Only when the west bank of the Don had been cleared and Stalingrad taken would phase four begin: a general advance into the Caucasus to capture the oilfields, the second main object of the offensive, the first being Ukrainian corn and industry.

It was a grandiose design that could hardly be expected to go exactly according to plan and a week before D-day there was a security breach that can be seen retrospectively as an omen of disasters to come.

Hitler's fanaticism in the matter of security was such that even commanders of divisions were not allowed to see their own corps orders until a battle had opened. The impossibility of working under this handicap was such that many corps commanders had fallen into the habit of unofficially giving their divisional commanders brief typed summaries "for eyes of divisional commander only." Such a commander was General Georg von Stumme, the commander of the XL Panzer

Corps, a key formation of Fourth Panzer Army due to spearhead the attack on Voronezh.

Stumme,[5] a thrustful tank general whose work-hard play-hard ebullience had earned him the nickname of "Fireball," had sent his three divisional commanders the usual short typed summary of the Corps plan—strictly for their own information. Stumme was a man who did not allow his high blood pressure to interfere with his attachment to good food and drink. He was enjoying a convivial evening in his Mess one week before the offensive was due to open when he was informed that a divisional staff officer had crashed in a reconnaissance plane over the Russian lines. The officer (against all orders) was carrying a marked map and General Stumme's unofficial typed summary of the Corps plan for the guidance of Divisional commanders. The Russians therefore had the Corps plan for the first phase of the attack on Voronezh and a marked map to go with it. General "Fireball" Stumme was, of course, relieved of his command and later court-martialled. After much anxious heart-searching the High Command decided that it was too late for the Russians to do much about it in the time and that the offensive must go on as planned. Nor is there any evidence that this lapse affected the course of the battle. But it did provoke such a security commotion from the Führer that it became even harder for senior commanders to brief their subordinates adequately enough to keep them in the larger picture.

The offensive duly opened on June 28 and by July 6 the greater part of Voronezh had been captured. But one part of the town was holding out strongly. It was noticed that the Russians had adopted new defence tactics. Instead of holding on to the last and allowing themselves to be destroyed by vast German encirclements as in the previous year, they were now holding fast with powerful rearguards and making sure that the bulk of their forces withdrew in the face of the usual German blitzkrieg tactics.

The first uncertainty now manifested itself in the German Command. The Army Group South commander (von Bock) had been suggesting to Hitler that it was pointless to waste time capturing Voronezh: he wanted his armies to bypass it and proceed to Phase Two of the offensive, the clearance of the left bank of the Don. Then he changed his mind and thought there was a chance to finish off Voronezh first. Hitler, unusually accommodating, authorized him to do what he thought best. But added that the XL Panzer Corps of Fourth Panzer Army must wheel southeast at once and start Phase

Two, the destruction of Russian forces west of the Don. Thus concentration of force was lost in both areas. The effort to complete the capture of Voronezh was weakened by the loss of the panzer corps; while Phase Two started prematurely at half-cock by having to be undertaken by a single panzer corps before Phase One had been completed. On top of this the weakening of the Fourth Panzer Army and some shortage of gasoline prevented that formation from effectively cutting off the Russian forces withdrawing in the face of Sixth Army's advance. Instead of being destroyed as intended, they were able to withdraw to the Don and cross it.

On July 10 a regrouping of German forces came into operation whereby Army Group South was split into two army groups. Army Group B (Field-Marshal von Bock) on the northerly part of the front consisted of Sixth (German) Army with Second Hungarian, Eighth Italian, and Third Rumanian Armies under command. Army Group A (Field-Marshal Siegmund List) comprised Seventeenth Army and, from July 14, First and Fourth Panzer Armies.

This meant that Phase Three of the offensive, the converging double thrust towards Stalingrad, would be carried out by Army Group B driving southward down the Don to form a pincer with Army Group A advancing from the Taganrog area across the lower Donets and Don towards Stalingrad. It was Army Group A therefore that would be making the main attack on Stalingrad as per Phase Three of the original plan. No sooner had this been decided than doubts began to be felt about the tactical feasibility of pushing two armies across the lower Donets. Army Group A was therefore ordered to advance northwards instead and on July 14 it established contact with Army Group B (moving south) at Millerovo, two hundred miles west of Stalingrad—the idea of a pincer attack on the latter now being abandoned. Instead Hitler ordered Army Group A to turn about and attack *south* towards Rostov. He was clinging to his belief that the Russians were at the end of their tether and that this drive on Rostov would cut off the Soviet forces retreating before Sixth Army and XL Panzer Corps between the Donets and Don where he was convinced he could fight a great battle of annihilation.

In fact it was becoming clearer that the Russians were not going to allow themselves to be trapped this time. They continued to hold specific points in strength for a time, but only to enable their main forces to withdraw east of the Volga and southeast into the Caucasus. This evasive strategy was confirmed when German Intelligence produced a report of a council of war in Moscow on July 13 at which it had been decided to withdraw the Russian forces to Stalingrad, the Volga and the Caucasus in order to compel the Germans to fight another winter campaign in the interior—the thing they dreaded above all.

Next day the two Panzer armies (First and Fourth) of Army Group B were across the Donets and well placed for a swift advance on Stalingrad as the original plan had envisaged. But Hitler persisted in dropping the Stalingrad plan and sending them in the opposite direction towards Rostov with the result that they were forced to line up for an annihilation battle in which there was in fact nothing to annihilate. It is almost certain that this about-face ordered by Hitler on July 13 threw away the one occasion when an armoured blitzkrieg against Stalingrad might have come off.

On July 16 OKW moved forward from Rastenburg (The Wolf's Lair) to Vinnitsa in the Ukraine (Werewolf). Hitler celebrated the change of location by sacking Field-Marshal von Bock, with whom he had been growing increasingly dissatisfied. General Freiherr Maximilian von Weichs took his place as Commander of Army Group B. But there was no sign that this change would deter the Führer from continuing to interfere daily and almost hourly in the running of an offensive that, to put it mildly, was not proceeding according to plan. It surprised none of his long-suffering staff when he decided that the task of attacking Stalingrad would now be carried out by the Sixth Army of General Paulus. The transfer of Russian heavy industry across the Urals to areas as far east as Siberia was nearly complete, and production of armaments of all kinds were rising. For Hitler a time of decision was at hand when it must become a question of now or never. It was not a time to split his forces. Yet not only had he split his main force as we have seen but at the same time he had ordered Field-Marshal von Mannstein's Eleventh Army (which had remained in the Crimea since its capture of Sebastopol earlier in the summer) to move to the northern front. On top of this Hitler insisted on two motorized divisions being sent to France in readiness for a possible British landing operation across the Channel. It was small wonder that Field-Marshal Rommel's grumbles about his supply difficulties in North Africa fell on deaf ears in the harassed headquarters at Vinnitsa.

The position in August 1942 may be summarized broadly in the following terms. The four-phase offensive in South Russia had been finally abandoned. Instead Hitler was conducting two offensives simultaneously in different directions: the Caucasus was being attacked with two German armies plus satellites, Stalingrad with another two, plus satellites. The German front line Voronezh-Tsymlianskaya-Rostov was already 750 miles in extent. If the Stalingrad and Caucasus offensives both achieved their revised objectives the new front line Voronezh-Stalingrad-Astrakhan-Baku-Batum would extend to no less than 2500. It was a strange time for Hitler to send his only spare southern army, the Eleventh, from the Crimea to the northern front to "finish off" Leningrad. It gave the final touch of grotesque fantasy to the huge project, now about to unfold in a form that seemed at last finalized, that it should start with this weakening of the already overtaxed forces available for its execution.

Yet in spite of the mercurial changes of plan, command and direction the invasion of the Caucasus, led by General von Kleist's First Panzer Army, got off to a brilliant start. By mid-August, only six weeks from the opening of the summer offensive at the end of June, von Kleist had reached the nearer oilfield area around Maikop. But the important oil centres were on the far side of the mountains—and the peaks of the main range of the Caucasus are from 14,000-18,000 feet high. The almost flashy initial success of von Kleist's penetration was soon spent and when he reached the mountains the advance ground to a halt, the difficulty of the terrain being aggravated by an increasing shortage of fuel and the weakening of the Army Group by its having to divert air and other supporting forces to the "rival" Stalingrad front.

In the blistering heat of late August 1942 the future pattern of events was inexorably forming. The attempt—in all the circumstances—to conduct two offensives simultaneously was already beginning to fail and one front was having to be weakened to reinforce the other. And since the formidable Caucasus enterprise could not safely be pursued without the cover of a secure northern flank to shield the Caucasus from Central Russia, the Stalingrad front soon began to establish its priority. Almost of its own volition the name of Stalingrad, "just a name on the map," began to sharpen in focus; becoming clearer and larger, until it filled the screen and was no longer a name on the map but the map itself, *STALINGRAD*.

Chapter 10

ENCIRCLEMENT ON THE VOLGA

□ About the 48th parallel of latitude the two great rivers of east European Russia—the Don flowing south to the Black Sea, the Volga to the Caspian—make, to their west and east respectively, sharp converging curves that bring them briefly within forty miles of each other after flowing some four hundred miles apart in their upper reaches and about the same distance at their mouths.

On the Volga, near the area where the "elbows" of the two rivers so nearly meet, stood the city of Stalingrad; formerly known as Tsaritsyn, subsequently renamed Volvograd, but unshakably immortalized in history—if not in current Russian ideological preference—as Stalingrad. The importance of this narrow isthmus of land between two great waterways, in general so far apart, is self-evident in a vast country renowned for its poor communications. At the turn of the century Tsaritsyn, a town with a population of about 50,000, acquired an importance, disproportionate to its size, as a distribution centre of raw materials and commodities, especially oil, timber, grain, and wool. It achieved fame and its first change of name in 1918 when it was heroically defended against the counterrevolutionary attacks of the Cossack commander Krasnov by the revolutionary leader Iosif Vissarionovich Dzhugashvili, better known as Joseph Stalin. It was a spontaneous military performance on the part of Stalin that augured well for his future as a war leader, for he was only a political commissar at the time with the administrative assignment of expediting the grain collection, and had had no previous experience of military command. The commemorating of the occasion through the subsequent name link between the town and its defender was to be of inestimable moral value to a new generation of defenders when the town was again threatened in 1942.

Under the regime of the premier whose name it now shared, Stalingrad developed during the 1920s and 1930s into one of the most important of the industrial cities of the new Russia till it extended for twenty miles along both banks of

103

the Volga with a population of half a million: a modern city of steel and concrete with factories turning out tractors in large numbers—at a time when the tractor was an almost mystical symbol of the new Russia—and later, when the need arose, tanks and guns. As a key centre of river transportation its dock facilities were greatly extended and improved and it was vital to the shipment of Caucasian oil to the main national centres of communication and distribution. It also grew into an important railway centre with extensive sidings, installations, and marshalling yards.

The surrounding country was steppe, bare and mainly flat, but scarred by deep ravines which, apart from the town buildings and the river, were from the military point of view, the distinguishing topographical feature of the place.

Such was the setting—the near-confluence of two historic rivers, the brick and concrete sprawl of a modern industrial city of half a million souls—where, from the stifling heat of high summer to the refrigerant paralysis of deep winter, this greatest of wars was to act out its climactic crisis; where the vaunting ambition, the dizzying changes of plan, the iron-clad virtuosity in combat, having exhausted their rage, would have to give up and withdraw. The breaking of the colossus was at hand and Stalingrad was where it would stagger and crack.

At the centre of the drama now beginning to unfold, its star actor was a man who emerges as possibly the most fascinating of Hitler's generals. Not merely because failure is nearly always more interesting than success; not merely because of the scale of the disaster and its consequences; but because of the man himself, the tragedy of circumstance in which he found himself, and the defects of his undoubted military virtues that contributed to his destruction.

General Paulus was a Hamlet-figure among the German commanders of the Second World War: a man of outstanding professional competence, a man noted for his modesty and charm as well as for his dedication to his job, but a man who carried within himself the seeds of his own undoing, an inability to make up his mind.

The drama of Stalingrad was momentarily to give tragic stature to the quiet self-effacing figure at its centre: a commander whose eminence had been attained in the background of events on the General Staff not, until his comparatively recent appointment to the command of Sixth Army, in the rough and tumble of field operations.

Friedrich Wilhelm Ernst Paulus was born in 1890 into a

middle-class family of farmers and minor civil servants; his father, the treasurer of a school for delinquents, being in the second category. Paulus wanted to make the Navy his career but that socially conscious Service, considering that his family background did not quite measure up to its fastidious requirement, turned him down. The Army proved to be more accommodating and after an orthodox military education he was in 1911 gazetted lieutenant in a respectable, but by no means distinguished, infantry regiment—the classier Prussian regiments at that time having the same sort of reservations about bourgeois backgrounds as the Navy. In his first year of regimental life Paulus became a close friend of two of his fellow officers, a pair of young Rumanians—brothers and members of an aristocratic family named Rosetti-Solescu —who had chosen to make careers in the German army. In 1912 Paulus married their beautiful elder sister Elena Constance and no doubt this brilliant match did much to help wipe out the memory of the snub administered by the Navy. As with so many other pre-war regular officers, the 1914-18 war brought him accelerated maturity as well as decorations, rapid promotion and the beginnings of a reputation as a promising staff officer. In the small Regular Army to which Germany was limited by the Treaty of Versailles, Paulus was soon attracting notice.

It could be said of him without exaggeration that he "had everything." He was tall, talented, extremely good-looking, industrious, and always so immaculately dressed that his family used to tease him about the whiteness of his collars, the almost excessive shine of his boots. His nicknames—the "Major with the Sex Appeal," the "Noble Lord"—are indicative of the impression he made on his brother officers. He was efficient, modest, and charming—and with a rich, patrician wife to supply the social push and "pull" that was the one advantage that seemed to have been denied him at birth. In the early 1920s Friedrich Paulus and another talented contemporary, Erwin Rommel, were both commanding companies in the 13th Infantry Regiment. Of the two, the much-decorated extrovert swashbuckling Rommel was the more flamboyant personality who generally seemed to catch the eye. But it was the company commanded by the modest meticulous Paulus that always came out top both at work and play. The two men, who were good friends, typified the essential difference between the staff officer and the man of action. A report on Paulus as adjutant of the 13th Regiment included the following: "A typical General Staff officer of the old school . . . good physique, extremely well turned out, modest (at times over-modest) . . . pleasant young man with good manners and a good mixer . . . exceptionally good and enthusiastic soldier . . . slow but very methodical . . . marked tactical ability though inclined to spend overmuch time on his appreciation . . . likes to study every situation minutely . . ."

It was a glowing report—except for the suggestion of hesitancy in making a decision that was to counterpoint the methodical progress of Paulus, though it did not prevent his rising steadily to the top.

Twenty years later Rommel and Paulus were again brought together in the line of duty—but at a rather higher level. In 1941 Paulus—by which time Paulus as *Oberquartiermeister I* was deputy to the Army Chief of Staff, General Halder—was sent by Halder to North Africa to report on the situation that had been created by the excessive zeal of his old friend General Rommel.

It will be recalled that Rommel, with the small armoured force that later grew into the Afrika Korps, had been sent to Tripoli to help the Italian ally to stabilize their front after their rout by the British desert army at the end of 1940 and the beginning of 1941. He had been given strictly limited objectives. Under the over-all command of the Italian Comando Supremo he was to restore the position and, if possible, to recapture Benghazi—but nothing more. The German High Command felt that they owed this much at least to their faltering ally, but, with the invasion of Russia impending, they were far too preoccupied to allow themselves to be drawn into anything serious in Africa. Rommel, however, had had other ideas. Having launched a surprise—and most successful—counterattack against the British he had, against orders, decided to follow it up and hang the consequences. In a series of brilliant and bold actions he had chased the British back to the Egyptian frontier, greatly overextending himself in the process. The High Command were pleased with his success but less pleased with the extra strain on their overtaxed logistics that it threatened to impose. So Halder sent his deputy, Paulus, to North Africa with orders that might be paraphrased as: "Go and see what that crazy fool Rommel thinks he's doing and tell him not to."

In his diary Halder noted [1] that he had sent Paulus on this mission because he was "an old and good friend of Rommel and is perhaps the only one who might, by his personal influence, succeed in putting the brake on that madcap!" The madcap however was not so easily braked. At the end of two-and-a-half weeks Paulus was forced to use his authority as Deputy Chief of Staff and to give Rommel a firm order to remain on the defensive for the time being and to confine himself to holding Cyrenaica. The report that Paulus presented to General Halder on his return prompted the latter to note in his diary:[2] "Situation in North Africa unpleasant. Rommel by exceeding his orders has created a situation with which present lines of communication can no longer cope. Ro. (mmel) is not up to the job." It became clear too that the "aesthete and the hearty"——Paulus and Rommel——were no longer quite such close buddies as Halder had assumed from their old regimental association in the past. The exasperated Paulus was heard referring to Rommel as a "thick-headed Swabian" who would not listen to advice and was incapable of seeing beyond his own front. On top of this the "modest, perhaps over-modest" Paulus could not restrain himself from airing his astonishment that "Rommel allowed himself to be surrounded all the time by a horde of war correspondents and press photographers." He conceded Rommel's outstanding gifts of leadership but doubted whether he had correctly appreciated the full implications of the North African front. So much so that he considered the possibility of recommending to the Army High Command that Rommel be replaced as C-in-C Africa and himself appointed in his place. As always he pondered the thought long and carefully before acting and it was actually his wife Elena Constance who sharply disposed of it, as soon as she knew what he had in mind, with a positive piece of wifely intuition:[3] "Keep your finger out of *that* pie! It won't do you any good to get put in the bag in Africa!" (Events were ironically to show just how wrong feminine intuition can sometimes be. But in fairness to Elena Constance Paulus it must be remembered that Russia had not yet been invaded and she was married to a golden boy headed, it was thought, for the highest his profession had to offer.)

The whole episode of the Paulus 1941 visit to Rommel and its sequel gives an illuminating insight into the character and personality of both men as well as the rigidity of the German General Staff in being unable to accommodate Rommel's ad hoc successes because they did not conform to the prescribed over-all plan. It was of course the General Staff, represented by Paulus, whose appreciation of the North African theatre was wrong, not Rommel.

It is the good fortune of historians that most generals, despite their own security regulations, are inclined to communicate volubly with their wives, or their diaries or both. Paulus, ever the exemplary staff officer, was an exception. His good manners, modesty, reticence, and meticulously correct behaviour at all times seem to have extended to his most private communications. He left behind little in writing on which the student of his actions and motives can base a close study. Walter Goerlitz, the German military historian, has perhaps come nearest to this in the short biographical sketch of Paulus that makes up the first third of his book *Paulus and Stalingrad*. In this he has assembled under various headings most of the known facts about Paulus from which it is possible to build up an impression of the man—a profile if not a biography.

Paulus was "in manner quiet, a thinker. Hardly anyone ever saw him excited, scornful or in a rage. He never showed his feelings. Was always self-possessed."

We learn that he was "always embarrassed and rather helpless in face of rudeness and ill-manners" so found it difficult to cope with Hitler.

We learn that he was "well-groomed and with slender hands, always beautifully turned out with gleaming white collar and immaculate boots."

But, as we have noted, there was also in his progress chart the recurrent nag of hesitancy. "This officer lacks decisiveness," wrote the director of an exercise who had tested Paulus for a quick decision and found him wanting. I have already quoted the favourable report on his regimental adjutancy which also, however, noted a "tendency to spend over-much time on his appreciation." And Walter Goerlitz remarks apropos the reticence of Paulus: "A man who ponders every factor thrice before deciding what is to be done is not usually inclined to lay bare his innermost thoughts."

It must be emphasized that these hints of indecisiveness are easier to form into a pattern in retrospect and with the advantage of hindsight than they may have appeared at the time. What is clear is that in the hard school of the German General Staff Friedrich Paulus was regarded as a brilliant and dedicated staff officer who seemed certain to rise to the top of his profession. For this reason, and in view of his ultimate fate, it is worth while looking for the weaknesses that may have lurked behind the success pattern. On investigation one discovers that the power of decision was wanting.

In view of such evidence as there is, and the final calamity which befell him, it seems reasonable to suggest that Paulus had a basic sense of insecurity deriving from his middle-class background and his early rejection experience with the Navy. It would explain his subsequent overattention to dress and personal deportment: a determination to be more perfect than perfect. His successful courting of an aristocratic wife no doubt helped him to overcome the sense of inferiority to some extent—but in a subtle way may subsequently have served as a constant reminder of it.

This, at all events, was the man whom Hitler appointed to command the crack Sixth Army in January 1942. That had been just after the autumn crisis of 1941 when the first Russian counter-offensive had saved Moscow and the first German withdrawal of the campaign had cost Field-Marshal von Rundstedt his job as C-in-C Army Group South. In the subsequent reshuffle Field-Marshal Walther von Reichenau, till then the commander of Sixth Army, moved up to command the Army Group in von Rundstedt's place so that a new commander had to be found for Sixth Army. The name of Paulus came up and von Reichenau strongly endorsed his suitability for the job, having had Paulus as his chief of staff at Sixth Army after the Polish campaign.

Paulus, after spending so long on the staff, was eager for an active command but as a result of his long confinement to staff duties had never commanded so much as a regiment in the field. His appointment to this "plum" command therefore caused a number of raised eyebrows among battle-scarred officers senior to him. It was another sign of the favour with which the gods seemed always to look on Friedrich Paulus that he slipped into this new appointment with his usual accomplished ease and (except among disappointed rivals) with high approval all round from Hitler down.

Paulus provided a complete contrast with his predecessor. Field-Marshal Walther von Reichenau was an able soldier. He was also a hard, ruthless, brutal man who had embraced the Nazi creed with zest from its early days and had prospered under it. He closely resembled the traditional caricature of the Prussian general: massive body on thick legs, cropped head, ugly red face with light blue eyes one of them supplemented by the usual rimless monocle: hard-living, hard-riding, hard-swearing: a man of great rages and great laughter. Extremely shrewd and in action capable of rapid decision but with no head for intricate staff work and therefore dependent on his chief of staff. When Paulus had occupied that position eighteen months earlier the two men had got on surprisingly well together, as complete opposites sometimes will, each supplying what the other lacks: as a gangster may become fond of the accountant or lawyer on whose superior mind and sophistication he depends.

But it is indicative of the difference between these two men, who nevertheless had had a good working relationship in the past, that one of General Paulus's first actions after taking over Sixth Army was to cancel von Reichenau's "severity order" issued to Sixth Army the year before and which included the following:[4]

> . . . The most important object of this campaign against the Jewish-Bolshevist system is the complete destruction of its sources and the extermination of the Asiatic influence in European civilization. In this connection, there devolve upon the troops tasks which go beyond the confines of normal military duty. In this eastern theatre, the soldier is not only a man fighting in accordance with the rules of the art of war, but also the ruthless standard-bearer of a national conception and the avenger of all the bestialities perpetrated on the German peoples. For this reason the soldier must learn fully to appreciate the necessity for the severe but just retribution that must be meted out to the subhuman species of Jewry . . .

This order had been von Reichenau's own brainchild. It had supplemented the notorious "Commissar Order" of Hitler himself early in the Russian campaign (the order, tacitly ignored by most of the generals, that political commissars with the Russian forces were not to be treated as prisoners of war but were to be taken aside and shot out of hand). Reichenau's order had naturally been highly approved by Hitler. It is to the credit of Paulus that this did not deter him from cancelling it.

As for von Reichenau he was not to have the opportunity to see how his protégé made out in his new appointment. A week before Paulus arrived to take over Sixth Army, von Reichenau was dead. The manner of his going did not exactly become him but it was a pointer to the kind of man he must have been. In that same January, only one week before Paulus arrived at Sixth Army Headquarters to take over, Field-Marshal von Reichenau went for what was described as "his usual cross-country run." The temperature was twenty degrees below zero; the Field-Marshal was in his late fifties!

When he came to the Mess for lunch he looked terrible, admitted he felt extremely unwell, ate very little. After lunch he had a heart attack and collapsed. Later that afternoon he was strapped to the armchair into which he had collapsed and carried aboard an aircraft to be flown to Leipzig for treatment. The aircraft was scheduled to make one stop on the way. It happened that the pilot had to make a crash-landing, during which the chairborne von Reichenau suffered a severe head injury. He died in a hospital that same evening.

That had been in January 1942. During the next few months Paulus showed himself to be as much at home with men as he had been dealing with paper. He developed as close a link with the rank and file as an Army commander can and indefatigably visited units and formations as often as possible. The Sixth Army and their commander were on terms of high mutual esteem and confidence when in the summer the time came to carry out Hitler's swiftly changing orders. On August 19 General Paulus began the attack on Stalingrad town forcing a double crossing of the Don on August 21 and by August 23 had broken through to the Volga at Rynok on the northern outskirts of Stalingrad. At the same time Fourth Panzer Army, diverted from the Caucasus advance and working their way up from the south towards the southern outskirts had likewise broken through to the Volga by the beginning of September, establishing a salient in the area of Yelshanka and Kuperosnoye. So by mid-September the Germans had established strong bridgeheads about five miles wide and about twenty miles apart in the extreme northern and southern outskirts of the city. It was only a matter now of turning inwards and advancing until they touched. But the Russian Sixty-second Army, reorganized and rallied by Lieutenant General (later Marshal) Vassili Chuikov began to offer stiff resistance. The Germans soon found themselves fighting for the city street by street, building by building, even room by room. It is the most unpleasant kind of fighting, this close-quarter street fighting in which normal tactical procedures go by the board and companies and platoons split up into small groups often working on their own, hunting out an enemy who may be on the roof of the next house or in the cellar of the one you are in yourself. In spite of Hitler's announcements that he had taken Stalingrad the fighting went on and by mid-November the Germans were still trying to finish off what they had begun by breaking through to the Volga on the northern and southern outskirts of the city. And soon—always the haunting nightmare of armies fighting in Russia—the weather would begin to turn cold.

On October 14 Paulus made the first of his two supreme efforts to take Stalingrad attacking on a narrow front of three miles with three infantry and two panzer divisions. The brunt of this attack was borne by Chuikov's Sixty-second Army which held the main Russian bridgehead covering the central part of the city and extending to a depth of only two miles from the west or right bank of the Volga. In this comparatively short distance between the Russian front line and the river lay the celebrated Tractor Plant (a sort of High Altar of Stalingrad) and the Barricades Artillery factory and it was on these two objectives that Paulus in the first instance directed the attack.

The Russian commander described it as a battle "unequalled in its cruelty and ferocity throughout the whole of the Stalingrad fighting." [5] To attack on so narrow a front, with an objective only two miles ahead, limited the number of divisions Paulus could deploy, and his plan was to use his attack force in depth, that is in successive waves supported by overwhelming artillery and air support. The battle opened early in the day. By nightfall the Luftwaffe had flown three thousand sorties. By nightfall the artillery and mortars which had been pouring out a murderous fire all day were preparing to keep it up all night. "It was a sunny day," Chuikov has written, "but owing to the smoke and soot visibility was reduced to 100 yards." The term "fog of war" takes on a new significance when an industrial city happens to be the battleground and streets of large buildings are being systematically smashed and churned up. Chuikov describes what it was like at the receiving end of the tremendous German onslaught:

> Our dugouts were shaking and crumbling up like a house of cards . . . The command and observation posts of regiments and divisions were being smashed by shells and bombs. At my Army's command post thirty people were killed. The guards scarcely had time to dig the officers out of the smashed dugouts of the Army HQ. The troops had to be directed by radio; transmitters had been set up on the other side of the Volga, and we communicated with them and they then passed on our orders to the fighting units on this side of the river.

By midnight the Germans had advanced one-and-a-quarter miles and captured the Tractor Plant, cutting the defending army in two. The day's fighting had cost both sides dear. Around the Tractor Plant lay three thousand German dead.

> We also (wrote Chuikov) suffered very heavy losses that day. During the night 3500 wounded soldiers and officers were taken across the Volga. This was a record figure.

Next day, October 15, Paulus resumed the attack with fresh troops and at one time his infantry came within three hundred yards of Chuikov's Army HQ but (in Chuikov's words):

> Was short of that one battalion which might have captured the Army headquarters only 300 yards away. And yet we decided not to move, and to fight on.

By the end of the day the two Russian divisions chiefly involved had lost 75 percent of their effective strength but during the night one regiment of a fresh division was ferried across the river under murderous fire to join in the battle and it was followed two nights later by the other two regiments.

On October 16, the third day of the battle, Paulus attacked again in great strength from that sector of the west bank of the Volga that he now tenuously held, attacking northwards and southwards to engage the flank and rear of the defending forces. But the attack was broken up by defenders prepared to fight till they died; by the devastating defensive fire of the Russian artillery reinforced by gunboats of the Volga fleet; and by the bravery of the Russian dive-bomber pilots who again and again flew suicidally through the German air umbrella to attack Paulus's panzer formations. Chuikov has this comment:

> The Germans were bold at the beginning of an attack, freely pursuing a defeated enemy, but were helpless in battle against even the remnants of a group of soldiers determined to die rather than let the enemy pass.

On October 19 and 20 Paulus continued the offensive, now concentrating its fury against the areas of the Barricades Artillery Plant and the Red October Blast Furnaces which lie in succession immediately south of the Tractor Factory: so that the three great factory areas together form a frontage of about five miles along the west bank of the Volga with a large suburb for its workers immediately behind each plant.

At last for the first time the Russians sensed that the German attacks were being pressed home without quite the same fury. The fighting was still relentless and savage but throughout the two days and nights of October 19 and 20 Chuikov was able to hold all the German attacks on the Barricades and Red October areas. This weakening of the German effort is reflected in the War Diary of the Luftwaffe's Fourth Air Fleet [6] of which the VIII Air Corps was supporting the Paulus offensive. On October 14, the day the offensive opened, the Diary noted that the attack on Stalingrad "is making good progress. The Russians seem to have been taken rather by surprise. The dreaded Tractor Factory has been captured and we've reached the Volga on a front of three kilometres." By October 19 the diaries of Fourth Air Fleet and its commander General Freiherr Wolfram von Richthofen were telling a different story:

> Stalingrad situation very confused. It seems that divisions have been too optimistic in their reports. No one knows exactly what the position is, and all the divisions are sending contradictory reports. Attack on Spartakovka has been halted north of Stalingrad. Fiebig [commander of VIII Air Corps] is furious, because the infantry don't exploit the chances his air raids make for them . . .

It is not unusual for inter-services recriminations to be bandied about at the lower levels—with soldiers complaining that air support is lacking or bombing the wrong targets, and airmen grumbling that the soldiers are too slow to exploit the openings made for them. But when these recriminations occur at the top it is a sure sign that things are going wrong. On November 1 von Richthofen, who manifested the same contemptuous arrogance towards the Army as his Chief, Goering, had a conference with Paulus and his chief of staff and afterwards recorded that they had "trotted out all the same old arguments (which are only partly true)—numerical inferiority, lack of training in this type of warfare, shortage of ammunition and so on." [7] He went on to say that the real trouble, apart from the extreme weariness of both the troops and their commanders was "that rigid Army conservatism, which still accepts without demur 1000 men in the front line out of a ration strength of 12,000, and which leads to the generals being content merely to issue orders, without bothering to go into any detail or to make sure that the preparations required for this type of fighting are properly made." The Air General admits that it did not endear him to Paulus when he spoke out along these lines at their meeting on November 1.

No less significant than the friction between the services was the changing mood of the German press at this time. The confident claims that Stalingrad had fallen or was about to fall had given way to reports describing the strength of the "Stalingrad fortress" and the appalling hardships being endured by the German troops. Typical was one in the *Deutsche Allgemeine Zeitung*: "A cruel battle is fought for every inch of ground; our soldiers, worn out, and with hollow cheeks, and their eyes red for lack of sleep, are praying for an end of the battle." This was the kind of thing that the German public was now being told. Even more significant perhaps were the press comments of the neutral countries: like the suggestion in Sweden that "Stalingrad has ruined all the German plans" and the Turkish comment that "Even if Stalingrad falls, it will not make all that difference now. The German timetable has been completely upset." This was the point. The Russian strategy of dragging out the summer campaign long enough to ensure that the Germans would have to fight through another Russian winter was succeeding. Several times it had been touch and go. The German army was still very, very good. But circumstances—vitally (and for the Germans fatally) influenced by Hitler's kaleidoscopic changes of plan in July—had so evolved that Stalingrad, almost by accident, had become the place where the issue had got to be worked out to a finish. Stalingrad was where Paulus had got to be stopped, no matter what it cost. Stalingrad was where the Russians must endure to the ultimate limit of desperation—until the Volga froze, and with it the pan-German hopes of Hitler. It was as simple as that.

To sustain resistance through its peroration of agony Chuikov had to throw into the battle almost anyone who could walk and hold a rifle—cooks, clerks, grooms in charge of horse transport, drivers, cobblers, butchers, tailors, tradesmen, and administrative personnel of every kind. This strange and bewildered array of non-combatants was ferried across the Volga under heavy fire every night in terrified batches, hurriedly given arms and ammunition and sent straight into action.

> These poorly trained or wholly untrained people (wrote Chuikov) became specialists in street fighting, as soon as they stepped onto the ground of Stalingrad. "It was pretty terrifying," they would say, "to cross over to Stalingrad, but once we got there we felt better. We knew that beyond the Volga there was nothing, and that if we were to remain alive, we had to destroy the invaders."

Formed into "storm groups" they quickly learned to make themselves useful supplementing the dwindling numbers of regular forces defending the city. And once they had overcome the "first time" fear of all soldiers facing their baptism of fire, and finding (as many always do) that it is not quite so terrifying as they had thought it would be, they became years older in a matter of hours and then they began to feel proud of themselves. In no time at all word of their deeds began to filter back across the river and it became, as one would expect, a matter of immense prestige to have fought on the right bank at Stalingrad. The cooks, the tailors, the storemen and the clerks were not exactly clamouring to be ferried across to the thunder and lightning of the right bank. But when it had become unavoidable and they had managed to survive their first hours alongside the real soldiers, there was no stopping them and in years to come their grandchildren would never hear the end of it.

Something less tangible was also animating the efforts of the defenders. Stalingrad was the crucible in which the Soviet citizen was discovering, with a profound sense of revelation, a new consciousness of being a Russian before he was a Soviet citizen. The Red Army was finding its soul and an identity as a national army rather than a mere political instrument of the Revolution. The most significant manifestation of this was the decision[8] of the Praesidium of the Supreme Soviet of October 9 that for the first time the Red Army was to be commanded by its own officers. The cumbersome and ineffective system of dual control by army officers and political commissars previously in force was now abolished. Furthermore, officers would henceforth be expected to look and behave like officers. In the testing extremity of battle the Soviets had found out the hard way that you cannot run an army on the egalitarian principle that had animated the Red Army from its inception: that a comradely relationship between officers and other ranks was desirable but not quite the same thing as the recent state of affairs where a great many Soviet officers were as slovenly in appearance and deportment (and therefore efficiency) as the men they commanded. From the blazing ruins and the smoke and the rubble of Stalingrad came new and much smarter uniforms, gold braid and a gleaming new image for the Russian officer. The Revolution was growing up. This build-up of the officer was not the least of the respects in which Stalingrad would be seen, in retrospect, as a watershed. There is a curious irony in the fact that while the revolutionary Russians were deliberately trying to re-create the officer class they had so meticulously expunged, Hitler was doing precisely the opposite: placing more and more Nazi political officers in headquarters posts to spy on the German officer class which had achieved so much for him but which he now increasingly mistrusted.

Meanwhile the hard fighting in the rubble of the streets and, especially, about the vast devastated areas of the three great factories continued through the rest of October and into November. To the other anxieties and trials of Paulus's hard-pressed assault forces was added the inescapable awareness that the air was getting colder. Whatever might happen to battle schedules, winter was going to arrive on time; a thought as awesome to the attackers as it was a comfort to the defenders. The approach of winter gave both sides, for opposite reasons, a deadline to work to. The Germans must win before it came; the Russians just had to hold on that long. Or this was how it seemed in the front line. For the Germans it was a grim thought that the Russian winter, with all that it implied, was inexorably approaching.

The Russians in Stalingrad felt that having survived this long they could hold out indefinitely so long as they had enough ammunition. The need for ammunition was the dominating theme of Chuikov's communications with his immediate superiors. A singleminded, blunt, fighting general with the fighting commander's impatience with staff and headquarters personnel, he had a difficult time persuading his rear echelons that ammunition was more important to him than food or winter clothing at this particular time. In his account of the battle he is especially hard on General Vinogradov, a well-meaning Deputy Chief of Staff

> who made the Sixty-second Army's rear units send
> us warm clothing, felt boots and provisions instead

117

of ammunition . . . I sent Vinogradov several telegrams with a categorical demand to stop interfering with the Army's supplies. But there was no stopping him: jerseys, caps with ear-flaps and felt boots were sent to us as priority cargoes. I had to turn to the Front Military Council . . . Only N. S. Khrushchev's intervention stopped the flood of ear-flaps and felt boots.

So everything on the Russian side was concentrated on the ensuring of the supply and distribution of ammunition. For there seemed no doubt that Paulus would make at least one more supreme effort to win the battle before the big freeze. He would not dare not to.

In this southern region of the Volga the advent of winter is no sudden affair; it extends over a matter of weeks like a screw tightening its grip imperceptibly with a turn every day or two. First there is a swift drop in the temperature, though it is some time before this affects the river. Even when the temperature has sunk to twenty degrees centigrade below zero the river will still be free of ice, but, because of the difference between its temperature and that of the air, steam will rise from it. This happens in late October and the next thing is that small pieces of ice form and flow down the river like rubbish. Then the pieces of ice become larger and gradually join together into sizeable ice floes till the river is no longer navigable except by powerful armoured vessels. Then at fifteen degrees below zero the ice floes become too large and packed for even these. For a time the river can be crossed only on foot by a few daredevil specialists from the Volga region who can cross it leaping from one floe to another, with a boat-hook in their hands to steady them, in the manner of lumberjacks riding a floating mass of logs.

It is at this stage; when the river is no longer navigable by even armoured boats, but is not yet frozen solid, and is therefore unable to bear loaded sledges; that the two sides are for a time completely cut off from one another except by bridges. This in fact was the stage at which the defenders of Stalingrad, who till then had been supplied each night from the left bank of the river, were completely on their own with such food and ammunition supplies as they had been able to hoard. It was at this moment, on November 11, that Paulus unloosed the second of his all-out offensives: his final desperate effort to finish off the battle. Now—while the exhausted Stalingrad bridgeheads were cut off from their comforting link with the left bank from which they had been maintained and to which their wounded had hitherto been evacuated—was the time for the supreme effort on the part of both armies: for as soon as the winter freeze-up was complete the problem would become a different one. And for the Germans it did not bear thinking about.

As on October 14 Paulus attacked on a front of three miles, initially using five divisions but with a further nine at hand to follow up. The air effort was again the biggest that could be made though, significantly, it amounted on the first day to a thousand sorties as compared with the three thousand of October 14. The German intention was to bulldoze their way through to the river by sheer weight of numbers and material and regardless of losses.

Once again the attack opened like a hurricane, with a saturation bombing of the defences followed by concentrated artillery fire with limitless ammunition. Once again Chuikov's battered Sixty-second Army braced itself against the shock. Stalingrad now imbued all of its assorted defenders with a unifying mystique. Not only the regular combatant soldiers that were the backbone of the defence but the Siberian sailors from the Pacific fleet who were now fighting with the infantry; the clerks and cooks and other administrative people from the rear; the young girls and women manning antiaircraft guns and signals units. Amid crashing factory chimneys, in the sewers, in the broken cellars and the bomb craters and the mountains of building rubble they fought the Germans for every foot of ground: how hard they fought may be gauged from the fact that one of the defending units (a regiment of a Guards division) was reduced by noon of the first morning from a strength of 250 to 6. Paulus was under pressure to force this attack home for it was now established at OKW that the Russians were carrying out considerable regroupings behind the Volga and that two new Army Groups (under Generals Yemenov and Yeremenko) were massing to the north and south rear of the Stalingrad area. Time was running out. The German High Command knew this better than the Russians defending Stalingrad. All that the defenders knew was that they had got to hang on at all costs, though Chuikov did have an inkling that something big might be brewing when he told his chief of staff that the High Command were satisfied with what his forces had done and therefore must have new plans. But this had been his only hint.

By sheer weight and power the first momentum of the

119

German attack of November 11 crashed through to the Volga bank—the third time this had been done and the defending army cut in two—but, as on previous occasions, the penetration was a narrow one and the attackers were unsuccessful in their attempts to exploit it by rolling outwards to clear the pockets of defenders to their right and left. As early as the middle of the second day it was clear that the attack could not succeed. The German momentum soon became noticeably weaker and though hard fighting was to continue for a few days longer the offensive had failed. Paulus was left to brood on the knowledge that the Russians were regrouping behind the Volga; that the north flank of his now depleted Sixth Army was only weakly held by Rumanian and Italian forces; and—perhaps the most bitter thought of all—that he had failed in his first object, to win the race with the Russian winter. It had been a close-run thing especially during the all-out offensives of October 14 and November 11. But he had finally lost the race with the Russian winter for possession of the Volga.

The ice floes of Stalingrad, transmogrifying into a single sheet of ice, might have symbolized at this time the fragmented hopes of the German Army hardening at last into a single barrier of frustration tinged with dread.

So skilfully did the Russians complete their regrouping behind the front that the Stalingrad defenders were as much in the dark as the Germans about where, when and how strongly any counterstroke was likely to be delivered. They could only assume that one was coming and, as the High Command seemed pleased with their efforts, Chuikov was not alone in concluding that whatever form it took it was going to happen soon. This feeling had been strengthened by a hint from Stalin, albeit a cautiously veiled hint, in a Special Order of the Day delivered early in November. By this time, Stalin was wholly a father-figure to the defenders of Stalingrad. In dire straits men crave the warmth and security of personal leadership. A later generation in different circumstances might invent the phrase "cult of personality" as a pejorative; in Stalingrad in November 1942 the cult in this particular instance was not only warm and encouraging but indispensable. The phrase of the father-figure that stuck in all their minds was the colloquialism, dropped casually into a Special Order of the Day: "There will be a holiday in our street too." It was a well-known saying in common use. It was as close as the Russian premier could come to saying "Hold on a little longer. There will soon be something to cheer about."

Two weeks after the Germans had made their last special effort at Stalingrad, Chuikov had a conference in his dugout to discuss with his subordinate commanders the increasingly acute problem of supplies and reinforcements: for it was now the in-between time when the Volga is not yet frozen hard but the ice floes are big enough and continuous enough to stop river traffic. During the conference Chuikov received a phone call telling him to stand by for an important order. Supplies and reinforcements were forgotten as, in an atmosphere tense with anticipation, the conference began to guess what the order was going to be. Then Gurov, the Divisional Commissar, slapped his forehead with that universal gesture that in any language means: "But of course! How stupid of me!" Then he said:[9] "It's the order for the big counter-offensive!"

In the early morning of November 19 two Russian army groups—that of General Vatutin's on the Southwest Front, General Rokossovsky's on the Don Front—rolled south towards Kalach on the Don forty miles west of Stalingrad. The next day new divisions of General Yeremenko's Army Group on the Stalingrad Front went over to the offensive thrusting northward towards Kalach to link up there with the other two forces. The masters of the gigantic encirclement were themselves about to learn what it felt like to be gigantically encircled.

The three Army Groups had been abundantly re-equipped from the new trans-Ural factories and the preliminary movements and dispositions had been made secretly, almost entirely at night, so that although German Intelligence had an inkling of what was in the wind they had no suspicion of its scale. Although about one million Russians were being projected at roughly the same number of Germans the Russian attack succeeded in achieving overwhelming superiority at the points of attack. It was as though the Germans were so mesmerized by Stalingrad as the be-all and end-all of their intent that they were caught completely off-balance by the size and weight of the Russian triple counteroffensive.

Within four-and-a-half days the Russian forces had effected their junction near Kalach. Paulus's Sixth Army had been encircled and cut off from the rest of Army Group B. In these few days of overwhelming counterattack the besiegers of

Stalingrad had been dramatically transformed into the besieged. There now began the slow tightening of the steel ring around the trapped Sixth Army, an ordeal that was to last two months: coinciding, as it happened, with the progressive tightening of that other steel grip, the Russian winter, now hardening into the pitiless, unforgiving agony that would reach its climax in January and February.

For General Chuikov's torn and battered Stalingrad garrison, so close to the end of human endurance, it was a sudden and magical deliverance: an instant mutation of despair into joy.

The encirclement of the German Sixth Army, completed by November 24, was the third and greatest of the three body blows which rocked the German war effort in the month of November 1942. For the other two we must look 1400 miles and 18 degrees of latitude south and slightly west of Stalingrad to Egypt.

Chapter 11

DESPERATION IN THE DESERT

☐ When, at the beginning of September 1942, Field-Marshal Rommel's last offensive in Egypt had been frustrated by General Montgomery at Alam Halfa ridge in the El Alamein defensive zone, he had lost not only a battle but the initiative on the Africa front: a foretaste of disasters to come.

The British victory in this (for them) purely defensive battle had been made possible by the crippling of the German-Italian supply system by the British naval and air forces; by British air superiority over the battlefield; above all by the galvanic effect on the Eighth Army of its new commander Montgomery. It was clear to everyone concerned that Rommel could never again take the offensive in Egypt unless there were a radical change in his supply and reinforcement situation and in the attitude of OKW to this campaign. However blind his superiors at Supreme Headquarters might appear to be, he would try once more to make them see the light in time, and realize the chance they were missing in Africa.

Rommel was now a very sick man indeed. The strain of the battle; awareness that the British had been revitalized by their new command, General Sir Harold Alexander the theatre commander and General Bernard Montgomery the field commander who had given the Eighth Army their much-needed first taste of victory in months; Intelligence summaries that daily brought news of more and more ship-loads of tanks, guns and ammunition passing through the Suez Canal for the British: all this had done nothing to im-prove the condition of a man suffering from dysentery, hy-pertension, and liver trouble. Not only were Rommel's doc-tors pleading with him to take sick leave but Hitler had now insisted that he do so. He was told that OKW would shortly be sending a deputy to take over in Africa. After which he was to take six weeks' sick leave and have his ailments prop-erly treated. He proposed to do this in Semmering, a moun-tain resort in Austria not many miles south of Vienna. But Rommel had something else in mind. He would make this trip an excuse to call at Hitler's headquarters and make one more impassioned plea for his seemingly lost cause, the Africa front, to be taken seriously.

Meanwhile there was hard and urgent work to be done before he could hand over. The colossal build-up that Mont-gomery was receiving could mean only one thing. The British were planning a knock-out offensive. He estimated that they would have a tank superiority of at least two to one, prob-ably more than that. Not only were they receiving more and more tanks but he knew that they included a substantial num-ber of the new American Shermans, the best tank they had so far had and the first that was likely to be qualitatively the equal of the best of the German tanks. It was no secret to Rommel's Intelligence department that a prodigal quantity of equipment and supplies of all kinds was streaming up the Suez Canal and filling Montgomery's base depots in the Nile Delta to the point of overflowing. And with the Luftwaffe fully occupied in Russia, and the Royal Air Force in com-mand of the Egyptian skies, there was nothing the depleted Axis air forces available could do to interfere with the un-loading of the British ships.

If he had to play a defensive role—and nothing was more alien to the audacious temperament of Rommel—then by heaven! he would do his best to make certain that what met the irresistible force, that Montgomery was clearly prepar-ing to unloose, would be as near an immovable object as he could make it. He would have preferred, of course, to fight a mobile defensive battle, using the open desert spaces and the speed, opportunism, and adaptability of his well-tried panzers which he still believed superior to the British in mobile tactics. But by stabilizing the front at El Alamein the British had ensured that the forthcoming engagement would be not a battle of manoeuvre but a static set-piece affair, a frontal slogging-match between El Alamein's two secure flanks, the sea in the north and the vast impassable Qattara Depression in the south; those happy wide outflanking movements of the past would not on this occasion be possible. Even if the ground allowed, he was forced to reflect ruefully, in the present parlous state of his gasoline stocks mobility was a luxury that would have to be strictly rationed.

So in the few days before his deputy arrived Rommel put in hand a defence plan designed to turn the flatness of the desert into a horizontal fortress in the sand. Its basis was to be the mine covered by the emplaced antitank gun and the dug-in tank. Three successive defensive zones were to be constructed to a depth of five miles along the entire thirty-eight miles length of the El Alamein front.

Rommel intended the mine and the antitank gun, working in concert, to have the same devastating effect on Montgomery's attacking waves of tanks as barbed wire and machine guns had had on the waves of British infantry in Flanders in the First World War. To ensure that his gunners and infantry would be able to continue to function, regardless of the constant aerial and artillery bombardment that the British could now sustain without giving a thought to the cost in ammunition, Rommel ordered his engineers to design and demonstrate suitable reinforced emplacements which were then prescribed for the entire German-Italian army.

Nothing perhaps was more symptomatic of the changing German mood everywhere at this time than that one of the army's most brilliant attacking generals should be rededicating his outlook to a strategy based on the mine, a wholly defensive weapon. Ominously it foretold what was for Hitler and Germany to be the story of this momentous autumn everywhere. The first slipping of the initiative, when it has been held as a matter of course and in overwhelming strength and confidence for three long years, is like the beginning of a wasting disease. To combat this would need all the powers of inspired leadership that could be brought to bear. It was particularly unfortunate, therefore, that this was the very moment the Panzer Army Afrika were to be deprived for several weeks of a leader who more than most had been able to inspire a personal loyalty that was almost devotional.

Having done everything possible to ensure that his defence plan was being put into effect exactly in accordance with his detailed instructions, Rommel handed over to his newly arrived deputy and prepared to depart on six weeks' sick leave.

The deputy turned out to be General Georg ("Fireball") Stumme, the ex-commander of the XL Panzer Corps fighting on the southeastern front in Russia. It will be recalled that Stumme had been held responsible as corps commander for the lapse of the staff officer in one of his divisions who had allowed himself to be shot down near the Russian lines while carrying an operation plan and marked maps of the opening of the German summer offensive the previous June. Only his excellent record of service and the intercession of senior officers at OKW had spared Stumme the full force of Hitler's wrath. He had narrowly escaped dismissal from the army with ignominy, and after his court-martial had been made available for posting away from the Russian front. It was a somewhat less effulgent "Fireball" who now found himself having to impress his personality on a "private army" that so clearly, and almost idolatrously, belonged to someone else. The Africa front was a long way from the mainstream of the German war. The Afrika Korps had developed that "forgotten army" complex of minority forces who fight distant campaigns for which they feel they are receiving insufficient credit and, more importantly, insufficient resources. Taking over the Panzer Army, and especially its most potent element the Afrika Korps, was like trying to replace the revered chieftain of an esoteric robber band who had been fighting a private war and would have liked to keep it that way. The unfortunate Stumme had arrived with a need to redeem himself in the eyes of the Führer. In addition he had to adapt himself to desert warfare, something totally different from the kind of fighting to which he had become accustomed in Russia. On top of all this Rommel told him before leaving that in the event of the British starting a major offensive he would return to Africa at once to resume command. It was not a happy take-over for General Stumme. Since, like the man he was replacing, he happened also to be a victim of high blood pressure (so often, it seems, the occupational complaint of senior military commanders and, in Stumme's case, aggravated by his summer of acute *angst*) the ruddy-complexioned "Fireball" had this too to add to his other difficulties.

Rommel left for Austria on September 23 but stopped off in Rome for a few days where he had talks with the Italian army chiefs, with Mussolini and with Ciano. In his talks with

Marshal Ugo Cavallero, the Italian Chief of Staff, he obtained specific promises of help in sending various urgently needed requirements to Africa, notably three thousand tons of rails and sleepers for railway communications.[1] Also the promise of a labour force of three thousand from the Italian army in Libya for the construction of new roads behind the front. None of these promises was kept.

In his talk with Mussolini, Rommel repeated what had become his standard plaintive speech on the inadequacy of the supplies being sent to North Africa. (He'd been making it off and on for eighteen months.)

> I left him in no doubt that unless supplies were sent to us at least on the scale I had demanded we should have to get out of North Africa. I think that, for all I said, he still did not realize the full gravity of the situation.

Apropos this meeting between Rommel and Mussolini, Ciano noted in his diary:[2]

> I have had a visit from Rommel, who said that he is taking six weeks' leave. Mussolini is convinced that Rommel will not come back. He finds Rommel physically and morally shaken. I didn't conceal from the Duce my estimate of the situation, synthesizing it in the following formula: "Our state of mind at the beginning of the winter is what, on the worst showing, we might have expected at the end."

To the growing pressures beginning to work against Germany there was now a new one—albeit a negative one and as yet slight—but something not to be discounted. This was the growing disenchantment of the Italian political and military chiefs. The Italian people and the Italian army (now hopelessly outclassed in its equipment) had always been disenchanted with the war but now the leaders in Rome were showing signs of this too. What Mussolini really meant when he talked to his son-in-law Ciano at this time was that Rommel had become a bit of a bore with his eternal complaints about not being sent the supplies he wanted. As for the Duce's hunch that the German would not go back to Africa, he may have had a hint of this from Hitler, as the Führer had decided that after his sick leave Rommel would be given a new appointment in the Ukraine. In the event this was not to happen but at the time Rommel was in Rome, the change was in Hitler's mind. Meanwhile the Italian solution appears to have been to humour Rommel and promise him more or less everything for which he asked and then do nothing about it. The specialist in this technique was Marshal Cavallero. The truth was that the Italian chiefs had difficulties about which they felt Rommel was showing too little understanding: the numerous sinkings, for example, in the Italian merchant navy. As Ciano noted:

> Replacements are slow and completely inadequate. In all, we have little more than a million tons left. At this rate the African problem will automatically end in six months, since we shall have no more ships with which to supply Libya.

This growing disillusion in Rome can be seen as the first foreshadowing of attitudes that were to come to a head one year later when the Italians would decide that Germany was no longer the best ally available.

What is certain is that Rommel's break of journey in Rome achieved nothing useful and vaguely irritated the Axis partner.

It was while Rommel was in Rome that the news came through that Hitler had finally dismissed the Army Chief of Staff General Franz Halder. This shocked the German Army, especially the officer corps, who had the highest professional regard for him. Halder was one of the few members of the military hierarchy to stand up to Hitler and he had clearly stood up to him once too often. There had been friction between the two for some time. The significance of the Halder dismissal was not lost on the Duce's entourage in Rome. "Halder," commented Ciano, "is a big figure in the German military world. An ugly sign." In place of Halder, Hitler had appointed General Kurt Zeitzler, previously von Rundstedt's Chief of Staff in the West. Zeitzler, according to Reichsmarschall Goering, was "a good National Socialist." The comment speaks for itself.

In passing one may note that one of the last entries in the OKH War Diary while Halder was Chief of Staff recorded that the Sixth Army advance on Stalingrad had worn itself to a standstill; that infantry companies were down to an average strength of sixty and panzer divisions down to between sixty and eighty serviceable tanks. And this was only the third week of September.

Having clearly made no impression on the Italians, Rommel moved on from Rome to the headquarters called Werewolf at Vinnitsa in the Ukraine, whither Hitler and his entourage had moved from the Wolf's Lair in East Prussia during the summer.

After the unsatisfactory talks in Rome during which Rommel, at heart a simple straightforward soldier, sensed that he was being subtly tricked by the smooth fast-talking Italians, it was a relief to be among Germans again—even though he never felt wholly at ease when visiting Supreme Headquarters.

Vinnitsa, like Rastenburg, was the usual austere layout of huts and bunkers buried in a forest and surrounded by high barbed wire fencing. Like all headquarters it teemed with officers and party officials whose function or usefulness you could not even begin to guess at. Dispatch riders and staff cars came and went but there was a sense of monastic isolation and tranquillity about the place that made it hard to believe that it had any connection with the blood and dirt that it was really all about. Everyone was much too formal, smart and well-dressed: so busy dealing with the torrent of paper flooding into and out of their offices: and always there was that tenseness of men who have learned to conceal what they are thinking. There could be none of that normal relieving of the feelings by grumbling at the follies of Higher Authority. It was too risky; the place was stiff with men listening for such indiscretions and eager to report them. In this atmosphere Africa all of a sudden seemed miles and miles away. There was nothing like OKW for making a plain honest-to-God fighting man feel badly dressed and out of place, a country yokel who has blundered into the royal palace: even if he happened to be a field marshal. For men like Rommel it always aroused a nostalgia for campaigning, for the rough blanket alongside his trailer or command tank in the open desert under the miraculous North African night sky.

But Rommel (Field-Marshal since Tobruk in June) had come here to Supreme Headquarters to state his case and state it he would. As he was one of the privileged few generals looked on with favour by Hitler he was soon invited to address a conference attended by most of the OKW hierarchy. Rommel made the most of his opportunity.

He gave an account of his last effort to break through the El Alamein line to Alexandria and Cairo and the reasons

128

for its failure. He stressed in particular the "tremendous superiority of the British in the air" and described the effect of the new Royal Air Force tactics i.e. carpet-bombing from a comparatively low level by tight formations of medium bombers. These tactics had imposed severe limitations on the use of motorized forces for it was the columns of "soft-skinned" supply and maintenance vehicles following up the assaulting spearheads that were most vulnerable to, and suffered most from, the bomber formations. The only way to counter the new enemy strength in the air would be to send strong German air formations to the Africa theatre at once.

He then dealt at length with the unsatisfactory supply position, telling Hitler and company what he had told Mussolini, "that we would be unable to keep going unless a radical improvement was made." He followed this up with detailed suggestions of how the improvement could be effected and said that a tonnage across the sea of 30,000 in September and 35,000 in October "was an indispensable condition for a successful defence against the forthcoming British attack." It is of particular interest that Rommel was no longer thinking in terms of renewing his own attack. That was now right out of the question. The build-up for which he was desperately pleading was to enable him to meet the British offensive. Times were indeed changing!

Rommel ended his report in the following words: [3]

> I quite realize that, with the present strategic sea and air situation in the Mediterranean, a very great effort will be required to ensure a safe and uninterrupted German supply to Africa. It will make the utmost demands of all German and Italian transport services and will require the reinforcement of the transport fleet. But it is only by the fulfilment of the conditions I have stated that the German troops, who are bearing the main brunt of the fighting in Africa, will be able to maintain their hold on this theatre against the finest troops of the British Empire.

There it was in a nutshell. Not how and when to renew the offensive, but how to muster the strength to defend and survive.

Hitler listened intently to what Rommel had to say and only Goering, of those present, was unsympathetic and sceptical; and inclined, when the opportunity arose, to suggest that the Field-Marshal was exaggerating his difficulties. Goering, of course, was annoyed by the references to the domination of the recent battle by the Royal Air Force. He had been stung quite early on when Rommel had paid tribute to the new carpet-bombing tactics of the British tactical bombers.

"Do you hear that, Goering?" Hitler had broken in, jeering. "Carpet-bombing in Africa!"

The Reichsmarschall, who regarded anything to do with the air as his personal and exclusive concern, was highly displeased. He was even more displeased later when Rommel needled him by telling the conference that British fighter-bombers had shot up his heaviest tanks with 40-mm cannon shells.

At this the Reichsmarschall exploded: "That's completely impossible. The Americans only know how to make razor blades."

"We could do with some of those razor blades, Herr Reichsmarschall," Rommel replied.[4]

He then produced from his briefcase a solid armour-piercing shell recovered from a crippled German tank. It had been fired at the tank by a low-flying British aircraft and had killed all except one of the crew.

Goering's reaction is not on record.

(Incidentally, the incorrect assumption that British aircraft would be firing American ammunition was perhaps indicative of the Germans' growing fear of American industrial potential though they had yet to meet the American soldier.)

Hitler's tone, when Rommel had finished, was propitiatory. He told him that his difficulties were appreciated and that he could rest assured that his supplies would be considerably stepped up in the coming weeks. This was going to be made possible by putting into service a large number of *Siebelfaehren*—a new type of flat-bottomed ferry designed by an engineer named Siebel. The feature of these craft was that they were of such shallow draught that torpedoes would pass under them without hitting. They also carried enough antiaircraft guns to render them reasonably invulnerable to low-level aerial attack. Their only disadvantage was that they could not be used in heavy seas—but in the Mediterranean this would not matter as heavy seas are infrequent.

This, Hitler seemed to imply, disposed of the little matter of Rommel's supplies. The *Siebelfaehren* would solve the problem. With regard to other help for the Africa front a brigade of *Nebelwerfer* (six-barreled rocket mortars) would shortly be on its way to Africa. This was a formidable new weapon now going into service and a brigade would amount to five hundred barrels. Another new development was the mammoth Tiger tank, the heaviest to date, and forty of these precious monsters would be allotted to the Africa front in the near future.

Rommel had the old soldier's scepticism about the promises of superiors that bigger and better is on its way. He would believe that all these wonders had come to pass when he saw them. Surely enough his account of this visit to OKW, written later, ends on this forlorn note.[5]

> Later it transpired that many of these promises had been given in a moment of over-optimism and on the basis of incorrect production figures, for it was neither possible to realise the building programme for *Siebelfaehren* on the scale provided for, nor to send the stated number of *Nebelwerfern* or Tiger tanks to the African Theatre.

His scepticism had not been misplaced though, fortunately for him, he did not know this when at last he left for Semmering for his well-earned rest and the proper medical treatment his circulation and liver illness so urgently needed. What he could not fail to know, after his short visit to OKW, was that the overriding concern there, eclipsing everything else, was Stalingrad. For, despite the conviction of Hitler that the Russians were beaten, and the hysterical predictions of the German radio that the city was about to fall, the Russians were defending it building by building as stoutly as ever. They did their best at OKW to show a polite interest in Rommel's difficulties but what was giving them nightmares was Paulus's failure to finish off the defenders of Stalingrad.

While Rommel tried to relax and forget his worries in the crisp mountain air of Semmering, Paulus was preparing his greatest attack yet on Stalingrad, the tremendous onslaught he launched on October 14 which has already been described. Meanwhile Stumme bustled about the El Alamein front implementing the defence plan laid down before his departure by Rommel, and striving to impress the clannish Afrika Korps, who could not accept him as anything more than a caretaker, with some of the qualities that had earned him the nickname of "Fireball" on the Russian front. In particular, of course, Stumme intensified the efforts of his Intelligence, especially his Air Reconnaissance, to pick up pointers to where and when the British would attack. It was air reconnaissance that gave him the important clue that the British were building a new water pipe line from the main pipe line near the coast to the southern sector of the Alamein front. It was an elaborate installation with reservoir and pumping stations; and its direction suggested that the offensive was intended to be launched in the southern part of the line. The state of the pipe line pointed to its not being completed until well into November. This probable date for Montgomery's attack was supported by the fact that there was no evidence of any considerable movement of transport to be expected before an offensive.

What Stumme could not know was that the water pipe line to the southern part of the front was a dummy deliberately intended to mislead him into thinking that that was where the attack would be launched whereas in fact it was going to be launched in the north. The dummy pipe line was in fact one of several devices in an elaborate British deception plan. The apparent lack of considerable transport movement was achieved by carrying out all forward movement of the many additional guns and tanks to battery positions or assembly areas previously filled with dummy guns and tanks or simply left vacant but camouflaged—so that the real guns and tanks could replace the dummies at the proper time or simply move into the empty camouflaged positions—these final moves all being made at night.

It was by such means that Montgomery was able to present to the inquisitive eyes of Stumme's daily air reconnaissance the impression that the ground picture of the British lines remained the same from day to day. Whereas in reality every night brought more guns, tanks and lorries into forward positions that were seemingly already occupied. The deception plan which preceded Montgomery's offensive at El Alamein was an outstanding essay in the art of camouflage: for the desert terrain—treeless and shrubless, with scarcely any variation of contour or configuration, without high ground, valleys, or gullies—is by its very nature more devoid of natural cover than any other kind of ground. To conceal the heavy movement of troops and material—the unavoidable prelude to an offensive—so as to deceive an alert enemy, both in the timing of the attack and the part of the front where it would be made, was a considerable feat of planning. Stumme accepted his Intelligence experts' belief that Montgomery was going to strike about the end of the second week in November and in the southern sector of the front.

That the Englishman should apparently not be aiming to attack sooner did not prompt Stumme to look at the evidence more closely. It fitted in with the general impression of the Panzer Army staff that the British commanders were cautious and methodical and never willing to start an offensive until supplies and reserves were overwhelmingly at hand and everything was "just right": an opinion shared, it must be said, and frequently aired by Prime Minister Churchill who was apt to explode with impatience whenever he was told that a commander was asking for more time. As for Montgomery, although they had formed a favourable impression of his professionalism and toughness after their first encounter with him, the German commanders had not failed also to discern from his conduct of the final stages of the battle of Alam Halfa that he too might be over-cautious; a man to play safe. All things considered it made sense that the British should carry on with their methodical build-up of strength and defer the opening of their offensive until mid-November. It therefore came, as it was intended to do, as a complete surprise when, at twenty minutes to nine o'clock (German Summer Time) on the night of October 23, the unique, poetic tranquillity of the desert was shattered by the traumatic discharge of nine hundred British artillery pieces.

The first of the three great blows that were to change the face of Hitler's war that autumn was on its way.

Chapter 12

EL ALAMEIN—DISASTER IN EGYPT

☐ Nothing like it had been seen, heard, or felt on the Africa front before. "Like the drumfire barrages of the First World War," was how Rommel afterwards described it— though he was not present that night or the night after and only heard about it later from some of its shaken survivors.

The night beyond the British lines simply exploded into a cadenza of shimmering flashes and a sustained tremble of thunder dissolving into the chromatic scream and crash of shells. It was awful for those at the receiving end, magnificent to those from behind whom, as they advanced, it came; beautiful and elating to a point almost of euphoria.

133

There is a cold classicism about the ancient arm of artillery. It is the intellectual of the battlefield, an instrument of appalling destructive effect planned on a drawing board with geometrical precision and cold detachment: a philosophical and mathematical discipline with an end product of flame and dirt that the mathematician will not personally witness. It is exact and unemotional in a way that aerial bombardment can never be. Science and modern technology have made it more than ever so and modern communications have given it a flexibility it never had before; so that a single observer can concentrate the fire of a hundred or more widely dispersed guns upon a single target in a few minutes. Like it or not this is one of the technological accomplishments of the age in which we live and the night of October 23, 1942—when the guns of El Alamein sounded their fanfare to a new phase of Hitler's war—was a watershed in its evolution. There would be bigger barrages in the years to come but El Alamein was the coming-out ball, so to speak, of Western gunnery in the Second World War.

The first cataclysmic fifteen minutes of the British shelling was directed against every known German and Italian gun position: its object, to destroy or paralyze the Axis artillery so that it would be unable to interfere with the British advance for at least the greater part of the night. Under cover of the bombardment the British infantrymen advanced to their start-line in no man's land and extended into assault formation for the advance proper. After a pause of five minutes—during which the attacking battalions made their final preparations—the guns resumed their work but more selectively now, supporting the particular groups to which they had been assigned. Leaning—as the soldier's phrase goes—on this barrage, the infantry advance now started or, to be more exact, various infantry advances started all along the line so as to confuse General Stumme for as long as possible about which was to be the one that mattered.

For his main effort that night Montgomery was using four infantry and two armoured divisions reinforced by two additional armoured brigades—a total of seven hundred tanks. It is of interest to compare this force with Paulus's three infantry and two panzer divisions for his "supreme effort" against Stalingrad nine days before. Paulus had attacked on a three-mile front, Montgomery launched his four infantry divisions in line abreast on a frontage of six.

It was an unnerving and bewildering night for the German-Italian Panzer Army. They had been completely deceived by the British cover plan and had not expected the offensive to open until the following month. The opening bombardment was in the most literal sense completely shattering. Its intensity took the defenders by surprise and it wrecked the army's communications for most of the night so that the Army Commander and his staff had little idea of what was happening. It knocked out many guns and wiped out whole sub-units of infantry by its sheer weight and density. But it did not paralyze the Axis batteries for the whole night: the Panzer Army had known what to expect. They knew by this time how fond of artillery, and how prodigal with ammunition, the British could apparently afford to be. They had not been idle during the weeks of preparation and despite the unhelpfulness of the desert in the matter of natural cover, they had done their best to ensure that men and weapons were lodged in emplacements that were well protected as tactical and engineering know-how could make them. Where the rock basis of the desert made digging below the sandy surface difficult or impossible they had been freely issued with explosives with which to blast good positions, and material with which to revet and fortify them. There had been more than six weeks since the last battle in which to construct and continually improve these defences, trying up to the very last to think of some final touch of ingenuity that would make them more secure, more cunning, more unexpected, more dangerous—perhaps through an electrically detonated booby trap—to a British infantryman stumbling into them in the dark.

So even when the British guns had done their best, or their worst (according to the point of view), the majority of Rommel's prepared defences had still to be taken by storm one at a time. Artillery cannot win battles by itself. But it can prepare the way. It was not easy for the men of Umbria and Campania, Thuringia and Saxony, to endure these massive bombardments and then—after cowering with their faces in the dust—to look up in their foxholes and watch successive waves of British infantry advancing steadily towards them with bayonets fixed and rifles held at the high port and Bren guns sputtering everywhere. White-faced from dust, some of them looked almost ghostly in their dust-whitened shorts, cardigan and steel helmet (the night attire of the desert combatant) so that the moving tableau of their advance through the dust, smoke, and bright moonlight was like the negative instead of the positive print of the grotesque picture they made on the surface of the night.

The dust uncannily whitened everything in the bright moonlight and, behind the advancing infantrymen, a gigantic dust-fog had formed and the ugly metallic clatter and roar that could be heard through it portended the host of tanks that were crawling through the minefields a little way behind the infantry. They too had to follow the teams of engineers perilously and laboriously making the gaps through the mines and, having made them, attempting to mark them with tapes that the slithering vehicles immediately churned back into the dust.

As a final touch of the barbaric or the merely bizarre—according to the nervous state of the German or Italian soldier who heard it—there could at times be heard through the other noises of that interminable night the skirl of bagpipes. One of the British assault formations was a division of Scottish Highlanders and their riflemen were being led through the mines and the dust not only by their officers but, as is their custom, by their regimental pipers.

The defence plan devised before his departure by Rommel and executed by Stumme had no option but to be static. A mobile defence, as we have noted, was not feasible because at El Alamein no outflanking of the line was topographically possible as it was elsewhere in the desert: and in any case the gasoline shortage imposed another limitation on the Axis army's mobility. For these reasons Rommel had been forced to resign himself to a set-piece frontal battle rather than one of manoeuvre, as he would have preferred. In the circumstances his plan was simple and basic, relying on thoroughness of preparation and the tenacity of his troops rather than on any flight of tactical imagination.

The plan was to man the entire line with infantry, alternating German and Italian units, and incorporating these infantry positions in a heavily mined defensive zone five miles deep: a horizontal fortress in the sand. No fewer than half-a-million mines were used to make the zone as nearly as possible tankproof. Some thousand antitank guns were shrewdly emplaced to pick off the British tanks as they inched their way through the vast minefield behind the mine-lifting squads that would have to precede them on foot.

The tanks were to remain some way behind the main defences so that they could race to any part of the line where a British breakthrough threatened. Because of the gasoline position (precluding extensive movement) and the obsolescence of the three hundred Italian tanks available (which

meant the German armour would have to bear most of the
burden) Rommel had been forced to distribute his armoured
strength to cover the entire front. He did this by forming
two groups each of one German, one Italian armoured division: one group to take care of the northern, the other of
the southern, sector of the line. The concentration of the two
veteran Afrika Korps panzer divisions that he and they
would have preferred was something that he could not risk
until the centre of gravity of the battle became established.

Montgomery's intention on that first night was for his infantry to penetrate the main Axis defences at the far side of
the minefield. His tanks, following closely behind them, were
then to pass through at first light and form a bridgehead beyond the minefield against which he hoped that the numerically weaker Axis armour would wear itself out making costly
counterattacks and sustaining losses it could not afford.

What in fact happened was that the British infantry failed
to complete the capture of the final objective line and by
dawn the main tank force was still well back in the minefield. With the arrival of daylight the Axis defenders recovered their balance after the night's hammering and began to
make things hot for those British elements that had secured
or nearly secured a tenuous hold on their objective line, but
now lacked the consolidating presence of the tanks that
should by that time have joined them there or passed through.
It took time for this situation to clarify sufficiently to perco-
late back to the respective army commanders. When it did
Montgomery simply ordered the Eighth Army to keep up the
attack until they had completed their assigned tasks and he
told his tank commanders that they would be expected to
break out of the minefield that night whether or not the infantry succeeded in making a gap for them.

For General Georg ("Fireball") Stumme the start to the
day was not so easy. After the exhilarating command of a
highly successful panzer corps in the southern Ukraine—the
weather warm and dry, the steppe proving ideal free-ranging
tank country, the army as a whole doing well—his initiation
into the desert war could scarcely have been less happy. He
had left the Russian front under a cloud—albeit not of his
own making. He had been sent here temporarily to take over
another man's army whose first allegiance was still to that
other man. Single-mindedly he had been forced to adapt his
naturally aggressive thinking and ideas to the unrewarding
task of defence against a stronger enemy. There was not a

hope of initiating anything: only of sitting tight and waiting for the other side to make a move. For the first time in his experience it was the enemy who had the air superiority, the unlimited stocks of ammunition, the great reserves of tanks. It was the enemy who had the initiative. On top of all this his Intelligence experts had now badly misled him. They had been insistent that a British attack was not imminent. They had been quite certain Montgomery would not strike for another two weeks or so. Nor had they given him any inkling of the weight of the attack to be expected. It was known that the British had been heavily reinforced, especially with tanks. But where had all those guns come from? How had Montgomery managed to conjure so many out of nowhere? Alternatively why had his own useless Air Reconnaissance not spotted them and warned him?

For Stumme it had been an appalling night. The British artillery had wrecked the Panzer Army's signals network and it had been impossible all night for Army HQ to find out anything definite about anything. Having spent what was destined to be his last unhappy night on earth vainly trying to find out what was going on, and no doubt deploring the palpable miscalculations of his staff, the General decided to visit the front as soon as it was light enough and try to find out for himself what was happening. The Chief of Staff advised him to take an escort vehicle and a signals truck as Rommel usually did but Stumme, perhaps wishing to make a gesture, said that the only escort he needed was the staff officer already detailed to accompany him: he intended to go no farther than the headquarters of 90th Light Division who were in a reserve position a few miles behind the front.

He left immediately after dawn and after visiting 90th Light Division headquarters and hearing what they had to say, he drove on to the front where he came under fire from the British lines. The staff colonel was hit and fatally wounded, Stumme jumped out to take cover at the moment the driver whirled the car round and started to withdraw rapidly. Stumme clung to the side of the car trying to climb back in but the effort proved too much for his high blood pressure. After a few yards he had a heart attack and fell to the ground. Panzer Army HQ were no better off than they had been before he had left. They still did not know what was happening. All they could do was to wait and see how the battle developed. And in the meantime make sure that ammunition supplies to the front were working smoothly.

Since daylight the Royal Air Force had come heavily into

the picture taking up the bombardment and strafing of the Axis gun lines where the artillery of the night before had left off. There was to be no let-up. During the day the British infantry and tanks kept up the attack with a further extravagant use of their artillery and now with continuous support from the air. During the day the Royal Air Force flew a thousand sorties in support of the ground attack while the German-Italian air force (one hundred German, two hundred Italian aircraft) scarcely came into the picture at all except for a few hit-and-run attacks. It was perhaps as well that the defenders, toiling away in their gun pits and regularly having to endure the "shuttle service" of the British bomber formations; and the panzers, perpetually harried by the cannon-firing fighter-bombers, could not know that at Stalingrad, just nine days earlier, the Luftwaffe had managed to support Paulus's "supreme effort" with three thousand sorties in a single day. (It does no good to a hard-pressed soldier's morale to fight under a sky that belongs to the other side. It does even less good for him to know that his own air force is doing magnificently on another front.) Nor would they have been particularly pleased to know about the three thousand Stalingrad sorties at Panzer Army Headquarters. There, after the confusion of the night and the new disruption caused by the death of the Acting Army Commander, they spent the morning trying to get some order out of utter chaos and trying to piece together a coherent picture of the situation. General Ritter von Thoma, Commander of the Afrika Korps, temporarily took over command of the Army in place of Stumme. It was afternoon before the first Axis counter-attack was launched. It was led by about forty German tanks but was easily disposed of by the British tanks of which there were now a substantial number well forward.

During the afternoon Rommel was telephoned by Field-Marshal Wilhelm Keitel from OKW and told that the British offensive had opened, and that General Stumme was missing. The purpose of the call was to sound out Rommel about whether he was sufficiently recovered to return to Africa and resume command if required. Assured by Rommel that he was, Keitel said that he would keep him informed of developments. During the evening there was another call to Semmering from OKW. This time the caller was Hitler himself, in a rather more considerate mood than usual. He said that Stumme was still missing—whether captured or killed no one seemed to know. Could Rommel therefore prepare to leave for Africa at once. But before taking off he was to telephone

OKW again and check as Hitler did not want him to interrupt his medical treatment unless "The British attack assumed dangerous proportions." Rommel ordered his aircraft to be ready to take off at seven the next morning. At midnight there was another call from OKW. It was the Führer again to say that in view of the way things were developing at El Alamein he felt obliged to ask Rommel to go back immediately and resume command of the Panzer Army Africa.

While Rommel made the most of his last sleep in the Austrian mountain air in readiness for his seven o'clock start, Montgomery was pressing home his attack with tanks and infantry, and regardless of losses. By the late afternoon of October 25, the third day of the battle, when Rommel reached Panzer Army HQ and began to hear from von Thoma and other members of the staff an account of what had occurred, he did not have to wait for very long to have his gloomiest suspicions confirmed—namely that the battle was probably lost already. Attacking continuously for two nights and two days Montgomery had made a dent six miles wide, five deep, in the strongest part of the Axis defence belt. That night he attacked strongly again having repelled, during the afternoon, an armoured counterattack in which one of the panzer divisions was temporarily reduced to thirty-one tanks. The position, Rommel soon learned, was as bad as he had feared. There were only three issues of gasoline at the front—an issue being the amount required to move the entire army a hundred kilometres. A large Italian tanker on which much hope had been based had just been sunk by the Royal Navy outside Tobruk harbour. On the 26th and 27th it seemed that Montgomery's first momentum had spent itself. (The British commander had in fact decided to initiate a new phase of the battle and was withdrawing some of his more battered formations for a brief rest before regrouping them for a new attack.)

This second phase of El Alamein opened on October 28 with a thrust northward to the coast as a preliminary to a drive west along the coast road. To cover the withdrawals and regrouping which preceded the new attack Montgomery left enough formations, including an armoured division, in the original salient charged with the task of keeping up the original frontal pressure as a cover for the new moves.

What is endearing about Field-Marshal Rommel is his extrovert simplicity. His letters to his wife are attractively revealing. Inside the grand Field-Marshal's uniform there remained to the last the figure of an infinite young soldier.

Sometimes he writes to tell his girl that being back is pretty awful after the wonderful time they had together on leave. Sometimes he is a defiant little boy telling his mother "I'll show 'em—you'll see!" or a distressed little boy crying on her shoulder when everything has become too much for him. The letters[1] he wrote on October 26, 27, and 28—the days of the hiatus between the end of the first phase of Montgomery's offensive and the beginning of the second—admirably display this emotional range.

October 26, 1942

Dearest Lu,

Arrived 1830 yesterday. Situation critical. A lot of work! After my wonderful weeks at home it's not easy to acclimatize myself to the new surroundings and the job in hand. There's too big a difference.

October 27, 1942

Dearest Lu,

A very hard struggle. No one can conceive the burden that lies on me. Everything is at stake again and we're fighting under the greatest possible handicaps. However, I hope we'll pull through. You know I'll put all I've got into it.

October 28, 1942

Dearest Lu,

Who knows whether I'll have a chance to sit down and write in peace in the next few days or ever again. Today there's still a chance.

The battle is raging. Perhaps we will still manage to be able to stick it out, in spite of all that's against us—but it may go wrong, and that would have very grave consequences for the whole course of the war. For North Africa would then fall to the British in a few days, almost without a fight. We will do all we can to pull it off. But the enemy's superiority is terrific and our resources very small.

Whether I would survive a defeat lies in God's hands. The lot of the vanquished is heavy. I'm happy in my own conscience that I've done all I can for victory and have not spared myself.

I realised so well in the few short weeks I was at home what you two mean to me. My last thought is of you.

141

It was probably this uncomplicated emotional candour (sometimes indistinguishable from naiveté) that enabled Rommel to embrace the Hitler mystique when so many of his brassbound Prussian Army colleagues were in private dismissing the Führer and his cronies as common riffraff they would not care to know socially.

The battle to which Rommel referred in his letter of October 28 was the prelude to the second phase of Montgomery's offensive, a development of the thrust northward intended to establish the firm base for the final drive west along the axis of the coast road. Correctly judging this to be the British intention Rommel quickly regrouped—unscrambling the German and Italian formations hitherto alternated—so that the complete Afrika Korps would be massed in the north ready to receive the blow. This involved moving the 21st Panzer Division from the southern sector of the front (where it had been immobilized throughout the battle) knowing full well that there was not enough petrol to move it back there should Montgomery suddenly attack in the south. It was a gamble and he took it.

While the British attack northward was working itself out Montgomery's Intelligence detected Rommel's massing of all his German units in the north. The British commander accordingly altered the point of his forthcoming attack further to the south where his Intelligence calculated that it would hit the junction between the now separate German and Italian elements of the Panzer Army. In the early hours of November 2 Montgomery unloosed what was to be the knockout with a new striking force compounded of rested or entirely fresh formations. Its climax was to be a dawn attack in which a brigade of tanks, after a long night approach march would surprise and smash through the last Axis anti-tank defences. The late arrival of one of the tank units delayed the start of the tank brigade attack by a vital few minutes. A surprise breakthrough in the mist and darkness at dawn became instead a sacrificial charge on the hard core of the Axis gun positions in rapidly developing daylight— the British Brigade losing seventy tanks in an hour. But there was a stream, a seemingly endless stream of tanks following behind. The greatest tank engagement of the battle now raged for the rest of the day until the Italian armour had been finally eliminated from the reckoning and the Afrika Korps had been reduced to thirty-five serviceable tanks. The battle was over and Rommel knew it, even though the British had still to break through the last crust of antitank defences.

The only hope now was to keep what was left of his army in being and withdraw to a new line where it could reorganize and hold on until it could be reinforced. Accordingly he gave the order for a phased withdrawal to start the next day to a line running south from Fuka, sixty miles back. This should forestall the destruction or encirclement of the Panzer Army that otherwise now seemed only a matter of time.

> The army's strength (Rommel wrote) was so exhausted after its ten days of battle that it was not now capable of offering any effective opposition to the enemy's next break-through attempt, which we expected to come the next day.[2]

The withdrawal, the timings of which had already been worked out in detail, was to begin early the next day November 3. This was to be Rommel's most difficult day. There is a hint of four-o'clock-in-the-morning despair in the first of the two letters he wrote to his wife, that day, probably in the sleepless early hours while the latest British attack was at its height:

> Dearest Lu,
>   The battle is going very heavily against us. We're simply being crushed by the enemy weight. I've made an attempt to salvage part of the army. I wonder if it will succeed. At night I lie open-eyed, racking my brains for a way out of this plight for my poor troops.
>   We are facing very difficult days, perhaps the most difficult that a man can undergo. The dead are lucky, it's all over for them. I think of you constantly with heartfelt love and gratitude. Perhaps all will yet be well and we shall see each other again.[3]

Rommel started the day "with an uncomfortable feeling that in spite of our unequivocal situation reports, our higher command had not drawn the proper conclusions from the conditions we were facing." In plainer words, what would happen when the Führer heard that Rommel had authorized a withdrawal the previous afternoon? He decided to send his aide, Lieutenant Berndt, to explain to Hitler in person.

> Berndt was to leave the Führer's HQ in no doubt about our situation and was to indicate that the Afri-

can theatre of war was probably already lost. He was to demand the fullest freedom of action for the Panzer Army.[4]

Rommel was determined not to let himself be encircled and destroyed and his plan was to fight "delaying actions in as many intermediate positions as possible" so that the British were forced to bring up their artillery and fight a set battle every time. He would try to keep this up and "avoid any decisive battle until either we had grown strong enough for it or the bulk of the African Army had been carried across to Europe, with only a small part left in Africa to cover the retreat." Lieutenant Berndt would fly to Führer HQ later in the day.

At nine Rommel went forward and spent the next three hours watching the opening stages of the withdrawal. During the morning there were eleven air attacks on the Afrika Korps and the last of them gave Rommel himself some anxious moments. At about midday he made his way back to his command post "only just escaping, by some frantic driving, a carpet of bombs laid by eighteen British aircraft." The prospect could hardly be bleaker but there was some satisfaction in knowing that the withdrawal was now under way and moving smoothly: that in a matter of hours his *aide* would be giving Hitler a firsthand account of all that had happened and was happening to the Panzer Army Afrika. Then came the shock. At 1330, to Field-Marshal Rommel from Adolf Hitler, by hand of officer, an order:[5]

It is with trusting confidence in your leadership and the courage of the German-Italian troops under your command that the German people and I are following the heroic struggle in Egypt. In the situation in which you find yourself there can be no other thought but to stand fast, yield not a yard of ground and throw every gun and man into the battle. Considerable air force reinforcements are being sent to C-in-C South. The Duce and the Comando Supremo are also making the utmost efforts to send you the means to continue the fight. Your enemy, despite his superiority, must also be at the end of his strength. It would not be the first time in history that a strong will has triumphed over the bigger battalions. As to your troops, you can show them no other road than that to victory or death.

144

"We were completely stunned," wrote Rommel adding that for the first time during the African campaign he did not know what to do. "A kind of apathy took hold of us as we issued orders for all existing positions to be held on instructions from the highest authority." All westward-moving formations were stopped. Stupefied subordinate commanders passed on the orders uncomprehendingly, wondering what madness had now taken a hold of "them." The chance of conducting an orderly withdrawal, before Montgomery's tank hordes broke through and turned it into a rout was now to be thrown away. Seldom can there have been more bitter exasperation in the immemorial soldier's grumble "It's all been changed again! No one seems to know what the devil's happening!"

It was Rommel's first experience of Hitler's interference at the crisis of a battle. It was his great awakening; his Road to Damascus but in reverse. The disillusion was the greater because the loyalty had till then been so unquestioning. Like that ever-lengthening list of German generals in Russia, Field-Marshal Erwin Rommel had in a single revelatory instant realized the kind of man to whom he had given his trust and personal oath of loyalty. That certain ingenuousness of Rommel, that has been noted, only made the shock greater; like the outrage of a trusting child deceived. From then on, Rommel admitted, devising ways of circumventing some of Hitler's orders became a regular occupational exercise. But that first instance of interference by Hitler in the tactical handling of an operation was a profound shock. During the afternoon he wrote the second of the two letters he wrote to his wife that day. The letter[6] seems beyond the ache and anguish of its immediate predecessors. It is as though Rommel, now resigned to the inevitable, has passed through his extreme bitterness into a defensive cocoon of fatalism and shrewd concern for his wife's practical welfare.

November 3, 1942

Dearest Lu,

The battle still rages with unspent fury. I can no longer, or scarcely any longer, believe in its successful outcome. Berndt flies to the Führer today to report.

Enclosed 25,000 lire that I've saved.

What will become of us is in God's hands . . .

P.S. Have Appel exchange the lire. Currency regulations!

This tidy piece of housekeeping at such a time suggests that Rommel was now prepared for any eventuality, including the strong possibility that he might not survive the next few days.

In the evening Lieutenant Berndt was dispatched on his delayed mission to Supreme Headquarters. His brief had been revised. He was now to report Rommel's emphatic view that if the Führer's "no withdrawal" order were upheld, the final destruction of the Panzer Army was certain. He was to add that the Army had already suffered great harm as a result of it.

The final breakthrough came early on the following morning November 4, when the armoured cars and tanks of three British armoured divisions surged through the opening made during the night by infantry. Owing to some initial slowness of the British pursuit to disentangle itself from the battle, and the traffic confusion caused by the size of the armoured forces involved, the German-Italian rearguards were able to help most of Rommel's motorized formations to get away. But by afternoon the stop-go withdrawal of the day before had been accelerated by the jubilant British tank hordes into headlong retreat. Early the following day a signal arrived from Supreme Headquarters authorizing the withdrawal that had been in progress for some time and now approximated to a rout. Rommel was on the run and destined to keep running for another 1500 miles before making his next serious stand against Montgomery at Mareth: though he was to fight a number of effective delaying battles on the way.

The decisive British defeat of Rommel's Panzer Army at El Alamein was the first of the three great counterblows that rocked Hitler and Germany in November 1942.

There was not long to wait for the second.

Part Three

THE WINTER THE TIDE TURNED

(November 1942-May 1943)

Chapter 13

ANGLO-AMERICAN LANDINGS IN ALGERIA, MOROCCO

☐ Between November 5 and 7, while Montgomery's pursuit of the defeated Rommel was gaining momentum, a convoy of 140 ships (including a powerful naval escort) streamed past Gibraltar into the Mediterranean, anxiously scanned, logged and analyzed by Axis eyes on both sides of the Straits. Its course indicated that it was another of the convoys with which the British had just managed, at heavy cost, to ensure the survival of Malta, their beleaguered island base in the Central Mediterranean—though it was much larger than any previous Malta convoy and included a number of vessels recognizable, beneath their grey warpaint, as big passenger liners that were clearly not principally carrying cargo.

The Comando Supremo immediately guessed that the convoy was headed for French North Africa and pressed this view on OKW. But by this time the views of the Italian High Command carried very little weight with their ally. After discussing the various possibilities with his staff, Hitler persisted in the view that it was a Malta convoy. The German-Italian air forces in Sicily could deal with it in the usual way when it came within range. Meanwhile OKW could concern themselves with the really important business of the moment, the climactic do-or-die offensive that Paulus was due to launch at Stalingrad in a very few days' time on November 11.

After dark on November 7 the convoy—the head of which was well past Algiers—abruptly changed course and split up. Early on Sunday morning November 8—and somewhat to the bewilderment of the few Arabs who happened at the time to be riding by on their donkeys—an Anglo-American invasion force—four-fifths American—which had sailed from British ports two weeks earlier, swarmed ashore from assault boats at Algiers and Oran 150 miles to the west. Simultaneously a third American force that had sailed direct from the U.S.A. in a separate convoy of eighty ships landed at Casablanca another four hundred miles west. There was practically no opposition from the French garrisons, except at Casablanca where some resistance continued till evening. By afternoon the three cities, their ports, docks, and airfields (except at Casablanca) had been occupied by the invading army which was under the supreme command of General Dwight D. Eisenhower.

This operation, which the Allies codenamed Torch, was the substitute "second front" on which President Roosevelt and Prime Minister Churchill, under pressure from Marshal Stalin, had decided during the summer when it had become obvious that a landing in northwest France in 1942 was out of the question.

The Allied invasion took the Germans completely by surprise. But not, as we have seen, the Italians whose growing distaste for their domineering ally was further irritated by this considerable I-told-you-so which they could now add to the action of Rommel four days earlier; when, in the chaos of defeat, he had commandeered a large part of the Italian front-line transport at El Alamein to speed the retreat of his favoured Afrika Korps, leaving many of the Italian infantry to walk or give themselves up.

It had always been obvious to the Axis partners that the long coastline of north and northwest Africa was wide open to Allied landings; and that an attempt might well be made to establish one or more bases on it from which an assault on Fortress Europe could be mounted, as it were, through the "back door." Although the Führer, psychologically and strategically orientated to Europe, could not accord this vulnerability of North Africa the same priority as his favourite danger coasts, Norway and France, he had at various times taken steps to improve the security of North Africa, though these had come to nothing.

First, during the Armistice negotiations with France in 1940, the Germans had tried to obtain a greater degree of control over French North Africa and the substantial colonial forces stationed there. But they had failed to do so: partly through their unwillingness to make concessions to the defeated French, partly due to the jealousy of Mussolini who refused to agree to any strengthening of French colonial forces so close to his own North African territories. So the negotiations had ended inconclusively with a general Axis acceptance that the French themselves should remain responsible for their colonial territories but should not be militarily strengthened there.

The next attempt to do something about North Africa

149

was at the end of the year, when Hitler tried to obtain General Francisco Franco's agreement to the passage of a German task force through Spain to seize Gibraltar. Grand Admiral Raeder, Hitler's Navy Chief, and the one member of the German hierarchy with strong views on the strategic importance of the Mediterranean, was an eloquent advocate of the Gibraltar project. Franco's Spain, however, was still bruised and bleeding from its own civil war so recently concluded. And though it may be presumed that his basic sympathies were with his two fellow dictators whose intervention had helped him to win it, Franco was determined not to involve Spain in any more trouble. He proved to be a shrewd and slippery negotiator; unique among top national leaders of the time in having outsmarted Hitler at the conference table when the Führer badly wanted something. The Gibraltar project had to be shelved.

Then came the attack on Russia and the total absorption of the German war effort in other directions: so that there was not enough to spare even to reinforce Rommel's successes in Libya and Egypt. The result was that, in the formative years of the war, North Africa lapsed by default into a sort of vague Achilles heel, that could be accepted as a reasonable risk so long as the Achilles head and arms were doing well; as indeed they were doing in 1941 and the first half of 1942.

During the summer of 1942 there were recurrent rumours of impending Anglo-American operations against North Africa but they worried the Italians more than they did the Germans. The OKW view was that an Allied expedition against Dakar in West Africa, and conceivably against the Atlantic coast of Morocco, was possible, but that action inside the Mediterranean against Algeria, or Tunisia was unlikely. Strangely enough it was the Vichy government which next began to agitate seriously about French North Africa—in June and again in September when they sought talks with OKW to discuss the strengthening of the defences in the French colonies. Hitler ignored the requests—partly, perhaps, because he was too immersed in events in Russia, but partly, without doubt, because Mussolini still automatically objected to any build-up of French garrisons on his own colonial doorstep.

By early in October 1942 the Italians seem to have had a pretty shrewd idea of what was going to happen. The Foreign Minister, Count Ciano, had a long talk in Rome with the head of Military Intelligence "who was distinctly pessimistic." In his Diary entry for October 9 Ciano wrote:[1]

> All the information and the conversations lead one to conclude that the Anglo-Saxons are preparing to land in force in North Africa, whence, later on, they intend to launch their blows against the Axis. Italy is geographically and logically the first objective.

It was a piece of shrewd anticipation on the part of Ciano who presumably did not keep it to himself. Yet, two weeks later, on October 21, Hitler was still stoutly reaffirming the OKW opinion that an invasion of Algeria or Tunisia was unlikely, quoting in support of this view an appreciation by his naval staff. This reiteration of the OKW view was made in a letter to General von Rintelen, the OKW liaison officer attached to the Italian High Command in Rome. The chief purpose of the letter was to urge von Rintelen to reassure Mussolini and above all to restrain him from taking measures on the Libya-Tunisia border which might "throw the colonial French into the arms of the Allies."

Four days later, on October 25, new information of an imminent Allied landing operation in the Mediterranean still failed to shake the German belief that the activity at Gibraltar merely portended a Malta convoy. If by any chance a landing was to be attempted, OKW now considered its likely objectives to be either Sardinia or Corsica or even southern France. This German view, dogmatically reiterated, was accepted by Mussolini in the face of the anxious hunches of his advisers in Rome. Neither he nor Hitler was alarmed when, on October 31, exceptional concentrations of Allied naval and merchant vessels were known to be assembling at Gibraltar.

During the next four days, when the battle of El Alamein reached its crisis and the spectre of impending defeat doubtless dominated the thoughts of both High Commands, neither saw reason to depart from the Malta convoy theory. It was not until November 4, when the 140-ship convoy passed into the Mediterranean, that the Italians at last decided that it must be heading for French North Africa. But even now Hitler would not have it. In a message to Commander-in-Chief South (Kesselring) transmitted via Goering he now decided that the Allied expedition, if not aimed at Sardinia or Corsica, was most probably intending to land much farther east at

Derna or Benghazi to cut off Rommel's retreat: that is if a landing *were* actually intended. On the whole he still preferred to think it was a Malta convoy.

Malta, Dakar, Western Morocco, southern France, Corsica, Sardinia; and now Benghazi and Derna! That the Führer for so long managed to consider (and to sway Mussolini into considering) almost every possibility except the right one was probably influenced by his overriding preoccupation with Stalingrad and his basic disinterest in the subsidiary Mediterranean theatre. But it was in large measure due to the efficiency of the deception plans with which Allied Intelligence and Counter-Intelligence covered the operation. In the words of the British Official Historian:[2]

> In short, the Allies had successfully spread a number of false plans and kept their real intentions secret. Hitler, misled into expecting possible landings elsewhere and obsessed by his views on probable French reactions, took no precautionary measures in North Africa and dissuaded the Italians from taking any.

The spreading of false clues was not the whole of the Allied deception plan. The operation was preceded by a secret American diplomatic mission led by Robert Murphy, the U.S. Consul General in Algiers, who concluded a deal with the French military command in North Africa whereby they agreed not to oppose the landings and later to join the invading forces when this became feasible.

The Torch invasion—in conjunction with the British victory at El Alamein, with which its timing had been co-ordinated in anticipation—marked the opening of the final phase of the war. It was the first large-scale Anglo-American enterprise jointly planned and jointly executed by all three services of both nations.

In its magnitude, complexity, and successful outcome it was a landmark in the evolving science of modern amphibious warfare and the blueprint for the bigger invasions that would progressively have to be undertaken on the way to the citadel and keep of Fortress Europe.

For the first time in the war American soldiers were about to meet the Germans on the field of battle.

Stalin might complain that this was no true "second front."

Nevertheless for the Anglo-American alliance this was the consummation.

News that the landings had started reached Hitler at two o'clock in the morning of November 8 in a railway siding in Thuringia. In his special train he had left his headquarters (now back at Rastenburg in East Prussia) the previous afternoon with senior members of OKW, including Field-Marshal Keitel, the Chief of Staff, and General Jodl, Chief of Operations. The train, which had halted for the night, was on its way to Munich where the Führer had to keep an important social engagement. The annual reunion of the Nazi Party "old faithfuls" was scheduled for the 8th and 9th. Hitler intended to grace the celebrations with his presence and a major speech.

Although the latest reports of the progress of the Allied convoy had been reaching the train during its long journey, the news, in the early hours of Sunday morning, that the invasion had started at three places in Algeria and Morocco, came as a complete surprise. As Keitel said later:[3] "We didn't even dream of it. Right up to the last day we were sure they were going through [the Sicilian Narrows]. . . . And then suddenly they turned about and made for the coast." At the conference to which Keitel and Jodl were immediately summoned from their beds it was gloomily agreed that for the moment the situation was at the mercy of the North Africa French. Messages were at once despatched to Marshal Pétain in Vichy exhorting strong resistance. A meeting of the Italian and Vichy French foreign ministers was urgently summoned for the following day in Munich. Field-Marshal Kesselring, Commander-in-Chief South, the only Axis commander in a position to do anything, was ordered to send strong detachments of the Luftwaffe to Tunisia immediately. An officer with the title Air Liaison Officer Tunisia flew into Tunis that afternoon and began to prepare for the arrival of the first squadrons. The only consolation for Hitler and his train companions on this difficult morning of Sunday, November 8, was that the German and Italian submarines, already ordered to race to the scene from the eastern Atlantic, should soon be in a position to attack the great concentrations of Allied ships.

On November 9 the Vichy government placed its Tunisian bases at the disposal of the Axis powers. But it was already clear that the French on the spot were not effectively opposing the Allies.

On November 10 Hitler made up his mind what to do and his plan to meet the situation was converted into operation orders by his staff. It embodied three main features: to establish immediately a bridgehead in Tunisia around Bizerte and Tunis; to occupy the hitherto unoccupied southern half of France; to occupy Corsica. During the day suspicions that the North African French were not going to be of much help to the Axis were confirmed by news of a cease-fire ordered throughout North Africa by—another sharp surprise for Hitler—Admiral Jean Darlan, the Vichy Commander-in-Chief! Darlan had happened to be in Algiers for family reasons on November 8. Seeing at firsthand the strength of the Anglo-American invasion and accepting it as a *fait accompli* this staunch Vichyite and Anglophobe had come to terms with General Eisenhower. As the only Frenchman of unquestioned authority on the spot, he had taken charge of the French side of the situation. Pétain immediately disavowed the cease-fire in a public announcement from Vichy but succeeded in getting a coded message to Darlan privately endorsing it.

Throughout these three hectic days the staff chiefs with Hitler were kept scurrying frantically between their offices on the train, now at rest in Munich Station; the house that Hitler used when in the town; and the notorious beer cellar—from which the 1923 Nazi *Putsch* had been mounted—currently the focal point and shrine of the Party Veterans' Reunion which was the reason for the Führer's being there in the first place. To add to their difficulties, the chiefs had to sort out the new orders and telephone them to their subordinates with the main body of OKW in East Prussia. It was doubly difficult for the Wolf's Lair to handle the new emergency in these circumstances—with the Wolf six hundred miles away and the chiefs with him never quite sure whether to find him at the station, in his Munich house, or joining in the tribal rites with the Party celebrants. (There was to be still more confusion ten days later when the Führer, having decided to put in some meditation on the new developments at his Berchtesgaden retreat, decided that the rest of OKW must transfer themselves and the "lair" from Rastenburg to Salzburg so as to be near at hand to the "Wolf." It must ever remain a source of wonder and awe that the German High Command could still somehow function comparatively smoothly despite the chaotic conditions imposed on it by the Führer.

In spite of all this—not to mention the meetings with Ciano and Laval to cover the political aspects of the new situation in North Africa—Hitler found time to do justice to the proceedings in the beer cellar. He made a Scale One speech to which Dr. Goebbels and the German press accorded the full treatment. It took the form of a hysterical paean of self-congratulation on having made himself the master of all Stalingrad.

Perhaps it was to reassure himself, even more than the Party "old comrades" and the German public, that he made this premature boast two days before Paulus made his final, and in the event unsuccessful, effort to rub out the narrow but still defiant Russian bridgehead on the right bank of the tormented city.

In North Africa events now moved rapidly. The opening surprises were over. The uncertainty about how the French would react—the key anxiety factor for both sides—had been resolved. It had become a straight race for Tunisia. The Axis, with fewer forces available, had to rush as many as they could a short distance by air. The Allies, potentially stronger but, until their follow-up convoys arrived, equally short of men and material, had to get enough of them a long distance by road. It was going to be a question of who got to Tunisia "the fastest with the mostest." For the time being both sides would have to forget any idea they might have of moving complete formations with their proper complement of men and equipment. Instead they would have to concentrate on rushing to the scene any units they could lay their hands on and organize them into small battle groups that could later be built up and expanded into something like an army. In the event the Germans won the race.

This was partly because of the shorter distance they had to travel (Sicily was only two hundred miles away). But also it was because quick reaction to a situation; and a talent for rapid decision as well as flexibility in command and planning to the point, if necessary, of improvisation; were conspicuous military virtues of the Germans in the Second World War.

The Allies on the other hand started with three disadvantages. They were extremely short of transport for the four-hundred-mile initial advance by road into Tunisia and would remain so until their later seaborne convoys arrived. The single-track railway, short of locomotives and rolling-stock and in a state of indifferent repair, could be of little use until their engineers had taken it over and had overhauled it. Precious time had been lost in the first few days of the invasion while certain of the French authorities, especially those in Tunisia, were still hesitating over what their attitude should be: and the Allied Command were bending over backwards to avoid upsetting them by precipitous or tactless action.

Nevertheless the Anglo-American spearhead, which included mixed forces of British and American tanks and infantry, were within forty miles of Tunis before the first major contact between the two armies occurred. The hoped-for seizure of the capital by *coup de main* was now out of the question: the Axis had got there first and had established a protective bridgehead. What is more it was backed by a powerful close support air force that had seized command of the Tunisian sky and was addressing itself with a will to its mission of holding up the Allied advance. It was going to retain this air superiority for some time to come, for the most forward Allied fighter field was seventy miles behind what was now about to be stabilized as the front line. In the last days of November and the first week of December the Anglo-American advanced forces actually fought their way forward to within ten miles of Tunis before they were successfully counterattacked and stopped. At the same time torrential rain, a notable feature of the Tunisian winter, hampered subsequent Allied efforts to resume the advance. Both sides went temporarily onto the defensive.

So ended the opening phase of Torch, the second of the three great blows sustained by Hitler during this disastrous November. The complete surprise of the invasion, and its almost bloodless accomplishment, represented a triumph of Anglo-American planning and a naval victory of the first magnitude. The less successful Allied follow-up, which initially fell short of its intention for reasons that have been indicated, was, apart from anything else, a triumph of German resilience and adaptability. Having glimpsed the event as a whole from the higher viewpoint of both sides it is illuminating to go back to November 8 and see the sequence of events on the Axis side from the time when the first orders began to go out from Hitler's train and the practised Supreme Headquarters Staff went methodically into action in their huts six hundred miles away.

As it is well established that Torch took the Germans by surprise and without any prearranged policy for dealing with such an eventuality, it may be wondered how it was that the Luftwaffe, alone of the Wehrmacht, was able to move into action so quickly and effectively. The answer is that it was a mixture of luck and intelligent anticipation—but anticipation of other dangers.

During October there had been a continual reinforcement

156

of Air Corps II, the Luftwaffe formation responsible f[...]
Mediterranean area. This was prompted in the first plac[...]
the critical position of Rommel in Egypt and the extre[...]
emergency measures that might eventually have to be taken
on his behalf. At the beginning of November, when it was
first reported that large Allied shipping concentrations had
been sighted near Gibraltar, there was a new reason to accelerate this air build-up in anticipation of the attacks on the
convoys that would have to be made when they approached
Sicily. As a result, it happened that by November 10 the operational strength of Air Corps II had been increased in a
month from 283 aircraft to 445.[4] At the same time the
number of transport aircraft had been increased from 205
to 673.

It was this formidable armada of fighting and transport
aircraft, so conveniently at hand—albeit for the wrong reasons—that made possible the swift sequence of events that
will now be described.

The invasion started early on November 8. In the afternoon
(as we have seen) an Air Liaison Officer flew into El Aouina—
the mellifluous name of the airport of Tunis—to prepare for
the arrival of the operational squadrons.

On November 9 the first of them touched down: twenty-
seven fighters, twenty-four Stuka dive-bombers. There were
more arrivals during the next two days together with a detachment of Luftwaffe troops and enough ground and technical personnel to set up the necessary ground organization
which, to begin with, was virtually non-existent.

On November 11 the Army began to arrive. First, a Colonel Lederer ordered to take charge of the ground forces and
to establish the protective bridgehead around Tunis and Bizerte ordered by Hitler. On November 12 came a trickle of
ground forces for the colonel to command: two companies
of 5th Parachute Regiment, one company of Panzer Grenadiers, and the first elements of an Italian division. On November 14 came a Parachute Engineer Battalion, a Reconnaissance Company, a Company of tanks and a detachment of
motorcyclists. Some of this motley assortment of early arrivals came from a pool of reinforcements held in southern Italy
for Rommel's army, others from reserve divisions and draft-
holding units in southern Europe. The large fleet of transports
amassed by Air Corps II paid off handsomely. From the first,
a daily airlift of 750 troops was maintained.

On November 15, at the end of the first week, in which
ground staff had been working day and night to make the

airfield itself as well as the arriving aircraft fully operational, the Air Commander Tunisia could count eighty-one fighters and twenty-eight dive-bombers of which fifty-two of the former and twenty of the latter were ready for immediate action.[5] In addition to the well-tried Messerschmitt 109 the fighters included a new one, the Focke-Wolfe 190. With about the same four hundred miles-an-hour top speed as the American Lightning and the British Spitfire, it was going to prove slightly their superior in manoeuvrability, armament, and armour. It was to prove a formidable accessory to the Luftwaffe's priority mission of holding up the Allied advance on Tunis.

At the beginning of the second week (November 16) a more senior commander, General Walther Nehring, flew in to take charge of the ground forces. Nehring was one of the younger panzer generals who had prospered under the aegis of Field-Marshal Rommel in the desert. He had been wounded on the second day of the battle of Alam Halfa at the beginning of September while commanding the Afrika Korps. He arrived in Tunis with one staff officer and established a headquarters for all land forces in Tunisia. It was somewhat grandly called 90th Corps Headquarters though corps was a big word for what it actually controlled at this time. To begin with, 90th Corps Headquarters consisted literally of Nehring and the single staff officer he had brought with him. They had neither signallers, clerks, nor even typewriters. Their transport was an ancient French taxi. For communications they had to make do with the existing civilian postal network and telephone service.[6]

One of Nehring's first actions was to dismiss his stop-gap predecessor, Colonel Lederer. Daunted by the difficulty of devising so much bridgehead with so little soldiery—Tunis and Bizerte are thirty-five miles apart—Lederer had limited his off-the-cuff plan to the defence of Bizerte only. This was not good enough for Nehring who reconnoitred a more ambitious defence ring and improvised small battle groups and suicide squads with which to man it. He was helped by the arrival during the week of some good troops as well as a continuing stream of "oddments." Two battalions of 7th Parachute Regiment; two and a half companies of the Barenthin Glider Regiment; three draft-holding battalions; Signals, Motorcycle, Antitank and Field Artillery, and twenty 88-mm Antitank-Antiaircraft guns—possibly the most comforting of his new arrivals. The "eighty-eight" was arguably the finest gun in its class of the Second World War, having an obsessive influence on the thinking of all Allied soldiers who encountered it. The British had learned to fear it in the desert and the Americans were about to develop a similar respect for it. The special feature of the gun, from the point of view of someone at the receiving end, was its high muzzle velocity. This was only enabled it to penetrate the thickest tank armour but for infantry had the unnerving effect of causing them to hear the crack of the exploding shell a fraction of a second before the thump of the gun being fired. Throughout the rest of the war, news of "eighty-eights ahead" could always be relied upon to diminish the élan of an advancing Allied column. With twenty of them to stiffen his bridgehead General Nehring could feel considerably more comfortable about the imminent Allied arrival in the area. Best of all, perhaps, there arrived during this week the first substantial contingents of armoured and motorized units. In all, fifty-two tanks arrived, mainly an assembly of small detachments from different formations but also including two-thirds (thirty-two tanks) of 7th Panzer Regiment of 10th Panzer Division. The rest of 10th Panzer Division was due to follow shortly—the first major formation of high quality destined for this front. All except four of these tanks were the Mark IIIs and IVs that had been Rommel's mainstay in the desert. The other four were rather special. They were the first specimens to reach Africa of the new Mark VI Tiger.[7] This squat, massive tank weighed 56 tons (compared with the 23 tons of the Mark IV) and its engine developed 700 hp (as against 300) while its 102-mm front armour was twice as thick as that of its two predecessors. Its main armament (additional to two heavy machine guns) was the dreaded 88-mm gun to which reference has been made. The Tiger was a formidable newcomer to the North African battlefield and would be even more so later for it was only just in service and had yet to get over its mechanical teething troubles. Even so it must have been galling for the deprived Rommel, who for so long had been told that there was nothing to spare, to learn that the Focke-Wolfe 190 fighter and the Tiger tank had reached the "other" North African front. In the second week of the new campaign there also arrived a further two thousand troops by sea in the ships that brought the heavy equipment: and some Italian contingents that arrived by sea and air to join the bridgehead force included a regiment of Bersaglieri and two battalions of Marines.

By November 22 when the Allied spearhead were ready to make their first attack to seize Tunis from the Medjez-el-Bab area thirty-five miles away, Nehring's scratch collection of oddments and remnants had somehow mutated into a homogeneous bridgehead, shrewdly positioned in the bare and rocky mountains which form a protective barrier some forty miles west and south of the city. In ten days of hard fighting the Allies fought their way to within twelve miles of the capital before being pushed back to the Medjez-el-Bab area from which they had started, and which became the pivot of a front which was to remain stabilized through the worst of the winter weather until well into the New Year, when both sides were strong enough to think again in offensive terms.

General Eisenhower had been frustrated in his effort to "rush" Tunis. The chief credit for this belonged to the Luftwaffe which had dominated the early proceedings in three ways. It had quickly established air superiority by blitzing the Allied airfields while they were trying to organize themselves, many aircraft being destroyed on the ground. Secondly, by continual attacks on road columns and troop concentrations which slowed down the advance and deprived the Allies of precious vehicles at a time when they could not afford to lose them. Thirdly, the smooth operation of the considerable airlift was a notable demonstration of planning and organization. In two weeks the Luftwaffe had conjured out of nowhere a scratch force of odds and ends that had been equal to the task of holding General Nehring's hurriedly but shrewdly planned bridgehead.

The Allies had won the first round of Torch. The Axis, by depriving them of the quick capture of Tunis for which they had hoped, had won the second; but in so doing had unwittingly ensured for itself a disaster in the long run; for once Hitler had secured a foothold anywhere he would never in any circumstances let go of it. There were those among his chief advisers who thought that Torch, following closely on the El Alamein defeat, was clearly the signal to get out of Africa altogether and concentrate on developing the defences of Fortress Europe. General Warlimont, Assistant Operations Chief, was one; Field-Marshal Rommel was another. Rommel had been watching his retreating columns inching their way through the bottleneck of the Halfaya Pass on the Egypt-Libya border when he heard the news of the Anglo-American landings at the other end of North Africa. His reaction was:[8] "This spelt the end of the army in Africa."

An alternative use for the 673 transport aircraft of the Luftwaffe's Air Corps II could have been to assist in mounting a "Dunkirk" evacuation of Rommel's army. But to Hitler withdrawal from anywhere in any circumstances was unthinkable. The interim success in Tunisia was just enough to persuade him that Tunisia was now the front to develop. The Tunisian bridgehead must be built up; and Rommel, fighting hard as he withdrew for another 1200 miles through Libya, would eventually become a part of it.

We happen to know that it was not so, but the failure of the first Allied attempt to seize Tunis might almost have been a clever calculated trap; so successful in the long run did it prove to be as an encouragement to Hitler to pour troops into a front which was of no real value to him and which merely gave a number of untried American and British divisions a gratuitous course of intensive battle training before they moved on to the battlegrounds of Europe.

The tide of war in the west had irrevocably turned and every thinking member of the High Command knew it except the Führer. From now on the Axis strategy had to pass to the defensive and everyone knew it except the Führer. So instead of cutting his losses in Africa—a front to which, in any case, he had never till then attached much importance—and instead of using those 673 planes to evacuate Rommel's panzer Army for future use, he used them to carry a second panzer army *to* Africa. It was a classic case of throwing good money after bad: or, in plain military terms, of reinforcing failure.

On November 23, as General Eisenhower's spearhead prepared to make their first attack on General Nehring's Tunis bridgehead, the third great blow of this disastrous month rocked the Germans. The Russian armies converging from north and south joined hands west of Stalingrad. The German Sixth Army was encircled.

That afternoon Hitler arrived back at OKW in East Prussia from his two weeks in Munich and Berchtesgaden to the news of the Sixth Army's encirclement and to be told by the new Army Chief of Staff, General Kurt Zeitzler, that Paulus was urgently requesting permission to fight his way out of the trap before it had time to close. Hitler directed that the Volga front and Stalingrad would be held at all costs.

The tide of war had turned in the west. Now it was perilously near its turn in the east. As usual everyone knew it except Hitler.

Chapter 14

THE GERMAN CITIES BURN
BY NIGHT

☐ It was not only on land that the initiative was being knocked from Hitler's grasp. During the second half of 1942 the stark reality of this phase of grim transition in the war situation was being brought home to the German people night after night by the constant stepping up of the British bombing offensive against their cities and homes. No one in Germany any longer remembered, unless as a sick joke, Reichsmarschall Goering's boast, early in the war, of his great defensive air barrier around Germany that no foreign plane would ever succeed in penetrating. The Royal Air Force had been penetrating it to bomb their towns since May 1940. The first time had been as long ago as the night of May 10-11 of that year when the town centre of Mönchen-Gladbach was attacked by a force of thirty-six bombers and four civilians were killed. There were more British raids in the next four months including eight on Berlin. The raiding forces were small, the damage and the casualties negligible. But Britain had taken the lead in launching unrestricted air warfare, though even today this fact is still not widely understood in the United Kingdom.

In the summer of 1940 Churchill was hitting back from extreme weakness with the only offensive weapon he then had. Britain's European allies had all been defeated. A small British field force stood by in Egypt to resist the expected Italian aggression against the Middle East and its oilfields. The main army, hurriedly reorganized, refitted and expanded after the Dunkirk debacle, stood by with the Royal Air Force's Fighter Command to resist Hitler's expected invasion of Britain. The Royal Navy guarded the approaches to the homeland, took care of the long sea lanes to the Far East and prepared to do battle in the oceans with the Axis navies. The mood was desperate, defiant, defensive. The Royal Air Force's Bomber Command (small, because at this time everything had to be subordinated to the production of fighter aircraft) was the only weapon with which the Prime Minister could hit at Germany immediately. So he struck out fiercely with it: much as a small boxer with little strength but with a long reach, fighting a huge opponent whom he cannot really hurt, may still aim painful jabs at his nose.

Hitler did not retaliate for four months. He was still hoping to persuade Britain to make peace and he did not want unrestricted bombing of cities to become general. It was not until after the fifth British raid on Berlin that he made an angry declaration to the effect that "If they don't stop bombing our cities we shall bomb theirs harder." He wanted to avoid the situation of both sides bombing each other's cities and he made efforts through neutrals to get some kind of an agreement to this. As more than one historian has observed it is unlikely that he was influenced by humanitarian motives so much as long-term self-interest. For he had no strategic bomber force of his own.

It must be explained that Germany and Britain had entered the war with two different conceptions of how an air force should be used. The Germans regarded theirs as an extension of the land arm. Its function was to give close support to the Army in the field; it was another kind of artillery.

The theory of the blitzkrieg with which the early campaigns were so swiftly won was based primarily on the shock effect of the armoured division working in close conjunction with the (Army) air force. With this in view the Luftwaffe had been equipped with the most suitable aircraft for the purpose, dive-bombers and fast medium-sized bombers. There was no strategic heavy bomber force as such.

The British strategists had approached the problem quite differently. Haunted by the 900,000 dead of the First World War, and above all determined to avoid another costly stalemate on land, they had conceived a doctrine of the offensive based on the strategic bomber as a means of attacking the heart of the enemy country to destroy at its sources (and at relatively small cost to the attacker) the enemy's power to continue the war. Co-operation with the Army was a secondary issue—though this part of the theory was amended halfway through the war. The Navy had its own air arm anyway. The air force existed in its own right, insisted the new strategists; not as an adjunct to the older services. It had a fighter command for defence and for escorting bombers. Its striking component was its bomber command. The striking-power of the strategic bomber (four-engined aircraft carrying eight or ten tons of bombs would shortly be available) was to make up for Britain's limited manpower and small army and were to win the war by destroying Germany's war industry, railways, oil installations. The United States also concurred with this strategic thinking. That, at any rate, was the theory and it was not unshrewd of Hitler in the summer of 1940 to promote the idea that it might be better all round if everyone agreed not to drop bombs on each other's cities.

On August 7, 1940, the Luftwaffe launched against the Royal Air Force and its bases the air offensive that came to be known as the Battle of Britain. Its aim was to obliterate the air defences of the United Kingdom and obtain command of the skies. This was the essential preliminary to the projected German invasion of England and the Luftwaffe was operating in what was, according to German doctrine, its orthodox role of supporting the Army. For one month, in the blazing sunshine of a perfect summer, the two air forces fought it out high over southern England in a series of fierce battles that took place several times daily. All this time Bomber Command, now more than ever the unglamorous poor relation of the R.A.F. in terms of equipment, strength and public interest, continued to make periodical modest night raids on German cities. By September 6 Hitler was forced to concede that the Luftwaffe's daylight offensive for mastery of the British sky had failed. It had been a "close run thing" but the R.A.F. had won. So when, on that day, he gave his air commanders permission—with some reluctance, it is said—to switch the offensive to night attacks on London and other British cities, he could fairly claim that it was a reprisal that the British had brought on themselves. Berlin had in fact been raided for the eighth time only the week before.

During the night of September 6-7 the Luftwaffe made its first heavy raid on London, concentrating mainly on the dock area. The gloves were off. The great air blitz on Britain had started, bringing a new dimension of war to the ordinary men, women and children of the only nation still willing to stand up to Hitler. Within a few weeks the blitz had settled into a grotesque way of life that was to make the British night hateful with fear, flames, heroism, and hideous destruction except when, mercifully, the weather was too bad for bombing. It was to continue through a long autumn and longer winter until the summer of 1941, when the German attack on Russia called for the presence of Hitler's air fleets elsewhere. Up to that time the main ports and industrial centres of the country were all blitzed in turn—Plymouth, Portsmouth, Southampton, Bristol, Liverpool, Manchester, Hull, Coventry, Birmingham, and other towns in the smoky industrial complex of the Midlands, the heart of the British engineering industry.

The bombing of London was almost continuous—a kind of running refrain to all the other visitations. The free world looked on in sympathy and in admiration of Britain's refusal to give in. The dramatic and moving accounts of the blitz which American correspondents cabled home to their newspapers probably did more than anything else to convince the general public of the United States that this was their war too and that their early involvement was inevitable though none knew just how, or precisely when, it would come about. Britain seemed to be proving that for all its horror, a brave and tough people would not be blasted into submission by the bombardment of its civilian population. But Britain was not to learn its own lesson.

Throughout the Luftwaffe's blitz on Britain, the R.A.F. maintained its own regular attacks on strategic targets in Germany: mainly on railways and industrial centres in the Ruhr. With monotonous regularity the communiqués reported attacks on factories, oil installations, refineries, railway marshalling yards. The vast marshalling yards at Hamm seldom went without a mention. Hamm became so familiar to the British public that it came to be regarded almost with affection and even as the subject of radio comedians' jokes. ("Why is Fritz looking so unhappy?" "Poor chap's just been promoted. He's to be the new stationmaster at Hamm!") This R.A.F. counteroffensive continued with more defiance than effect through the last six months of 1940 through 1941 and into 1942. It was some comfort to the morale of the ordinary Londoner to know that while he was going through his own greater ordeal something was being thrown back at his tormentors. But the British bomber raids during these eighteen months were still neither heavy nor accurate. The heavy four-engined Halifax and Lancaster bombers that were promised would not be ready to come into service until 1942. As for accuracy, although the communiqués maintained the pretence that military and industrial targets were being accurately hit every time, the truth was different. So far from it being a question of hitting the right pinpoint target, two-thirds of the crews were not getting within five miles of it. Although Germany was bombed 109 times in the second half of 1941, up to January 1942 the bombing scarcely began to be felt by the German people and was felt not at all by German war industry. It was understandable that Churchill was pressing his scientific advisers to hurry up with the various aids to bombing accuracy with which they were then experimenting.

Like the British the winter before, the German city dwellers came to terms with air raids as a part of normal life in wartime. They augmented their antiaircraft defences, their fire and rescue services and an ever-growing army of air raid wardens to cope with them.

This was the situation at the end of 1941 when Pearl Harbor precipitated the United States into the war and the German people were confronted by the prospect of American bombers joining in the assault on their cities before long.

Early in 1942, while Hitler's frost-bitten legions were enduring the misery of their first Russian winter, the soldiers began to receive news from home of the increased night terror being unloosed on their families. In February the British war cabinet, dissatisfied with the ineffectiveness of their strategic bombing during the previous eighteen months, and with the first of the promised heavy bombers now coming off the production line, initiated a new phase of severity in the air war. It directed that, starting as soon as possible, the bombing offensive against German towns was to be greatly intensified. The implementation of the new offensive was entrusted to a newly appointed chief of Bomber Command, Air Marshal Sir Arthur T. Harris.

Harris was an ideal front man for that element in the higher British councils who believed in bombing as the road to speedy victory. "Bomber" Harris, as he was soon to be nicknamed, was a singleminded and ruthless believer in the capacity of Bomber Command to win the war almost singlehanded. He was undeterred by the failure of bombing to defeat his own countrymen the year before—all he asked for was more and better bombers, and bigger and better bombs. With these he would bomb Germany into submission. He was the Cato of the British Military hierarchy. *Carthago est delenda,* Cato had monotonously advocated after the Roman victory in the Punic Wars. If Harris is not on record as having actually said *Germania est delenda* his actions were soon saying it for him.

The first attack in the new schedule was on the night of March 28-29, 1942 when a heavy raid was made on the historic Hanseatic port of Lubeck on the Baltic. This ancient medieval city, rich in historic buildings, was no centre of war industry. According to *The Royal Air Force in the World War,* Vol. IV, by Norman Macmillan, Lubeck was chosen for experimental reasons. "The old part of the city that was the target area was almost completely islanded. It was therefore a comparatively simple matter to assess accurately the scale of damage."

The attack, in bright moonlight, lasted three hours. Some 320 people were killed, 785 injured. Over a thousand houses were destroyed, more than four thousand seriously damaged.[1] The twenty-five public buildings destroyed included the twelfth-century cathedral. The official communiqué was able to cover itself by claiming that large quantities of military stores intended for shipment to the Eastern front had been destroyed. But what interested the chief of Bomber Command was that the raid had convincingly demonstrated that fire was a better weapon against towns for his purpose than high explosive: liquid incendiary bombs, as well as the ordinary stick variety, had been used for the first time and had proved most successful.

One month later in the period of the next full moon the neighbouring and similar Hanseatic port of Rostock was heavily attacked on four successive nights: not only the Heinkel and Arado aircraft factories but, as in the case of Lubeck, the inner town of narrow streets and ancient buildings, which was gutted.

Hitler was stung by Lubeck into ordering reprisal raids on what he took to be equivalent historic English cities. The first of these so-called Baedeker raids coincided with the first British attack on Rostock. While five hundred R.A.F. bombers were on their way to the first of the four raids on the Baltic port, twenty-five bombers of the Luftwaffe—all that were available—attacked Exeter. In the next few nights heavier raids were made on Exeter, Bath (twice), and Norwich by units specially withdrawn from the Eastern front for the purpose. These raids continued intermittently through the summer. Having made his point Hitler then allowed the Baedeker reprisal raids to lapse: the Luftwaffe, fully extended on the fighting fronts, just could not spare the squadrons to carry them out. The new British bomber offensive continued. Its pattern was now set. There was no longer any pretence of aiming at specific targets related to the German war effort. This had now been accepted as useless. The new idea was for pathfinder aircraft, flying ahead of the main force, and manned by the most skilled navigators, to mark with flares an area about one mile square centred on the middle of the town, and for the following bombers to drop their high-explosive and incendiaries into the area marked out. An area so large could not be missed and if the burning and devastation were thorough they would be bound to take in a genuine military target or two. If you burned enough haystacks you could hardly fail to scorch a few of the needles hidden in them. And if the fires were big enough they would make useful aiming guides for more bombers the following night and the night after that. The formula was established. "Area bombing" had come to stay.

At the end of May—four days after Rommel launched his last successful desert offensive, the one that was to take him to the threshold of victory in Egypt—Air Marshal Harris staged the most spectacular set piece to date in the air war: the first thousand-bomber raid on a German city. On the night of May 30-31, 1,130 aircraft dropped 2000 tons of bombs (two-thirds of them incendiaries) on Cologne, then the third largest city in Germany: 460 people were killed, 45,000 lost their homes, 12,000 fires were started, 5000 acres in the centre of the city were devastated.[2] The British communiqué claimed severe damage to 250 factories—but it was the centre of the town that had been devastated and most of the factories ringed the outskirts.

It was of course a tremendous feat of organization and navigation to marshal this huge air fleet from more than fifty airfields and direct them to drop their bomb loads on this one target in ninety minutes. Churchill had hesitated before authorizing the operation on the grounds that it would be too expensive, estimating a loss of at least a hundred aircraft. It was not the least part of Harris's triumph that he was able to report that he had lost only thirty-seven aircraft, or 3.3 percent of the attacking force. The scale of the attack prompted the Germans to conclude that the American Air Force must also have participated in it. The discovery in due course that this was not so was indeed grimly disturbing. If the British could mount an effort of this size alone, what lay ahead for German cities when the bombing fleets of the United States did join in?

As if to show that his Cologne attack was no fluke, Harris dispatched another thousand bombers twenty-four hours later to drop their load on Essen, the great armaments centre and hub of the Krupp industrial empire. This was at least a legitimate military target. The damage inflicted was again devastating and it was when announcing this second thousand-bomber attack to the House of Commons that Churchill commented:

In fact, I may say that as the year advances German cities, harbours and centres of war production will be subjected to an ordeal the like of which has never been experienced by a country in continuity, severity and magnitude.

Within three weeks a third thousand-bomber attack was made, this time on Bremen.

So began the long and fearful expiation of the German people for having submitted to Hitler and the Nazi philosophy. They had little option in the matter. For the regime was activated and supported by the comprehensive machinery of a police state that reflected in full measure the German genius for discipline, organization and administration. "Theirs not to reason why"—the line had been updated and invested with a new poignancy.

The tragic irony of strategic bombing, intended by its Anglo-American sponsors to shorten the war, failed in both the respects through which this desirable end was supposed to be achieved.

First, it did not destroy German war production. It did not even slow it down. *The United States Strategic Bombing Survey (European War)*, published in September 1945, states that "German fighter production continued to increase during the summer of 1944, and acceptances reached a peak of 4375 in September." A nation that could produce this number of fighters in one month at the end of its fifth year of a war it had nearly lost, could scarcely be said to have had its war industry crippled. Senator Harley M. Kilgore's *Statement on German Industry*, published by the U. S. Office of War Information, London in August 1945 and based on "The official report of the Reich's Ministry for Armaments and War Production for 1944," shows that three times as many armoured fighting vehicles, more than three times as many fighter-bombers and eight times as many night-fighter planes were produced in 1944 as in 1942.

A failure in its attempt to cripple German war industry, strategic bombing was equally unsuccessful in its secondary objective, the "undermining of civilian morale" as it was euphemistically defined at the Casablanca conference; i.e. making life so unbearable for the civilians that they would give up and topple the regime. The lesson of London had not been learned. So far from undermining civilian morale the bombing of the towns merely stiffened it. In addition, at the very time when the German armies were beginning to be disillusioned and dejected after their first major reverses, the news of what was happening to their families at home merely angered them and gave them a new motive to fight to the last. Strategic bombing was destined to be a failure, destroying neither war production nor civilian morale. Was it therefore justifiable when, in the words of Liddell Hart [3] it ". . . involved the paradoxical course of seeking to preserve European civilization through practising the most uncivilizing means of warfare that the world has known since the Mongol devastations?" The answer must be yes, of course it was. The first duty of any belligerent in any war is to win it.

Total war is by definition totally terrible. The decisions of those charged with running such a war can be justly considered only in the war context: only if the prevailing mood and circumstances of the time are recreated. The Allies, it cannot be too often repeated, were fighting back from a position of weakness against the most powerful military machine in history when it was at the height of its success. Everything had to be tried. The strategic bomber appeared to the Allied war leaders to provide a means of achieving victory more quickly and more cheaply. It was not till afterwards that they could know whether it had been a success or a failure. With hindsight we know it was a failure. Those who had to make the decision did not unfortunately have the benefit of hindsight. The decision they took was the right one at the time. In total war the operative word is total.

The supremely distressing irony of the whole business was this. That to atone for the criminal power lust of Adolf Hitler it was the women and children of Germany who had to be nailed to the cross by those fighting the Nazi curse in the name of humanity and civilization.

Thus, in the last weeks of 1942, as the once invincible German army reeled before successive blows and the war on land approached its turning-point, the very citadel itself of Fortress Europe blazed with apocalyptic fires. Moreover, the scourging of the Reich was only just beginning. In a few weeks the Americans, too, would be dropping their bombs on the German towns.

There was one gleam of consolation for the Führer at this time. November was the most successful month of the war for his navy in its campaign against Allied shipping. A record tonnage of no less than 700,000 (representing 117 ships) had been sunk by U-boats, while a further 100,000 tons had been disposed of by mines and other means.

At sea, where paradoxically Germany was weakest, the war could still be won. It was small wonder that Churchill, appalled by these figures, was ordering the most urgent consultations between his naval and air chiefs and those of the United States and Canada to discuss how they might tighten up their joint counter-measures against the German submarines.

Chapter 15

DISASTER AT STALINGRAD: PAULUS CUNCTATOR

☐ In the Stalingrad cauldron—as they called the area, twenty-five miles in diameter, where the resurgent Russians had cut off twenty divisions of the Sixth Army—General Paulus wanted to break out before the trap closed and withdraw to the Don or its tributary the Chir. The Russian counteroffensive was already developing strongly on the Don front some seventy miles to his left rear and he had decided as early as November 22 that a break-out to join the main body of Army Group B was imperative if Sixth Army were to be saved from isolation and inevitable destruction when the Russians had consolidated the encirclement which, to begin with, was incipient and insecure.

The Army Group Commander (General von Weichs) and General Zeitzler, the Army Chief of Staff who had recently replaced Halder, both supported Paulus's appreciation. Zeitzler promised to do his best to persuade Hitler that this would be the right thing for Paulus to do. He accordingly sought permission for Paulus to be given freedom of action. The answer, predictably, was negative. The Volga front was vital. Sixth Army must form defensive "hedgehogs" and hold on at all costs. There would be NO repeat NO breakout. There could be no question of freedom of action for Paulus. A relieving force would be sent to break through to Stalingrad.

The last nail in what was to be the coffin of the doomed Sixth Army was hammered in with characteristic irresponsibility by Reichsmarschall Goering, who finally sabotaged the efforts of Zeitzler to make Hitler see reason by airily assuring him that the Luftwaffe could keep Sixth Army supplied by air. This view was not shared by General Wolfram von Richthofen, the air commander who would be responsible for implementing Goering's wild promise. He had only 298 aircraft left in Fourth Air Fleet and the airlift would need 500. The new liability of the Tunisia bridgehead was absorbing far more aircraft than the Luftwaffe had to spare. Stalin may have been unwilling to treat the recent Anglo-American venture in North Africa as a "second front." To the German air generals now made responsible for the supply and maintenance of the Sixth Army at Stalingrad, it was annoyingly like one.

The truth was that Hitler was now landed with the consequences of his dispersion of effort in the summer when, after too many changes of mind and orders, he had finally decided to direct simultaneous offensives in two divergent directions—against Stalingrad and the Caucasus. As has been related, the chance to take Stalingrad "on the run" in July, before any substantial defences had been developed there, was thrown away by his decision to divert to the other front part of the armoured force that might, at that time, have managed it; a golden opportunity that was never to recur. The price was now being paid for personal overambition that had led inexorably to military overextension. Aiming at two exacting and widely separated objectives, Hitler had achieved neither.

Meanwhile the two fronts turned out to be more closely interrelated in failure than they had been in the spectrum of Hitler's now fading summer dream. For if the Stalingrad-Volga front collapsed the main line of communications through Rostov to Army Group A in the Caucasus would be threatened and an even more disastrous encirclement would threaten. A firm Stalingrad-Rostov axis on the Caucasus northern flank was the essential defence against this threat. It made military good sense that the cornerstone of the southeast, the Stalingrad-Rostov axis, should be stabilized and strengthened to meet the rapidly developing situation. Hitler's plan for achieving this was first, to form a new army group in the southeast, Army Group Don which came into existence on November 24 under General Field-Marshal Erich von Mannstein and absorbed Sixth Army four days later: and secondly, to insist that the firm holding of the Stalingrad pocket was integral to the new plan. When, on November 28, Sixth Army came under command of the new Army Group, von Mannstein, with an anxious eye on the Caucasus and the imminent likelihood of his having to withdraw some of the forces there through Rostov, had no choice but to echo Hitler's view of the vital importance of the related Stalingrad front standing firm. A collapse at Stalingrad might endanger the whole position in the southeast, and result in the larger Army Group A being cut off and stranded in the Caucasus. The Field-Marshal could only reiterate Hitler's orders to Paulus and promise him that relief would shortly be on its way to him. But in his *Memoirs* published after the war, von Mannstein expressed the view that Paulus should have made a tactical withdrawal, without permission, right at the beginning, on November 19. The implication of this later comment on Paulus is that though von Mannstein could not authorize a withdrawal if Paulus had gone ahead anyway, he would have backed him up later as his Army Group Commander. It was now too late. Hitler's reasoning was being vindicated by events now that danger was actively threatening in the Caucasus.

One of the subtler aspects of military command is the ability to recognize when it is better *not* to ask permission, but to go ahead and explain your way out of the consequences later. The Hamlet in Paulus had reached his to-be-or-not-to-be point and unfortunately he had opted for the slings and arrows of outrageous fortune—destined to become more outrageous still.

The attempt to relieve Stalingrad was planned in two phases, the second of which was to follow immediately after the first. In the first phase, codenamed Winter Storm, the 57th Panzer Corps of General Hermann von Hoth's Fourth Panzer Army was to cut a corridor to the encircled Sixth Army from a point about seventy miles south. When Hoth's tanks were within twenty miles of the bridgehead, Paulus was to complete Winter Storm by sending a strong panzer group out of the bridgehead to make contact with them. As soon as this had been done Paulus was to launch the second operation, Thunderclap—a general breakout by the entire Stalingrad garrison.

The first operation Winter Storm was launched on December 12 when Hoth's spearhead, the three divisions of 57th Panzer Corps, started its advance in a temperature of 20° below zero. After seven days of hard fighting they had forced their way to the intermediate objective of the river where superior Russian forces were well entrenched to bar further progress. The relieving divisions had fought their way to within forty miles of the perimeter of the cauldron and this was as near as they were to get. Von Mannstein thought the time had come for Paulus to complete Winter Storm by sending his armoured group out of the bridgehead to make contact with the relief force. He told Paulus to set them moving as quickly as possible and also to make all necessary preparations for the follow-up operation Thunderclap, the breakout, as it might be necessary to act at short notice if the first operation finished according to plan.

Paulus hesitated. He said he could not send out his panzer group as he was desperately short of gasoline: his tanks had enough for only twelve miles. The airlift had fallen hopelessly short of his requirement. He had been receiving an average of a hundred tons of supplies a day instead of the five hundred he needed. He said he would now like to forget about the last phase of Winter Storm and launch Thunderclap, the general breakout, at once. It was von Mannstein's turn to hesitate. The over-all position, he said, had not changed. The full breakout could not be initiated without orders from above. Paulus then asked if he could make "psychological preparations" for it without indicating what on earth he meant by this. Again von Mannstein stalled, telling him to wait until they were in touch later that night. The upshot was that Hoth's relief group got no nearer to the bridgehead. No tanks came out to meet it. No permission for a fighting breakout was given.

The indecisive dialogue (by teleprinter) continued for another two days with Paulus reiterating his plea to be allowed to fight his way out, von Mannstein continuing to regret that he had no authority to give this permission. The Russians now broke through on the northern flank of the Don front and one of Hoth's three relief divisions had to be hurriedly diverted from Winter Storm to assist at the new danger point. This was December 23. The remaining two divisions of the relief force were still no nearer to Stalingrad having been strongly counterattacked and contained.

That day von Mannstein had a slightly different idea. He asked Paulus if he thought he could break out with his tanks and join up with Hoth as planned if extra supplies of gasoline were flown into the bridgehead. Paulus said that it was impossible to judge from where he was just what chance of relief there now was; that the best course, from his point of view, would still be to break out with his entire garrison as

174

soon as possible; could he take it that von Mannstein was now authorizing him to do so?

The Field-Marshal replied that he still had no authority to give the word for Thunderclap, the general breakout. What he was trying to find out was whether Paulus thought that, if he was sent the extra supplies, he *could* break out in sufficient strength to join up with Hoth. Paulus said it looked as though there was no alternative.

On December 24 the Chiefs of Staff of Sixth Army and Army Group Don took over the dialogue, when the latter said that, although the High Command had still not authorized Thunderclap, von Mannstein had told him to advise Sixth Army "to make up its mind that Thunderclap would be the solution." As Sixth Army had been clamouring for a month to be allowed to do just this, the wording seemed needlessly circumspect. (No doubt it had to be so for the record. Whether you called it a breakout or a withdrawal, it was not a felicitous word to bandy about in the highest circles of the Wehrmacht.)

So at last von Mannstein had taken the responsibility or nearly had. Sixth Army had been given the chance. The breakout would be more difficult now than it would have been a month before. But far better a fighting chance, even with 50 percent losses, than the slow death that was the alternative. But it was not to be quite so simple as that. There was a catch at the end of the message from von Mannstein, relayed by his Chief of Staff. There would have to be an improvement in the weather (the message concluded) before the extra supplies could be flown into the bridgehead. It was Christmas Eve and the weather looked unlikely to improve for a long time.

On Christmas Day hope of relieving Stalingrad finally died. The Russians had broken through a second time on the Don front and von Mannstein had to transfer to the new crisis sector a second division from the dwindling Stalingrad relief force, still forty miles away. This left only one panzer division. Hope of fighting through to Paulus was now out of the question and this division had to be pulled back before it suffered a private encirclement and destruction of its own.

At the same time Army Group A were being pushed back in the Caucasus by yet another Russian offensive which had opened three weeks before. The withdrawal of the Army Group through Rostov was now the main concern of the High Command, bent on abandoning the Caucasus as painlessly as possible and reconstituting the entire southeast front with the three Army Groups, A, B, and Don.

The new developments meant that it was now more than ever essential for Sixth Army to hold out and contain the large Russian forces at Stalingrad for as long as possible, to help the Caucasus withdrawal. It was von Mannstein's unpleasant duty to signal Paulus firm orders to this effect only one day after he had told him to prepare to break out as soon as the Luftwaffe had been able to replenish his fuel stocks. On the face of it Hitler's strategy had been vindicated. It can only be a matter of speculation whether Sixth Army could not have done even more good after the brief tactical withdrawal to a better position that Paulus had wanted to carry out at the start of the Russian counteroffensive.

At least the latest orders meant that Paulus had been rescued from his dilemma of conscience. There could now be no question of his breaking out on his own responsibility. He was under firm orders and therefore relieved from the necessity to make any higher decisions. The indications are that he was happier that way. For the last agony of Stalingrad, which was to drag on for five weeks, Paulus resumed his normal persona of the punctilious and considerate staff officer turned field commander.

On January 8 the Russians demanded his surrender. With the concurrence of his corps commanders he refused. (It was characteristic of him that from the beginning of the encirclement he treated these senior subordinates as a kind of consultative inner cabinet.)

On January 22 the Russians opened their final offensive against a garrison now half-starved, half-frozen, convinced that they had been wantonly sacrificed by Hitler and with little left to fight with except the habit of not giving in that is ingrained in the well-trained soldier. It took the Russians nine days to cut the bridgehead in half. When at last, on January 31, they appeared outside Sixth Army's last headquarters, which was in Red Square, Paulus and his Chief of Staff surrendered and the headquarters garrison laid down their arms. It must have been of little comfort to Paulus that it was as a Field-Marshal that he surrendered; his promotion had come through the day before; presumably because Hitler was feeling guilty about him. The remnant now cut off in the northern pocket of the cauldron surrendered two days later, on February 2.

Of an original paper strength of 300,000, Sixth Army's fighting strength in the cauldron at the beginning of the encirclement on November 22 was 220,000. Of this number 72,200 were killed or died of wounds, sickness, starvation, or cold; 42,000 (35,000 wounded, 7000 specialists and technicians) were evacuated by air during the siege; 17,000 were taken prisoner during the final nine-day offensive in January; 91,000 (including one field-marshal and twenty-four generals) marched or rode into captivity after the surrender.

German historians are divided in their views on whether Paulus should or could have acted differently. His actions are likely to be a continuing subject of historical argument. In most respects he seemed the epitome of military orthodoxy and yet he remained an enigma. At least it may be said that the size of the occasion and the personal dilemma in which he found himself merit a verdict not of pity but of compassion.

There is a postscript to the Paulus story. In the summer of 1943 certain German senior officers in Russian hands and under Soviet influence formed the *Bund Deutscher Offiziere* (Federation of German Officers) as a section of the *Nationalkomitee Freies Deutschland* (National Committee of Free Germany). The Soviet government pressed their star prisoner Paulus to support the Free Germany movement but he refused for a year, faithful to the German officer code of non-involvement in politics. In 1944 when he heard about the unsuccessful July plot to kill Hitler, and the subsequent grisly fate of some of the conspirators who had been his friends in the Army, he decided to co-operate fully. He adopted the communist "faith" and spoke on the radio for the National Committee. Having given the matter his usual protracted deliberation before deciding, he had finally decided unshakably and forever that the hope of mankind now rested on the Soviet ideology. When he returned to Germany after the war it was in East Germany, in Dresden, that he chose to live out the rest of his days, dying in 1957 of a rare type of organic cerebral sclerosis.

One is tempted to think of him as Paulus Cunctator (the "Delayer"), the nickname the Romans bestowed on their General Fabius for his strategy of exhaustion against Hannibal, based on delaying or avoiding action. But whereas Fabius Cunctator avoided giving battle, what Paulus Cunctator liked to avoid was making decisions. In the sombre context of Stalingrad he emerges as a tragic figure, if a minor one. The too meticulous, too logical habit of weighing all the possibilities more than once before deciding had in the end proved his undoing. His acknowledged professional excellence in other respects had been fatally flawed by this inherent weakness of hesitancy at moments of supreme decision. It was this which held him back from fighting his way out, regardless of the consequences to himself, when he might or might not have got away with it, but would have saved his army anyway. He was the victim of his own virtue as a staff officer who in the crucial test failed as a commander in the field.

In a way, more than any of the others he symbolized the eventual self-stultification of the German General Staff by its own virtues carried to the last extreme so perilously near to absurdity. In every other respect the Complete Soldier— impeccably efficient, painstaking, considerate, and brave— he went down with his ship because he could (rather than would) not order everyone to the lifeboats without permission. He was too well-trained; almost a computer; and the programmer had said "hold on." So he stayed where he was, leading such resistance as could still be offered, until the Russians appeared outside his headquarters. Then he surrendered. It was at that time the logical thing to do. So logically and courteously this logical man did it.

That in outline was how the end came at Stalingrad. That was how the battle ended for those who had to give the orders. What were the thoughts and feelings of those who received them? What were the last days in the cauldron like as food stocks dwindled; as the unburied dead piled up; as the number of the wounded and the sick outpaced the diminishing means of succouring them; as they realized that the Führer had finally let them down?

What did they think about as the ring steadily tightened, the cold became colder, and many of those outside Stalingrad were limping and crawling back into the stricken city to seek better shelter in the cellars, sewers, and craters within its foetid ruins? What went on in the minds and hearts of those left in the condemned cauldron during this white Christmas that for the German soldier was the blackest Christmas there had ever been?

Circumstances, macabre and grotesque, have made it possible for us to know a little about some of these men and of how they faced the end.

Shortly before the Russians overran the last airstrip, a plane left the Stalingrad cauldron with a load of mail that the senders knew would be their last letters home. The warped genius of Dr. Goebbels, Reichsminister of Propaganda, saw this as a unique opportunity to carry out an accurate survey of Army morale and at the same time an unprejudiced popularity poll of the Nazi leadership. An opportunity like this might never recur. It was a market researcher's dream. It was like an advertising man's having the chance to go round the death cells of his country's main prisons finding out which cereal the condemned men would choose for their last breakfast.

When the plane touched down seven bags of mail were impounded by order of the High Command and handed over to the Army Bureau of Information for examination. After removing the address and sender's name, the ABI closely analyzed the letters and finally sorted their findings into five categories.

1. Positive Attitude towards the Leadership   2.1%
2. Doubtful Attitude towards the Leadership   4.4%
3. Negative Attitude towards the Leadership   57.4%
4. Actively Opposed   3.4%
5. Indifferent   33.0%

The result was not quite the hosanna of Heil Hitlers for which the High Command had hoped. Nevertheless the letters (clearly a baby that no one wanted to be left holding) were processed, reprocessed, minuted, examined again, checked, stamped, handed on, initialled, signed for, left in pending baskets, passed from department to department and exhaustively submitted to that curious, intermittent and often totally inexplicable transmigration of paper peculiar to the rear echelons of all armies: until they landed, with half a ton of other documentation pertaining to Stalingrad, in the care of the Army Press Corps, which was given the task of producing an authentic history of the Battle of Stalingrad. It was obviously hoped that the High Command would show up well in this work. To their credit the APC historians found it impossible to produce an account of the battle pleasing to their masters.

When Dr. Goebbels saw the fruit of their labours he refused to authorize publication. At the end of their interminable interdepartmental manhandling by the bureaucrats of the Army and the Party, the Stalingrad letters were finally consigned to the limbo of the Army archives at Potsdam from which photocopies were rescued shortly before the fall of Berlin in 1945. A selection of them was published [1] in Germany in 1954 and in the United States and Britain shortly afterwards. These fragments from a doomed army add their own poignant footnote to the Stalingrad story. But perhaps their greatest value is to remind those who read them that beyond the Nazi indoctrination and the Prussian military stereotype, the German soldier, like the other citizen soldiers he fought, was a human being who thought and felt as a human being, and was in the end as much a victim of Hitler's overweening ambition as they.

A melancholy astronomer writes to Monica, his "best friend"—best, he implies, because *only*. He jokes wanly about men having always avoided his company because he was too serious, too dedicated to his telescope and his study of the stars, his one overriding enthusiasm. At Stalingrad he is in a small meteorological unit.

> There are four of us . . . What we do is very simple. Our job is to measure temperatures and humidity, to report on cloud ceilings and visibility. If some bureaucrat read what I write here, he would have a fit . . . violation of military security. Monica, what is our life compared to the many million years of the starry sky! . . .
>
> Around me everything is collapsing, a whole army is dying, day and night are on fire, and four men busy themselves with daily reports on temperature and cloud ceilings. I don't know much about war. No human being has died by my hand. I haven't even fired live ammunition from my pistol. But I know this much: the other side would never show such a lack of understanding for its men. I should have liked to count stars for another few decades, but nothing will ever come of it now, I suppose.

There is a letter which begins

> I took out your picture once again and looked at it for a long time. I remember the experience we shared that lovely summer evening in the last year of peace.

and ends

> When you receive this letter, listen intently to it, perhaps you will hear my voice then. They tell us

that our struggle is for Germany. But there are only a few here who believe that this meaningless sacrifice could be of use to our country.

A pianist, whose wife Margaret has suspected that something has happened to his hands and whose letters have been probing for an answer, now tells her the truth.

So it is well that this letter should reach you, and that you know, in case I should turn up some day, that my hands are ruined and have been since the beginning of December. I lost the little finger on my left hand, but worse still is the loss of the three middle fingers of my right hand through frostbite. I can hold my drinking cup only with my thumb and little finger. I am quite helpless; only when one has lost his fingers does one notice how much they are needed for the simplest tasks. The thing I can still do best with my little finger is shoot. Yes, my hands are wrecked. I can't very well spend the rest of my life shooting, simply because I'm no good for anything else. Perhaps I could make out as a game warden? But this is gallows humour; I only write it to calm myself.

Kurt Hahnke, I think you remember him from the Conservatoire in '37, played the Appassionata a week ago on a grand piano in a little side street close to Red Square. Such things don't happen every day. The grand piano was standing right in the middle of the street. The house had been blown up, but feeling sorry for the instrument, they must have got it out beforehand and put it in the street. Every passing soldier hammered away at it. I ask you, where else can you find a place with pianos in the streets? As I said, Kurt played incredibly well . . . If the boy gets home, we will soon hear about him. I certainly shall never forget these hours—the kind of audience and the situation were unique. Pity that I am not a writer so that I could describe how a hundred soldiers squatted around in their great-coats with blankets over their heads. Everywhere there was the sound of explosions, but no one let himself be disturbed. They were listening to Beethoven in Stalingrad, even if they didn't understand him. Do you feel better now that you know the full truth?

181

Only when the fate of the garrison is certain does one artillery officer feel justified in telling his wife.

> For a whole week I have avoided writing this letter; I kept thinking that uncertainty, painful though it is, still keeps a glimmer of hope alive. I was the same way in thinking about my own fate . . . Now things are different; since this morning I know how things stand; and . . . I want you also to be free from apprehension and uncertainty.
>
> I was shocked when I saw the map. We are entirely alone, without help from outside. Hitler has left us in the lurch. If the airfield is still in our possession this letter may still get out . . . The men of my battery have some inkling of it too, but they don't know as clearly as I do. So this is what the end looks like. Hannes and I will not surrender; yesterday, after our infantry had retaken a position, I saw four men who had been taken prisoner by the Russians. No, we shall not go into captivity. When Stalingrad has fallen, you'll read and hear it. And then you'll know that I shall not come back.

A soldier, urged to lay down his arms by a politically minded friend, writes back angrily:

> . . . Just don't bother me with your well-meant advice. . . . It is easy to give good advice; but it just won't work the way you think it will . . . The time to act was in 1932; you know that very well. Also, that we let the moment go by. Ten years ago, the ballot would still have done the trick. Today, all it will cost you is your life.

A young dupe of the Hitler myth, now tormented by disillusion, tells his girl:

> No one can tell me any longer that the men died with the words "Deutschland" or "Heil Hitler" on their lips. There is plenty of dying, no question of that; but the last word is "mother" or the name of someone dear, or just a cry for help . . . I have seen hundreds fall and many belonged to the Hitler Youth as I did; but all of them,

if they still could speak, called for help or shouted a name which could not help them anyway.

The Führer made a firm promise to bail us out of here; they read it to us and we believed in it firmly. Even now I still believe it, because I have to believe in something . . . So leave me my faith, dear Greta; all my life, at least eight years of it, I believed in the Führer and his word. It is terrible how they doubt here, and shameful to listen to what they say without being able to reply, because they have the facts on their side.

A chaplain tells his wife about his celebration of Holy Communion on Christmas Eve with eleven soldiers.

It was not easy to find them in the herd of doubting, hopeless and disappointed. But those I found came happily.

His altar was an ammunition box.

Yesterday the box still held anti-aircraft shells; today my hand spread over it the field-grey tunic of a comrade whose eyes I closed last Friday in this very room . . . I read my boys the Christmas story according to the gospel of Luke . . . gave them hard black bread as the holy sacrifice and sacrament of the altar . . . the true body of our Lord Jesus Christ . . . The men sat on footstools and looked up to me from large eyes in their starved faces. They were all young except one who was 51.

The chaplain's letter contrasts with another last letter, addressed to another man of God—a pastor in Germany—by his son.

In Stalingrad, to put the question of God's existence means to deny it. I must tell you this, Father, and I feel doubly sorry for it. You have raised me, because I had no mother, and always kept God before my eyes and soul . . . I have searched for God in every crater, in every destroyed house, on every corner, in every friend, in my fox hole, and in the sky. God did not show himself, even though my heart cried for him. No, Father, there is no God . . . and if there should be a God, He is only with you in the hymnals and the prayers, in the pious sayings of the priests and pastors, in the ringing of bells and the fragrance of incense, but not in Stalingrad.

A gunner writes to a friend in a tone of forced jauntiness.

Here I am: still in one piece, with a fairly normal pulse, a dozen cigarettes, had soup day before yesterday, liberated a canned ham today from a supply bomb (there is no more regular distribution; everyone is on his own), am squatting in a cellar, burning up furniture, 26 years old and otherwise no fool, one of those who was mighty keen on getting his bars and yelled "Heil Hitler" with the rest of you; and now it's either die like a dog or off to Siberia. That wouldn't be so bad. But to know that it is done for something utterly senseless makes me see red.

But let them come. The Third still has 26 rounds and their commander an 08 with six shiny bullets . . .

There is a stiffly controlled letter from an officer to his father, a colonel on the General Staff:

The word is out that we can write today. For one familiar with the situation that means that we do it just once more.

You are a colonel, my dear Father, and a member of the general staff. So you know what this means, and I needn't go into explanations which might sound sentimental. This is the end. It will last perhaps another week, I think, then the game's up . . . The reasons are now altogether unimportant and pointless. But if I am to say anything about them, it is this: do not look to us for an explanation of the situation, but to yourselves and to the man who is responsible for it. Don't knuckle under—you, Father, and all those who think like you. Be on guard so that a greater disaster does not overtake our country. . . .

And now to personal matters. You can be sure that everything will end decently. It is a little early at thirty, I know. No sentiment. Handshake for Lydia and Helene. Kiss for Mother (be careful, old man, think of her heart trouble), kiss for Gerda, regards to all the rest. Hand to helmet, Father. First Lieutenant——respectfully gives notice of departure.

There is another letter, rather different in tone from most of the others: an officer's letter, written, one feels, with the stiffest of upper lips, and still mindful, in its carefully general wording, of military security even now when it cannot any longer matter. It begins:

> . . . You are the wife of a German officer; so you will take what I have to tell you, upright and unflinching, as upright as you stood on the station platform the day I left for the East . . .

He has never been much of a letterwriter, he says—never more than one page. And he and his wife Augusta have never shown their feelings much. But the truth was that

> this is the grimmest of struggles in a hopeless situation. Misery, cold, renunciation, doubt, despair and horrible death.

He'll say no more. He did not talk about it on his leave and he has not mentioned it since in his letters. He's not complaining, he's just telling her the truth. Then comes a surprising sentence:

> I cannot deny my share of personal guilt in all this. But it is in a ratio of 1 to 70 million. The ratio is small; but it is still there. I would not think of evading my responsibility; I tell myself that by giving my life, I have paid my debt. One cannot argue about questions of honour.

After exhorting Augusta to be strong and not to give way to bitterness he adds:

> I am not cowardly, only sad that I cannot give greater proof of my courage than to die for this useless, not to say criminal, cause.

One can almost hear the heel-click and see the stiff little bow as he signs off with an injunction not to forget him too quickly.

It was perhaps as well that the "dear ones" referred to never received the rather terrible letter from the weeping gunner on the threshold of breakdown. This is one of the few letters that do not blame Hitler and the Supreme Command directly or indirectly; indeed the writer seems hardly aware of the main situation. He is clearly an introvert on the edge of a complete crack-up:

> . . . During the last few nights I have wept so much that it seems unbearable even to myself . . . On Tuesday I knocked out two T-34s with my mobile anti-tank gun . . . It was grand and impressive. Afterwards I drove past the smoking remains. From a hatch there hung a body, head down, his feet caught, and his legs burning up to his knees. The body was alive, the mouth moaning. He must have suffered terrible pain. And there was no possibility of freeing him. Even if there had been, he would have died after a few hours of torture. I shot him, and as I did it, the tears ran down my cheeks. Now I have been crying for three nights about a dead Russian tank driver, whose murderer I am . . . I'll never be able to sleep quietly, assuming that I shall ever come back to you, dear ones. My life is a terrible contradiction, a psychological monstrosity. . . .

There was one other 'last' letter[2] from Stalingrad. It was not among those impounded for analysis. It was from the recently promoted Field-Marshal Friedrich Paulus to his Rumanian-born wife. It has not survived and is presumed to have been destroyed by Frau Paulus when the Gestapo were on their way to arrest her at the end of 1944. But it has been established that it contained this sentence:

> "I stand and fight—those are my orders!"

Having regard to all the circumstances, for a soldier of Stalingrad, it was not a bad epitaph. It was an epitaph for an army.

The midday conference at OKW on February 1, 1943, lacked cordiality. To add insult to injury first news of the Sixth Army's capitulation had reached Hitler and his entourage by courtesy of the Russian Radio. The Russians did not forebear to mention that Field-Marshal Paulus, his Chief of Staff, General Rudolf Schmidt, and a number of other generals (all of whom they named) were included in the bag of 91,000 prisoners. There was no question of sympathy or gratitude to Paulus for holding on as long as he had in an impossible situation. It was not so much a conference as a diatribe by Hitler with the Army Chief of Staff, General Kurt Zeitzler, acting as feed to the soloist by cautiously agreeing, after every few sentences, and giving the angry monologue the semblance of a discussion.

The shorthand transcript [3] of the conference conveys between the lines the fury of an enraged child sobbing with hate.

> *Hitler:* They have finally and formally surrendered there. Otherwise they'd have concentrated, formed square and shot it out using their last bullet on themselves. When you think that a woman's got sufficient pride just because someone's made a few insulting remarks to go and lock herself in and shoot herself right off, then I've no respect for a soldier who's afraid to do that but would rather be taken prisoner . . .

Zeitzler agrees but wonders whether it is true. Paulus might be lying there wounded.

> *Hitler:* No, it's true. They'll be taken straight to Moscow and put into the hands of the GPU and they'll blurt out orders for the northern pocket to surrender too. That man Schmidt will sign anything. A man who hadn't got the courage at a time like this to take the road that every man has to take one day won't have the strength to stand up to that. He'll suffer mental torture. We put too much emphasis on education and too little on character training.

Zeitzler agrees that it is impossible to understand that type of man.

> *Hitler:* . . . In peace-time about 18,000 or 20,000 people a year choose to commit suicide although none of them are in a situation like this, and here's a man who sees 45,000 to 60,000 of his soldiers die defending themselves bravely to the end—how can he give himself up to the Bolshevists?

187

Zeitzler thinks it is something quite incomprehensible.

> *Hitler:* But I had my doubts before. It was at the moment when I heard he was asking what he should do. How could he even ask such a thing? . . .

Zeitzler agrees that there is no excuse; when his nerves looked like breaking down he should have shot himself first. Hitler repeated that when one's nerves broke down there was nothing to do but to shoot oneself.

> *Hitler:* There will be no more field-marshals in this war. We'll only promote them after the end of the end of the war. I don't go on counting my chickens before they're hatched . . . What hurts me so much is that the heroism of so many soldiers is cancelled out by one single characterless weakling—and I'll tell you what the man will do now. Think of it! He arrives in Moscow and think of the rat trap he's in! He'll sign anything. He'll make confessions, issue proclamations. You'll see. They'll now plumb the depths of lack of character . . .

> *Hitler:* (later): Any minute he'll be speaking on the radio—you'll see Seydlitz and Schmidt will speak on the radio. They'll shut them in that rat trap and two days later they'll have got them so conditioned that they'll speak straight away. And there's this beautiful woman,—Hitler now assumes the idiom of a Vaudeville comedian telling a funny story—a really very beautiful woman, who is insulted by some words. Straightaway she says—it was only a triviality, so I can go; I'm not wanted. Her husband answers "get out, then!" So the woman goes off, writes a letter of farewell and shoots herself.

There is speculation about what has become of some of the other senior officers involved and some discussion of the communiqué to be issued to the foreign press. But Hitler is soon back to his main theme.

> I can't understand how a man like Paulus wouldn't rather die. The heroism of so many tens of thousands of men, officers and generals is cancelled out by a

man like this who hasn't got the character when the moment comes to do what a weakling of a woman can do.

For the fourth time the Führer is cued back to what seems to be his favourite comparative image—that of beautiful weak women ever willing to point a pistol at their heads, while cowardly field-marshals lack the courage to do so. It was an obsession. He was ready with yet another example.

There were a man and wife living together. Later the man died a painful death. Then I got a letter from the wife; she asked me to look after the children. She said she couldn't go on living in spite of her children. Then she shot herself. That's what a woman can do; she's got the strength and soldiers haven't.

So the battle of Stalingrad, which in terms of human endurance at times came close to the sublime, ended squalidly in the sobs and ravings of the man whose folly had brought it about in the first place and had been the main cause of its ending as it did.

Chapter 16

EASTERN FRONT REORGANIZED: FOCUS ON TUNISIA

☐ The student of the Second World War is likely to be struck, even mystified, by the apparent multiplicity of turning points with which it has been credited by different historians. A global war, which lasted so long, and was conducted through so many disparate and widely separated campaigns, inevitably provided a series of crisis points to which the historian could point and say: "This was *the* occasion after which nothing could ever be the same again!" So we find that the Battle of Britain, Pearl Harbor, Midway, El Alamein, Stalingrad, and Tunis have all been so described, sometimes without the specific amplification the term calls for if it is to have meaning. This is not an idle digression into semantics but a preliminary to attempting to set the German catastrophe at Stalingrad in proper perspective.

In the most literal tidal sense of the term it was clearly the turning point of the German aggression on Russia: the point at which the aggression, having reached its "high tide" on the Volga, was forced to withdraw, never again to advance so far into the heart of the country. In the literal sense of attack and withdrawal on the ground and the figurative sense of the tidal ebb and flow of success it was undoubtedly the turning point for Germany on the Eastern front. But it was by no means the military turning point of the Russian campaign.

A single army had been liquidated. Three Army Groups still remained in the southeast and the front was being reorganized and contracted to arrest the Russian counteroffensive. In charge of this reorganization was the highly competent man whom his peers as well as the more knowledgeable foreign military experts were in the habit of calling Germany's finest military brain, Field-Marshal Erich von Mannstein. The military showdown in Russia had still to come and it would be some months before it did. It was *psychologically and politically* that Stalingrad could, without qualification, be called the turning point of the war for it was the occasion that destroyed the Hitler myth of infallibility from the top to the lowest ranks of the German Army. There are many witnesses to the almost hypnotic spell he exercised over senior commanders who came to him disgruntled and prepared to speak their minds, but were then completely won over by him in private audience: Stalingrad ended this. Similarly the almost mystical hold over the loyalty of the lower ranks had been shaken. The Stalingrad let-down was not something that could be kept quiet and forgotten.

Politically, Stalingrad's importance was in its effect abroad. It was the end of the German military myth not only for Germany's opponents, and for the neutral countries, but, especially, for her allies. The remnants of dispirited Italians, Hungarians, and Rumanians—whose positions on the flanks of the main Sixth Army zone had been the weaker sectors against which the Russians had shrewdly aimed their first counterblows—were now all too aware of the price of fighting an alien tyrant's war.

These were the factors which entitled Stalingrad to be considered a turning point. The military turning point was something else again. It would have to wait its turn. There was no question yet of Germany being forced to take the defensive in Russia.

At OKW in Rastenburg the war had to go on. An army had been liquidated. Its commanders had been duly denounced and their names were not to be mentioned again. Stalingrad was soon as stale as the day before yesterday's newspaper. The war had to go on. The urgent need now was to complete the withdrawal of Army Group A from the Caucasus, a withdrawal already in progress.

While the Stalingrad battle had been attracting all the attention in the last weeks of the year, the second and simultaneous German offensive in the Caucasus had ended abortively in November in the high mountains that barred the way to the oilfields that were its objective.

At the end of November, Hitler carried out what seemed to have become his annual pre-Christmas reshuffle of generals appointing Field-Marshal Erich von Mannstein, as we have seen, to command the new Army Group Don. At the same time he promoted General Paul Ludwig von Kleist (who had been commanding First Panzer Army, one of the formations of Army Group A) to command of the Army Group itself.

Army Group A was stretched out over many hundred miles of this vast area with its head in the main mountain range beyond Mozdok, where the offensive had ended in stalemate in November. It was not long before von Kleist was having to earn his promotion.

Just maintaining itself was difficult enough when the Russian winter developed its full severity at the end of the year: leading to such extreme absurdities as the necessity to use mules to carry gasoline to fighting vehicles stranded in remote mountain passes for want of it and camels elsewhere for the same purpose. When the Russian counteroffensive developed in the south it threatened the tenuous snake of Army Group A at its head near Mozdok; in the middle near Lake Elista, 175 miles south of Stalingrad; and towards its rear base and main supply centre Rostov. It was the thrust from the Stalingrad area down the Don towards Rostov that was the most dangerous, as Russian possession of the Stalingrad-Rostov axis could cut off the entire army group.

When the Russians were only forty-five miles from Rostov and the centre of his Army Group four hundred miles east of it von Kleist received an order from Hitler that he was not in any circumstances to withdraw. The threat to his flank and rear would be taken care of by a Rumanian army group under Marshal Ion Antonescu. To von Kleist, who would be only too well aware of what was happening at Stalingrad, this order was "a sentence of doom." But the Rumanians, after their mauling on the Stalingrad front, were for the time being in no position to provide a force of any value. To von Kleist's relief neither Marshal Antonescu nor any army group presented themselves for duty. Instead there was a new order from Hitler. Von Kleist was to retreat with all his equipment as quickly as possible to the narrowing Rostov bottleneck and withdraw through it to join the rest of the armies in the south. Better still was the news that Field-Marshal von Mannstein, not Hitler, was now effective in supreme command of the southern front. With von Mannstein's close co-operation and support at the receiving end von Kleist effected the withdrawal of his Army Group in three weeks and with relatively small losses of men and equipment in spite of the growing Russian pressure and the extreme difficulties and hardship imposed by the winter weather. The withdrawal was one of those operations within an operation which are dismissed in a few sentences because they are wholly successful. Had it been disastrous it would no doubt have been added to the list of remembered "epics" of the Russian campaign. By the end of Frebruary von Kleist had pulled back as far as the Dnieper and in March he was ready to turn over to the attack.

The southern wing of the Russian advance, its momentum now slowing down, had formed a precarious salient south of Kharkov. Von Mannstein decided that the time had come to deliver a strong counterattack—not only for the good of the morale of the whole Army Group South after its gruelling three months, but also to administer an effective rebuff to the Russian offensive now that it was weakening. With an army of twenty-five divisions (half of them armoured) von Mannstein accordingly struck three successive blows at the Russian salient, forcing the Russians to withdraw to the Donets and then back across it. Instead of chasing after them he ordered the most westerly of his three army groups to attack and recapture Kharkov. On March 13, the third battle of Kharkov ended with the Germans again in possession of what remained of the city. Their winter offensive having now spent its force, the Russians were glad to go on the defensive and accept the winter lull which was not to end until mid-summer.

It was clear evidence that the German armies in Russia were still a force to be reckoned with and it emphasized that Stalingrad had not been the military turning point. The armies withdrawn from the Caucasus had played their full part in von Mannstein's judiciously planned and executed counterblow. And von Kleist now had a field-marshal's baton to show for his achievement in bringing the Caucasus withdrawal to a successful conclusion: despite Hitler's threat only a few weeks before, that he would make no more field-marshals until after the war.

The stand of the Sixth Army at Stalingrad, and the Russian forces it had tied up, must have had a beneficial influence on the concurrent withdrawal from the Caucasus. It can be only a matter of idle speculation whether a breakout by Paulus might have helped von Kleist even more. What seems beyond doubt is that the successful completion of the Caucasus withdrawal, and the subsequent switch to the offensive culminating in the recapture of Kharkov, owed much to the fact that Hitler had little to do with either, for once leaving the two experienced professional soldiers, von Mannstein and von Kleist, to get on with it.

Third, Kharkov, coming so soon after the end of 1942—the great year of strategic transition—was an ominous reminder that the Germany Army, despite recent reverses, was still a powerful and resilient force. There was no reason at this time of renewed confidence and success to suggest that this would in fact prove to be Germany's last victory on Russian soil. But time was to confer on the third battle of Kharkov this extra distinction.

With the Eastern front subsiding into that winter lull against which even the most modern and technologically advanced warfare is not proof, the focus of attention now switched to North Africa—and another winter lull for two other armies.

The Allied year in the Mediterranean began with the Casablanca Conference attended by President Roosevelt, Prime Minister Churchill, and their Chiefs of Staff. Among the various policy decisions arrived at there were three of far-reaching importance that must be singled out.

First it was decided that the Allies' next move after the defeat of the Axis in North Africa would be the invasion of Sicily as a steppingstone to a landing in Italy. This decision was not reached without considerable renewed discussion and argument: much discussion having already taken place in London and Washington. Certain of the American chiefs—Admiral Ernest J. King and, to begin with, General George C. Marshall—were opposed to a Mediterranean strategy (of which Churchill was the staunchest advocate) on the grounds that it would delay the final invasion of Europe across the English Channel by diverting too much Anglo-American strength to a secondary theatre that might prove to be a dead end. But this school of thought was finally won over by the hard (and agreed) fact that there was now no possibility of the cross-Channel invasion being mounted before 1944.

Secondly, it was decided that the strategic bomber offensive against German towns would be greatly intensified with the United States Air Forces now joining in. With the R.A.F. stepping up their night bombing and the U.S.A.F. very shortly starting an equally heavy programme of daylight raids, the cities of the Third Reich were now to experience the new horror of round-the-clock bombing. Ominously, the objective of the new Allied bombing offensive was defined in these words:[1]

"The progressive destruction and dislocation of the German military, industrial, and economic system, and the undermining of the morale of the German people to a point where their capacity for armed resistance is fatally weakened."

Pretence and euphemism had been finally set aside. It was now an openly stated part of Allied policy to weaken the German will to resist by bombing civilians. It was a callous decision that in simple terms meant that the innocent masses were to be punished even harder for the crimes of the guilty few. It could only be explained, if not excused, by the grim inescapable fact that at the beginning of 1943 Hitler's armed forces were still hugely strong in spite of their reverses in the last half of the previous year: and the bomber was still the only weapon with which the Allies could communicate directly with the German civilian population.

It must also be remembered that, although the full horror of the concentration camps was still to be revealed, enough was already known of them and of the oppressive Nazi subtyrannies established in the occupied countries, of the treatment of Resistance fighters and guerrillas, of the vast importations of slave labour into Germany, and of such emotive episodes as the massacre of Lidice, for a climate of such angry hate to have been generated in the free world that the mildest of men and women, hearing of the devastation of Germany, could not rise above a heart-felt "Serve them right!" Nevertheless, it is an appalling incidental comment on the Second World War that the defenders of freedom were forced to subvert the cry "Women and children first!" so far from its ancient and merciful significance.

The third far-reaching product of Casablanca was the announcement by the Allies that they would accept nothing less than "unconditional surrender."

This decision has been heavily criticised as a major blunder which, by depriving the German people of any hope, merely stiffened their will to resist. It was certainly presented to them in this way by Dr. Goebbels, to whose propaganda ministry unconditional surrender came as a godsend, capable of every kind of distorted and malign elaboration. In retrospect it does seem a foolish prospect to have presented to people beginning to show signs of weakening under the hammering they had been receiving from the sky.

Churchill, explaining to the House of Commons in 1944 what the Allied leaders had had in mind, offered this amplification:[2]

> The term "unconditional surrender" does not mean that the German people will be enslaved or destroyed. It means however that the Allies will not be bound to them at the moment of surrender by any pact or obligation. . . .
>
> Unconditional surrender means that the victors have a free hand. It does not mean that they are entitled to behave in a barbarous manner, nor that they wish to blot out Germany from among the nations of Europe. If we are bound, we are bound by our own consciences to civilisation. We are not to be bound to the Germans as the result of a bargain struck. That is the meaning of "unconditional surrender."

Put that way, and in the reassuring prose of Winston Churchill it sounded more reasonable than it did in the fiery polemics of Dr. Goebbels. But what worried the German people (and somewhat blurred the effect of Churchill's well-meant definition) was that they would be unconditionally surrendering not only to the Americans and the British—but also to the Russians.

The Allied leaders discussed many other matters, of course, at Casablanca in addition to the three items singled out. They discussed in some detail, for instance, the conduct of the two campaigns now converging on Tunis. But perhaps the burden of Casablanca was that it proclaimed, almost with a fanfare of trumpets, that, 1942 having been the year the initiative was wrested from Germany, 1943 was going to be the year of coming to grips with Fortress Europe and forcing the first entry. Not only was the writing on the Atlantic Wall: it was there in electric lights.

The Axis year in the Mediterranean opened in gloom and bitterness. This is graphically reflected in Ciano's diary notes for January 1943. There were the depressing communiqués covering the last days of the Stalingrad disaster. There was particular bitterness over the terrible mauling of the Italian Eighth Army holding the Don flank of the Stalingrad position when the Russians overran it. There was now frequent talk in Rome about asking for a separate peace as soon as a convenient opportunity to do so could be contrived. In addition, Montgomery was preparing his final attack on Tripoli, Italy's main base port in Libya, and it was likely to fall any day. Rommel was discredited. The Italian services chiefs were now thoroughly disenchanted with their German allies. Practically the only members of the Axis on speaking terms any more were Mussolini and Hitler who continued to keep up their pretence of undying friendship and mutual loyalty— perhaps because neither of them any longer had anyone else whom he could call friend or could really trust.

On January 23, three months after the start of El Alamein, Montgomery took Tripoli, 1400 miles west of it. Rommel withdrew to Tunisia to prepare his next stand in the Mareth line, a zone of fortifications built by the French colonial army in peacetime. Here he could at least make contact with the other Axis army in Tunisia, holding Eisenhower's Anglo-British advance towards Tunis.

In December this Tunisian bridgehead force had been taken over by Colonel General Dietloff von Arnim, a corps commander from the Russian front. It was in the process of being built up to an army of seven divisions and was named the Fifth Panzer Army, with 10th Panzer Division as its most formidable component. As already noted, the torrential rains of the Tunisian winter had brought offensive operations to a halt in the Tunis bridgehead and von Arnim was using the lull to build up his strength most of which had still to be brought in by air.

At Supreme Headquarters in Rastenburg there was a growing conviction that the North Africa front was a costly nuisance that might eventually lead to a catastrophe; that the best thing would be a complete withdrawal from the theatre while this was still possible. Otherwise there was a risk of eventually losing a number of excellent formations that more than ever could not be spared.

This notion, widely held at OKW, had been strongly planted at the end of November by Field-Marshal Rommel, when he made a surprise appearance at the Wolf's Lair. It was his first visit since his defeat at El Alamein. He had not been invited. His reception—compared with the favourite-son treatment Hitler normally accorded him—was noticeably chilly. But Rommel's view made an impression on the staff if not on the Führer, and the feeling that his view was the correct one received an extra impetus when Tripoli fell to the British in January, and Rommel pulled his army hurriedly back into Tunisia. But despite the fact that the loss of Tripoli now made even more desperate the already difficult Axis logistical link with North Africa, Hitler chose to regard the presence of the two Axis armies in Tunisia as a splendid opportunity to start offensive operations there. He was additionally beguiled into this attitude by the ever-optimistic Kesselring who made the usual comforting noises supporting Goering's reckless assurances that the Luftwaffe would be equal to all demands made upon it.

In February, General Warlimont, Assistant Operations Chief to General Jodl, was sent to North Africa to go thoroughly into all aspects of the situation and to bring back a firsthand impression on which OKW could base a complete reappraisal. He spent ten days on the trip, visiting both armies, talking at length to their commanders and staffs. He also had full discussions en route with top men at Comando Supremo in Rome. He reached the firm conclusion that Rommel was right; that the only solution was to evacuate North Africa at once.[3] A front would have to be written off but two substantial armies would be saved to fight elsewhere. On the way back he called on Kesselring, Commander-in-Chief South, to report his findings and try to convince him that they were right. Kesselring, however, refused to be persuaded. During the return journey the next day Warlimont finalized his thoughts and prepared his report. He made up his mind, Kesselring's disagreement notwithstanding, to recommend to Hitler as strongly as he could that North Africa be evacuated as soon as possible. There would be a chance to say this to Hitler at the usual midday conference on the day after his return. But when Warlimont arrived at the conference to give his report, he was astonished to find Kesselring was there ahead of him. The C-in-C South had beaten

197

him to the draw, and it was to him, naturally, that Hitler turned for an up-to-the-minute report on the Africa situation. Kesselring, the renowned optimist, was telling Hitler all the things he wanted to hear. Everything was fine. Both armies in Tunisia would shortly resume the offensive. Difficulties in the command set-up were being ironed out. The Luftwaffe could handle the supply and reinforcement position. Warlimont never had a chance to speak. A sympathetic aide, realizing that he had something he badly wanted to say, tried to arrange a private audience for him later in the day, but he was unsuccessful. That evening the Führer left for a four-weeks' stay at his advanced headquarters in the Ukraine! Field-Marshal Kesselring, the Luftwaffe officer who, as Commander-in-Chief South, controlled the destiny of two German-Italian panzer armies, had successfully forestalled their evacuation at the one time, never to recur, when it might have been achieved comparatively painlessly.

At this point it is appropriate to give a brief idea of the topography and terrain of the country now destined to be a centre of world attention for four months. Tunisia is a small, narrow country squeezed between the much larger territories of Algeria to the west and Libya to the east. It can most conveniently, if roughly, be visualized as an oblong 150 miles wide and 350 miles long from north to south. It is situated at a point where the generally west-east lie of the North African coast takes a sharp right-angled jink south to the wide Gulf of Syrte. This means that Tunisia has two distinct coasts. A north coast 150 miles long, an east coast extending 350 miles southward. Tunis, the capital, is in the right angle which links the two coasts at the northeast corner of the country.

Tunisia is generally mountainous though very few peaks exceed three thousand feet. A poor road system makes rapid movement of motorized forces difficult. The mountains and the comparative paucity of small plains and substantial valleys between them favour a defending army, which can dominate large tracts of ground with comparatively few troops holding the dominating high ground.

The Fifth Panzer Army of von Arnim was mainly concentrated in the mountainous north in a bridgehead barring the breakout of Eisenhower's Anglo-American spearhead onto the thirty-five-mile plain leading to the capital. The German-Italian Panzer Army of Rommel (four and a half German Afrika Korps divisions, three Italian, but later to be increased) was busy improving and developing the Mareth line which straddles the coastal route into Tunisia near its southeast corner. The Mareth was a system of natural defences improved by the pre-war French Army with blockhouses and other fortifications to protect Tunisia against invasion from Italian Libya. It was a formidable barrier now to be overcome by Montgomery after his 1600-miles pursuit before he could threaten Tunis from the south.

Kesselring's strategy was to make spoiling attacks on both the Allied armies in turn; taking advantage of the interior line of communications now connecting the two Axis armies, to concentrate the armour of both as required. Eisenhower and Montgomery were to be attacked in turn primarily to delay their own offensive plans. But there were factors which complicated Kesselring's ideas. In the first place the command set-up was awkward. For political reasons Comando Supremo was still in control of operations. In the second, Rommel and von Arnim did not like each other and each wanted to play the situation in his own way.

The first effective Axis action within the new strategy was an attack on the central part of the Allied line between Kasserine and Faid where Major General Orlando Ward's U.S. 1st Armored Division was in position. The Axis commanders saw the danger of a determined American thrust breaking through to the sea, only seventy miles away, thus driving a wedge between the two Axis armies. To forestall this, von Arnim was ordered to attack the American position and he was given Rommel's veteran 21st Panzer Division to carry it out. The inexperienced Americans were taken by surprise and in what became known as the battle of Kasserine lost 150 tanks and 1600 prisoners in addition to many killed and wounded. But 21st Panzer did not rapidly exploit the success—as they would certainly have been made to do if Rommel had been in charge—and the Americans had time to recover and fight back. Nevertheless this success enabled Rommel to move other forces into the Kasserine area, from which he considered that a decisive outflanking of the whole Allied front could be carried out if the armoured and motorized formations of both Axis armies were now concentrated in the area from which the Americans had withdrawn.

Such an attack would aim first at Tebessa, road and rail centre and important forward Allied base on their more southerly front; and from there it would strike north right across the Allied communications. Rommel sensed a psychological advantage. The American soldiers had been shaken by their first encounter with *his* panzers (even though they were on loan to von Arnim at the time); the American generals were inexperienced in handling the quick-thinking mobile operations of which he, Rommel, was the acknowledged master. The Americans, in fact, were in rather the situation the British had been in two years before in the desert. This, thought Rommel, was the moment to exploit that inexperience and establish a moral ascendancy.

But Rommel's enthusiasm was soon damped. His opposite number von Arnim did not see it that way—"probably," said Rommel,[4] "because he wanted to keep the 10th Panzer Division in his sector for a small private show of his own." So Rommel decided to submit his plan straight to Comando Supremo and Commander-in-Chief South. "I put my faith in the habitual overoptimism of Kesselring and the Italians."[5] In the former he was not disappointed, Kesselring at once agreed: but the Italians took their time and had to be sent an urgent reminder before they finally approved the operation—but with a small modification that completely deprived it of its point. The place-names are unimportant, but the point was that Rommel should send the entire armour of both armies northwest so that it would strike well *behind* the Allied front and across its lines of communication. Comando Supremo insisted on the direction being northward, which would bring it hard up against the Allied reserves close behind their front line. This was precisely what Rommel had wished to avoid and the attack failed because it ran into stiff opposition almost at once. To make matters worse, von Arnim's dog-in-the-manager attitude to parting with his 10th Panzer Division had caused him to send only half the division to take part, and under an ineffective commander whose inefficiency contributed to its failure to play a useful part in the proceedings. Applying their reserves to the threatened or breached points with great skill and tenacity the Allies stopped the advance though considerable losses were sustained. At the climax of the attack Rommel asked von Arnim if he could have the nineteen Tiger tanks which Fifth Panzer Army had been sent. These monsters, newly in service, might have turned the scale at this crucial stage of the battle. But von Arnim refused, on the grounds that all the tanks were in workshops for mechanical reasons. Rommel did not believe this, assuming that this was something else that von Arnim was keeping back for his own future operations.

After a week's hard fighting the Americans had made a

fine recovery after the early disaster at Kasserine, and the Allied front had been restored.

Not without justification, Rommel blamed Comando Supremo for ordering the fatal change of direction which prevented "a thrust deep into enemy territory to collapse the whole of their Tunisian front"—as he had intended. And he added that "Clumsy leadership by certain German commanders, and the absence of the forces which had been held back by the rivalry of Fifth Army, led to a premature check in our attack."

The same evening the difficulty of the command situation was corrected by an order from above that the two armies were now regrouped as Army Group Afrika with Rommel in command—an Italian, General Giovanni Messe, taking over Rommel's German-Italian Panzer Army which would now be renamed the First Italian Army. Had this obvious step been taken a month earlier it might have resulted in a different ending to the battle just concluded. But at that time Rommel was out of favour and it was not until Kasserine that, in his own words, he "ceased to be *persona non grata*." [6]

Three days later, on February 26, the Fifth Panzer Army opened a new offensive against the main Allied front in the north. This was von Arnim's "private show of his own" to which Rommel had referred when they were squabbling over who was to have which armoured division.

Striking at six points, von Arnim gained some early successes and it soon became clear that he ws intending to develop a pincer attack on Beja, the forward Allied base in the north as Tebessa was on the southern front. The Allies hit back and the positions where penetrations had been made were soon counterattacked and with one exception, restored. In a week's hard fighting von Arnim, whose efforts were hampered by heavy rain, never succeeded in causing the Allies more than temporary and local anxiety and when he was forced to break off the offensive his losses were greater than those he had inflicted. The Allied line was still intact except for the one penetration in the north which was held. The Commander of Army Group Afrika was not impressed by the showing of General Dietloff von Arnim. Nowhere, wrote Rommel,[7] did the offensive develop into a smooth-running tactical manoeuvre; it was, in fact, "a mere waste of strength."

It made me particularly angry to see how the few Tigers we had in Africa, which had been denied for our offensive in the south, were thrown in to attack through a marshy valley, where their principal advantage—the long range of their heavy guns—was completely ineffective. The heavy tanks either stuck fast in the mud, or were pounded into immobility by the enemy. Of the 19 Tigers which went into action, 15 were lost. It was the same with all the other tanks that went into that narrow valley, large numbers of which were destroyed by the British. I very soon gave orders to Fifth Army to put a stop to the fruitless affair at the earliest possible moment.

The counteroffensive in the centre of the southern part of the front had failed. The effort in the north had failed. Army Group Afrika had one more effort to disrupt and delay the offensive plans of the Allies. Rommel decided to attack Medenine, Montgomery's assembly area for his forthcoming set-piece assault on the Mareth line in the far south of the front. Concentrating the Army Group's three panzer divisions, 10th, 15th, and 21st, he launched the attack early on the morning of March 6. "If it failed," he wrote on the eve of the battle, "in its object of breaking up the Eighth Army's assembly areas and thereby postponing their offensive, the end of the army in Africa would be close." The attack, which struck at Montgomery from three sides, came up against a well-prepared defence incorporating five hundred tanks and as many antitank guns. The panzers kept at their task all day but could make no impression on an unshakable defence. In the evening Rommel, having lost forty tanks totally destroyed in addition to those disabled, called off the attack, depressed that, like the others, this final offensive effort had failed to interfere with Montgomery's preparations.

A great gloom settled over us all. . . . For the Army Group to remain longer in Africa was now plain suicide.[8]

Two days later he handed over the Army Group to General von Arnim and on March 9 he left Africa for Hitler's Headquarters via Rome. As the plane headed out over the Mediterranean Rommel did not know it but he was leaving Africa forever.

For some weeks the Field-Marshal had been mentally and

physically run down and his doctor had been pressing him to ask for sick leave. It was imperative (the doctor said) that he go back into hospital at Semmering for at least eight weeks to resume the treatment that had been cut short by his sudden recall to Africa early in the battle of El Alamein. As Rommel would not ask for sick leave, the doctor had been forced to communicate secretly with Frau Rommel and less secretly with OKW acquainting them with the position. So decisions were being taken of which Rommel as yet had no inkling.

When he set off on the long and familiar journey to Führer Headquarters (in Russia at the time) intending to make the usual stop in Rome, there was no thought of sick leave in his mind. The object of his journey was to bring home to the two dictators the realities of the situation in Tunisia and, if they insisted on continuing a campaign that he personally considered already lost, to obtain authority at least to shorten the present 250-mile front of his Army Group to a tight defensible hundred miles covering Tunis and Bizerte and the northeast corner of the country.

In Rome, Rommel went first to Comando Supremo and talked to General Vittorio Ambrosio, the new Chief of Staff who had recently replaced Marshal Ugo Cavallero; then he had a meeting with Mussolini.[9] He was surprised to find that these two seemed to know more about his future than he did. Both seemed certain that he would not be returning to Africa, but would be sent on sick leave by Hitler. Rommel did his best to make Mussolini face the harsh facts of the situation in Tunisia. The Duce humoured him, offered to send another division to Tunis. Rommel replied tartly that it would be more helpful to send some adequate equipment to the divisions that were already there. The conversation, according to Rommel, then became less cordial, and he later heard that Mussolini had considered his attitude "defeatist," and in consequence had withheld the Italian Gold Medal for Military Valour which he had been going to give him that day. Rommel made preparations to leave for the Führer's headquarters. Goering, who happened to be in Rome, offered to give him a lift in his special train. Rommel declined the offer as he wanted to see Hitler alone without the Reichsmarschall sitting in and making his usual fatuous and overoptimistic interjections that would wreck the import of what he himself had to say. He left Rome on March 10 in his green and yellow Heinkel bomber, reaching Hitler's forward HQ in Russia in the afternoon.

Hitler invited him to take tea with him in the evening. They had a long private session together in which Hitler began by referring gloomily to Stalingrad and then went on to offer some reflections on how defeat tended to warp judgment. He could not accept Rommel's appreciation of Tunisia and what ought to be done about it: Rommel, he thought, had become a pessimist. Rommel strenuously argued that the North Africa divisions should be re-equipped in Italy to enable them to defend the southern flank of Fortress Europe. "I even went so far," he wrote,[10] "as to give him a guarantee—something which I am normally very reluctant to do—that with these troops, I would beat off any Allied invasion in Southern Europe." Hitler was not impressed. He told Rommel to go away and take some sick leave and get thoroughly well again so that he could again take command in North Africa —for operations against Casablanca! Self-delusion had seemingly inflated itself so far that the Führer was quite seriously visualizing a counteroffensive in the summer which would drive the Allies out of Tunisia, all the way back across Algeria and into Morocco—the grand climax to be the recapture of Casablanca. Rommel took off for his temporary family home in Weiner Neustadt, near Vienna, where he was met at the airfield by his fourteen-year-old son Manfred. But it dimmed the joy of the schoolboy, as they warmly shook hands, when the father he idolised said:

"The Führer won't let me go back to Africa again; von Arnim is taking over the Army Group." It seemed incomprehensible to the boy that his father, the admired and famous Rommel, could be in some kind of disgrace.

Two days later the Field-Marshal left with his wife for Semmering to continue the treatment that had been interrupted by El Alamein six months before. Manfred, at school during the week, would visit them each weekend.

It was from the radio, in the sitting room which the hospital placed at his disposal, that Rommel received his only news of the final Allied offensive which, in the next six weeks, brought upon the Axis armies in Tunisia the disaster of which he had for so long been vainly warning his superiors.

Chapter 17

TUNISGRAD

☐ The Allied Supreme Command, like their Axis opposite numbers before them, had been learning, during the early months of the Tunisian campaign, that running an alliance is perhaps the most difficult operation of war. Paying for one's own mistakes is always preferable to paying for what one believes to be the follies of one's friends. Especially in the drastic exigencies of war, and especially when the impulse to blame them has to be curbed by tact.

A front of more than three hundred miles, mainly mountainous and deficient in roads, was being held (at least for the first three months) by dispersed Allied forces of three nationalities distributed in small packets to hold the key pieces of ground. British and American staffs and field commanders, at all levels down to platoon, were operating together for the first time. Despite the potent personal example of General Eisenhower and his official insistence on differences being fused and integrated into a completely Anglo-American outlook and spirit, in the early days there were—not unnaturally—certain clashes of method, style, psychology, personality, and idiosyncrasy which had to be smoothed out. The "barrier of a common language" is not something that can just be treated as if it doesn't exist—as Austrians, for example, know only too well. An added complication was the presence of the French Corps, the Cinderella of the Allied armies—under strength and starved of modern equipment—whose situation *vis à vis* the over-all French political context at this time called for especially sensitive handling. The result was a tentative fighting front lacking cohesion and unified command and this became all too apparent when Rommel and von Arnim began to attack it during the winter and to expose its weak spots.

General Eisenhower, enthroned in Algiers at the far end of the long line of communications from the front, was primarily concerned with the higher logistics of the campaign and the proconsular and political responsibilities of Supreme Command. He therefore could not exercise close control over the day-to-day course of operations at the front. To resolve the problem and to tighten up the whole operational structure of the Allied effort, it was decided at the Casablanca Conference in January to bring in General Sir Harold Alexander (then British C-in-C Middle East) as Eisenhower's Deputy C-in-C with executive control of all fighting forces in Tunisia, which were now to be unfied into a new group of armies to be known as 18th Army Group.

On February 20, Alexander took over 18th Army Group, consisting of the British First Army, which also controlled the U.S. II Corps and the French XIX Corps, and the British Eighth Army which had recently arrived in the south-east corner of Tunisia in the course of its long march from El Alamein. The new Deputy Supreme Commander was an outstanding professional soldier whose military talent was supplemented by a flair for diplomacy and for handling human relationships with firmness and charm. These qualities made him, like Eisenhower, eminently suited to the task of commanding mixed forces.

When Rommel and von Arnim started their winter counter-offensives to disrupt the Allies' own plans, it was Alexander's overhaul of the fighting front, and his rapid adjustments of positions and movements of formations to meet successive tactical crises, that enabled the Allied line to hold firm against the various efforts to break it. There was a new cohesive purpose about the front that had not been there before. By the third week in March he was ready to take the initiative himself and to launch 18th Army Group into the closing phase of the campaign.

He struck first in the southeast on March 20 with a set-piece assault by Montgomery's Eighth Army on the Mareth line. It was Montgomery's most difficult assignment since El Alamein. His plan was to make a frontal attack on the coastal sector of the fortified line to initiate a "dogfight" which would draw the reserves of General Messe's First Italian Army into a battle of attrition. This was Rommel's old army fighting its first battle under its new name and commander and it included the four-and-a-half German divisions of the Afrika Korps who were likely to be prominent in the counterattacks that Montgomery could expect. When the battle had been in progress for a few days and Messe was fully committed, Montgomery intended to surprise him with the second part of his plan: an assault on his rear flank by a strong armoured force dispatched on a wide outflanking march behind the mountain massif which extends twenty miles to the West of Mareth. The "left hook" was to be the trump of the attack and the force assigned to it set off on its circuitous route before the battle opened so as to be in position to launch its assault from the rear when Montgomery gave the word.

As a prelude to the battle the U.S. II Corps under Major General George S. Patton, Jr. was to strike eastward from the Gafsa area towards Gabes on the coast, twenty-five miles north of Mareth. If Patton got through to Gabes he would cut off the Axis line of retreat from Mareth. If, as was more likely, his move provoked an immediate attack from the 10th Panzer Division a short distance to his north, he was to engage that division with all his strength with a view to preventing its moving down to join in the Mareth battle. In the event this is what happened. Patton did not get through to the coast. He did fight a hard battle with 10th Panzer which successfully kept it from helping at Mareth.

Montgomery's left hook was delivered in the afternoon of March 26. On March 28, the eighth day of the battle, the Italian First Army was in full retreat, having lost seven thousand prisoners and (mainly from continual air attack) a large quantity of heavy equipment, especially transport. General von Arnim was now forced to watch the left wing of his Army Group Afrika retreating by rapid stages through the incomplete stop lines at Gabes, Akarit, Sfax, and Sousse until they came to the last prepared defensive position before Tunis, which was at Enfidaville—a hundred miles up the coast from Mareth and only fifty from the capital. Here, von Arnim was confident, Montgomery could be held. It remained to be seen whether Alexander would order Montgomery to attack Enfidaville or whether he would resume the offensive on another part of the front. Von Arnim rather thought it would be the latter. He was right, and he had not long to wait.

The Eighth Army was effectively blocked at Enfidaville. The position was overlooked by mountains and Montgomery's men, seasoned in desert fighting, were out of their element when confronted by mountains. Their first attempts to rush the position failed. Alexander decided it was time to attack on the left and centre of 18th Army Group.

The front of the Tunis bridgehead was now reduced to a hundred miles across the northeast corner of the country. The climactic offensive would be launched by (from right to left) the French XIX Corps, the British First Army, and the U.S. II Corps. Only on the far right would the British Eighth Army hold fast where they were—with the task of maintaining enough local pressure to prevent von Arnim from withdrawing any troops from the Enfidaville sector. Alexander issued his directive on April 16 ordering British First Army to capture Tunis, U.S. II Corps on their left to take Bizerte. On April 20 Kesselring issued a Special Order of the Day exhorting Army Group Afrika to put its trust in the Führer and brace itself for the coming blow. On April 22 Alexander struck.

It was not the kind of offensive that newspapers can report colourfully in terms of place names and spectacular daily mileages. The names were the most unpronounceable Arabic names of unimportant mountains or mountain villages: Djebel this, and Djebel that. It was a grim foot by foot struggle in which the Allied columns—French, American, and British—had to battle for peak after peak, crest after crest, through a complex of razor-back ridges, escarpments, and rocky peaks until they had forced their way to the far edge of the defensive crust. Then and only then could they gather themselves for the final break into the plain that led to the capital. Fifth Panzer Army had been established in this mountain bridgehead all winter. They had worked on it continuously, improving it all the time until their defences were as secure as experienced military engineering could make them. Fifth Panzer Army by this time disposed six German divisions, four Italian. Rent additions included the Panzer Division Hermann Goering (contemptuously described by Rommel as Goering's Praetorian Guard) which, with 10th Panzer, provided the main armoured strength of the army. At every stage the advance was heavily counterattacked. The Allied infantry became discouraged by their slow progress. Fifth Panzer Army became more and more confident. They felt increasingly that if the ammunition supply held out they could stay where they were forever. But then the last crucial heights before the plain were taken in bitter hand to hand fighting. On the left the Americans could now glimpse Bizerte from their observation posts; the British could almost see Tunis. Alexander thought it was time for the knockout and he proposed to deliver it up the axis of the main road from Medjez-el-Bab to Tunis—across the heart of the plain, overlooked by the mountains which the Axis Army had turned into a barrier and which the Allies, recapturing each height at great cost, had transformed into a firm base from which their last shock attack could be launched. The heights that till a few days before had hidden westward-facing German and Italian gun barrels were now filled with American and British guns, facing the other way and ready to support the last advance.

What Alexander now did was to switch two Eighth Army divisions—one armoured, one infantry—from the static Enfidaville sector, grouping them with an armoured and an infantry division of First Army. This assault force, attacking on a narrow front astride the Medjez-Tunis road; with five hundred guns behind them, and an availability of three thousand American and British aircraft to give them round-the-clock support for as long as they needed it; opened the last attack in the early morning of May 6 with its two infantry divisions. By noon they had taken the ridge that was the intermediate objective and by nightfall the two armoured divisions were eight miles ahead of them in the jump-off positions from which they would deliver the knock-out blow the next day. Early on May 7 the two armoured divisions went in for the kill. By early afternoon the British tank men were arguing about who had been first into Tunis—before some of them raced on into Cap Bon, the promontory forty-five miles long, just south of the capital, to cut off and mop up von Arnim's shattered armies now streaming into it. A conforming attack by Major General Omar N. Bradley on the far left carried the American spearhead into Bizerte about the same time.

On May 8 it was all over except for the final mopping-up and the organization of the great numbers of prisoners that were streaming in. On May 13 the formal capitulation of all German and Italian forces in Tunisia was complete.

To the Allied soldiers the shock ending in the brilliant sunshine of May was euphoric. No one who was there would ever forget the hysterical welcome in the streets by the dense crowds of cheering weeping Tunisians proffering jugs of wine and throwing flowers. Generals to their embarrassment were stopped and kissed. After the long winter in foxholes on the barren rainswept mountains, the French-Arab elegance of Tunis, which wartime shabbiness could not entirely obscure, seemed positively Elysian. Tunis was the first ecstatic liberation of a major enemy-held capital. The word *liberate* was still fresh and spontaneous and innocent. It was only later that it turned into a newspaper cliché and then finally degenerated in Northwest Europe into a sick joke.

Most astonishing of all to the victors was the spectacle of the endless truckloads and marching columns of German and Italian troops, moving in disciplined groups without any escort, to give themselves up to anyone who would accept their surrender and tell them where to go. Most of them were smiling, many were laughing and singing. Many were fine physical specimens, smartly dressed and seemingly in excellent heart; certainly bearing little resemblance to an abject defeated army. This was particularly true of those who wore the proud brassard of the Afrika Korps. They had fought desperately to the last: but having now been authorized to surrender they seemed delighted to do so. The Italians were inclined to resort to that garrulous and histrionic cynicism to which the Italian temperament is prone when it thinks it has been let down by its bosses. The Germans were able to converse easily and without embarrassment about their situation as though it were no more than a good game of football which they had happened to lose. Many of them made no secret of their relief that they were headed for prisoner-of-war camps in America or Britain—and not in Siberia.

Tunis restored to the Allies full control of the Mediterranean and the entire North African shore; it rescued the island base of Malta from its long siege; rendered obsolete the danger to Britain's Middle East oil supplies and restored the short sea route to the Far East by way of the Suez Canal.

In the proving grounds of Tunisia the American army, like the British and the Russians the year before, learned the hard way the implications of pitting themselves against the experience and professionalism of the German Army. In Tunisia the Anglo-American alliance passed from a shy and nervous consummation to the total involvement of a happy quarrelsome working marriage. Tunisia saw the re-entry of France into the war. The French corps commanded by General Alphonse Juin—the bluff outspoken gendarme's son who was to become a Marshal of France—was to begin with little more than a hopelessly underequipped token of France's former military glory. But regaining its confidence as it went along, and completely refitted and equipped to full U.S. scale at the end of the campaign, it was to play an important part in the Alliance when the war moved on. Finally, the Tunisian climax, when three thousand Allied aircraft sustained a canopy of complete air supremacy over the battlefield, was a demonstration, as congenial to the Allied soldiers as it was daunting to their opponents, of the "rich man's war" the Allies could now fight and in the months to come would increasingly fight.

Field-Marshal Kesselring, Commander-in-Chief South, summarized the causes of defeat in the following terms:[1]

. . . the main error, in my opinion, lay in a total misunderstanding of the importance of the African and Mediterranean theatre.

The second mistake was the insufficient protection of our sea transport and the gradual breakdown of our supply lines.

The third handicap seemed to me the difficulties of waging a coalition war. Too much giving way and too obvious intransigence were equally harmful . . .

The fourth, and perhaps the most disastrous, error lay in our attitude to France, whose African colonies Hitler incomprehensibly regarded, and insisted on our regarding, as taboo.

Kesselring thought these mistakes "all the more to be deplored because they were largely avoidable." But he did not mention that his own persistent optimism was one of the reasons why they weren't. His summary of the consequences was frank:

"The final battles," Kesselring said, "left the enemy with a sense of superiority which gave an extraordinary boost to his morale." He thought that the loss of Tunisia so soon after that of Tripolitania had greatly shocked the Italians and awakened them to the danger now threatening their motherland, "till then scarcely affected by the war."

Germany, he said, "had accepted the inevitable extension of the war to important parts of the Mediterranean with a certain lethargy and had missed the chance of exploiting her one opportunity to deal a mortal blow at England in a part of the world vital for her."

"Great Britain, the classical Mediterranean power," Kesselring concluded, "had been able, with the aid of the Americans, to establish a jumping-off base for an assault on Europe from the south."

The final statistics of the defeat vary slightly—no official Axis figures being available. The British Official History[2] gives the following record of unwounded prisoners actually held on May 25:

German	101,784
Italian	89,442
Nationality unspecified	47,017
Total:	238,243

The History also quotes an 18th Army Group calculation of prisoners taken between March 20 (the start of the battle of Mareth) and May 13 which gives:

German	157,800
Italian	86,700
Total:	244,500

The United States official history gives an estimated total of 275,000.

Whichever figure is preferred, it was by any reckoning a catastrophe for Hitler on the scale of Stalingrad. His war had reached the end of a tremendous chapter; a chapter that had opened on the snowbound threshold of Moscow at the end of 1941. What Winston Churchill's supercharged rhetoric later called the "hinge of fate" was not turning any more: it had turned. Hitler's enemies were at the southern as well as the western wall of Europe. The storming of the fortress could not be long delayed.

Part Four

SUMMER OF DISCONTENT
THE ENEMY WITHIN THE GATES

(May 1943-June 1944)

Chapter 18

DEFEAT OF THE U-BOATS: KURSK—CATASTROPHIC TURNING POINT IN THE EAST

☐ The role of *farceur* does not commonly suggest itself in connection with the words or deeds of Adolf Hitler. Yet it seems the only term appropriate to an address[1] which he gave to officers on the Eastern Front not long after the collapse in North Africa. He said he had given a great deal of thought to the question whether the Tunisian enterprise, with its losses of men and equipment, had been worthwhile and had decided that it had. By the occupation of Tunisia, he had succeeded in postponing the invasion of Europe for six months. More importantly, Italy, as a result, was still a member of the Axis.

It was a vintage example of the classic technique of explaining a military defeat by suggesting that it was really a subtle kind of victory. Within four months the Führer's words were to seem even more foolish than they did at the time. Tunis was not only the end of the most critical chapter of the war, it marked the start of a summer of discontent in which Hitler was to sustain four more serious setbacks in as many months. The first of them occurred only eleven days after Tunis when he was forced to accept that his U-boats had lost the all-important Battle of the Atlantic.

We have seen how in the previous November, when he was recoiling before the successive hammer blows of El Alamein, the Anglo-American landings in North Africa, and the Stalingrad counteroffensive, his one consolation had been the record of the U-boats, which had sunk 800,000 tons of Allied shipping during the month. This naval blockade of Britain—now, apart from everything else, the unsinkable aircraft carrier and indispensable launching pad from which the final assault on Europe must be mounted—was still something that could still win the war for Hitler. At Casablanca, in January, Roosevelt and Churchill reaffirmed as axiomatic the principle that the U-boat offensive in the Atlantic would have to be defeated before an invasion of Western Europe could be attempted. Accordingly, they urged the Antisubmarine Warfare Committee that they had set up in the summer—and consisting of U.S., Canadian, and British naval and air chiefs and scientific advisers—to hurry up and find a solution to the submarine. They also ordered the United States and British air commanders in Britain to divert substantial forces from other strategic bombing to an assault on the Atlantic ports where the German submarine pens were located: an order received with some annoyance by the air commanders who by this time had come to think that every bomb not dropped on Germany was a bomb wasted.

The Allies' first objective in the Battle of the Atlantic was to reduce the monthly sinkings to a lower rate than their monthly capacity to replace the tonnage lost. It was like a monstrous version of the schoolchild's mathematical teaser about filling a bowl with a hole in it. By the end of 1942 this preliminary goal had not been reached. During the year Allied sinkings[2] totalled a gross tonnage of 7,699,000 while the year's shipbuilding output was only 7,182,000: an adverse gap of 400,000 tons. The "hole" in fact was still emptying the basin faster than the tap could fill it.

In the early part of 1943 the German Navy retained its command of the situation. Admiral Karl Doenitz, who had replaced Grand Admiral Erich Raeder as Commander-in-Chief, by now had four hundred U-boats to draw on. The heavy bombers, brought into the battle as a result of the Casablanca discussions, started an offensive against the U-boat pens at the French Atlantic ports of Brest, Lorient, Saint-Nazaire, La Pallice, and Bordeaux from which the German submarines operated. They dropped 11,000 tons of high explosive,[3] and 8000 of incendiary in four months but with little or no effect, as Air Marshal Harris himself had predicted. The pens were tunnelled into cliff bases, banks, and docks and so heavily protected by concrete as to be virtually invulnerable.

In March the U-boats threatened to equal their record figure of sinkings in the previous November. The area of greatest vulnerability to the Allies was the "air gap" in the middle of the North Atlantic out of range of all their aircraft whether based on the United States, Iceland or Britain. It was to cover this area that Doenitz sent thirty-eight U-boats at the beginning of March to molest convoys known to be sailing from New York and Canadian ports. In the first ten days of the month they sank 229,949 tons (forty-one ships), in the next ten, 282,000 tons (forty-four ships). With losses in other waters this brought the Allied sinkings in three weeks to a total of 627,000[4] tons. There was gloom in London.

Then, as if in support of the adage that it is "darkest before the lights go on" there was a dramatic change. In the last days of the month the battle began to turn against the U-boats and this trend continued through April. In May the Allied losses fell to 260,000 tons. This was still, in truth, serious enough; but there was a vital difference from previously. To achieve this reduced success Doenitz lost forty-one U-boats. This ratio was unprecedented; the German Navy could not stand such a loss rate; Doenitz withdrew his submarine fleet from the Atlantic. Like so many battles that for a long time seem to be a deadlock that will never be resolved, the end, when it came, was sudden—almost an anticlimax.

It had been a curious eerie battle that had gone on silently and invisibly (except for the participants) and of which the ordinary people of Britain and America were hardly aware. There was no ringing of bells when it ended, no victory march to mark the occasion. Its nature was such that time was bound to elapse before the winners could even know that they had in fact won. In June there were grounds for thinking that perhaps they had. In the whole month no attack was made on an Atlantic convoy; moreover seventeen U-boats were sunk.

It was a simple question of arithmetic. Admiral Doenitz worked out that up to a few weeks previously the cost of sinking 100,000 tons was one U-boat, a good return on his investment. By the third week of May the return on one U-boat lost had fallen to 10,000 tons. The investment was no longer profitable. So he withdrew his submarines from the Atlantic. This was not the end of submarine warfare. The U-boat war would continue; but with a different motivation. Henceforth the U-boats would concentrate on distracting and containing Allied naval forces. They would try to harass and interfere with amphibious operations throughout the world. They would never give up their ceaseless efforts to make the Allied sea lanes as hazardous as possible. But the crucial battle of the Atlantic had been lost.

What had caused the sudden transformation in March? There seems to have been no single cause. It was a combination of various new ideas, tactical and technical, which had been coming into operation over a long period and which seem to have come to fruition in concert at that particular time.

Tactically, there was the introduction of naval support groups for the better protection of convoys. These groups were miniature battle fleets and most of them included an aircraft carrier. In the technical field an improved radio location network made it possible to monitor all messages and orders received or transmitted by the U-boats—a considerable aid to their speedier detection. The use of longer-ranged aircraft, as they became available, made it possible to reduce the "air gap" in mid-Atlantic. The detection of U-boats and direction-plotting by escort vessels were made almost infallible by new high-frequency radar equipment. The effectiveness of depth charges was enhanced by the introduction of a projector enabling them to be fired in salvos and also by new types of depth-charge that could be detonated in deeper water than hitherto or, alternatively, could be fused to explode at a shallow depth. Once these new Allied techniques for hunting, locating, and attacking the U-boat packs had surmounted their teething troubles and had come into practised use at the end of March, life quickly became unbearable for the German submariners.

It may be an exaggeration to suggest that at this comparatively late stage, success in the Battle of the Atlantic could have won the war for Hitler. What is beyond dispute is that, by cutting this umbilical lifeline between Britain and America, the German Navy could have grievously—perhaps fatally—delayed and disrupted the Allied schedule for the climactic invasion project of 1944. It was a defeat for Hitler not less important than that which had been sustained by his armies in Tunisia a short time before. That he did not seem particularly aware of this was further evidence that sea power—its importance and its implications—was something he never understood.

With the trend of events in the West, the realities of a two-front war were beginning to be seriously felt by the German leadership. The dichotomy in the higher direction of the war effort on land was not the least of it. From the start, the campaign in the East had been under the immediate control of the Army High Command, *OKH:* all other land fronts came under the higher Armed Forces Headquarters, *OKW*, Hitler alone being common to both as C-in-C of the former and Supreme Commander of the latter. OKH, controlling some two hundred divisions in a gigantic campaign in which they had almost lost the initiative, had a whole-time occupation and could hardly be expected to take seriously what might be happening to a handful of divisions in the Mediterranean. For OKH and their Chief of Staff, Kurt Zeitzler, there was only one war. At OKW, on the other hand, the large Allied Army, Navy, and Air Forces now within easy reach of the whole of southern Europe were exceedingly disturbing: especially as no one, from Hitler down, had much doubt that the Italians would soon desert their ally. Hitler was hardly the stabilizing influence to hold the balance between the conflicting preoccupations of East and West, i.e. between OKH and OKW, that would now become even more necessary: the more especially as his fanatic obsession about security always ensured that left hands under his command were never allowed to know what right hands were doing.

At OKW the immediate question was where the Allies would go from Tunis. Sicily, to some of the Axis strategists, seemed an obvious choice not only as a steppingstone to the Italian mainland, from which it is separated by only the three-mile Straits of Messina, but also to secure the northern side of the Sicilian narrows, thus clinching the Allied clearance of the Mediterranean. An invasion of Sicily could be supported by a simultaneous landing in Calabria, the "toe" of Italy. In addition Sicily was within range of fighter air cover from Tunis, only eighty miles away. On the other hand (thought others) Sardinia would be a better choice from the point of view of subsequent operations against the mainland north of Rome. Corsica was another strong possibility. It had the advantage of being even farther north, and would make a jump-off area for an invasion of northern Italy or southern France. Yet another possibility was the Balkans, with a view to an advance northeastward to strike at the rear of the German armies in Russia. The Balkans, however, could not be invaded directly from North Africa (anyway not with the air cover it was assumed the Allies would require); but an attack on this quarter could be made from southern Italy. Field-Marshal Kesselring who—as C-in-C South—was the commander primarily concerned, favoured Sicily because, as an airman before he became a land commander, it came naturally to him to assume that air support would be the decisive factor governing the Allies' choice. Marshal Pietro Badoglio and other senior Italians—perhaps to assert their superior knowledge in regard to their own territory—maintained that Sardinia would be the militarily correct place to make for if Rome was to be an early objective. The Balkans theory was successfully stimulated by a felicitously macabre ruse of British Intelligence which arranged for an English corpse to be washed up on the Spanish coast; the corpse apparently that of a courier whose plane had been shot down. The skilfully faked plans and maps found on the body related to an invasion of Sardinia and the Peloponnese. The

Spanish authorities handed over the papers to the Germans who were partly taken in, at least to the extent of reinforcing Greece from the Eastern Front with an armoured division that could neither be spared from Russia nor perform any useful function in the mountainous terrain to which it had been sent.

On June 22, General Frido von Senger und Etterlin presented himself,[5] as instructed, for an audience with Hitler at OKW. The headquarters was at the time on the Obersalzburg for one of those interludes when the Führer needed the spiritual comfort of his eyrie at Berchtesgaden to listen to a little Lohengrin and to feel, perhaps, on his brow the soothing hand of his housekeeper-mistress Eva Braun. Though a veteran of both world wars, von Senger was comparatively junior in command, having lately commanded the panzer division in Russia which came closest to Stalingrad during the unsuccessful attempt to relieve the Sixth Army at the end of the previous year. A tall, scholarly intellectual with the long legs and slight stoop of many cavalrymen, he was the antithesis of what is commonly imagined (outside Germany) to be the "typical German officer." His tall spare body, topped by a round head conspicuous for its beaky nose and large deep-set round eyes, gave him the aspect of a kindly but melancholy outsize bird. He loved Italy and spoke the language well, so he had been an obvious choice to serve as a German liaison officer on the Franco-Italian Armistice Commission which sat in Turin in 1940 after the defeat of France.

Among those in attendance on the Obersalzburg were General Warlimont, the Assistant Chief of Operations and Field-Marshal Keitel, OKW Chief of Staff who was more privately regarded as Hitler's most senior lackey; the infinite yes-man who had the gift of being able to agree with Hitler even before he had said anything. It was Keitel who told von Senger why he had been summoned to this august company. The Führer had decided to make him responsible for the defence of Sicily against a possible Allied invasion. That was the assignment, but in deference to Italian sensitivity at this particular time, von Senger was to perform his assigned task in the capacity of liaison officer to the Italian commander on the spot, General Alfredo Guzzoni.

He then saw Hitler privately, when the Führer held forth at length on the feasibility of defending Sicily with two German divisions without having to call on the Italians. Hitler made it clear that he thought the defection of his Italian ally was imminent as a result of "the machinations of the

219

Court, Society, the General Staff, et cetera." [6] In addition to the two divisions—one already there, the other on the way —there were 30,000 other German troops in the island; anti-aircraft units, Luftwaffe ground staff, supply, ordnance, and administrative people of various kinds; and Hitler discussed with von Senger the practicability of turning some of these into combat personnel and forming them into what he called "alarm units." He concluded with a critical assessment of the strategy of the Allies who "through failing to leap across to Sicily immediately after their landings in North Africa, had already lost the struggle in the Mediterranean." General Warlimont, with whom von Senger lunched after his session with Hitler, took a more practical view of the Sicily assignment. In the event of a major Allied operation against Sicily (Warlimont suggested) it would be best to evacuate as many German troops as possible to the mainland, leaving their heavy equipment behind.

From OKW von Senger went to Rome to continue the discussion with his new C-in-C, Field-Marshal Kesselring, who radiated his customary optimism. Like others who had professional dealings with the Field-Marshal, von Senger thought that he was a little too optimistic about the prospect of defending Sicily with two German divisions and an Italian garrison, but approved of his continuing faith in the loyalty of the Italians. Kesselring refused to take for granted, as the rest of the German Hierarchy appeared to be doing, that the defection of Italy could be expected at any moment. In any case he took the realistic view that for the time being the only possible course open to the scanty German forces charged with the defence of the Italian islands was one of maximum co-operation with the faltering ally. It was easy for Kesselring and von Senger to be in accord about this as both of them happened to like the Italians. But if the Italophile Kesselring managed, as was his way, to view too optimistically the prospect of defending the three islands, his considered view (which he recorded later) was less glowing.

On the maps everything was in order . . . But the only construction work done was mere eyewash. There were no prepared positions on the islands, which were inadequately defended, and had unguarded tank obstacles more likely to hamper the defenders than to check the enemy—all so much gingerbread.

The coastal divisions I inspected were on a par with

the fortifications. With such troops in these defences it was hopeless to offer resistance. There were differences: Corsica was the best, then came Sardinia; Sicily and the Calabrian coast left much to be desired.[7]

From Rome, Kesselring and von Senger flew to Sicily where they met General Guzzoni, C-in-C of the Italian Sixth Army, to discuss with him the defence plan. In addition to the two German divisions, one still in transit, Guzzoni had four understrength Italian mobile divisions and six so-called Coastal Defence divisions. Kesselring's opinion of this Italian garrison and its coastal defence preparations has been noted. With engaging candour, General Guzzoni admitted that he was relying on the two German formations (15th Panzer Grenadier and Hermann Goering Panzer Divisions) as the mainstay of his defence. He proposed to concentrate them and hold them well back as a main counterattack force, using two of the Italian mobile divisions to blunt the edge of the first advance of any landing force. Kesselring had no authority to change this but persuaded the Comando Supremo to do so. The revised plan divided the German divisions between the east and west of the island. Kesselring told the German divisional commanders: "It makes no difference whether or not you get orders from the Italian Army HQ at Enna. You must go into immediate action against the enemy the moment you ascertain the objective of the invasion fleet." This was in line with German anti-invasion doctrine that the landing must be smashed immediately; on the beaches if possible. General von Senger noted that, while Kesselring retained his habitual air of optimism, General Guzzoni remained stubbornly sceptical.

By the beginning of July the Sicily defences were as ready as they would ever be except for one detail. Field-Marshal von Richthofen (now C-in-C of Second Air Fleet) believed that Kesselring was wrong and that Sardinia was most likely to be the next Allied objective. With the characteristic, and often impudent, independence of the Luftwaffe, he had therefore moved the bulk of his air strength to that island instead of Sicily.

Thus Sicily, unhappy impoverished Mafia-ridden Sicily; stamping ground through many centuries of many conquerors—Greek, Carthaginian, Roman, Turk, Norman, Spaniard, Frenchman, Moor; Italy's forsaken Deep South, the chronic bane and immemorial problem child of every Italian government, lay back, like a woman to whom rape has become habitual, and fatalistically awaited her newest conqueror. Of all those who waited in some tension to see whether this was where the Allies would next invade, those who manifested the least concern, and in some cases welcomed the prospect, were the Sicilians themselves. Despite their long heritage of conquest and occupation, they had had enough of the corrupt tyranny of Fascism and the administrative neglect and indifference that went with it. They had had enough of the recent occupation by the German armed forces (mostly Luftwaffe) many of whom regarded them, in the Hitlerian manner, as a sub-human species. On the other hand many Sicilians had been to America or had been visited by relatives and friends who had emigrated to the United States. They had a naive conception of the U.S.A. as a great dreamland across the sea where everyone was rich and everything perfect. If the Americans did decide to append themselves to the long inventory of Sicily's conquerors, they would be surprised to find in almost every village a man ready to welcome them in that uniquely quaint brand of broken English that combines with comical infelicity the cadences of Palermo and the Bronx.

In the first hot days of July, as Italian soldiers—their tunics unbuttoned, cigarettes dangling from their lips—lounged listlessly against Sicily's unfinished defence works; and as the master minds of OKW endlessly debated where and when the Allies would strike and how soon the Italians would secede from the war; Hitler's "other" headquarters OKH—now becoming, as we have seen, almost a rival to OKW—abruptly seized the centre of the stage. On July 5 it initiated on the Eastern Front an offensive of such concentrated power and fury that it eclipsed anything that had gone before. It was as if OKH were determined to assert their priority, to show once and for all that theirs was the real war, the war that mattered. For the new offensive was not Hitler's idea, nor was it OKW's and there were divided counsels about its wisdom. It was General Kurt Zeitzler, the Army Chief of Staff, who was its most persistent champion from first to last; almost as if he were determined to push it through if only to score a victory for OKH at the expense of OKW. It was called Operation Citadel and it had a long involved history.[8]

It will be recalled that, after the Stalingrad disaster and the withdrawal from the Caucasus at the beginning of the year, Field-Marshal von Mannstein had stabilized and reconstituted the front of Army Group South and had eventually halted the Russian winter offensive. He had then demonstrated the recuperative power of his army group by hitting back at the Russians and recapturing Kharkov in March. This left the Russian line with a U-shaped salient about eighty miles wide with Kursk in its centre and Orel and Bielgorod on its northern and southern shoulders respectively. An immediate pincer attack on the Kursk salient from north and south had been considered by von Mannstein but was rejected for various reasons, the chief of which was the imminence of the spring thaw which would transform the steppe into a glutinous morass impossible for tank operations. But Operation Citadel had been born and General Zeitzler, who was to become its most fervent and persistent advocate, made sure that the baby was nourished and cared for.

In April—by which time von Mannstein was thinking in terms of alternative offensive ideas—Zeitzler brought up Citadel again and carried it a stage farther by submitting a memorandum about it to Hitler. He proposed the same pincer attack on the salient from north and south, Army Group Centre (Field-Marshal von Kluge) to attack the northern corner of the bulge using Field-Marshal Model's Ninth Army; Army Group South (Field-Marshal von Mannstein) to attack the southern end using General Hoth's Fourth Panzer Army. Zeitzler suggested that ten or twelve panzer and a similar number of infantry divisions should be sufficient for the task. Hitler hesitated, considering the suggested amount of armour inadequate. It would be unwise, he thought, to undertake further offensives until the new Panther tank—now being nursed through its teething troubles—became available in quantity. The victory at Kharkov in March had been due in the main to the surprise debut of the Tiger tank. The Panther (thought Hitler) might have the same shock effect this time.

At this point the Citadel discussion was thrown open "to the floor" and furious argument pro and con took place. Zeitzler, whose pet project it had become, was passionately in favour and promoted it as if he were defending the honour of OKH. Field-Marshal Gunther von Kluge, whose Army Group Centre had been on the defensive since late 1941, was strongly in favour of it as an opportunity for his own personal glory. But Field-Marshal Walther Model, von Kluge's subordinate, the Army commander who would actually be carrying it out, had reservations and was against it unless he could be greatly strengthened: he thought the plan rather obvious and what he had seen of the Russian preparations in his sector made him think that they too thought the project obvious and would have prepared thoroughly and extensively to meet it. Model was partly won over by the promise of substantial numbers of the new Panther tanks but he was still not over-keen.

Jodl, who as Operations Chief of OKW had to view the war broadly and as a whole, was strongly against Citadel on the grounds that it would absorb too many armoured reserves at the precise time when they were likely to be needed to meet the imminent Anglo-American activities in the West. The conflict between Zeitzler and Jodl was bitter and personal and epitomized the rivalry, already referred to, between the two headquarters and the conviction of the Eastern generals that theirs was the only war that counted.

The most outspoken opponent of Citadel was—voice from the past—General Heinz Guderian, Germany's finest tank general and foremost tank theorist; architect of the early blitzkrieg victories based on armoured pre-eminence; the German general who had absorbed and developed the theories of armoured warfare, expounded between the wars by the British military philosopher Liddell Hart, and had brilliantly realized them on the battlefield. Guderian was one of those who had been frivolously dismissed in the "purge of the generals" at the end of 1941 after the failure before Moscow. As he was still the German Army's greatest tank expert, both practical and theoretical, Hitler had been forced to recall him from the wilderness earlier in the year. Since the beginning of March he had been Inspector General of Armoured Troops with the double task of overhauling the panzer arm and its tactics for the final phases of the war; and of collaborating with Albert Speer, the Minister for Armaments and War Production, in the choice and development of new types of tank.

In the interminable arguments of the summer for and against Citadel, an additional complicating factor was a bitter personal feud between General Guderian,[9] vigorously *against* it, and Field-Marshal von Kluge equally strongly *for*. The feud dated back to the events before Moscow in 1941. Guderian believed that his dismissal had been precipitated through his being reported by von Kluge to Hitler as disloyal. Guderian had never forgiven him. A Citadel conference in Munich at the beginning of May brought the two men together for the first time since 1941. The Field-Marshal's greeting was unfriendly. Guderian returned the compliment with equal frostiness. Later there was an acrimonious exchange of words when von Kluge asked Guderian to explain his attitude and Guderian replied curtly that the Field-Marshal had never put right his action of 1941, though Guderian had subsequently been completely vindicated. No more was said on this occasion but some time later Guderian was astonished to hear from a Führer aide that von Kluge had written to Hitler informing him that he was challenging Guderian to a duel and would the Führer please act as his second! There devolved upon Hitler of all people the appeaser's task of metaphorically banging two of his senior generals' heads together and ordering them to stop being silly. With unconscious humour Guderian comments: "Herr von Kluge knew perfectly well that duelling was prohibited and that Hitler would never have countenanced two of his generals fighting one another in wartime. All the same he requested Hitler to act as his second." (Letters of apology and conciliation eventually closed this bizarre embellishment to the great Citadel controversy.) Meanwhile the argument went on, Hitler—which was unusual for him—remaining undecided and justifying his indecision by blaming it on the uncertainty about the Panthers. On May 10 some of this uncertainty was dispelled.

On that day Guderian attended a meeting at the Chancellery in Berlin at which an official from the Armaments Ministry was to report to Hitler on tank production. He reported that the industry could guarantee 324 Panthers by May 31. Guderian, who had been attending field trials, nevertheless remained unconvinced that the Panthers were yet battleworthy. As this was one conference at which none of the Citadel enthusiasts was present, Guderian took advantage of the occasion to make a personal plea to Hitler to drop it:[10]

> After the conference I seized Hitler's hand and asked him if I might be allowed to speak frankly to him. He said I might and I urged him earnestly to give up the plan for an attack on the Eastern front; he could already see the difficulties that confronted us; the great commitment would certainly not bring us equivalent gains; our defensive preparations in the West were sure to suffer considerably. I ended with the question: "Why do you want to attack in the East at all this year?"

Here Keitel, ever at hand with a sycophantic banality, chimed in with the comment that they must attack "for political reasons." Which brought from Guderian the blistering reply:[11]

> How many people do you think even know where Kursk is? It's a matter of profound indifference to the world whether we hold Kursk or not. I repeat my question: Why do we want to attack in the East at all this year? Hitler's reply was: "You're quite right. Whenever I think of this attack my stomach turns over." I answered: "In that case your reaction to the problem is the correct one. Leave it alone!"

Boiled down to its simplest terms, this was the essence of the argument about the Kursk offensive, Citadel.

The lobby in favour (OKH and a majority of Eastern generals—but not Model and not von Mannstein) believed that they must beat the Russians to the draw and deliver a crushing blow that would cripple their army for months: that to do this they must concentrate everything they could lay their hands on.

The opposition (OKW and Guderian, who was directly concerned in his capacity of Inspector General of Armoured Forces) held that it was folly to put all the armoured eggs in the Eastern basket at the very time the Anglo-American armies with their vast material strength were about to move in the West.

But it was the "Easterners" to whom Hitler in the end gave way and Citadel proceeded to its final sequence of delays, postponements, and last-minute alterations of plan. These endless continuing delays made von Mannstein, hitherto cagily noncommittal, turn firmly against the offensive. When at last it opened on July 5, few operations had so deservedly merited that definitive lament of the much messed-about soldier, "It's all been changed again!"

The German plan was still essentially the same; its aim to iron out the Kursk salient by a pincer attack on its northern and southern flanks by two armies. But since the first plan the forces to be used had been greatly strengthened by milking the rest of the Front of its armour and delving deep into the central reserve. The final line-up was formidable indeed.

Field-Marshal Model's Ninth Army, which was to attack the north shoulder of the salient from the area of Orel, had been built up to seven panzer, two panzer grenadier and nine infantry divisions: General Hoth's Fourth Panzer Army would assault the salient's southern end from the area of Bielgorod with ten panzer, one panzer grenadier, and seven infantry divisions. This meant a total of seventeen panzer divisions in the two converging armies each of which had about fifty miles to advance before they met east of Kursk. Not only was there this unprecedented preponderance of tanks which would be led by the Tigers and followed up by the Panthers, which the Russians would be meeting for the first time: but the infantry were the best fighting formations on the Eastern Front, including the fanatical and ruthlessly efficient regular divisions of the Waffen-SS, the *Das Reich, Liebstandardte,* and *Totenkopf* Divisions. These immensely strong armies, each of eighteen divisions, constituted a pincer without precedent in concentrated power. Mindful of the ease with which the first onrush of the German summer offensives had initially swept all before them in the previous two years, it was taken for granted that this third summer offensive would prove as irresistible as its predecessors. Nothing, it had become customary to assume, could ever withstand the first shock of a German all-out offensive. This time however it was not irresistible. What went wrong?

There is no need to be a military expert to understand why the accepted vulnerability of a salient (or bulge) in a line of organized defences is a basic military cliché. Any salient automatically creates two flanks forward of the main line. By attacking both at once, the attacker can trap or destroy anyone and anything in the pocket which becomes a compact, convenient killing ground. From this fundamental principle one may go further and say that a salient is a salient is a salient—for those within as well as those outside. Because its vulnerability is so obvious, the defender may choose to exploit this very fact. He may go so far as to flaunt the salient as a standing temptation to the attacker to try to squeeze it out, thereby channelling his attention and diverting him from surprise attack elsewhere. He may then pack the area with defences so strong that the salient acquires a fortress-like identity capable of withstanding siege and breaking up the attacks made upon it. This was what the Russians did.

Ever since March they had taken it for granted that the Germans would sooner or later try to smooth out the Kursk salient. The Germans liked order, tidiness. The salient made the front untidy. They would be sure to try to rectify this. Very well, then. The Russians would make sure that any attempt to eliminate the salient would find it a hard proposition. For three months they developed defences in depth from the outer perimeter. Half a million railway wagons brought in men and heavy equipment. By July there were four Soviet armies defending the salient under Generals Rokossovsky, Popov, and Vatutin with a tank army in reserve. The artillery concentration was vast—with 20,000 guns of all types and 900 multiple rocket projectors. Mines were laid in thousands. The Kursk salient had been transformed from a supposedly tender scab into an impregnable fortified bridgehead surging forward of the rest of the line like a huge disguised dreadnought broadside on. The defenders were rehearsed and rehearsed again in exercises covering every possible variation of attack that they might have to face. Every foot of ground was exhaustively reconnoitred. Crossing places over streams and rivers were signposted. No detail was overlooked.

By July 5 the Kursk salient had become quite the most prickly sector of the Russian front on which to attempt a battle of annihilation. Nevertheless the two German armies, assembled at such cost in reserves to the army as a whole, rolled forward into the great ocean swell of ripening corn which the south Russian steppe becomes at this time of year. From the start the offensive began to go wrong. The first thing was that neither German army succeeded with its initial onslaught in making the irresistible first penetration that was taken for granted. Always in the past the enemy had crumpled before the terrible opening shock attacks. This time they did not crumple. The High Command had fatally miscalculated. The brave but bewildered and unskilled hordes they had so easily overwhelmed in each of the two previous summers had matured through experience and training into an efficient professional army whose war industry, now safely re-established behind the Urals, was providing it with unlimited supplies of equipment at least equal, and often superior, to the German. From the start the irresistible force met the immovable object at both ends of the salient and it became a brutal fight to the death between mammoth and mastodon. The second German miscalculation was that they produced no new tactical ideas. They were relying mainly on their new and nearly new heavy tanks, accompanied by close-support infantry, to have the bulldozing effect of the Macedonian phalanx.

The Tigers, though equipped with the deadly 88-millimetre gun and thick frontal armour, were slow; the Russians who had met them before had evolved a new artillery tactic of quickly concentrating several antitank guns on a single tank. The new Panthers, being used in the follow-up waves of the attacks, were (as Guderian had warned) not yet wholly ready for battle. They developed mechanical faults and caught fire too easily. The third new armoured fighting vehicle on which the Germans were relying was the Ferdinand, a heavy (100 millimetre) mobile gun mounted on a modified Tiger tank chassis. There were ninety of these monsters ready in time for the battle and they were all given to Model's Ninth Army in the north. Formidable though they undoubtedly were, they had a fatal weakness: they had no secondary armament of a machine gun—unlike the tanks which they so closely resembled. With their huge gun they were devastating against tanks, pill-boxes, fortified buildings: but once they had broken through to the infantry positions they had (in Guderian's words) "to go quail-shooting with cannons." The Russians soon discovered this weakness. The Ferdinands had to withstand not only the new antitank gun tactics of the Russians, as well as the curtains of defensive fire laid down by the rest of their artillery, they had also to reckon with Russian infantry brave enough to let them pass through their positions before emerging from their foxholes to shoot them from behind with bazookas.

After four days Model in the north had bogged down after penetrating only six miles into the salient. Hoth in the south had done little better: at great cost Fourth Panzer Army had penetrated nine miles on a fifteen-miles front. The two armies were still about eighty miles apart. Appalling losses in men and machines had been sustained by both sides. The last crust of the Russian defensive belt still defied the panzers' efforts to break out. The German nutcracker had closed not on a nut but on a granite boulder: and the nutcracker it was that cracked.

General Hoth, the more successful—or the less unsuccessful—of the two Army commanders decided to make a final supreme effort to drive the tanks of Fourth Panzer Army through. He formed a new assault force by grouping together all the survivors and spare units he could muster from his battered and exhausted Panzer divisions and launched them in a do-or-die effort to break out of the Russian defence ring at no matter what cost. Marshal Zhukov, the Front commander, now played his trump. As the battle-weary six hundred German tanks clattered forward through the choking dust, the pitiless heat and the ubiquitous, almost tangible, miasma of

150,000 unburied dead, they met not the last screen of a hard-pressed defence, but the entirely fresh Russian Fifth Tank Army of whose existence they did not even know, and which Zhukov had kept in reserve for just this contingency. The two tank armies—one fresh, the other worn out—fought the issue out for eight hours. It was the final showdown. By the end of the day Hitler's offensive capability in Russia had been broken for ever.

The Germans had lost not less than 2000 tanks and 70,-000 men killed in a week's fighting. The Russian losses were almost as heavy—but they had unlimited replacements. Hitler's central armoured reserve had been prodigally wasted away in a battle he himself did not want and which his saner advisers had strongly advised him against undertaking. Kursk was the true military turning point of the war in the East that Salingrad had not been. Next day Hitler called off Citadel. Almost at once the Russians hit the Germans on the rebound with a counteroffensive that took them flooding out of the Kursk salient at Orel and Bielgorod and far beyond, in an advance on a broad front that was to continue until the end of the year. The High Command of the German Army had tried to forestall this offensive by crippling the armies that would carry it out. Instead, they had seen their own armies crippled in the Kursk salient, which had turned out to be the graveyard of the panzers and the panzer legend in Russia. But Hitler now had new worries.

On July 10, the fifth day of Kursk, the Western Allies invaded Sicily.

Chapter 19

INVASION OF SICILY— CALCINATION OF HAMBURG

□ To the Germans it was a question of *where*—Sicily? Sardinia? South Italy? Greece?—and they had finally placed an each way bet on Greece and Sardinia, helped in reaching this conclusion by the British corpse (referred to earlier) that had been washed up, by arrangement, on the Spanish coast and handed over by the Spanish authorities together with the bogus plans for landings in Sardinia and the Peloponnese which the corpse was carrying.

To the Italians it was more a question of *when*. They had not the slightest doubt that the invasion of Italy was near and it did not matter much which of the offshore islands was used as the steppingstone. It would be dreadful anyway. They felt increasingly that they had "had" the war and had also by this time "had" their tiresomely keen, hearty and rather over-bearing allies. In the first week of July, as the Allied Mediter-ranean air forces, now swollen to an operational strength of four thousand aircraft, began a systematic round-the-clock devastation of all Axis airfields in Sicily, Sardinia, and South-ern Italy, it was still no clearer which of these particular areas was to be honoured by the actual assault; but it did now seem beyond doubt that they would not have to wait long to find out.

On July 9, a moderately strong *tramontana* was blowing. This is the cool, sometimes cold, northerly wind which can suddenly blow up in southern Italy: the Italian counterpart of southern France's *mistral* which blows southward off that country's central plateau. Like the *mistral* the *tramontana* can blow hard and cold, even under a cloudless summer sky, swiftly whipping the sea into a flurry of white-capped waves. When this happens the Italians become fretful and irritable. For, like all people who are habitually warmed and spoiled by taken-for-granted sunshine and a summer climate that is generally close to perfection, they react impatiently and even with anger when the weather happens briefly to fall from grace. "*Fa bruto!*" they grumble, turning up their col-lars and shivering histrionically, "*Fa cattivo!*" But when, on July 9, 1943, the *tramontana* bore down upon Sicily, the Ital-ian soldiers who were manning its 475 miles of coast fore-bore this once to curse it and cry "*Fa cattivo!*" Instead, they were cheerfully calling to one another, "*Va bene!* They will not invade tonight. It is too rough for a landing." After days of false alarms, latrine rumours, practice alerts and contra-dictory orders, the Italian soldiers felt confident that the heavy swell provoked by the wind in the Sicilian narrows would guarantee them at least one quiet night, perhaps more, for a *tramontana* could last for several days. For once they blessed the *tramontana*.

One man who was not blessing it was the Royal Navy's Admiral Sir Andrew Cunningham, whose flagship was riding the agitated waters somewhere off Sicily. Cunningham was in command of the vast armada of 2600 Allied ships forming up in the narrows for the assault on Sicily. Cunningham had to make an unenviable decision. As the hours of July 9 ticked away and the weather worsened he had to decide whether or no the invasion could go in early next morning as planned. Provision had been made for an alternative plan in the event of a postponement proving unavoidable, but the decision would have to be made not later than noon on the 9th. It was after this deadline had passed that the weather deteriorated. There was gloom at Eisenhower's Advance Headquarters in Tunis, and in London and Washington, as the meteorological reports became increasingly unfavourable through the afternoon. It may be assumed that Cunningham directed at the *tramontana* (if not by that name) some of the choicer nautical curses for which seafaring men have ever been celebrated. When the Admiralty in London again asked him at 2000 hours what he had decided, he signalled: "Weather not favourable, but operation proceeding." Fortune, as is proper, favoured the boldness of his decision. From midnight the weather steadily improved, and the wind died away leaving only the uncomfortable swell that it had kneaded in the central Mediterranean.

The invasion fleet that came together to invade Sicily was the largest to date of the Second World War. The 2600 vessels ranged from the largest American and British battleships and aircraft carriers, to the smallest assault landing craft, motor torpedo boats and armed trawlers. The expedition was mounted in Gibraltar and Malta and in nearly every North African port from Casablanca to Suez. Enough transports had to be found to carry the assault waves of an army group consisting of six divisions of General George S. Patton's U. S. Seventh Army and seven of General Montgomery's British Eighth Army. In each case one of the divisions was armoured, with all that that implied in terms of exorbitant shipping space. The 1st Canadian Division joined Montgomery direct from Britain, the U. S. 9th Division, commanded by Major General Manton S. Eddy, came direct from the States pausing only at Casablanca. All these components of the armada, prepared in such wide dispersion, had to be escorted by naval units from their ports of loading to their final assembly position in the Sicilian narrows. Units of Major General Matthew B. Ridgway's U.S. 82nd Airborne Division and the British 1st Airborne Division were to precede the invasion by dropping to seize bridgeheads and key positions in front of their respective armies.

Sicily is an isosceles triangle lying on its side. Its long sides (north and south coasts) are about 175 miles long, its base (east coast) about 120. On the east coast are the ports of Augusta, historic Syracuse, Catania, and Messina, the ferry-port connecting with Reggio on the "toe" of Italy. Palermo the capital is near the western tip of the north coast. Etna, the 10,700-foot volcano, the island's most dominating physical feature, is in the northeast corner and bars the roads to Messina from south and west. The interior of the island is hot, mountainous, arid, and almost roadless—ideal for a defender fighting a delaying action.

The two Allied armies, under General Eisenhower's supreme command but under the executive control of General Alexander's 15th Army Group, both landed in the southeast of the island: Montgomery, on the right, headed first for Augusta and thence northward to Catania and the airfields on the plain inland from it; Patton at several points from sixty to eighty miles to Montgomery's left near Gela and Licata. The airborne landings were the least successful part of the venture, many gliderborne troops being dropped by their towing aircraft into the sea, paratroop units suffering heavy losses and excessive scattering for the few successful results achieved. But the main invasion proceeded without much difficulty. The bad weather of the previous day, and the consequent belief of the Italians that no invasion could take place, enabled the invaders to achieve surprise. The low quality coastal defence divisions of whom little had been expected offered even less; they resisted hardly at all and seemed delighted to seek out the comparative tranquillity of the prisoner-of-war cages. The only serious resistance was offered by the one German division in the east of the island, the Hermann Goering Panzer Division which counterattacked the American invaders at Gela with tanks and infantry and drove them back to within five hundred yards of the beach before being forced back themselves. The other German division, 15th Panzer Grenadier, positioned (on Kesselring's orders) in the west of the island was kept there, during the vital early hours, by a feint attack designed to make the defenders expect a major landing in the west. Thereafter their move to the east was further delayed by Sicily's inadequate interior roads. This was how the invasion seemed to Field-Marshal Kesselring the Axis commander.[1]

One disappointment followed another. The Italian coastal divisions were an utter failure, not one of their counterattack divisions reached the enemy in time or even at all . . . The commandant of the fortress of Augusta meanwhile surrendered without even waiting to be attacked.

On July 12 Kesselring flew to Sicily after ordering the German 1st Parachute Division to fly to the island from Calabria immediately. He also ordered General Hube and the headquarters of XIV Panzer Corps to move to Sicily and take charge of the three German divisions now there or on their way, and in addition he asked OKW to let him have a fourth division, 29th Panzer Grenadiers, also in Italy. The Germans had feared that any landing in Sicily would be supported by landings elsewhere, in particular in Calabria where a landing would have cut off at a stroke all their forces in Sicily. Kesselring later criticized the Allies for missing this trick.

The absence of any large-scale encirclement of the island or of a thrust up the coastline of Calabria gave us long weeks to organize the defence with really very weak resources.[2]

This is Kesselring writing about the campaign in his *Memoirs*. But at the time he was grateful that the Allied advance was manifesting the methodical orthodoxy the Germans had come to associate with the performance of General Montgomery; and equally grateful that the difficult Sicilian terrain was no kind of country in which the volatile, impulsive General Patton could display his panache in the command of tanks. There were only a few areas in Sicily where tanks were of any use at all.

It took Kesselring only forty-eight hours to decide with relief that no collateral landing in Calabria was intended by General Alexander, so that he could immediately begin to transfer to Sicily the two divisions (1st Parachute and 29th Panzer Grenadier) that had been held there against that eventuality. These divisions took some time to complete their move. But on the fifth day of the invasion, by which time Montgomery and Patton had joined up to form a continuous front of a hundred miles across the southeast corner of the island, Kesselring had most of four German divisions on a defence line anchored to the Etna massif and barring the Allied advance towards Messina and Italy. The pretence that General Guzzoni was still in command was diplomatically sustained, but General Hube and his XIV Panzer Corps Head-quarters, newly arrived from Italy, were in fact now running the battle and Guzzoni seemed only too happy to let them do so. Kesselring was under no illusion that he could win. His declared purpose was simply to delay the much stronger Allied armies for as long as possible before withdrawing to Italy, and in this he was splendidly assisted by the terrain. Sicily became the German workshop for the study and development of rearguard techniques. In this campaign Kesselring perfected the science of holding up a stronger advancing army by frequent demolitions on mountain roads, the booby-trapping and mining of abandoned towns and villages, the employment of mobile guns, leap-frogging back from one twist in a mountain road to the next, so that the advance was constantly held up by the necessity to build bridges, create traffic diversions around road gaps, or by the necessity to mount set-piece attacks with artillery and air support.

The sheer wealth of artillery and air support on which the Americans and British could call, and the limitless quantities of ammunition that they could squander, encouraged them to substitute destructive extravagance for tactical guile and it became commonplace for every village and town to be flattened by bombing and artillery before being attacked and, on capture, to be found to have been already vacated by the Germans who were probably never actually in it anyway, but holding the high ground behind it. At which stage the first entry into it of the victors would have to be made by bulldozers to clear a way through the obstructive rubble created by their own bombers and guns. This became the regular pattern of operations in Sicily.

Once more, after the initial failure of the Allied airborne operations, Montgomery tried to speed up his advance by a air drop ahead of it, sending a gliderborne force to seize ground in the Catania plain. A third of the first British glider force, the one which had supported the invasion, had in error been dropped by their American towing aircraft into the sea. The second force, now sent into action nearly a week later, were equally ill-fated. The dropping-zone chosen for them chanced to be the very ground on which a unit of the German 1st Parachute Division, flying in from Italy, had just landed. As the frail gliders of the British 1st Airborne Division swooped noiselessly to land, the riflemen and machine-gunners of the German 1st Parachute Division were presented with a gift target of which they took the fullest advantage. Within seconds the sky was filled with blazing coffins.

After two weeks of hard fighting in temperatures approaching 100 degrees Fahrenheit—and with malaria beginning to compete with shells and bullets as a cause of casualties—Montgomery's advance in the east reached a deadlock against Hube's four German divisions now firmly established with their backs to the gigantic wall of Etna. To break the deadlock Montgomery proposed to deliver a "left hook" round the western shoulder of Etna with his reserve division, the British 78th, which Alexander had just brought over from North Africa. The 78th had earned a big reputation for mountainfighting in Tunisia and it was to be used to break the deadlock in the Catania plain south of Etna by outflanking it by way of the tortuous mountain route over Etna's western shoulder. During the temporary lull in the east while the new initiative was being prepared, General Patton struck out on Montgomery's left. Taking advantage of the comparative lack of German opposition he was able to overrun the centre and west of the island, capturing the shattered remains of the once-beautiful capital Palermo, and, launching an advance eastward along the north coast, to join up eventually with the Montgomery left-hook over the mountain's lower slope. Kesselring used this lull on the Etna sector to accelerate the concentrations of antiaircraft batteries he was crowding into both sides of the Messina Straits (antiquity's Scylla and Charybdis) to protect the Germans' final withdrawal to the Italian mainland when it could be delayed no longer. The summer of Hitler's discontent was grinding relentlessly to its climax. Not less terrible than the Hollywoodesque Armageddon of the Kursk salient, infinitely more terrible than the extinction of the U-boats in the Atlantic and the fighting withdrawal of the German soldiers in Sicily, was the one-sided air battle of Hamburg which engaged the Royal Air Force and the people of Germany's second city for four nights and three days in the last week of July.

The strategic bombing offensive against Germany had taken a step forward in May 1943 when for the first time American bombs fell on industrial objectives. But there was a fundamental difference between the British and American approach to strategic bombing. This Anglo-American difference, which extended to almost all branches of strategy, can be summed up as a difference in national outlook and temperament conditioned by the respective wealth and resources of the two nations.

In general the Americans preferred the direct approach:

"perfidious Albion," inclined to the devious. For example the American approach to the conquest of Germany was an invasion across the Channel by the shortest route and a direct drive on Berlin. The cost might be heavy but men and machines were expendable; there would always be more forthcoming; therefore why not tackle the objective by the shortest and most direct route?

Britain, on the other hand, historically conditioned to tackle stronger continental powers by indirect and peripheral attacks based on her naval superiority, and mindful of the need to conserve both her limited manpower and her smaller industrial potential, preferred to attack Germany in the first instance via the Mediterranean. This was one difference of opinion that has already been briefly touched upon.

Tactically it was much the same. The American generals preferred to launch their ground attacks in daylight against objectives their soldiers could see. They did not think first of the cost in casualties: they thought a daylight attack would be easier, quicker, and better. The British preferred the night attack, navigationally and administratively more difficult, but cheaper in casualties because darkness enhanced the scope for surprise and hampered the defender in his defensive fire.

The same doctrinal difference extended to the war in the air. The British, who had been bombing German towns since 1940, believed that night bombing was the only way to avoid crippling casualties (even if it was at the expense of accuracy) and their heaviest bomber, the Lancaster, was the product of this thinking. Nothing more than a four-engined bomb carrier, it could carry 10,000 pounds of bombs for 2250 miles or 14,000 pounds for 1660 miles. The Americans thought it senseless to bomb invisible targets in the dark and geared their policy to daylight operations. Since daylight bombers would attract heavy enemy fighter opposition they equipped their bombers with a heavy armament. Thus the B-17 (Fortress) carried twelve 5-inch machine guns giving all-round fire—hence its better-known name Flying Fortress—but this armament meant a sacrifice of load-carrying capacity. The Flying Fortress could carry only 4000 pounds of bombs for over 2000 miles; the B-24 (Liberator) 2500 pounds of bombs for 2850 miles.[3]

Strong British efforts were made to persuade the Americans to change their minds and supplement the night bombing offensive of the Royal Air Force, but without success. The strongest of these representations was made by Churchill at the Casablanca conference when he tackled General Ira C.

Eaker, Commander of the U.S. Eighth Air Force in Britain.[4] The United States had been in the war for a year, chided Churchill, and the Eighth Air Force had been deployed in Britain for six months, yet it had not dropped a single bomb on Germany. Eaker refused to be hustled, defended the Eighth Air Force policy which aimed not only to achieve greater accuracy by bombing in daylight, but to attract the Luftwaffe to battle and inflict on it heavy losses with the defensive armament of the Liberators and Fortresses. (It was not to work out quite like this, as we shall see later, but before the U.S. bomber offensive opened that was the idea and the hope.) This brief background is sketched in partly because it is an important element in the total context of Allied strategic bombing, partly because it seems proper to establish for the record that any operational success or moral obloquy that may be thought to attach to the Hamburg operation belongs to the British leadership alone.

It was codenamed Operation Gomorrah with a horrible tastelessness that probably seems worse now than it did at the time: its purpose to destroy as a functioning entity the port of Hamburg, Germany's second city, with a population of 2,000,000. Hamburg was not unused to air raids. By July 1943, it had lived through 137, and in a recent one no fewer than 1500 separate fires had been put out. Hamburg had one of the most efficient and experienced fire and civil defence services in Germany. Its regular fire brigade was 3600 strong and equipped with 305 of the most modern fire engines and fifty fire ships in the harbour. In addition there were 935 auxiliary pumps in such key situations as factories, stations, office blocks, warehouses, and public buildings and manned each night by locally found fire parties. The various rescue services had a strength of 8000 men and women, there were 1800 police and 12,000 soldiers. Neighbouring fire brigades could (and on this occasion did) bring the total number of available firemen up to over 14,000. Hamburg considered itself ready for anything that might come.[5]

The operation named Gomorrah was Air Marshal Harris's *pièce de resistance* in his dedicated mission to prove to a hierarchy that still included doubters that strategic bombing could destroy the German will to resist. The attack consisted of three catastrophic raids each by over seven hundred Royal Air Force bombers, between which there were two daylight raids by a total of 235 aircraft of the U.S Eighth Air Force. It was rounded off by a lighter and less successful night attack by 350 R.A.F. aircraft on August 2-3. It was assisted by two technical devices.

The first was the now perfected and long-awaited radar direction-finding device called H2S. The Pathfinder force—the R.A.F.'s elite of experienced and outstandingly skilful bomber crews who led the way in all attacks and then found and marked with skymarkers the target areas for the less talented—now flew only in aircraft fitted with these costly and complex devices and could almost infallibly find the right targets. Gomorrah began on the night of July 24-25 with an attack by 740 bombers which dropped their load in two hours and twenty-eight minutes. It was a stiflingly hot night, the afternoon shade temperature having been 77 degrees Fahrenheit. The attack achieved surprise through a second technical device used for the first time that night. This consisted in the dropping by the bombers of showers of strips of metal foil which had the effect of blinding the radar of the German antiaircraft defences on the ground and in the air where the night fighter aircraft were as frustrated as the antiaircraft batteries. As Air Marshal Harris described it,[6] this was the effect of "Window":

> . . . The Radar-controlled searchlights waved aimlessly in all directions, the gunfire was inaccurate, and in England the stations which intercepted the enemy wireless traffic were immediately aware of hopeless confusion in the German ground control stations. In fact ground controllers gave the whole situation up, their instruments behaved as though the sky was filled with thousands of hostile aircraft. . . .

In less than two and a half hours this first shock attack raised a pall of smoke and dust that would blot out daylight from Hamburg—even in this exceptional heatwave—for more than a week. And it was only just beginning. Two nights later a second attack was made with 738 aircraft which dropped their bombs in three hours. In this attack six times as much High Explosive and seven times as many incendiaries (both stick-type and liquid) were dropped with the intention of saturating the fire services as totally as "Window" had nullified the defenders' radar. In this the attackers were successful, though the firemen, with reinforcements rushing in from all over, never gave up. There was more to come. Two nights later a third attack was made by 726 bombers. In

239

these three main attacks the R.A.F. dropped 7196 tons of bombs of which the unusually high proportion of 4300 tons were incendiaries. Fire, the most ancient weapon of siege warfare against cities, had come back into fashion with the chemical expertise of the mid-twentieth century. Hamburg would burn for days.

Rescue workers, many of whom had been on duty for forty-eight hours, were still putting out fires and pulling the dead and the dying out of the shambles of the first attack when the second was launched with its overwhelming preponderance of incendiaries. The calcination of Hamburg now began in earnest. The temperature anyway had soared to 90 degrees Fahrenheit that night. By the time the incendiaries had been raining down for some minutes heavy stone buildings were scorching up to temperatures of 1000 degrees and more. Above all, this second attack of Gomorrah introduced a new horror of warfare, the fire-storm. The fire-storms were caused by large numbers of smaller fires, beyond the capacity of the fire services to extinguish them, merging into larger general conflagrations which then led to a fire-storm. Air Marshal Harris quotes a contemporary German document which explained the fire-storm on which, at this moment of history, the Hamburg physicists were undoubtedly the world's greatest authorities: [7]

> . . . Through the Union of a number of fires, the air gets so hot that on account of its decreasing specific weight, it receives a terrific momentum, which in its turn causes other surrounding air to be sucked towards the centre. By that suction, combined with the enormous difference in temperature (600-1000 centigrade) tempests are caused which go beyond their meteorological counterparts (20-30 centigrade). In a built-up area the suction could not follow its shortest course, but the overheated air stormed through the street with immense force taking along not only sparks but burning timber and roof beams, so spreading the fire farther and farther, developing in a short time into a fire typhoon such as was never before witnessed, against which every human resistance was quite useless.

The fire-storms swept before them anything movable and much that was not. There were several instances of trees being uprooted by them. It was while the inferno was at its height and the fire-storms were snarling unstoppably through the white-hot nightmare that the water supply gave out. The city's mains had been hit 847 times. Anyway by now it was impossible to get anywhere near many of the fires so intense was the heat. Air Marshal Harris had to contain his impatience for some time before his air reconnaissance experts could give him an idea of how successfully Gomorrah had emulated the thoroughness of the Lord God Almighty in the case of its namesake:[8]

> It was some time before the smoke of the burning city cleared away and air photographs of the damage could be taken. When this was done there was at last revealed a scene of unimaginable devastation . . . 6200 acres in the most densely built-up district had been destroyed, 74 percent of the most closely built-up parts of city. All four of Hamburg's main shipbuilding yards . . . were severely damaged, and it was clear that all work and tranport in the city had been stopped.

Greatly exaggerated estimates of the casualties and results of the Hamburg holocaust were made by both sides at the time. But the Germans, among other things, are diligent and conscientious archivists and researchers. It took ten years of postwar research to arrive at something approximating to a definitive inventory of Hamburg's catastrophe in the last week of July 1943. The true figures are terrible enough to need no exaggeration.

The number of people killed was 30,482. Another 17,372 were unaccounted for and presumed to have perished in the flames.

Despite the previous evacuation of large numbers of children from the city, seven thousand died in the July holocaust and ten thousand lost one or both parents. In the first forty-eight hours 900,000 people were rendered homeless; 277,330 dwelling houses were completely destroyed, 170,000 were in varying degrees damaged, only 114,757 survived Gomorrah wholly undamaged. All public services were temporarily out of action. Destruction other than in the residential sections of the city included severe damage to 580 industrial buildings, 2632 business premises, 76 public-service depots, 24 hospitals, 277 schools, 58 churches. All four main shipbuilding yards were badly damaged and 180,000[9] tons of shipping were sunk in the harbour and docks. As is to be expected at a time of full mobilization the number of women killed was 40 percent higher than the number of men.

The United States Strategic Bombing Survey, after observing that the Gomorrah raids were "amongst the most devastating of the war" reported that nevertheless . . . "Hamburg as an economic unit was not destroyed. It never fully recovered from the bombings, but in five months it had regained 80 percent of its former productivity, despite the fact that great areas of the city lay . . . in dust and rubble. As in the case of industrial plants, when it was found much easier to destroy the buildings than the machines in them, so also it is much easier to destroy the physical structure of a city than to wipe out its economic life."

The U. S. Strategic Bombing Survey is not necessarily to be taken as Holy Writ. But it did represent a cool and methodical piece of research carried out by a specialist unit while the war was still going on and the facts were still fresh.

In corroboration of the effectiveness of Gomorrah (and, by implication, of the success of strategic bombing) Air Marshal Harris quotes in his memoirs a statement apropos Hamburg made by Speer, Hitler's Minister of War Production, under Allied interrogation in 1945.[10]

> "We were of the opinion that a rapid repetition of this type of attack upon another six German towns would inevitably cripple the will to sustain armament manufacture and war production. It was I who verbally reported to the Führer at that time that a continuation of these attacks might bring about a rapid end to the war."

What one would like to know is what Hitler said in reply —if Speer did actually say this to him. We are not told. But it is surely not irrelevant to point out that in the course of 1943, the year of the greatest strategic bombing to date, German industry produced six thousand tanks including new models over which there were many delays and changes of policy, and this figure was 1700 more than in 1942. In 1944 production was to rise again by more than three thousand to 9161 tanks.

There is good reason to think that if Speer did in fact address his Führer on the lines he claimed during his end-of-war interrogation, the reaction is unlikely to have been more helpful than that of Nero (whatever it may have been) to the person who broke the news to him that Rome was burning.

The reason for surmising this is a reported conversation about the time of Hamburg between Hitler and Field-Marshal Rommel, whom this narrative left at the commencement of two months of sick leave in Austria in March. By May 10 Rommel was well enough to return to duty but he was given no new appointment at once and spent the summer months as a kind of floating senior officer without portfolio, attending conferences at Supreme Headquarters, passing time at the Army Command Office in Berlin and for the first time learning at firsthand the true nature of what was being done in Germany's name by people like Himmler. He was shocked by what he was finding out. Like most of the orthodox German Army commanders he had no doubt had his suspicions and had adopted a prudent policy of asking no questions and getting on with his job. In any case the almost pathological secrecy with which the Nazi hierarchy shrouded its activities would make it quite possible for a commander, most of whose service had been outside Europe, to remain in ignorance of the full nature and extent of the activities of the SS (whose arrogant independence of attitude the Regular Army generals always resented).

Rommel left no connected account of these summer months of 1943 but his English editor, Sir Basil Liddell Hart, was able to piece one together as a result of his conversations after the war with Rommel's widow, Lucie, and their son Manfred, still a schoolboy in 1943. Both were able to recall that the Field-Marshal had been particularly impressed by two conversations with Hitler during this period. In the first Rommel, in a gloomy appreciation of the war situation had taken the opportunity to recapitulate the disasters of the last few months—Stalingrad, Tunis, a monthly loss of thirty or more U-boats. He referred to the immense material strength of the Allies. He had ended by asking pointedly how long Germany could keep pace with the whole world. To all this Hitler had listened "with downcast eyes." Then to Rommel's surprise he said he knew that there was now very little chance of winning the war. "But the West would conclude no peace with him —certainly not the people who were then at the helm. And the people who would have been prepared to negotiate with him had no power. He had never wanted war with the West. But now the West would have their war—have it to the end."

Frau Rommel remembered her husband telling her how, as Allied military pressure increased in the East and the West, "Hitler whipped himself up into a pathological impotent hatred, which allowed the demoniac side of his personality to emerge, the side which had remained hidden in the days of his success."

The second conversation with Hitler—that Rommel's wife and son vividly remembered him to have found "no less shattering"—took place at the end of July at the time of the immolation of Hamburg. As Liddell Hart (quoting Manfred Rommel) recorded it:

" 'If the German people are incapable of winning the war,' Hitler had said, 'then they can rot.' In any case the best were already dead. If he was to be beaten, he would fight for every house, nothing would be left. A great people must die heroically—it was a historic necessity."

To which Rommel's son added: " 'Sometimes you feel that he's no longer quite normal,' my father commented when he spoke of this incident."

It must have been the understatement of the Second World War.

So the ordinary men, women, and children of Germany were to be punished for failing to win Hitler's war. Let them all perish in the fire-storms, the Herr Schmidts, the Frau Heinzes: let them all be calcined in the 1500 degree inferno of their own streets. It was a "historic necessity." They could expect no sympathy from their beloved Führer. It was, after all, *they* who had let *him* down by failing to win.

Chapter 20

A SLIGHT CHANGE OF ALLIES

☐ From the catharsis of Kursk, the fire-storms of Hamburg and the torrid dry infantry cut-and-thrust on the Sicilian lava slopes (which could wear out a pair of army boots in a day and the hearts of normally patient pack mules in half that time) it is a relief to turn to the one important episode of the Second World War that had rich overtones of comedy. This was the sequence of events known as the defection of Italy.

If a novelist of genius should some day wish to write the definitive work of art exposing the nature of war to its ultimate horror and absurdity, his work might well be based on the total Italian experience in the Second World War. The Italian people were the "fall guys" of the Fascist-Nazi era. Arguably the most civilized—if, emotionally, the least stable —people of Europe it was their fate to experience what was easily the most unsatisfactory war of all the belligerents. Duped by a braggart windbag and their own emotional susceptability, they had been dragged into a first league war for which they had no stomach, armed with obsolete second league equipment. They had had the worst of campaigns in Greece, Albania, Ethiopia, and North Africa where the loss of Tripoli at the beginning of the year had completed the liquidation of a colonial empire into which they had in fact put much creditable and constructive work. The army they had sent to fight in Russia had come to grief at Stalingrad. Tripoli had been the last straw and since then there had been an ever-growing conviction at all levels of the population (not least the practising military population) that the time had come to disengage from the war, at least at the side of the German ally. The lack of alacrity with which the Italian defenders of Sicily had failed to fling themselves at the Anglo-American invaders had been indicative of the Army's feeling about things. In the highest circles of Italian life more positive action was taking shape. When Hitler, briefing General von Senger before sending him to Sicily, had forecast the early defection of Italy as a result of "the machinations of the Court, Society, and the General Staff," his intuition was for once hitting the nail on the head. It was precisely these three elements[1] that were plotting the change of leadership that must precede any change of policy towards the war.

First there was Princess Maria José, wife of Crown Prince Umberto. A haughty patrician in a land where this quality, when it exists, is displayed without apology or compromise, she had loathed Mussolini for a long time, considering him a common upstart. Not long after the fall of Tripoli she went to work on her father-in-law King Victor Emmanuel urging him to take action against the Duce. The King, less impetuous than she, said that the time was not yet right, and Maria José had for the time being to content herself with furthering opposition to the regime in the high circles of Roman society where intrigue is of the very stuff of existence. There were many who thought like her both at Court and in the higher echelons of the armed services.

One such was Marshal Pietro Badoglio. Badoglio was the conqueror of Ethiopia who had taken over from Marshal Emilio de Bono and brought that campaign to a successful conclusion in 1936. In 1940 when he was Chief of Staff he had been blamed for the failure of the Albanian campaign and had been sacked by Mussolini—since when he had nursed a deep grudge against the Duce. Another leading supporter of the growing revolt was General Vittorio Ambrosio, the Chief of the General Staff of the Armed Forces, who had replaced the Germanophile Marshal Cavallero at the beginning of the year. The Chief of Staff of the Army, General Roatta, and General Castellano, also of Comando Supremo, were two more. At Court the conspiracy had a powerful supporter in Duke Pietro d'Acquarone, Minister of the Royal Household. Political sympathisers within the Fascist hierarchy itself were led by Count Dino Grandi, a former Ambassador to Britain, and Count Galeazzo Ciano, who had owed his political advancement to the post of Foreign Secretary to the circumstance of having married Mussolini's daughter Edda. But Ciano had recently fallen from favour and had been reduced to the sinecure post of Ambassador to the Holy See. With the King counselling patience, and playing his own part with the coolest of non-participating poker faces, the conspiracy smouldered warmly but in well-kept secret.

It was remarked earlier in this narrative that one of the more difficult operations of war is being an ally. It may here be added that quite the most difficult of all is changing allies in mid-war without getting too badly hurt. It was this most delicate manoeuvre to which Italy was about to be committed. It was to call for all the genius in natural histrionics and guilelessly guileful double-talk which makes the Italians at once the most endearing and the most exasperating of people to their friends.

Not for nothing was Italy the birthplace of the Renaissance in which great art flourished so stupendously on a foundation of political intrigue and commercial skulduggery. Not for nothing were the city states of Pisa, Venice, and Genoa able to found flourishing maritime empires not so very long after the time those later maritime imperialists, the British, were still painting themselves with woad. The Latin spirit, imprisoned for so long like a genie in an iron bottle, was about to escape with the purposeful pop of a champagne cork. The sombre chronicle of the war was to be lightened for a short time by an *intermezzo* to be treasured for a long time by the connoisseur of stylish duplicity.

The invasion of Sicily on July 10, and the poor showing of the Italian troops, brought matters to a head. The King, who was in touch with the different strands of the conspiracy and had passed through a number of changes of mind without reaching a conclusion, now made up his mind to take the lead and arrest Mussolini. He was egged on to this decision by General Ambrosio and the Duke d'Acquarone. At the same time the new development in Sicily had affected the Fascist hierarchy in the same way. They too had decided that the time had come for action. Mussolini must be pinned down to give a report on the war situation to a full meeting of the supreme constitutional body, the Fascist Grand Council. The meeting was fixed for July 24 and the King was informed. But five days before this there was a meeting between Hitler and Mussolini (at Hitler's request) at Feltre in the Dolomites. Mussolini's advisers, especially Ambrosio, urged the Duce to take the opportunity to tell Hitler flatly that Italy was finished and could not continue to fight unless sent considerable help. Mussolini failed to pluck up the courage to say this. Instead, Hitler delivered a fierce monologue saying that the fight must go on and Italy must place herself wholly under German command. While the inconclusive meeting was in progress—with Mussolini contributing less and less to it—the news came through that Rome had been bombed by the Allies for the first time. The railway station and yards had been heavily damaged, and many people killed. This gave the thoroughly dejected and discomfited Duce an excuse to leave the meeting on the grounds that his place was with his people in Rome now that this terrible new calamity had befallen them. The killed numbered at least a thousand. The Feltre meeting therefore achieved nothing except to give Hitler an opportunity to add to Mussolini's general discomfiture and to remind him that it is easier to become involved in criminal activities than it is to disengage from them.

On July 24 at a specially convened meeting of the Fascist Grand Council,[2] Italian Fascism and the bombastic dictatorship of Benito Mussolini formally ceased to guide the destinies of the Italian people. The twenty-eight members of the Grand Council met in their black shirts at the Palazzo Venezia and the meeting lasted for nine hours. Ostensibly its purpose was to provide Mussolini with an opportunity to give an up-to-date report on the war situation. In reality it was to be the occasion for forcing his resignation by Count Grandi and his fellow plotters. In its twenty-first year Fascism was to be brought to an end not in the bloodshed and civil war expected of toppling dictatorships, but constitutionally.

Mussolini, as was traditional, opened the proceedings with his report which his biographer Christopher Hibbert described as a "long rambling speech of a quite astonishing opacity. Complacent, disingenuous, sometimes arrogant, often accusatory, self-justifying and misleading, he spoke in an unrelieved monotone without conviction or regard for truth . . ." [3]

Other speeches followed, mostly of a petty bickering nature. Then Grandi read out his resolution which was the "object of the exercise." It was a formal No Confidence resolution which, after a wordy preamble, came to the point in carefully moderated language. Its key proposal was that the King should assume command of the Armed Forces and "supreme initiative of decision": a polite way of saying that Mussolini must quit. After a lengthy and at times angry debate the Resolution was carried by 19 votes to 7: one member abstaining, another choosing to vote for an alternative resolution of his own. The only course open to Mussolini was resignation. He would have an opportunity to hand it to the King the following day.

The King, his power of executive decision having been restored, began to exercise it. After the Grand Council had voted, Grandi telephoned the Minister of the Royal Household, Acquarone, with the result to pass on to the King. He suggested that Marshal Enrico Caviglia, a distinguished senior soldier, might be a suitable head of government. Only to be told that the King had already decided to appoint Marshal Badoglio. Grandi, architect of Mussolini's downfall, had been neatly blocked at the very start of his new career of kingmaker. Furious at what he considered a royal double-cross he immediately turned his back on public life and on Italy, and left for Portugal.

The next afternoon Mussolini heard the King say among other things[4]: ". . . You can certainly be under no illusion as regards Italy's feeling for you. At this moment you are the most hated man in the country. I am your only remaining friend. That is why I tell you that you need have no fears for your own safety. I will see you are protected." The Duce was then arrested by *carabinieri* whose presence at the Villa Savoia had been organized by General Ambrosio. An ambulance took the deposed dictator at high speed and under escort from Rome to Gaeta and from there he was shipped to the island of Ponza.

Shortly after eleven o'clock that night the rumours with which Rome had been seething all day were confirmed by a radio announcement:

> His Majesty the King-Emperor has accepted the
> resignation from the office of Head of the Govern-
> ment and Chief Secretary of State, of His Excellency
> Cavaliere Benito Mussolini, and has nominated as
> head of the Government and Chief Secretary of
> State Cavaliere Marshal of Italy Pietro Badoglio.

There was an outburst of spontaneous rejoicing.
Many people ran into the streets and there was much singing and dancing and cheering, Mussolini had been dismissed
and no one now had a good word to say for him.

> There was little violence and no one was killed.
> The mood was one of gaiety rather than of revenge
> . . . crowds of people sang and danced as at a *festa*.
> "Fascism is dead" they called happily to each other.
> And it was true. Not a single man died in Rome that
> night in an effort to defend it.[5]

Everyone, it seemed, including Fascist diehards, had made
an instant discovery that he had always been an anti-Fascist.
Fascism had gone out not with a bang and not even with a
whimper. It was just as if it had never been there at all!

While many made merry in the streets, even more remained at home and heard Marshal Badoglio's first proclamation as Head of Government: heard him remind the nation that the war would continue and that Italy would remain loyal to her German ally. This was the bitter reality that
had to be faced. The first part of the Italian conspiracy had
been successfully completed. Mussolini had been deposed
without fuss or bloodshed. The second part could now begin
and it was going to prove trickier. The Germans had to be
delicately double-crossed while remaining fully persuaded that
their loving allies were with them to the last. The real game
was about to begin.

The Germans in Rome were taken by surprise by the sud-
denness of Mussolini's downfall. Kesselring lost no time in
seeking an interview with the King that very night but was
told that the King could not possibly see him before the next
day July 26. Before presenting himself to the King he called
on Badoglio who gave him heartfelt assurances that Italy's new
regime would prosecute the war with even more energy
and determination than before. When Kesselring asked for

the present location of Mussolini, Badoglio replied that this was something known only to the King. A few minutes later King Victor Emmanuel was as fervent as Badoglio in assuring Kesselring of Italy's continuing friendship and her determination to continue the Axis fight with all her might. He spoke with passion and emotion. Germany would not find her ally wanting. Kesselring asked where Mussolini was at that moment. The King said regretfully that he had no idea: it was a secret known only to Marshal Badoglio.[6]

Hitler exploded when he heard the news. It was all the fault of those fools in Rome with their softness and their idiotic policy of making friends with the Italians. The chief services liaison officer with the Comando Supremo, General von Rintelen, and the Ambassador, Hans-Georg von Mackensen, were recalled from Rome in disgrace as "dupes" of the scheming Italians. Kesselring, down as an Italophile, was under a cloud of suspicion. "That fellow Kesselring [according to Hitler] is too honest for those born traitors down there." In the first flood of his fury Hitler ordered the 2nd Parachute Division in southern France to land south of Rome and cut it off from the south; and he proposed to order the 3rd Panzer Grenadier Division, forty miles north of the city, to "drive without any ado into Rome and arrest the Government, the King—the whole bag of them—especially the Crown Prince and Badoglio."[7] More prudent voices, however, including that of Kesselring persuaded him that it would be more sensible to forget about the drive on Rome and to build up German strength in the north of Italy first. So he confined himself to ordering eight divisions to move into northern Italy from the south of France and Austria with the primary task of securing the Alpine passes. And he gave orders that the withdrawal of the Sicily divisions to the south of Italy should be accelerated. But he still ordered 2nd Parachute Division to drop south of Rome. There was one surprise. The eight German divisions now scheduled to move into northern Italy were to come under command not of Kesselring, the suspect Italophile, but of Field-Marshal Rommel and a new northern command designated Army Command B; Rommel and his HQ remaining for the time-being in Munich. Rommel, back in favour, was the man who would stand no nonsense from the Italians! So far it was a game of chess with loaded chessmen. The Parachute and Panzer Grenadier divisions now lay respectively south and north of the capital and five Italian divisions were between them in the Rome area. In the north Rommel's occupation had secured the passes and forestalled a possible plot to cut off all the Germans in Italy. Badoglio had now reached the point where he had to reassure the Germans as publicly and vehemently as possible that he was one hundred percent with them and at the same time contrive somehow to drop a hint to the Anglo-American leadership that he was anxious to talk business.

In connection with the first part of this proposition he sent Hitler a telegram to suggest a top-level meeting in northern Italy, now that the new government had taken oath. The King would attend.

Hitler replied curtly that he did not think there was anything to add to what had been said at the previous meeting at Feltre. But he agreed to a conference between the foreign ministers and Services chiefs. This would take place at Tarvisio on August 6. But Hitler shrewdly declined to risk a personal appearance on Italian soil in case the Italians had in mind a coup similar to that which they had carried out against his dear friend Mussolini! [8]

In connection with the second aim of Badoglio's duplex plan he sent to Lisbon the Marchese d'Ayeta, an experienced diplomat, with the additional qualification of having American relatives, to make contact with the British Ambassador. D'Ayeta's mission was to give an account of recent events in Italy and Italy's plight as a result; to make it clear that German suspicions were fully aroused and that one false step could provoke a bloodbath; that the only course open to Badoglio was to "play along" with the Germans and keep them sweet for as long as possible. This was what he was trying to do. Hence the forthcoming meeting at Tarvisio which had been called solely to reassure the Germans, and the Allies were to take no notice of whatever emerged from it. Frankly, Italy was in a desperate situation and longed for the Allies to come to the rescue.

Two days later, while the Tarvisio talks were actually in progress, a second Italian emissary named Berio saw the British Ambassador in Tangier. He went further than his colleague, saying that he had been invested with plenipotentiary powers to put out peace feelers.

Meanwhile the meeting at Tarvisio achieved little except to enable the Italian delegates to gain a little time by rhetorical, filibustering protestations of loyalty to the Axis. The new Foreign Minister, Raffaele Guariglia, was successful in convincing Ribbentrop but General Ambrosio and his military colleagues were less successful with Keitel and the German military delegates in whom any susceptibility to glib Italian sales-

251

talk was constantly stiffened by ferocious telephone calls from the Wolf's Lair. They were not, for example, taken in by Ambrosio's bland suggestion that Rommel's eight divisions in the north should be brought under the control of Comando Supremo and transferred to the south to be joined there by the Italian occupation forces now in the south of France, and the Balkans. The reason Ambrosio gave for this suggestion was that the south was where the Allies were almost certain to land so that this was where the defensive strength should be concentrated. But the Germans thought this could not be other than a dastardly Italian ruse to draw as many German divisions as possible into the south and then persuade the Allies to land in the north and cut them all off. There was some cautious you-go-first bargaining. The Germans said they might send more troops to the allegedly threatened south if the Italians withdrew some of theirs from the north where they now threatened the German line of communications. So the talks ended with loud reaffirmations of loyalty by the Italians, unallayed suspicions by the majority of the Germans, and nothing much achieved.

News of the two tentative peace feelers reached Churchill when he was at sea on his way to the "quadrant" conference in Quebec with Roosevelt. The British Foreign Secretary, Anthony Eden, had attached to his report a draft reply to Berio for Churchill's approval which included this sentence:[9] "Should we not then reply that, as is well known, we insist on unconditional surrender, and the Badoglio Government must as a first step notify us that Italy surrenders unconditionally? Subsequently, at a later stage, if the Badoglio Government was to do this, we should then inform them of the terms on which we would be prepared to cease hostilities against Italy."

Churchill found himself scrawling in red ink in the margin of Eden's note, "Don't miss the bus" and "If they surrender immediately we should be prepared to accord conditions as acts of grace and not as a bargain." It was as though the Prime Minister had instinctively sensed a situation in which horsetrading and generosity might both be called for and that the stiff, prosaic approach of the Foreign Office must not be allowed to spoil it. He cabled Eden preliminary approval of what he had done and sent him a fuller reply when he reached Canada two days later on August 9:

1. Badoglio must state that he is prepared to place himself unreservedly in the hands of the Allied Gov-

ernments, who have already made it plain that they desire Italy to have a respectable place in the New Europe.

Reference should also be made to General Eisenhower's offer of the return of Italian prisoners of was taken in Tunisia and Sicily, provided Allied prisoners are speedily set free.

2. The object of the above is to convey to the Italian Government the feeling that, while they have to make the formal act of submission, our desire is to treat them with consideration, so far as military exigencies allow. Merely harping on "unconditional surrender" with no prospect of mercy held out even as an act of grace may well lead to no surrender at all. The expression "honourable capitulation" has also been officially used by the President, and I do not think it should be omitted from the language we are now to use.[10]

The President also endorsed Churchill's instructions to Eden when the Prime Minister had had an opportunity to inform him of the Italian overtures and his exchanges with the British Foreign Secretary.

The next development was on August 12 when General Castellano and a small military staff—impeccably disguised in civilian clothes as a mission to meet the homeward-bound Italian Ambassador to Chile—took the diplomatic train to Lisbon but stopped off at Madrid where Castellano introduced himself to the British Ambassador, Sir Samuel Hoare. Castellano was empowered to carry the deal a stage further. He was instructed by Badoglio to say that the moment the Allies landed on the Italian mainland the Government would like to join them and take up arms against Germany.

"We are not in a position to make any terms," Castellano said. "We will accept unconditional surrender provided we can join as allies in fighting the Germans." As an inducement Castellano said that if the Allies were agreeable to what he suggested he would be pleased to suply them with a complete location state of all German units in Italy together with details of their strength and armament.[11] What gave this proposition a certain piquancy was the fact that in Italy at this very time the Italian Army chiefs had just completed yet another session of staff talks with their German opposite numbers—this time at Bologna—in which they had continued

253

their inconclusive charades to gain time with the German delegates who were now displaying increasing impatience and even truculence. One concession which the Italians did gain at this meeting was German agreement to their withdrawing their Fourth Army from the French Riviera. This provoked General Jodl into asking sarcastically whether they wanted it to fight the Anglo-Americans in the south or the Germans in the north.[12] Whereupon General Roatta blazed back at him: "How dare you! We are no traitors to go over to the enemy in the middle of a battle!"

As Churchill and Roosevelt were still conferring in Quebec, the Castellano proposal had to be relayed to them by London, and they immediately sent instructions to Eisenhower to send an American and a British officer to talk to Castellano in Lisbon on August 19. Eisenhower nominated his Chief of Staff, Major General Walter Bedell Smith, and the British head of his Intelligence Staff, General Kenneth W. D. Strong. The meeting took place at the British Embassy in Lisbon. Bedell Smith informed Castellano that Eisenhower would accept his government's unconditional surrender on terms that would now be given to him. He then handed the surprised Castellano the document. Castellano protested that the purpose of his visit had been to discuss how Italy could enter the war against Germany. Bedell Smith replied woodenly that he could only discuss unconditional surrender.

On this meeting Churchill comments significantly:

> It is difficult to make hard-cut military negotiations fit in with flexible diplomacy. The Italian envoy general at Lisbon was placed in a hopeless position.[13]

If war, as Clemenceau suggested, is too serious a matter to be left to the generals, peace is even more so. West Point and Sandhurst are admirable institutions for producing the kind of man an army normally needs and wants. But by definition their teaching is not conducive to flexibility of mind nor to the development of imagination outside certain well-defined limits. On top of this it must be remembered that Britain and America have a common heritage of puritanism. This is particularly noticeable in the dedicated Regular soldiers of the two nations. It is difficult to avoid the suspicion that this quality was now in evidence; that its manifestation, albeit unconscious, was unhelpful to the peace discussions; that the straight and honest Eisenhower and his

British colleagues actually disapproved of what the Italians were doing and were rather shocked by it. The Allied military leadership lacked the imagination and adaptability to play the situation "by ear" and exploit to the full a golden opportunity for which the Army manuals of West Point and Sandhurst had made no provision. The elimination of Italy from the war had been laid down as one of the major Allied objectives for this year. It was now being offered on a plate without the need to fight for it; and there seemed an almost relentless determination to drop the plate. "We can only discuss unconditional surrender." Admittedly they were under orders as was Eisenhower himself. But there seems to have been little imaginative thinking about the situation by those required to handle it.

Churchill knew the score. He had seen the danger instantly as his marginal notes on Eden's first letter had shown. But Churchill was the only Allied leader with a Renaissance grasp of mind capable of assimilating a Renaissance situation; and he was in Quebec and in any case could not decide anything alone.

Meanwhile the Sicilian campaign ended on August 16 in what the Allies were pleased to consider a great victory, though it would be nearer the truth to say that it ended because the Germans were ready to withdraw their four divisions across the Messina Straits to Italy where they were now more urgently needed. Their thirty-nine-day delaying action, followed by a smooth withdrawal with minimal losses, could be claimed by Kesselring as a moral victory. Leaving behind a final remnant of only seven thousand prisoners, they succeeded in evacuating 60,000 troops under an arch of antiaircraft protection that successfully held off the overwhelmingly superior Allied air forces.

General Castellano was unable to return to Rome for some days after his unsatisfactory talks with Bedell Smith. For security reasons he had to travel by the same train as the Italian Ambassador who was returning from Chile, and the Ambassador's ship was delayed. It was August 28 before he could report to Badoglio. There was great disappointment in Rome when Badoglio and his colleagues heard what Castellano had to say. There they were on a razor's edge, just managing to keep the Germans happy and still while they planted the knife between their shoulder blades, and here were those

255

impossible Anglo-Saxons fussing about unconditional surrender! Instead of welcoming Italy as an ally the terms brought back by Castellano demanded access to any part of Italy for the purpose of continuing the fight against Germany, surrender of the Navy and Air Force and evacuation of Italian occupied territories. Eisenhower would anounce the armistice by radio from Algiers six hours before the invasion of Italy began. The Badoglio government would be expected to follow with a similar announcement. He was given till August 30 to reply.

On August 31 Castellano met General Bedell Smith in Sicily. The Commedia dell'Arte was approaching its *dénouement*. Castellano began by saying that if only the Italian government were free agents they would accept the Allied armistice terms without hesitation. Unfortunately the Germans had sent in more troops since Lisbon and Italy was now, for all practical purposes, an occupied country. It would therefore, said Castellano, be impossible for the armistice to be announced before the main Allied landing in Italy. Speaking of which (said Castellano) it would be most helpful if the Italian government could be told some details about the landing. Where, for instance, would it be made? And in what strength? His government had in mind something in the order of fifteen divisions. A landing a little north of Rome would enable the government and the King to feel a little more comfortable about those two German divisions within reach of Rome. So ruminated Castellano aloud and persuasively but Bedell Smith would not be persuaded.

He stated firmly that he could not continue the talks on the basis of the armistice being announced *after* the Allied landing: nor could he give any details of the landing itself. (The Allies could hardly be blamed for regarding the Italians as something of a security risk at this time!) In that case, said Castellano, he would like an adjournment so that he could go back and consult his government.

He was given forty-eight hours: until midnight on September 1; by which time he must be back with an unequivocal Yes or No. He flew back to Rome that evening but not entirely emptyhanded. Eisenhower, realizing that the Italian government was losing its nerve and needed some kind of reassurance about the strength of the forthcoming Allied invasion offered to land an airborne division in the Rome area on condition that "the armistice is signed and announced as desired by the Allies;[14] that the Italians will seize and hold the necessary airfields and stop all antiaircraft fire; that the

Italian divisions in the Rome area will take action against the Germans."

On September 3, in a Sicilian olive grove, Castellano finally signed the armistice document. Bedell Smith then told him that the invasion of Italy had started that very morning with an unopposed landing by Montgomery's Eighth Army on the "toe." This was the subsidiary operation designed to draw the Germans south. The main landing would take place further north. *Now,* pleaded Castellano, he could surely be told something definite about that main landing. The armistice had been signed. His government had accepted all the Allied terms. Surely they could now be let into the secret. Bedell Smith pretended at last to relent. Well, he said, some time between September 10 and 15 and it might possibly turn out to be around the 12th. In fact General Mark W. Clark's U.S. Fifth Army was due to land at Salerno, south of Naples, on September 9. Castellano reported back to Badoglio that the 12th was the day, and Badoglio accepted it as a firm date.

Eisenhower reported to the President that the armistice had been signed. Churchill, staying at the White House for a few days before returning to England, therefore heard the news at the same time and together they drafted a reply instructing Eisenhower that "the agreement having been signed, you should make such public announcement regarding it as would facilitate your military operations." [15]

In the afternoon of September 8, Marshal Badoglio had an unexpected visitor who brought with him a shattering piece of news. Brigadier General Maxwell Taylor was the Deputy Commander of General Matthew B. Ridgway's U.S. 82nd Airborne Division, detailed to carry out the forthcoming drop on Rome. General Taylor, who had come to Rome in a cloak-and-dagger manner the night before, was there to finalize arrangements for the air drop with General Carboni who was commanding the corps of four Italian divisions in the Rome area. There was something near to panic when Taylor informed him that the main Allied landing was scheduled for the following morning September 9. The Italians had taken at its face value Bedell Smith's deliberately misleading hint that the 12th was D-day. They were now caught unprepared. In particular, Carboni's corps had not yet been brought up to its operational requirement in fuel; the Chief of Staff was out of town on family business; worst of all Rome's four airfields were firmly in the hands of the Germans. If only they had been told to be ready *any time:* but they had been led to think that they had until the 12th. Badoglio agreed

257

that the airborne operation would now be a disaster. Taylor at once reported to this effect to Eisenhower who without hesitation cancelled it.

There was worse to come. In a few hours, i.e. on the eve of the invasion, General Eisenhower would proclaim the armistice on the radio. This was the last straw. What could the Allies possibly imagine they would gain by presenting the Germans with this information *before* they landed? Badoglio dispatched a desperate radio signal to Eisenhower in Algiers begging him not to announce the armistice until at least three days after the landing. When the Badoglio message was received in Algiers it caused what military men call a "flap." Eisenhower was at his forward headquarters in Tunis. His staff forwarded the message to Tunis. Eisenhower replied to Badoglio "in a peremptory telegram" in which he stated curtly that he proposed to go ahead with his announcement at 1830 and that if Badoglio did not make a simultaneous announcement of his own "Italy would have no friend left in the war." [16] The Eisenhower proclamation was duly made but not before further confusion had been caused in Rome by a premature announcement of the armistice by the British Broadcasting Corporation forty-five minutes earlier: the confusion being caused by the fact that most of the Italian government—and notably the Minister of Propaganda—were not in on the secret and had no idea of what had been going on for the last six weeks!

The affair of the Italian armistice must rank as one of the more ineptly mismanaged Allied efforts of the war. In what way did anyone at the Eisenhower headquarters think it would benefit the entry into Fortress Europe?

Its main consequences, all predictable and all inimical to the Allied purpose were these:

The Germans were given twelve gratuitous hours in which to set in motion their prearranged plan to occupy Rome, take over all airfields, disarm the Italian forces, close the exits in the Alps, and take over the defences against the expected Allied invasion. With Rommel's eight divisions in the north and Kesselring's six in the south they were well placed to prepare for an Allied invasion.

The second consequence was that the Allied invasion forces, which heard the announcement a few hours before storming the beaches at Salerno, were lulled into a relaxed belief that they would be meeting little or no opposition. It was correspondingly demoralizing when General Clark's Fifth Army found themselves vigorously opposed from the start by a fully alerted panzer division that seemed to have been expecting them.

The third was that the Italians were effectively prevented from contributing such help as might have been within their capability. The only gainers from the affair of the Italian armistice were the Germans, its intended victims.

So the Allied powers, in a mixture of tragi-comedy and opera bouffe, "missed the bus."

In only one respect did the Germans come off worst. The Italian fleet was a prize greatly coveted alike by the Allies and by Hitler, whose own Navy was meagre. The story of its failure to come into his possession added the final harlequinade to the *commedia dell'arte* of August and early September. Badoglio's Minister of Marine was Admiral de Courten. Kesselring liked and trusted him. Though partly German on his mother's side he had the Italian gift for reinforcing vehement affirmation with tearful protest. On September 7 he called on Kesselring. It could not be long, he said, before an Allied invasion fleet approached the Italian mainland. At such a time, he continued with emotion, the Italian Navy could not remain idly in harbour. There was only one honourable course open to it; to sail out to sea and bring the enemy to battle or perish in the attempt. It would sail at once to the sea area west of Sicily to fight the Allied invaders. Both Kesselring and his Chief of Staff, Siegfried Westphal,[17] have reported how passionately and sincerely de Courten spoke; how his eyes misted with tears when he spoke of his German blood on his mother's side.

On the following night September 8 just after dark the La Spezia Squadron—three battleships, five cruisers, fifteen destroyers—slipped quietly out of La Spezia Harbour led by Admiral Carlo Bergamini flying his flag in the battleship *Roma*. The squadron, which was joined by some light units from Genoa, made for the west coast of Sardinia and sailed south until it made contact, by prearrangement, with a British naval patrol about 0900 the next morning, when it continued on its southward course. During the day the absence of the fleet was noticed and the Luftwaffe sent a force of bombers to find it. In the middle of the afternoon the bombers located and attacked the fleet. The battleships *Italia* and *Roma* were both hit, the *Italia* being only slightly damaged, *Roma* the flagship severely. Shortly afterwards a second direct hit on *Roma* found the magazine. There was a sheet of flame and she sank in half an hour, Admiral Bergamini and most of the crew going down with her. Leaving a cruiser to pick up survivors, the Second-in-Command led the La Spezia Squadron without further incident to Malta where it was received by the British with naval honours and the cheers of British sailors.

On September 10—the day after the landing at Salerno— Admiral Sir Andrew Cunningham transmitted to his masters, the Lords of the Admiralty in London, one of those terse yet curiously moving naval signals which sometimes have a kind of unconscious poetry:

"Be pleased to inform their Lordships that the Italian Battle Fleet now lies at anchor under the guns of the fortress Malta."

And so the first portentous breach of the walls of Fortress Europe—the great and long-awaited day of days—was in the event something of an anticlimax; born of a mixture of intrigue, political ineptness, and high tragi-comedy.

It was as though the Trojans, trying to oblige the Greeks, had supplied their own wooden horse filled with Greek-loving Trojans only to find Achilles and Agamemnon squabbling about the quality of the wood.

Chapter 21

THE HARDNESS
OF THE SOFT UNDERBELLY

☐ The fracture of the Axis and the vaunted "pact of steel" —however ineptly it may have been exploited by the Allied Supreme Command from the military standpoint—was still a major political happening on the journey to the end of the war. Hitler certainly thought so, however cynically and without surprise his advisers took the news.

Having to make some sort of political face-saving gesture quickly, he sent for General Kurt Student, his chief of Airborne Forces, and ordered him to mount as soon as possible a commando-type airborne operation to locate and rescue his friend Mussolini. After temporary incarceration on the islands of Ponza and Maddalena, the deposed dictator—now an abject, thoroughly deflated figure, sick in body and spirit

—had been moved finally to a lonely and remote mountain hotel on the Gran Sasso, a high plateau in the northern Apennines. Here, on September 12, a company of Germany glider-borne paratroopers made a daring landing, snatched the bewildered Duce from the hotel and from those who were supposed to be guarding him, bundled him into a light aircraft and took him to Hitler's headquarters. There he was "installed" as head of a Fascist government-in-exile which was to function under close German supervision on the shores of Lake Garda in north Italy. Totalitarian honour had been satisfied!

At about the same time King Victor Emmanuel and Marshal Badoglio, who had escaped from Rome shortly before the Germans moved in, set up *their* Italian government at Brindisi in the southeast with the Allied military administration in close attendance. Though longing to be accepted as a full ally and actively to direct at his late comrades what remained of his belligerence, the disconsolate Badoglio was forced to resign himself to the temporary status of probationary ally under supervision who could not yet be elected a full member of the club.

The failure of the Allied Supreme Command to make the best use of the opportunity afforded by the Italian collapse was a symptomatic prelude to a campaign that was to have its full share of misfortune and misjudgment. The basic reason for this was the divided thinking of the Americans and the British in regard to its purpose. Brief reference has already been made to this Anglo-American difference of strategic opinion in respect of the Mediterranean theatre. As the Italian campaign was its least felicitous end-product, a recapitulation of the disagreement is essential to an understanding of the campaign and must now be given before we revert to the main narrative.

We have seen that there was a basic suspicion in the minds of the American Chief of Staff, General George C. Marshall, and several of his colleagues, notably Admiral King, that Churchill's preference for the indirect approach to Europe via the Mediterranean created a danger of America's strength being diverted from the ultimate main aim of a cross-Channel invasion of France into a wasteful sideshow. Marshall had hoped for the cross-Channel assault in 1943. By the beginning of this year at Casablanca the Americans as well as the British had been forced to face the fact that Overlord, as the cross-Channel operation was now known, could not be mounted before summer 1944. The question was what to do after the expected victory in Tunisia. Churchill pressed for an invasion of Sicily as a preliminary to the invasion of the Italian mainland. The Americans agreed to Sicily but were chary of continuing into Italy, a move that they thought might escalate into just that costly secondary campaign (at the expense of the eventual cross-Channel invasion) that they were determined to avoid.

The dialogue was continued at the "trident" conference in Washington immediately after the Tunis victory or "Tunisgrad," as the Germans now called it. The size of this success had exceeded all expectations and the British wanted Eisenhower to be directed to exploit the forthcoming Sicily enterprise to the full with a view to eliminating Italy from the war—which implied an onward move into Italy itself. Churchill persuasively pressed the British view on the grounds that, with a year to wait before Overlord, the large and victorious Anglo-American forces now in command of the North African shore should not simply remain idle. They *must* go somewhere and fight the Germans. Not only was this necessary as a preliminary to Overlord itself but, as he later told the House of Commons: "We have got to fight them somewhere unless we are just to sit back and watch the Russians." The obvious "somewhere" seemed to him and his Chief of Staff, General Sir Alan Brooke, to be Italy, the "soft underbelly" of Fortress Europe.

General Marshall and his colleagues were chary of going into Italy. They preferred to go from Sicily into Sardinia and then to stop. The farthest that they would go was to agree that Eisenhower should "mount such operations in exploitation of the attack on Sicily as might be calculated to eliminate Italy from the war." What these operations might be was left unclear, but there was a firm stipulation that, before he embarked on any, Eisenhower must first obtain the authority of the Combined Chiefs-of-Staff. Churchill's eloquent advocacy of Italy as a way to meet the Russians in Central Europe or, alternatively, as a springboard for operations in the Balkans that might bring Turkey into the war, scared rather than persuaded the Americans who, with their eyes firmly fixed on the English Channel, felt that this kind of Churchillian flight of strategic fancy was precisely the kind of diversionary activity they feared and that might jeopardize the main effort Overlord.

As a further brake on any ambitious ideas that Eisenhower might develop under Churchill's potent influence, the American Chiefs decided at Washington that substantial air and naval forces and a number of the precious landing craft should be diverted to Burma and the Pacific after Sicily: and that seven divisions (four American, three British) and still more of the scarce landing craft were to return to Britain to be held there for Overlord. Eisenhower, caught between the beguiling persuasions of Churchill and the determination of his own Chiefs not to be beguiled by them, said he would reserve his own judgment regarding an Italian invasion until he had seen how the Sicily venture fared.

It took him only one week of the Sicily campaign to make up his mind that Churchill was right and that Italy should be invaded. On July 20 the American members of the Combined Chiefs of Staff gave their approval—but stultified it by simultaneously insisting that the transfer of air, naval, and land forces laid down at the Washington conference must proceed as arranged. Eisenhower went to work and decided that he could make his landing at Salerno, a little to the south of Naples, provided that the necessary resources could be made available.

> Accordingly, the British Chiefs of Staff, on their own account, issued a temporary standstill instruction to all aircraft and shipping which were under orders to leave the Mediterranean. This produced an outburst in Washington, where Marshall and King insisted on July 24 that the original movement orders must be carried out.[1]

Next day the news of Mussolini's downfall came through. Wilmot continues:

> Invasion of the mainland in strength was imperative and urgent, but Eisenhower's forces were deeply committed in Sicily and to his dismay he discovered that with the shipping allocated to him he could make no large-scale landings before the first week of September.

Thus it was the American Chiefs of Staff, not the Commander on the spot, who prevented the proper exploitation of the Italian collapse and it must be inferred that the stubbornly blind eye that they turned to so obvious an opportunity can be explained only by their deep-rooted *idée fixe* that no good would come of involvement in a new Mediterranean campaign. As General Marshall put it during the Washington discussions: "The Mediterranean is a vacuum into which America's great military might could be drawn off until there is nothing left with which to deal the decisive blow on the Continent." But, as Colonel Rudolf Böhmler—German combatant officer and historian of the Cassino battles—later commented: "The divergence of views among the Allies as regards their Mediterranean strategy came as a rare godsend to the Germans and was much to the detriment of the Allied cause."

In the circumstances it was perhaps not so surprising that Eisenhower, frustrated by his own Chiefs, should have been testy and short-tempered when Badoglio was throwing out blithe suggestions that the Allies should invade north of Rome with "at least fifteen divisions!" For his initial assault at Salerno he would be able to land only five with three to follow up.

It was out of this misalliance of strategic intent and viewpoint that the love-child (or love-hate-child) named the Italian Campaign was born. The verdict of the English military critic Major General J. F. C. Fuller[2] that it was "a campaign which for lack of strategic sense and tactical imagination is unique in military history" is arguably too dogmatic and harsh. There is no doubt, however, that it was fought under an initial and continuing handicap which it never wholly overcame. It was never accorded more than second-class status (and therefore support) yet it was fought in terrain of exceptional difficulty that always demanded first-class performance.

The German who emerged with most credit from the Italian defection and its confused aftermath was Field-Marshal Albert Kesselring, the discredited "dupe of the Italians" and Commander-in-Chief South with seven divisions at hand and an eighth in the process of being withdrawn from Sardinia. A difficulty was that there were two Commanders-in-Chief in Italy. Rommel, now as much in favour as Kesselring was out of it, was earmarked by Hitler to take over-all command in November. Rommel, thought Hitler, would know how to deal toughly with the Italians. Under Rommel's influence he had decided that the place to establish his main defence line was across the Apennines south of the Po Valley on the line Pisa-Rimini. This presupposed that the Allies with their great sea and air power would land well up the peninsular and with this in mind Hitler was prepared to write off Kesselring's divisions in the south, though there were eight of them. Hitler did not depart from this strategic intention even when the Allies in fact made their main landing in the early hours of September 9 at Salerno, thirty miles south of Naples.

That morning General Mark W. Clark's U.S. Fifth Army invaded with five divisions (three American, two British) supported by Rangers and Commandos; two more American divisions and one British division being at sea ready to follow up the assault wave. Montgomery's British Eighth Army, which had landed two divisions in the extreme south six days previously, was to press forward in order to join up with the Salerno landing as soon as possible. As soon as the Italian armistice was announced—a few hours before Clark's landing—Rommel in the north addressed himself energetically to the prearranged task of disarming the Italians. The Allied invasion, as far as he was concerned, was part of another war, Kesselring's war. Kesselring, with an invasion on his hands and the additional task of disarming his share of the Italian Army, considered the double assignment excessive. He would at the same time have to resist an invasion and disarm Italian forces that numerically outnumbered him. He used both his intelligence and the ability to "get on with the Italians" that had lately earned him so much abuse at OKW. Through his old Italian contacts he arranged a private surrender of the Italian Army in the south whereby, in return for laying down their arms and agreeing to offer no resistance, he would let the soldiers return to their homes unmolested—the one thing they wanted above all to do. This amicable and successful settlement of the problem contrasted with Rommel's action in the north where the Italians found themselves rounded up in prison camps, evacuated to Germany or forced to run away and join the bands of partisans that the Communists were busy organizing.

Having thus cleared the decks for General von Vietinghoff's Tenth Army, as the divisions in the south had been designated, Kesselring made strong representations to OKW to send two of Rommel's northern divisions to the south to help Tenth Army, but the request was refused. For three days the U.S. Fifth Army were made to fight desperately for their initial beachhead. On the fourth day, September 12, Kesselring was ready to launch his major counterattack to drive the invaders into the sea. It was spearheaded by 16th Panzer Division and directed at the gap between the U.S. and British sectors. For three days it was touch and go. To break up the German counterattacks the Fifth Army called on massive artillery fire, the continuous support of their air forces, and the guns of the two navies. The British battleships *Warspite* and *Valiant* sailed inshore to throw in the weight of their fifteen-inch guns—a hazard not normally encountered by the Panzer crews. The Luftwaffe retaliated with a surprise, new to the Allies, a radar-controlled glider bomb of a rocket type. Bombs of this new kind caused severe damage to *Warspite* and to the American cruisers *Savannah* and *Philadelphia*. Allied reinforcements poured in. General Ridgway's 82nd Airborne Division parachuted a force into the struggling beachhead and another behind the German lines on the road to Naples. The British 7th Armoured Division began to land, and Major General Lucian K. Truscott's U.S. 3rd Infantry Division was shortly to follow. Kesselring was raging at OKW and Rommel for refusing to send him even one division from the north that might have made all the difference. By September 15 the crisis was over. The Allied beachhead was secure and the advance to capture the port of Naples could proceed. On September 16 the two divisions of Montgomery's Eighth Army that had landed in the "toe" of Italy made contact with the Fifth Army near Salerno. They had advanced two hundred miles through the heat and the arid mountains of Calabria against harassing rearguards by two German divisions. It had taken them a day under two weeks. To the hard-pressed Fifth Army it seemed a long, long time.

In the meantime General Alexander, whose 15th Army Group controlled the Fifth and Eighth Armies, had shipped his two reserve British divisions—1st Airborne and 78th Infantry—to Taranto to open a new front on the Adriatic side of Italy. Their purpose was to take some of the strain off the Naples front and also to advance to capture the Foggia airfields, an early objective of the campaign. From Foggia the Allied strategic bombers would be able to reach southern Germany, Austria, and the Ploesti oilfields in Rumania.

By October 1, General Alexander had reached "first base": the great port of Naples and the complex of airfields at Foggia. Clark's Fifth Army were continuing their advance up the west side of the country: Montgomery's Eighth up the east coast. Kesselring, aggrieved at being denied the reinforcement with which he thought he might have turned Salerno into an Allied disaster, was preparing a winter defence plan to show the Allies that the road to Rome was longer than they might think from the map; that the "soft underbelly" of Europe was a great deal hornier than they had been led to believe; and to prove to Hitler and his co-Commander-in-Chief Rommel that Italy *could* be effectively defended south of Rome, in spite of their dogmatic assertions to the contrary a few weeks before. With the two Allied advances up the two coasts now slowing down to a stop-go progress from river to river and ridge to ridge, with always a new ridge or river or mountain just ahead of the last, the Italian campaign assumed a pattern of warfare that was to continue for many months. This pattern was dictated, like all patterns of war, by topography. Italy is a peninsula about a thousand miles long, 120 wide. A dorsal range of mountains runs down its centre, and a succession of fishbone ridges run down to the coast from either side of it. The only flat country, until the northern valley and plain of the Po are reached, is the narrow coastal strip on either coast. On the western side the central mountain range is farther from the coast than it is on the eastern side. The western coastal strip can therefore be as wide as twenty-five miles, whereas on the eastern side it is seldom more than ten. Lateral roads across the mountains are few. A military advance is therefore confined to the two coastal strips of plain and these are intersected every few miles by the lateral spurs and ridges leading like ribs off the central range, and by the streams and rivers running beside them.

On October 24 Alexander said in a situation report:[3]

> Today the situation is that eleven Allied divisions are fighting a frontal battle in country favouring the defence against an immediate strength of nine German divisions, which can be reinforced at any moment.

Earlier in the same report, which was presented to Eisenhower, he said:

> The obvious present German intention is to hold a line south of Rome, where the country favours defence and allows no scope to the deployment of our superiority in armour or artillery. Coming bad weather will limit the employment of our air forces, as indeed it has done already . . . It would therefore appear that we are committed to a long costly advance to Rome, a "slogging match," with our present slight superiority in formations on the battlefront offset by the enemy opportunity for relief. . . .

What Alexander's armies needed was infantry, for in this kind of country and with torrential rains now developing, it was going to be an exercise in pure infantry warfare. Already tanks could not move off the few roads, artillery with its flat trajectory was beginning to disclose its limitations in mountains and the weather was already grounding the air forces. Infantry was what was needed. Bombers were what ceaselessly arrived in the early weeks of the campaign. The Allied obsession with the heavy bomber as the supreme war-winner now extended to this difficult new front apparently to be favoured with everything but soldiers. From the moment Foggia was captured the Strategic Air Force and its needs were given priority of shipping space from the Allied bases in North Africa and Sicily and they retained it throughout the first vital weeks when Clark and Montgomery were striving to drive their land offensive forward. This situation provoked Churchill to understandable protest when he learned what was happening. He sent a sharp note through General Sir Hastings Ismay to the Chiefs of Staff Committee: [4]

It is surely altogether wrong to build up the Strategic Air Force in Italy at the expense of the battle for Rome. The strategic bombing of Germany, however important, cannot take precedence over the battle, which must ever rank first in our thoughts. Major tactical needs must always have priority over strategic policy. I was not aware until recently that the build-up of the Army had been obstructed by the forward move of a mass of strategic air not connected with the battle.

A week later he exploded:

The monstrous block of air, in its eagerness to get ahead, has definitely hampered the operations of the Army.

The Prime Minister might well be worried about "his" campaign. First the Combined Chiefs of Staff had insisted on the return of seven Allied divisions to Britain for Overlord. Now the divisions that were still left in North Africa were prevented from reaching the Italian battlefield because the available ships were bulging with the wherewithal to bomb southern Germany and Rumania.

And now the weather deteriorated rapidly. Great gales swept southern Italy. In the mountains cold and exposure began to rival bullets in claiming casualties among the forward troops while in the plains vehicles bogged down in glutinous mud reminiscent of the classic morasses of Passchendaele in the earlier German war.

On the German side the prospect was considerably brighter. The difficult situation created by the Italian defection had been surmounted with what must inevitably be called "typical German efficiency" and with little bloodshed. Field-Marshal Rommel's Army Group B now numbered ten good divisions in the northern half of the country. In the south Field-Marshal Kesselring, though he had failed to prevent the Allies landing, had been agreeably surprised by the relatively small forces with which they had done so. With little help from his superiors he had gained a grip on the situation in the south, was already effectively delaying the double Allied advance—with much the same tactics as those he had practised and perfected in Sicily—while he prepared a winter defence line that he was confident would hold up the advance throughout the winter. By mid-November (at the time Churchill was complaining to his Chiefs of Staff about the surfeit of bombers and the paucity of soldiers) Kesselring was back in favour. Having until then adhered to his intention to appoint Rommel supreme commander in Italy and post Kesselring elsewhere, probably to Norway, Hitler now suddenly changed his mind. Kesselring was given the appointment and Rommel was posted to France to take over the completion of the Atlantic Wall and eventually to command an army group in its defence against the Allied cross-Channel invasion. Kesselring's new title was C-in-C South-West and Army Group C—to avoid confusion with Army Group South in Russia and Army Group B, now being relinquished by Rommel in north Italy.

Hitler also embraced with enthusiasm Kesselring's strategy for the defence in depth of Italy. First, the Gustav line, a river and mountain line halfway between Rome and Naples through Cassino. Second, the Pisa-Rimini line (later called the Gothic line by the Allies) barring the way to the Po Valley and the plain of industrialized north Italy. Lastly there were the Austrian Alps. Between these three main stop lines were an unlimited number of minor ones covering all road routes like the baffle plates of an automobile silencer.

Italy was no longer the lyrical dream of the travel posters, the cradle of European art, religion, and culture. It was a topographical extension of the Third Reich, projecting one thousand miles southward, scaly-backed with mountains, ridges, ledges, and valleys that might have been specifically designed by nature for the one military purpose of enabling the few to obstruct the movement of the many. Italy was now just a lump of ground providing the hardest possible route to Germany from the South. "Soft underbelly," the off-the-cuff description used by Churchill when Mussolini was its protector, had become a grotesque irony. It is arguable that this was what General Marshall had instinctively been afraid of.

Kesselring was for the time being a contented man. He had been given control of the Italian theatre. His armies had been heartened by the fact that they were now to face the enemy and stand fast after the continuous withdrawal that had been their lot since El Alamein. The atrocious weather was working in Kesselring's favour. First, it gave him more time to prepare the Gustav line. The Gustav defences were to follow the river line of the Garigliano-Rapido, which barred both the main highways to Rome, the Via Appia and the Via Casilina, and also the entrance to the Liri Valley through which the latter runs. Some fifteen miles inland from the west coast this river line abruptly reared upward at Cassino into a mountain line running inland into the heart of the Abruzzi Mountains until the Gustav again ran downwards towards the east coast along the River Sangro. The combination of river line and mountain near Cassino, one complementing the other, made this the key sector. In addition to his own engineers Kesselring had been allotted units of the Organization Todt to carry out the more elaborate construction work on the Gustav.

Secondly, the bad weather made it easier for him to delay the Fifth Army advance before it even reached Cassino and the Gustav. This stretch of the road to Rome ran through or past a series of hills and mountains guarding it like massive sentinels ideally placed for a succession of blocking actions in depth. The Allied advance could be blunted and bled and frequently stopped some way before it came up against the main defences. Kesselring was confident that his defenders could hold on till summer at least.

If the weather-assisted *rallentando* of the Allied advance in Italy made some sense (as we have suggested) of General Marshall's prior apprehensions about the campaign, events elsewhere were giving point to Churchill's argument about the necessity to fight the Germans "somewhere unless we are just to sit back and watch the Russians." The Russians had been providing plenty to watch all summer. After crushing at birth the German summer offensive at Kursk in July, and immediately hitting back with their own counteroffensive, they had been rolling forward on a wide front as inexorably as that steamroller to which their army used to be likened in the First World War. They retook the much-taken much-retaken Kharkov on August 23, Poltava on September 22, Smolensk on September 25. It was a war of "placenames" again for the convenience of the newspapers. By the end of September, when the Italian campaign was three weeks old, the Russians had reached the Dnieper, that long wide, curving, comforting waterway which the Germans were inclined to regard as one trusty barrier on which they could rely as a firm winter line—their East Wall. But not so. Not waiting to mount a set-piece attack with special amphibious transport, assault boats, bridging and other specialized equipment which the Americans and the British liked to bring to bear on such assignments, the Russians just swarmed across the river s'khodu, as they called it, meaning "on the march": using anything and everything that would float—small boats, large boats, rafts, barrels roped together, stray bits of timber, anything. On November 6 they recaptured Kiev, the capital of the Ukraine. They had advanced 250 miles since July.

It could hardly have increased Stalin's wary regard for his Western allies if the large Anglo-American armies now in existence had watched all this happen from comfortable grandstands in North Africa and Britain. Churchill had a valid point when he foresaw the possibility of this, and offered it as an additional reason for the Allies to go into Italy.

As he watched the Gustav line growing daily stronger, while the mud and the mountains of central Italy increasingly delayed the Allies' approach to it, something of his old optimism returned to Kesselring. He had a naturally confident disposition and Italy was now his exclusive responsibility. There was no need for him to think beyond it. But if Kesselring, with his limited and clear-cut brief—to hold the Anglo-Americans and defend Rome and the Reich on the Cassino line—could take a rosy view of the war situation in late 1943 he was by this time just about the only senior German officer or political leader who still could.

On three successive days in September Dr. Goebbels had revealing notes in his copious diary. On September 20 he noted the latest consolidated German casualties for the Russian campaign. Between June 22, 1941, when it opened and the end of August 1943, two years and two months later, the German losses were 548,480 killed or died, 1,998,991 wounded, 354,967 missing. Next day his entry included the sentence:

> It gives one the creeps to look at the map and compare what we had under our dominion about this time last year with the distance we have now been thrown back . . .

And on the day after that:

> At the moment things look very bad on the Eastern Front. Our retreats are no longer orderly and troops naturally lose a lot of equipment owing to the speed of their movement. Once again there is a serious crisis.[5]

Goebbels the diarist, as opposed to Goebbels the propagandist and professional cheer-leader, was understandably despondent. He was not alone. The OKW operations staff, especially its chief General Jodl, who was responsible for all fronts other than Russia (which remained the province of General Zeitzler, the Army Chief of Staff), was also despondent. Jodl was engaged in the increasingly exacting process of military "inflation" which might be defined as trying to garrison too many danger fronts with two few troops.

In addition to the main commitment in Russia where some two hundred divisions were fighting the Red Army, there was the following distribution on other fronts in November 1943.[6] In the Balkans there were twenty-four; in Italy twenty-two; in France, Belgium, and Holland fifty; in Norway and Denmark eighteen; in Germany itself another fifteen which should have been a strong central reserve but tended to be skeleton formations in the process of being re-formed. Many of these so-called divisions were by this time divisions in name only. It was Jodl's thankless task to maintain these various fronts and to reconcile the dwindling central reserve with Hitler's allergy to any withdrawal, even a tactical withdrawal to shorten a line and thereby reduce the number of troops needed to hold it. Italy was a case in point. By settling for the line through the Apennines as Rommel had suggested and Hitler had originally accepted, the front—which had to be reinforced from France—could have been held with half the troops. But Hitler insisted on defending every part of Fortress Europe on its outermost perimeter from the Reich. Once the idea of defending the Cassino line south of Rome had been planted in his mind its defence to the death became an end in itself, an article of faith. To this extent the Allied strategy of drawing German divisions from France was successful, though General Alexander pertinently noted in his Italian campaign report that he had to ask himself every day "who was containing whom."

Jodl's problem was more than a question of mathematics —of making the available number of troops go round. As a result of the Allied successes during the year, the occupied countries had taken heart and had been encouraged to offer more active resistance to the occupying power than hitherto. The Allies were beginning to have some success in their efforts to foster these resistance movements. Tito's partisans in Yugoslavia, for example, were not only being actively assisted by Allied guerrilla fighters, but were now being supplied across the Adriatic by the Allied armies in Italy and were able to evacuate their wounded to Allied military hospitals, where the tough handsome Yugoslav girl soldiers hobbling about on crutches, and frequently without one or more limbs, were a never-ending source of sympathetic wonder to their western allies. Norway's Resistance had always been active and useful but now Denmark was giving trouble for the first time. The French Resistance, nourished and helped by the American Office of Strategic Services (OSS) and its British equivalent Strategic Operations Executive (SOE), had now developed an active presence that was more than a mere token as it had been previously. Jodl had therefore not only to keep the existing garrisons of Fortress Europe up to strength but to increase them.

The recurrent German nightmare of the two-front war had not merely come home to roost: it had roosted and had fledged as many fronts as there were occupied countries. In the Führer's Fortress were many mansions; and in each a time bomb or Trojan horse was making ready to erupt when the time was ripe. The retributive grip was tightening. But as 1943, the year of crisis, moved through its last weeks into 1944, the year of decision, it was not the East and the South that were uppermost in Hitler's apprehensions though these were the fronts that had dominated the autumn. It was his old bogey the West that riveted once more his attention: and in particular the significantly insignificant strip of water called the English Channel (or La Manche) where he knew that the climax, the supreme climax of all his dreams, hopes, aspirations, efforts and ambitions must be played out. The wheel had come full circle. Once again Adolf Hitler looked out over the English Channel to England, as he had done in 1940. On that occasion it had cheated him, this English moat. Now it must be made to reverse its role and, as the moat of Fortress Europe, thwart in turn *his* enemies.

But after three-and-a-half years the circumstances were slightly different. The "scepter'd isle" of Shakespeare's high-flown imagery had turned into an unsinkable Anglo-American aircraft carrier, a vast armed camp and a trial ground on which the technology and industrialization of destruction were being brought to the highest degree of proficiency that human ingenuity had ever reached.

As the year of decision loomed ahead with the majestic inevitability of an iceberg on a collision course Hitler issued the 51st of the numbered Führer Directives that provide so useful a continuity of insight into his character, mentality and military direction. In its preamble, Directive 51, which was dated November 3, 1943, summarized his thinking at this time. In 1941 he had attacked Russia with the intention of achieving there a quick conquest as a preliminary to settling finally with Britain and the West. The lightning conquest had not been achieved and in not achieving it he had lost 3,000,000 German soldiers dead, wounded or missing. The resurgent Russians had now driven relentlessly westward and by November were less than four hundred miles from the eastern ramparts of Fortress Europe. Yet it was upon the English Channel, and the invasion that would soon be directed across it, that Hitler's thoughts and fears were obsessively fixed.

The Führer.   Führer Headquarters,
                                              3rd November 1943
                                                   27 copies

Directive No. 51

The hard and costly struggle against Bolshevism during the last two and a half years, which has involved the bulk of our military strength in the East, has demanded extreme exertions. The greatness of the danger and the general situation demanded it. But the situation has since changed. The danger in the East remains, but a greater danger now appears in the West: an Anglo-Saxon landing! In the East, the vast extent of the territory makes it possible for us to lose ground, even on a large scale, without

274

a fatal blow being dealt to the nervous system of Germany.

It is very different in the West! Should the enemy succeed in breaching our defences on a wide front here, the immediate consequences would be unpredictable. Everything indicates that the enemy will launch an offensive against the Western front of Europe, at the latest in the spring, perhaps even earlier.

I can therefore no longer take responsibility for further weakening the West, in favour of other theatres of war. I have therefore decided to reinforce its defences, particularly those places from which the long-range bombardment of England will begin. For it is here that the enemy must and will attack, and it is here—unless all indications are misleading—that the decisive battle against the landing forces will be fought.[7]

The "long-range bombardment of England" was to be carried out by two secret weapons. These were the FSG 76 (known to the British as the V-1 Flying Bomb), a pilotless monoplane 25 feet long and carrying a ton of explosive: and the A-4 ballistic missle (the British knew it as the V-2 rocket), a 4-ton rocket 46 feet long with a range of 200 miles and a velocity in descent of 2200-2500 miles an hour.[8] The V-weapons were intended as a retaliatory measure to pay back the British for the great fire raids on German cities. Hitler's original intention was to discover by experiment which of the two "secret weapons" was the more effective, but eventually he decided to order both. By the middle of 1942 Allied intelligence was on the trail and had discovered that Peenemunde on the Baltic was the station where the research and experimental work was being carried out. Thereafter an intensive bombing of Peenemunde and continuous air reconnaissance forcing it to be dispersed delayed the German effort and disclosed the launching sites for the Flying Bombs on which a vast tonnage of Allied bombs was then expended. But in the end the chief delay was caused not by Allied countermeasures but by the natural technical difficulties incurred by both these highly complex experimental projects in the natural course of their research and development.

Hitler had hoped to launch his new terror on London and the south of England early in 1944 while the Anglo-American invasion was in the last phase of its preparation. The notion of raining flying bombs and rockets on England at this crucial time was understandably appealing. But science was a difficult mistress to hurry. She had to take her time. General Heinemann, now in charge of the army formation responsible for both offensives, reported at the end of 1943 that a considerable amount of work remained to be done both on the launching sites and the Flying Bombs themselves and that they would not be ready for a mass bombardment until May or June. As for the A-4 (or V-2) Rockets, they were unlikely to be ready before the end of 1944. You could not after all perfect a thing like that to order. Though Heinemann could not know it his A-4 was the historic forerunner of the Sputnik, the harbinger of the space age. Unfortunately for all concerned too many of the missiles were still blowing up in the air. There was still much work to be done.

This was what Hitler meant by the long-range bombardment of England to which he referred in his Directive 51. Since the beginning of the war he had made a habit in his propagandist speeches of uttering terrible threats of "secret weapons." "Hitler's secret weapon" had long been a favourite catchphrase of the Allied wartime comedians. Now it seemed that he really had produced not one but two secret weapons of formidable potential. Unfortunately for him both were going to be too late to make any difference.

In Führer Directive 51 Hitler wrote the prologue to the last act of something that had started to go against him just two years before outside Moscow. As if to symbolize the sense of climax, to provide, as it were, the theatrical roll of drums, the bombing of his capital began in earnest in the middle of the same month. The bombing of Berlin had been taking place intermittently since the summer of 1940. But it had not been heavy and by this time the total weight of bombs dropped over the long period was no more than five hundred tons. On the night of November 18 the Royal Air Force initiated a series of sixteen heavy attacks, using between seven hundred and nine hundred bombers each time, dropping a total of 25,000 tons of bombs. The attacks were made between mid-November and March 1944 and the intention was to inflict on Hitler's capital an experience similar to that suffered by Hamburg in the summer.

From the German point of view the Battle of Berlin, though highly destructive and costly in lives, was for a number of reasons less concentrated and therefore less calamitous than the fire-storms of Hamburg had been. The ground area of the city had a diameter of between twenty and twenty-five miles. The distance from England required the longest nights of the year for the round journey. Berlin was the most heavily defended of German cities and since Hamburg there had been a tightening up and improvement of night fighter tactics. On the way, the attackers had to run the gauntlet of successive zones of antiaircraft defences covering other areas. The corollary of having to attack when the nights were longest was that the weather was at its seasonal worst. In the words of Air Marshal Harris:

> The whole battle was fought in appalling weather and in conditions resembling those of no other campaign in the history of warfare. Scarcely a single crew caught a single glimpse of the objective they were attacking.[9]

Dependent wholly on their radar aiming equipment the British bomber crews (for whom the Battle of Berlin was an epic test of courage and endurance in extreme difficulties) devastated three and a half square miles of the city, seriously damaging forty-three important factories and 282 others.[10] Casualties to the population were 6166 dead and 18,431 wounded. These figures would have been worse from Berlin's point of view had 1,000,000 people, including large numbers of women, children, and elderly people not been evacuated from the city in the early stages. To discourage them from drifting back the schools were closed and remained closed.

The cost to the Royal Air Force of the sixteen attacks was three hundred[11] aircraft and four thousand men. Production, however, was hardly affected, and morale was not damaged. The sceptical satirical brand of humour for which Berliners are noted almost flourished in circumstances that provided so much scope for their caustic sense of humour. Not until March did the weather clear sufficiently for good photographs of the damage to be obtained. "It fell short of what had been achieved at Hamburg," wrote Churchill shortly. And as it had been achieved at a cost to the R.A.F. that they could not have sustained anyway, even if the bombing squadrons had not now been required for other purposes, the great Berlin raids could on balance be counted a victory for the Luftwaffe. In the Battle of Berlin the German night fighters gained for the first time an ascendancy over the British bombers, assisted, of course, by the long distance the latter had to travel, but also because of the success of their latest tactics. (A night raid on Nuremberg at this time cost the British 94 aircraft.)

As March 1944 marked a change of direction in the air war—the Allied bombing effort now being switched to support for the coming cross-Channel invasion—two comments by the Official British Historian of the Air War, Noble Frankland,[12] may relevantly be quoted. The first is general to the theme of Strategic Bombing to date, the second is particular to the sixteen attacks known as the Battle of Berlin:

> By March 1944, the night offensive of Bomber Command, despite its enormous successes, had failed to achieve a decisive reduction in German war production or a decisive break in German morale . . .
> . . . by March 1944 the German air defences had got on top of the night bombers and were inflicting an insupportable casualty rate upon them.

As if to balance this temporary thwarting of the British night bomber, the Battle of Berlin provided the occasion for a heartening return to duty of the American day bomber. As already noted, the U.S. Eighth Air Force had opted for the greater accuracy of day bombing, a policy which had assumed that the defensive armament of the Flying Fortress and Liberator would be able to take care of the fighter attacks that day bombers would be bound to attract. Unfortunately this assumption proved to be false. From the start of their day attacks in the spring of 1943 the Eighth Air Force sustained heavy losses, which continued through the summer, and reached a terrible peak in the disastrous October raid on Schweinfurt, centre of the German ballbearing industry, when no fewer than sixty out of an attacking force of 291 Flying Fortresses and Liberators were shot down, and another 138 returned to England damaged. This brought the Eighth Air Force's total losses in four raids carried out within six days to 148. The American offensive had to be called off until such time as there became available a long-range fighter force that could escort the day bombers all the way to and from their targets. The problem was to produce an aircraft with the long range of the strategic bomber and the manoeuvrability of a fighter, produce it fast and produce it in quantity. It was a tall order but it was met in six months.

There happened to be in Britain a fighter named the 73 Mustang that the British had ordered from North American Aviation in 1940 when they were desperately short of aircraft. The U. S. Air Force rejected the Mustang because its performance was not considered good enough. By the time the Royal Air Force received its first operational Mustangs in 1941 it, too, decided that the Mustang performance was now inadequate. The despised plane was passed to the less exacting field of Army co-operation. Rolls-Royce now appears in the story as Fairy Godmother. Rolls-Royce thought that there was nothing wrong with the Mustang that a more powerful engine would not put right. Prolonged tests and experiments were therefore carried out in 1942 with five Mustangs fitted with Rolls-Royce's well-tried and successful Merlin engine. Out of these tests, and with certain modifications to the airframe, there emerged the P-51B Mustang with a Packard-Merlin engine giving it a range (with long-range tanks) of 1500 miles and a top speed at 30,000 feet of 455 miles per hour—a distinct lead on its main German rivals the Focke-Wolfe 190 and the Messerschmitt 109 G. But Cinderella had not quite reached the Ball yet. In July 1943 General Henry H. Arnold, Commanding General of the U. S. Air Forces, conceded, but without enthusiasm, that the P-51B Mustang was for the moment probably the best answer to the need for a long-range fighter but he ordered only a modest 180 to be provided for the Eighth Air Force in England. Then came the expensive raids of late summer culminating in the crippling Schweinfurt disaster and the crisis that followed in the U. S. Air Command. The Mustang was at last recognized for what it was—one of the finest fighter aircraft produced by any country during the war. A crash production programme was now put in hand with that dynamism in which American industry excels. Cinderella had arrived at last at the Ball. By the end of the year Mustangs were flying with the Eighth Air Force and undergoing their final modifications.[13] By February the Eighth Air Force had resumed its daylight offensive against German industrial centres, escorted to and from the most distant targets by their Mustang fighters. One of these raids was the daylight attack made by 672 Flying Fortresses and Liberators on Berlin as the R.A.F.'s programme of sixteen night attacks was drawing to a close. Compared with October, when the Eighth Air Force losses per raid had reached the insupportable peak level of 9.1 percent, their losses from February 1944, thanks to the Mustang escorts, were now down to 3.5 percent.

It was a good augury for the new air offensive that was to prepare the way for the Allied invasion. It helped, as has been said, to make up for the ascendancy that the German fighters had been gaining over the British night bombing offensive.

Part Five

THE FINAL CRACK-UP

(June-August 1944)

Chapter 22

ATLANTIC WALL:
TWENTIETH-CENTURY BULWARK,
RAMPART, AND BARBICAN

☐ As the last weeks of 1943 dissolved into the first of 1944, the squeeze around Europe, the once indestructible—seemingly not even hurtable—fortress, steadily tightened into a hug that was physically an increasing strain on those in charge while pressing claustrophobically on their nerves.

Certain key Allied commanders quietly disappeared from the Mediterranean theatre to assume new duties in Britain. From Italy went Generals Eisenhower (to exchange one Supreme Command for a bigger) and Montgomery and Air Marshal Sir Arthur Tedder: from North Africa, Generals Bradley and Patton. Also on the move to Britain were the seven Army divisions and the four air groups that had been scheduled during the summer. These moves did not long remain unknown to the Germans. Their significance was not difficult to guess and it did not lessen the strain on the German Supreme Command.

Admittedly these changes proclaimed rather publicly that the Allies had downgraded the status of Italy, their Southern Front. But lest the Germans draw the wrong conclusions from this the Allied army group there retained its "First League" commander, General Alexander, as well as the Fifth Army's General Clark; powerful reinforcements continued to arrive from North Africa to strengthen the Fifth and Eighth Armies; and a major offensive against the German winter line at Cassino opened at the beginning of 1944. The contribution of the Southern Front to the encircling squeeze would not be negligible.

In the East the Russian offensive that had been driving westward since the breakout at Kursk and Orel in July had not, from the German point of view, worked out as a well-behaved summer offensive should. It had obstinately declined to bog down for the winter after the first crossings of the Dnieper in December. In January it had liberated Leningrad after the city's nine hundred days of siege and near-starvation and had then pushed the German Army Group North back to the border of Esthonia. In the centre the First and

Second Ukrainian Fronts of Generals Ivan Koniev and Nikolai Vatutin had also declined to stop for winter. Having completed some sizeable encirclements, bringing the Russian centre within striking distance of Poland and East Prussia, they had swung southwest to defeat Army Group South in what the Russians named the "Mud Offensive." Their momentum was not exhausted until March, by which time they had crossed the Bug, Dniester, and Pruth and had reached the northern border of Rumania—leaving well to their rear the German Seventeenth Army, cut off and stranded in the Crimea.

At every crisis Hitler, as usual, had ordered his commanders to hold fast rather than make the timely tactical withdrawals that might have saved their armies. As usual, when the "summer" offensive had at long last spent itself in March, he sacked the generals—this time the two remaining senior East Front veterans Field-Marshals von Mannstein and von Kleist, who departed with the customary severance pay-off—the Swords Clasp to their Knight's Crosses.

In the West the active pressure (as opposed to the psychological pressure across the Channel) came from the air during the first weeks of 1944. The Royal Air Force's sixteen night bombing attacks on Berlin were being pressed home despite the adverse weather conditions that were making this distant and difficult target more difficult still. As we have seen, the night offensive on the capital was less successful than some others. The British lost three hundred bombers in Berlin raids and two hundred in others so that by the end the German night fighters had gained an ascendancy that made the loss-rate uneconomic. On the other hand large areas of Berlin were devastated; public services were badly disrupted for weeks; scores of factories, dwelling houses, commercial premises, and administrative buildings were severely damaged; one million people had to be evacuated, and most of the rest spent sleepless nights in air-raid shelters at the time of year when the nights are longest and coldest. The people as well as the leaders and the soldiers were being made increasingly aware of the implications of fighting almost the whole world.

These pressures, working in concert, exposed the nakedness of Hitler in respect of reserves. As successive emergencies arose in Russia or Italy the gaps had to be plugged with divisions from the West which the West—with the invasion looming ahead in the near future—could not spare. There were simply not enough divisions to go round. The reserves, the most precious kind of military capital, had been squandered at Kursk in the summer during the abortive offensive that Hitler had not wanted but had allowed himself to be talked into. Now, like a man who has spent his spare capital, Hitler was desperately having to rob Peter to pay Paul only to have to rob Paul immediately afterwards to pay Peter back. The fighter aircraft sorely needed in Russia and Italy had to be retained in Germany to defend the Reich against the Allied bombers. Of course Hitler could have made his dwindling capital go farther by pulling back his Italian front to the northern Apennines where he had originally intended to place it. By doing this he could have held Italy with fewer divisions thereby making more available for use elsewhere. Instead his refusal ever to withdraw from anywhere caused him to play the Allies' game by putting more and more into Italy. But it was a waste of time for any of his close advisers to point out as Jodl often did such obvious ways of saving the manpower that was now stretched to the limit. The Allied policy of keeping him at full stretch on all fronts was amply vindicated.

But if spare soldiers were in short supply—something which bothered his staff, desperately striving to fill gaps and replace losses, more than it appeared to worry Hitler—war material had never been so plentiful. Production figures for 1943 [1] issued by Albert Speer's Ministry of Armaments and War Production showed a huge increase in all the main categories over those for 1942. Ammunition, for instance, had risen from 1,270,000 to 2,258,000 metric tons. Production of automatic weapons was up by 25 percent. Artillery of all kinds had more than doubled: 26,904 guns as compared with 11,988 in 1942. Armour (tanks and their near-relations mobile guns) had also more than doubled: 11,897 compared with 5573 the year before. The aircraft figure was very nearly double that of the previous year: 22,050 compared with 12,950 in 1942. (Apart from any other consideration, these figures supply their own comment on the efficacy of strategic bombing.) Hitler's problem was not how to maintain his war industry at full pitch. It had become a question of how to find enough trained men to handle the superabundance of weapons and machines of war that Reichsminister Speer was so capably providing.

It was against this background of steady concentric pressure, and in an atmosphere of impending climax, that Field-Marshal Rommel arrived in the West towards the end of the year with the mission of inspecting the Atlantic Wall from Denmark to the Spanish border. The focus of German anxiety and tension had swung back to the English Channel. There was a dreadful inevitability about it. Two and a half years earlier Hitler had set off on a rapid conquest of Russia as a preliminary to settling at his leisure with Britain which had not yet been joined by America. Now the position was in principle the same—but the roles of West and East had been reversed. The coming Anglo-American invasion, which now overshadowed all other thoughts, had to be annihilated on the beaches on the first day. (If they failed the first time, thought Hitler, they certainly would not try it again.) Then he would swing everything back to the East and deal with Russia at his leisure. It might take a little longer to win the war than he had originally hoped but with the new secret weapons that would soon be ready he could still win—once this tiresome business of an Anglo-American invasion had been disposed of in the English Channel.

It was Rommel's first important assignment since his return from Africa nearly a year before. He had since been out of favour, not so much because he was blamed for the final defeats in the Mediterranean, but rather because events had justified his many unheeded warnings that unless certain steps were taken they were bound to occur; to be proved right is never the best way of winning friends. During the summer, when a series of time-filling headquarters jobs had brought him into more frequent contact with the Führer, he had returned to favour despite some outspoken criticism of the blacker side of Nazi activity for which Himmler was responsible, which Rommel was for the first time learning about in detail; and which he was bold enough to tell Hitler would in the end lose him the war if allowed to continue. In spite of all this he was sufficiently popular again to be given Army Group B in northern Italy. This proved an unsatisfactory appointment because of the difficulty of having to "share" the theatre with Kesselring, a second commander-in-chief of equal standing. The eventual decision to make Kesselring C-in-C Italy and to give Rommel the task of inspecting the Atlantic Wall solved the problem for everyone. Hitler's growing concern about the West had been eased by the knowledge that the best possible man was now going there. Kesselring was delighted to have Italy to himself. Hitler was additionally pleased to have found suitable employment for his youngest, most energetic field-marshal. Rommel himself was delighted to be given this important role in what everyone now recognized to be the crucial operation of the war.

"Our last chance in the East," he remarked in the course of a conversation[2] about the future with General Bayerlein, "lies in equipping the Army thoroughly for an unyielding defence . . . But the West is the place that matters. If we once manage to throw the British and Americans back into the sea, it will be a long time before they return . . ." This last sentence was to be the dominant theme of his thinking from the moment he arrived in the West at the end of 1943. To carry out his inspection and any necessary action resulting from it Rommel was allowed to keep the headquarters staff of Army Group B which accompanied him from northern Italy and was now designated "an army group for special employment responsible directly to the Führer." It was typical of Hitler's policy of *divide et impera* with his commanders that Rommel should be responsible to him even though he would be operating within the sphere of responsibility of Commander-in-Chief West, Field-Marshal von Rundstedt. Rommel's position was not clearly defined and von Rundstedt was told almost nothing about what he was supposed to be doing. Western Command had to find out deviously that there were apparently three main reasons for Rommel's special mission: to direct his dynamic personality and energy into the overhaul and development of the Atlantic Wall; to utilize his popularity with people like the Minister of War Production, Speer, and the Organization Todt to procure their maximum co-operation in providing any constructional defence works he might call for; and, not least, to make full use of Rommel's long experience of fighting the British and his knowledge of their methods and psychology. So the oldest and the youngest of Germany's field-marshals—von Rundstedt, at sixty-nine almost old enough to be the father of Rommel, fifty-one—found themselves jointly responsible for the German arrangements for the most momentous battle of the war, the direct assault on Fortress Europe in the West where it was strongest. It was a dichotomy of command similar to that which Rommel had recently experienced in Italy. Rommel was to report directly to Hitler on the Atlantic Wall and what he thought should be done about it. But von Rundstedt was still the Commander-in-Chief West. Who, in the last resort, was in charge? It was an awkward situation that worked for a short time only because of the mutual respect the two men felt for each other as soldiers. And also because the sophisticated von Rundstedt, the sage and senior father-figure of the German Officer Corps, had learned, in his two comfortable years of "peacetime" soldiering in Paris, to take resignedly in his stride almost anything perpetrated by "Corporal Hitler" and the riffraff that surrounded him. Field-Marshal Gerd von Rundstedt was old, and feeling his age, and beginning not to care any more what new folly emanated from the leadership for which he had felt such uncompromising contempt for so long. He was a soldier. He would obey and do what he had to do. But no one could make him love or respect those who compelled his obedience.

Towards the end of 1943 the impossibility of the command set-up became more and more apparent as the subordinate commanders found it increasingly difficult to discover whether they were responsible to Rommel or to von Rundstedt. The latter accordingly asked OKW to clarify the position. An entry in the OKW Operations Diary on the last day of the year shows that they did so by activating Army Group B into a fighting Command responsible for the vital sector from Holland in the east, to the Loire in western Brittany, and comprising the Netherlands Command; Fifteenth Army (General Hans von Salmuth) between the Scheldt and the Seine; and Seventh Army (General Friederich Dollmann) which took over from the Seine to the Loire. Thus Rommel's Army Group B now took in the whole of the Dutch, Belgian, and north French coastline—at some point of which the invasion was almost certain to be directed—and it included the two large peninsulas of Normandy (with the port of Cherbourg) and Brittany (with Brest at its northwest corner). This 1300-mile sector seemed certain to be the part of the Atlantic Wall that mattered: and though surprise possibilities, such as a landing in Scandinavia or southern France, had to be borne in mind, all military logic seemed to indicate that either the Fifteenth or the Seventh Armies (or both) were bound to be the recipients of the coming invasion. The order which thus placed Rommel in command of the invasion coast also reaffirmed von Rundstedt as C-in-C West. Rommel was to press ahead with the task of strengthening the Atlantic Wall (in which he now had a more personal and proprietary interest) but from now on he was to address his reports, recommendations, and demands to von Rundstedt instead of to Hitler.

This order clarified the command relationship between the two field-marshals primarily responsible for preparing Fortress Europe for its supreme test. But a more serious difference between them was not to manifest itself. They differed in their views of how the defence of the West was to be conducted. As this strategic disagreement critically influenced the German defence policy both before and during the event it is necessary to summarize its essence before resuming the narrative of the preparatory months.

Von Rundstedt believed with Frederick the Great that "he who would defend all defends nothing. . . . Little minds want to defend everything, sensible men concentrate on the essential." Faced with the problem of defending 2500 miles of Atlantic and Mediterranean coasts he considered that it would be a waste of time to attempt to defend it all. With their current strength and with their complete superiority on sea and in the air, nothing (he thought) could stop the Allies making one or more successful landings. The time to attack them was *after* they had done so and before they had had time to consolidate a beachhead. Therefore, the proper defence was to keep a strong armoured reserve some way inland ready to rush to the invaded point and counterattack the landing force while it was still weak.

Rommel believed that the time to smash the invasion would be while it was in progress. It must be broken on the beaches. If the Allies once secured a footing their immense material strength would soon build up and ensure that they could not be dislodged. They must at all costs be prevented from securing that first footing. He countered von Rundstedt's idea of keeping the main armoured reserve inland— to race forward to counterattack any penetration—with the argument that, in the face of the Allies' command of the air, the panzers would never even reach the battle.

Both men were influenced by their experiences earlier in the war. Von Rundstedt was remembering how in 1940 he had exposed the folly of fortified lines by the ease with which he had turned the celebrated and supposedly impregnable French Maginot line. Rommel was remembering the paralysis of his panzers in North Africa from the time the British had achieved air supremacy at Alam Halfa. On the other hand he was also remembering how his deep minefields at El Alamein had held up Montgomery's vast numbers of tanks for days. The beach obstacles which he was planning could and must do the same for the coast of France.

The argument continued and eventually led to some unhappy compromising. Some people saw it as a typical conflict —common to all areas of existence—between an older man, rigid and conservative in outlook, and a dynamic younger man with livelier ideas and a sharper sense of the immediate present. For the time being Hitler favoured Rommel's idea —it naturally accorded with his own hold-fast-do-not-yield-an-inch outlook. So Rommel continued to chivvy his soldiers, his engineers, and the workmen of the Todt Organization into working harder than they had ever worked before to make the Atlantic Wall prickly and impenetrable. Von Rundstedt wrestled with the interminable problems of higher logistics in order to conjure enough good troops from somewhere to defend the West properly: and occasionally in an unguarded moment was heard to say that the Atlantic Wall was nothing more than a Propaganda Wall—a great bluff.[3]

Chapter 23

HITLER'S INTUITION ABOUT NORMANDY

☐ At the beginning of 1944 German manpower was stretched to the limit. There were 179 divisions in Russia, twenty-six in the Balkans, twenty-two in Italy, sixteen in Scandinavia, eight in Finland, three in the Low Countries, and fifty in France.

In a letter to his wife written shortly before Christmas, Rommel remarked:[1] "I hear that the call-up is going to be extended to the fourteen-year-olds. The lads will be sent to labour service or defence according to their size and physique." The question of boys now having to be conscripted to do man's work was understandably in Rommel's mind at this time. His own son Manfred, now fifteen, had received his call-up papers and was due to report to his assigned antiaircraft battery on January 6. The sort of letter the Field-Marshal wrote to his wife on Christmas Day 1943 was doubtless being written by many German fathers at this particular Christmas:

> . . . The big news was Manfred's call-up on the 6th January. He is sure to be pleased, but for us, and above all, for you, it's painful to see the youngster leave home, and it will take us a long time to get used to the idea.
>
> I wish you both a happy Christmas. Enjoy the time you still have together. . . .

At the end of January Rommel wrote a man-to-man as-one-soldier-to-another kind of letter to his son:[2]

Dear Manfred,

I was particularly pleased with your first letter as Luftwaffe auxiliary, because you have settled in so well to your new conditions. It is not easy for an "only child" to leave home. Perhaps you'll be getting a few days' leave in February and then you must give us a full report. There's still an endless amount of work here before I'll be able to say that we're properly prepared for battle. People get lazy and self-satisfied when things are quiet. But the contrast between quiet times and battle will be tough and I feel it essential to prepare for hard times here.

I'm out on the move a lot and raising plenty of dust wherever I go.

All the best to you and warmest greetings,
Your Father.

These human incidentals are mentioned because they illuminate the over-all German situation at this time more vividly than abstractions like "manpower shortage." They also illuminate the character and off-parade nature of the soldier who was the key man in Hitler's defence of the West, even though he was not the commander-in-chief.

The garrison of fifty divisions under Field-Marshal von Rundstedt's command in France in January was a self-perpetuating manpower problem on its own, as it had been for two years. The difficulty was that Western Command was not only responsible for guarding the western ramparts of the European fortress against any Allied initiative across the English Channel, but it had long been regarded as the most convenient and accessible source of reinforcements for the Eastern, and more recently the Southern, Fronts. Since the beginning of 1942 France had been a combination of rest and rehabilitation centre and reinforcement camp. Divisions decimated in Russia came to France to be rested, replenished with men and equipment, and retrained before being sent back. At any given time therefore von Rundstedt's garrison, though the number of formations did not vary much numerically, was always variable in quality and actual strength as opposed to strength on paper. The number of so-called "divisions" might be impressive but many of them were "coastal defence" formations of inferior quality: while ordinary divisions of supposedly first-class level were much below standard in the equipment that could be spared for them. Most divisions in France had to rely on horse-drawn transport; panzer divisions, unless about to depart for Russia or Italy, were below strength in tanks; some were skeleton formations back from a mauling in the East and now waiting to be issued with new tanks and guns; others were green units from German training and reinforcement centres who had been sent to France to complete their advanced training before being sent to one of the fighting fronts. The coastal defence divisions were often brought up to strength with Russian prisoners of war who found the role of "anti-Bolshevik volunteer" more congenial than the various alternatives open to prisoners captured on the Eastern Front. So the custodians of the Atlantic Wall included a substantial number of Armenians, Ukrainians, Georgians, Tartars, and Cossacks. They also included numbers of German officers and noncommissioned officers who had been medically downgraded as a result of wounds or sickness on the Eastern Front. There was one division consisting almost entirely of men with stomach complaints developed in Russia: a bizarre example of German efficiency —this grouping presumably being intended to ease the division's victualling requirement. There was an ever-growing number of officers and noncommissioned officers with artificial limbs in the static coast units. But perhaps the most eloquent clue to this heterogeneous Western army was the average age of its personnel—thirty-one and a half years, or six years older than the average age that year of the U. S. Army.

The weakest of these divisions, however, had its cadre of experienced German officers and noncommissioned officers to take charge of it and hold it together, to site the weapons and give the orders. In purely static defence they could perform adequately because all they had to do was to stay in their well-protected positions aim straight, and squeeze the trigger when they were told to. But much of von Rundstedt's energy as Commander-in-Chief was spent trying to convince Hitler that the apparent mass of divisions indicated by the clusters of little flags on a small-scale map gave a most misleading impression of what was actually on the ground. He was particularly, and almost permanently, worried about the number of panzer divisions which fluctuated according to the successive demands for them made by the Russian and Italian fronts. At one period of March 1944 von Rundstedt had been reduced to only one, though after this the position improved and by June his total of fifty-nine included nine panzer divisions.

Having to cut his coat according to his cloth—cloth that was not only insufficient but was liable to be tweed one day, so to speak, and threadbare silk the next—von Rundstedt had long since accepted the dictum of Frederick the Great already quoted: namely, that it was a waste of time to try to be strong everywhere; that the only course open to him was to make sure of being strong in the most threatened places. He had therefore paid special attention to certain danger areas: the Pas de Calais—the coast nearest to Britain, from which long-range artillery had been shelling the English coast since 1940 and where the launching sites were being placed for the forthcoming V-1 Flying Bombs that would soon be sent against London; the coast on either side of the estuaries of the Somme and the Seine; the ports, especially Le Havre, Dieppe, Calais, Boulogne which were designated as "fortresses." Hitler frequently directed that various places should be converted into "fortresses"—the Channel Islands of Jersey, Guernsey, and Sark which were close to the coast of France were among the fortresses. The Cotentin peninsula in Normandy was not one of von Rundstedt's chosen coasts for strong defences though Cherbourg itself was a "fortress" as was Brest at the corner of the Brittany peninsula to the west.

Hitler's fortress complex became a family joke with von Rundstedt's staff at Western Command. In the words of General von Blumentritt, his Chief of Staff:[3]

> The "fortresses" on the coast were amazing spectacles. Hitler had a passion for fortifications: the word "Fortress" had a reassuring effect upon him—but not on Rundstedt, who set little store by them. "Promotion" to fortress, as we on Rundstedt's staff humorously called it, was not really very helpful . . .
>
> Hitler devoted much time, material and labour to the extensive construction of his "fortresses." Rundstedt knew that the enemy would never be so foolish as to attack a fortress *direct* from the sea. He could take it much more easily if he landed on the open coast outside its area and then attacked the port from the rear. . . .

There were supposed to be between one and two divisions defending the larger fortresses and one in the smaller ones, but von Rundstedt was lucky if he could find one or two coastal defence battalions to garrison them: nor was his task eased by the fact that he had no power to give orders to the Navy, the Luftwaffe, or the naval artillery. The problem became worse when Hitler suddenly began to appoint trusted officers as "fortress commandants."

"These unfortunate men," continues von Blumentritt,[4] "had to swear affidavits to hold the 'fortresses' at all costs, and these were sent to Hitler. But the commandants had no forces with which to hold their 'fortresses!' These were only imperfectly built and, above all, the commandant had no absolute powers inside his 'fortress' because the naval commandant also had a say in the matter."

This infatuation with the very word itself points strongly to the probability that Hitler himself is to be credited with the grandiose concept of Fortress Europe, first bandied about OKW at the end of 1941. As with many grand delusions with a psychopathic impulse, time and usage had gradually transmogrified the shadow into substance. Hitler had become the supreme victim of his own propagandist bluff. Call something a fortress often enough and it would become one!

Thus von Rundstedt, comfortably settled in his villa at Saint-Germain, enjoying his garden and his daily walks, retained his urbane, faintly contemptuous aloofness. He duly obliged by "promoting to the rank of fortress" such places as Hitler ordained—but put his greatest effort into building up an armoured reserve with which to destroy the invading force after it had landed—for he persisted in the view that none of this would do any good; that his efforts must be concentrated on collecting as many first-class divisions as possible—especially armoured divisions—so that he could effectively hit back at the invasion force: which no power on earth, he thought, could prevent from landing.

Meanwhile Rommel, spending all day and every day travelling up and down his Army Group front harrying, driving, persuading, and inspiring his engineers and frontline soldiers and Todt building workers, began to make the north coast of France look like something that might deter an invader. Soon the foreshore bristled with spiky obstacles designed to wreck the flat-bottomed landing boats in which the Allies would assault. These obstacles included stakes driven at an angle into the sea bed, many of them tipped with an antitank mine; concrete pyramids, with steel blades or mines at their apex; antitank obstacles of railroad metals; and various other submerged hazards designed to damage any men, boats, and tanks that encountered them. One of the most ingenious was the "nutcracker" mine, which consisted of a stake slotted into a concrete housing containing a heavy calibre shell. An assault boat hitting the stake would press it down on the shell which in turn would strike a firing pin which would detonate it. Work on these new devices started too late for Rommel to complete the ambitious plan for them that he conceived; but by the middle of May, 517,000 foreshore obstacles had been sited on the north French coast of which 31,000 incorporated mines.

Mines, the value of which Rommel had learned in Africa, were to dominate his second line of obstacles. His master plan for mines consisted of a first belt, a thousand yards deep covering the beach and the coast behind. In this first belt he aimed at a density of twenty mines per yard and he reckoned it would require 20,000,000 mines to cover the whole of the French coast in this way. The second belt of mines was to continue to a depth of eight thousand yards inland and for this he wanted 200,000,000 mines. Fortunately for the Allies shortage of time as well as supplies limited his achievement to 4,193,167 mines in all by May 20.[5] Within these minefields were placed stationary tanks, strongpoint groups and resistance nests and the invaders, while picking their way through them, would also receive the full weight of the artillery's defensive fire.

The third item in Rommel's obstacles plan was to have all likely landing grounds for paratroops and gliders planted with what quickly became known as "Rommel's asparagus." The "asparagus" consisted of poles, ten feet long and a hundred feet apart, connected by wires that would detonate shells or clusters of mines when subjected to pressure.

That Rommel was able to make a noticeable difference in the short time available was due both to his boundless energy which would never admit to difficulties and to his personal taste for technical ingenuity and inventive improvisation. If mines were in short supply then they must be contrived out of the large stocks of surplus shells and explosives that had once belonged to the French Army. He took an almost schoolboyish delight in any new contraption the engineers came up with—for instance, the "nutcracker" mine. His greatest difficulty was the undergrowth of bureaucracy and red tape through which he had to hack his way to obtain his authorizations. He asked for complete authority over all Army, Navy and Todt Organization personnel working on the Atlantic Wall but it was sharply refused. He had to apply for everything he wanted through the "proper channels." He and von Rundstedt both used to speak with wistful envy of General Eisenhower with his unified control of all Army, Navy, and Air Forces. To a German commander in 1944 this unified command seemed the most wonderful and enviable notion imaginable. It was about this time that Field-Marshal von Rundstedt led a subordinate commander to the window at his Saint-Germain headquarters and snapped: "You see that guard posted outside. If I want to post him to the other side of the house, I must first ask permission of Berchtesgaden." [6]

While work on the Atlantic Wall proceeded, the strategic argument about how to make the best use of it remained undecided. Hitler in principle seemed to support Rommel's wish to concentrate the strongest forces near the coast; von Rundstedt's desire to keep the Panzer divisions well back was supported by General Geyr von Schweppenburg who was in command of Panzer Group West (later to become operational as Fifth Panzer Army). The problem was to get a firm decision out of Hitler.

In these early months of 1944 it was generally agreed by von Rundstedt, Rommel, and OKW that the invasion was most likely to take the short sea route across the Straits of Dover, with the result that Fifteenth Army's sector of the Atlantic Wall had so far received the greatest attention. Perhaps to correct any tendency to treat an invasion here as a foregone conclusion Hitler, in an address on March 20 to the Commanders-in-Chief of all three services in the West, warned them against taking anything for granted. And for the first time he mentioned Normandy:

". . . It is evident that an Anglo-American landing in the West will and must come; how and where it will come no one knows. . . . At no place along our long front is a landing impossible, except perhaps where the coast is broken by cliffs. The most suitable and hence the most threatened areas are the two west coast peninsulas, Cherbourg and Brest, which are very tempting and offer the best possibilities for the formation of a bridgehead, which would then be enlarged systematically . . .[7]

After emphasizing that "The most important thing for the enemy will be to gain a port"—as indeed it had been in

North Africa, Sicily, and Italy; but, unknown to Hitler, would not be on the next occasion—the Führer said:

> . . . The enemy's entire landing operation must under no circumstances be allowed to last longer than a matter of hours or, at the most, days, with the Dieppe attempt as a model.

(Hitler, again deceived by his own propaganda, had grown to believe that the Canadian raid on Dieppe in 1942 had been an invasion attempt that failed; although Canadian orders captured on the day had made it clear that the operation was no more than a limited one, a reconnaissance in force.) But Hitler still avoided a final decision on the big issue that everyone wanted settled: whether the strategy was to be von Rundstedt's keep-the-panzers-behind policy or Rommel's concentrate-everything-near-the-coast alternative. Encouraged by the Führer's address on March 20, especially the passage about the landing not being allowed to last more than a matter of hours, Rommel quickly put in a request for armoured reserves to be placed under his direct control near the coast. Next day Hitler agreed to this. The day after, he changed his mind which goaded Rommel to exclaim in exasperation: "The last out of his door is always right!"

So the long wait continued in tense uncertainty: hampered by indecision at the top, interservices disunity at the higher command level and the fog of administrative bureaucracy obstructing arrangements of commanders like Rommel who were striving tirelessly to win what had become a race against time. Then in April there was a significant development. General Warlimont has written[8] that in that month Hitler "suddenly, and without apparent reason" gave Normandy top priority in his list of probable landing areas.

It was by no means the first time Normandy had been mentioned. As we have seen it rated a special mention in the Führer's address to Commanders-in-Chief on March 20. But previously it had been automatically included in long lists of possible landing areas. In show business parlance it had been one of several "featured" names in routine precautionary orders and directives. Now all of a sudden it was elevated to "star" billing and was to rate equally with the much-fancied Pas de Calais sector.

According to Warlimont, Hitler never gave any reason for his change of view other than that increasing information about troop dispositions in southern England "made it appear likely that there would be a landing in Normandy, where was the great port of Cherbourg and where the Cotentin peninsula could easily be cut off." Warlimont (who hardly ever left OKW) claims that there is "still no completely satisfactory explanation of what led Hitler suddenly to attach such greatly increased importance to Normandy": that it might have been his renowned "intuition"; or he may have received information (unavailable to anyone else) from the Secret Service, now transferred to the Reich Central Security Office of the SS.

Characteristically he gave orders for the defences of Normandy (Seventh Army front) to be rendered impregnable forthwith but not at the expense of the Calais sector (Fifteenth Army) which was equally important—thus presenting Rommel with a new dilemma of making too little go too far.

Chapter 24

THE DISPUTED PLACING
OF THE PANZERS

☐ While von Rundstedt and Rommel went ahead with their preparations hampered by policy disagreements, interservices schisms and a command structure that seemed specifically designed to create difficulties rather than to solve them, those engrossed in the equally feverish activity on the other side of the Channel were at least spared these particular problems; though the magnitude of what was about to be attempted created difficulties enough.

Through trial and error and long experience in the Mediterranean the Allies had evolved a pattern of integrated command of which Operation Overlord, the invasion, was the summation. An American soldier, General Dwight D. Eisenhower, was Supreme Commander of the invasion enterprise and all land, sea, and air forces assigned to it. His Deputy Chief Commander was a British airman, Air Chief Marshal Sir Arthur W. Tedder. A British sailor Admiral Sir Bertram Ramsay RN was in charge of the Allied naval forces; another Briton, Air Chief Marshal Sir Trafford L. Leigh-Mallory, was in command of the Allied Air Forces. On all staffs at all levels American and British naval, military, and air officers were intermixed.

Credit for this integration and the spirit behind it was chiefly due to General Eisenhower, to whom the principle of what might be termed *Allies uber alles* had been sacred from the time he had first arrived in England in 1942 to take command of an Allied army. To Eisenhower it was not merely a polite courtesy or a diplomatic gesture: it was an article of faith. You cannot eliminate national differences by order, but Eisenhower came close to doing so; creating a climate of feeling in which it became almost a question of bad taste to speak of the British or the Americans. The correct and compulsory word was *Allies*.

It is unlikely that history will remember Eisenhower as one of the Great Captains in the traditional sense of that term; his service did not give him the appropriate opportunities in the field. He will certainly be remembered with honour as a great Commander-in-Chief and architect of an alliance. To the organizational magnitude and technical complexity of mid-twentieth century warfare he brought, in addition to basic soldierly virtue, something of the quality of an impresario, handling a cast of temperamental individualists; something of the quality of the executive vice-president of an industrial corporation—a corporation whose business happened to be the manufacture of invasions. Eisenhower's cultivation of an alliance mystique was inspirational, almost devout; and it percolated from his headquarters down. In an England that had become one vast continuous camouflaged military camp, except in those open parts that were one vast continuous camouflaged airfield, the "barrier of a common language" had virtually ceased to exist. American soldiers had taken to drinking tea: British housewives to smoking Chesterfields. The social phenomenon known as the "GI Bride" was a growing feature of Britain's export charts. These things may be trivial but they were symptomatic of something bigger, something that Hitler's New Order never even began to achieve: as Hitler—with the Russians now uncomfortably close to occupied East Europe—was beginning to realize. The personal influence of General Eisenhower in all this should not be underestimated.

In addition to his devotional flair for alliance as such; and in addition to a deep conviction that he was leading a crusade (he called his account of it *Crusade in Europe*): this basically unsophisticated God-fearing man also disposed, in the spring of 1944, 11,500 aircraft which had been allotted to him for the invasion. Both morally and practically he was singularly well-equipped to praise the Lord and pass the ammunition. At the beginning of April 1944 he began to do so.

Whatever else may be said about the final storming of Fortress Europe in 1944 one thing can be stated with certainty. Without the gigantic two-month air offensive which proceded it, the landing could never have succeeded. The bare statistics of the air effort indicate its scale. Between April 1 and June 6 the Allied air forces flew over 200,000 sorties over northern France dropping 195,400 tons of bombs. They lost 1933 aircraft of all types and destroyed 1850 enemy machines in combat or on the ground. This preliminary offensive had four main objectives:

The first was to gain and hold indefinitely absolute mastery of the air. Implicit in this aim was to prevent enemy aircraft penetrating to photograph the Allied preparations.

The second was to isolate the coming battlefield of Normandy from the rest of France by destroying the French railway system and all key points of the road system for ninety miles from the coast and so cripple the German ability to supply the front.

The third was to destroy the Luftwaffe's Third Air Fleet in the air and on the ground to the point where it would be of negligible use when the invasion started.

The fourth was to hammer the defences of the Atlantic Wall, and all military installations connected with it, including the launching sites of the forthcoming V-weapons, right up to the moment of the landing.

The offensive involved every kind of air activity from carpetbombing by heavy bombers to precision swoops by fast fighter-bombers: from fighter sweeps to low-level reconnaissance.

The isolation of the battlefield, known as the Transportation Plan, envisaged heavy and repeated attacks on all railway bridges, junctions, depots, sidings, and tunnels while cannon-firing fighters would ceaselessly patrol, seek out, and attack trains and create a crippling shortage of locomotives and rolling stock to supply the front along a railroad that was by then virtually unusable. That was the aim. As for the roads the aim was to destroy all bridges over the main rivers, especially those on the Seine and the Loire. Saboteurs of the now eager and alerted French Resistance would supplement and sometimes complete the demolition work of the bombers—in cases, for example, where a bridge, despite repeated bombardment, obstinately remained intact: or where an awkward target like a tunnel could not be satisfactorily dealt with from the air.

The part of the offensive concerned with softening up the invasion coast was closely interwoven with the main deception plan for Overlord. This plan had two aims: to convince the Germans that the invasion was going to be directed across the narrow Straits of Dover against the Pas de Calais coast and secondly that it was timed for late July. The deception rested on two main stratagems. The first concerned the preliminary air offensive that has just been described. For every attack on the true invasion coast, the Normandy sector of the Atlantic Wall, two attacks were made at the same time on the Pas de Calais. The second stratagem was more complicated. A fictitious American Army group was simulated in the southeast corner of England by setting up the appropriate radio signals network which buzzed with traffic some of it calculatedly indiscreet for the benefit of the German monitors intended to pick it up. The picture of the bogus army group and its activities and intentions was filled in with appropriate continual troop and vehicle movements between the imaginary headquarters. In addition concentrations of dummy invasion craft were established in the southeast ports for the Luftwaffe to photograph. Apart from these two stratagems the deception was disseminated through Intelligence channels and the network of agents and resistance units in all the occupied countries now looking forward to the day of liberation.

A refinement of the plan also put about, was that there would be a diversionary landing in Normandy but this was intended to be no more than a diversion: the main landing would definitely be in the Pas de Calais.

We have already seen something of how the deception was affecting the estimates and guesses of Hitler and von Rundstedt. The Commander-in-Chief already accepted the Pas de Calais because it seemed logical to him: it was the shortest crossing, the coast where the V-1 launching sites were located, and it was the direct route to the Ruhr. As the deception plan gained momentum von Rundstedt would become more convinced by it because it would be only reinforcing an opinion at which he had already arrived by his own reasoning. As for Hitler, his sudden emphasis on Normandy in April (for which Warlimont says there was no reason) would seem to indicate that Allied Intelligence had got through to his intelligence organization with its subsidiary notion of a diversionary landing in Normandy prior to a main effort in the Pas de Calais—for Hitler had then followed his order for a strengthening of the Normandy sector with an admonition that there must be no relaxation of effort in the Pas de Calais.

Nothing can change the historical record that the Allied invasion of Hitler's Europe opened on June 6, 1944. Yet it would be truer to say that it began on April 1, when General Eisenhower unleashed the huge preliminary air offensive that was really its opening phase. It was now apparent why Air Chief Marshal Tedder had been appointed as his Deputy. It was upon Tedder—perhaps the outstanding air tactician of the war—that Eisenhower would rely to run this offensive. So in April it started: the pounding of the coastal batteries, the destruction of the radar installations which, in the absence of an effective Luftwaffe, were the coast artillery's only early warning system; the battering of the bridges, the trouncing of the troop and tank concentrations, the cutting up of the roads, the cannon-firing swoops on every train caught riding the French railroads, the churning up of the V-weapon sites, the pounding of the pill-boxes, bunkers, beach obstacles; the shattering of the marshalling yards, locomotive roundhouses, and depots, the airfields and the aircraft. It was now a rich man's war without precedent. In addition to the 11,500 aircraft of his "private" Expeditionary Force air armada Eisenhower could also call on another two thousand heavy strategic bombers if required. For German civilians, at least, there was relief from raids for a few weeks. The bombers were fully occupied elsewhere.

One vital item in this air programme was that under its cover Allied photoreconnaissance aircraft constantly flew sorties a few feet above the waves to provide an almost hour-by-hour record of Rommel's progress with his beach obstacles and shore defences. This photographic coverage of the beaches would also ensure that the assault divisions could be provided not only with overprinted maps showing German defences, but with photo enlargements of the beaches they would attack, showing in detail the defences as they would look from a landing craft as the invaders ran in. The running commentary on the growing defences by daily air reconnaissance was supplemented by naval frogmen who slipped across the Channel at night, in midget submarines or motorboats, and brought back details of depth soundings, tide variations, types and consistency of sand, measurements and the nature of the different beach and foreshore obstacles. Because they quickly took control of the air the Allies could provide their armies with this comprehensive pre-invasion service and at the same time prevent the Luftwaffe from doing anything remotely comparable for the defenders in France. They seldom broke through to see what was happening in the ports of Britain and the invasion assembly areas near them. When they did it was more often than not because the Allies wanted some misleading aspect of their deception plan photographed and reported; for example, the concentrations of dummy landing vessels in the southeast ports.

With time running out, Rommel continued to nag OKW into giving him a panzer reserve close to the coast. Still Hitler would not give a decision.

"You have no idea how difficult it is to convince these people," he once said to Bayerlein.[1] "At one time they looked on mobile warfare as something to keep clear of at all costs, but now that our freedom of manoeuvre in the West is gone, they're all crazy [about] it."

On April 23, when the Allied air offensive was three weeks old, he tried once again—in a long letter to Jodl,[2] the letter of a man whose patience is being sorely tried:

> If, in spite of the enemy's air superiority, we succeed in getting a large part of our mobile force into action in the threatened sectors in the first few hours, I am convinced that the enemy attack on the coast will collapse completely on its first day. Very little damage has so far been done by the heavy enemy bombing to our reinforced concrete installations, although our field positions, dugouts and communication trenches have in many places been completely obliterated.

After commenting that this showed the importance of getting concrete over as many positions as possible, Rommel returned to his main theme, by this time familiar to everyone:

> Contrary to myself, General Geyr von Schweppenburg, who may well know the British in peacetime, but has never yet met them in battle, sees the greatest danger in an operational airborne landing deep inside France, and so wishes to be in a position to mount a quick counter-operation. His forces have been located mainly with that end in view . . . I have disagreed very violently with General von Geyr over this question and will only be able to exe-

cute my ideas if he is put under Army Group command early enough. . . .

After enlarging on what he considered the weakness of the Panzer Group Commander's appreciation, and his exaggeration of the airborne danger, Rommel ended with a solemn warning that coming events were to prove prophetic:

> The most decisive battle of the war, and the fate of the German people itself, is at stake. Failing a tight command in one single hand of all the forces available for defence, failing the early engagement of all our mobile forces in the battle for the coast, victory will be in grave doubt. If I am to wait until the enemy landing has actually taken place before I can demand, through normal channels, the command and dispatch of the mobile forces, delays will be inevitable. This means that they will probably arrive too late to intervene successfully in the battle for the coast . . .

Once again OKW took little notice. After all, Rommel's notes, memoranda, and letters of protest and entreaty had been a familiar feature of the OKW IN trays ever since before El Alamein. At OKW they were inclined to think that Rommel protested too much, even though he was once again a Hitler favourite. Hitler warmed instinctively to Rommel's idea of smashing the invasion on the first day. But under other pressures he could not decide about the panzers.

It is possible that Jodl never showed him the letter. For we know that in the last week of April the Führer was in Berchtesgaden concerning himself with an investiture followed by a short "pep" course in *Weltanschauung* ("world view") for senior officers attending to receive their decorations. This we know because one of those ordered to hand over their commands for a short while and attend was General von Senger und Etterlin from the Italian Front.

This narrative last encountered von Senger when he was sent to organize the German defence of Sicily for the Italian Commander-in-Chief nominally in charge of it. After performing this task and assisting in the German withdrawal from the island von Senger was next entrusted with the evacuation of the German garrisons from Sardinia and Corsica to fight in Italy.

He was then appointed Commander-in-Chief of the XIV

Panzer Corps, the formation which was to bear the brunt of the German defence in the great battles of Cassino during the winter of 1943-44. On April 18 he handed over his command temporarily in order to attend the investiture and course on the Obersalzburg.

As we noted earlier, von Senger was a man of culture and sophistication who had completed his education at Oxford University where he had spent a year as a Rhodes scholar before the First World War. His account of the investiture at Berchtesgaden on the Obersalzburg is one of the few intimate close-ups of Hitler on such an occasion that we have by an articulate regular officer who had always been impervious to the Hitler spell. It is therefore a portrait sketch of some interest: this was how he described the investiture at which he received Oak Leaves to his Knight's Cross:[3]

It was impressive in rather a negative sense when the selected candidates were received on the Obersalzburg. The impression made by Hitler was utterly depressing, and involuntarily I wondered how the young officers and NCOs attending the ceremony would react. This man, to whose fiendish tenacity and nihilistic will the German people were committed, was still regarded by many of these young officers as a demi-god, a man deserving of complete confidence, whose handshake inspired new strength. He wore a yellow military blouse with a yellow tie, white collar and black trousers—hardly a becoming outfit! His unprepossessing frame and short neck made him appear even less dignified than usual. His complexion was flabby, colourless and sickly. His large blue eyes, which evidently fascinated many people, were watery, possibly due to his constant use of stimulating drugs. His handshake was soft, his left arm hung limp and trembling by his side. Yet a striking feature, contrasting with his notorious screaming during speeches or fits of rage, was the quiet and modulated voice that almost inspired compassion since it barely concealed his despondency and weakness.

But von Senger admits he was impressed by Hitler's objectivity when he reviewed the war situation to "a small circle of fortuitously assembled frontline soldiers when he sat down with them at a round table." The Führer was frank about the "disastrous situation" on the Eastern Front, frank about the failure of the Battle of the Atlantic, frank about "his anxiety over the impending invasion in the West and the prospect of a second front that would use up his forces." The only consolation he could give was "a muttered sentence to the effect that all difficulties must be surmounted through 'faith'." "There was not even a comforting allusion to the hopes centred on the famous secret weapons, hopes on which the ordinary German citizen was being constantly nourished . . ." As a colleague and kindred soul of von Senger's put it: "The government and the Army are finished—defeated over and over again in the field, damned by history, heading for downfall—and they know it."

The kindred spirit with whom von Senger shared the strange interlude at Berchtesgaden was an eccentric from the Italian Front by the name of General Baade, commander of the 90th Panzer Grenadier Division which had been chiefly responsible for stopping the first Allied attack on Cassino in January. Baade was in the most literal sense a gay cavalier. A regular cavalryman, he and his wife had been renowned before the war in European show-jumping circles. In his military career Baade had a lighthearted approach to soldiering that is not commonly to be found in German officers. He was one of those natural and popular leaders whose unconventional methods and escapades inspire legends and about whom a crop of anecdotes circulate. On the North African desert, he used to lead armoured night patrols wearing a kilt over his breeches and with a holstered Luger pistol hanging in the place normally reserved for a sporran. Once, it was said, he broke into the British lines, kidnapped an officer to guide him safely back through the British minefield, then put him down, shook hands and thanked him and told him to return to his own lines. It was said that he sometimes ended his night forays up to the enemy outposts with a message over the British radio net: "Stop firing. On my way back. Baade." More than once, it was said, his enemies had obliged. Only last January von Senger, who by then was Baade's corps commander, had received a telephone call from an agitated adjutant at OKW demanding to know whether it was true that General Baade had accepted an invitation to eat Christmas Dinner with the enemy at Cassino. Of course it was not true, von Senger reassured OKW. But he did not add that all General Baade had done was to radio New Year's greetings to the enemy in English.

Most of the stories were no doubt apocryphal or at least embroidered. The personality who inspired them was clearly

not. He was of that supreme military aristocracy, the gifted
leaders who can succeed brilliantly in war without losing their
sense of fun. It is somehow reassuring to know that—Moltke
and Schlieffen notwithstanding—the German Army also had
its stylish eccentrics. (And since few war stories are permitted
a happy ending it must further be recorded that General of
Panzers Baade—international equestrian, gifted leader of
men, and joker extraordinary—died of wounds sustained in
an Allied air attack on the road along which he was driving
to his home: on the very last day of the war.)

Both generals found the senior officers' course in *Weltan-
schaung*, which followed the investiture, expectedly tedious.
In von Senger's words:[4]

> During these sessions the atmosphere remained
> oppressive, despite Field-Marshal Keitel's optimistic
> speeches and the artificial joviality of the "Reichs-
> führer SS" Himmler. I was aware that certain officers
> of the OKW . . . were anything but enthusiastic
> at having to listen to such propaganda nonsense at a
> time when the general situation was nothing short
> of disastrous. But these officers thought it best to con-
> ceal their feelings. Fear of a revolution had made the
> die-hard followers of Hitler keep an eye on the "un-
> reliable generals."

While these officers from the Italian Front stifled their
yawns at the "propaganda nonsense" being dispensed on the
Obersalzburg—heartened only by the knowledge that they
would be rewarded by a few days' leave with their families at
the end of the course—Rommel pursued his tireless efforts
in France.

The headquarters of Army Group B was in the Château
La Roche Guyon, built against steep chalk cliffs on a bend of
the Seine about forty miles north of Paris. La Roche Guyon
was the ancient seat of the Ducs de la Rochefoucauld. Allowing the family to remain in residence, Rommel took over
only enough apartments to accommodate himself and a few
of his most senior staff, the rest of the headquarters being
quartered outside. Had the Field-Marshal been of a more reflective turn of mind he might have derived some ironic satisfaction from perusing in the evenings the maxims of the
most celebrated of the Ducs de la Rochefoucauld; and savour-
ing the seventeenth-century Duc's elegantly cynical philosophy, promulgated through the famous collection of mots and

aphorisms—mostly suggesting that self-interest is the principal motive of human behaviour. Rommel might have taken his mind off the Atlantic Wall by choosing suitable La Rochefoucauld maxims to fit the Nazi hierarchy whom he was finding it increasingly difficult to serve.

No man is more frequently in error than he who cannot bear to be wrong. Motto to hang in Hitler's bunker?

A man of good sense is almost always one who shares our views. Explanation of why Field-Marshal Keitel and General Jodl retained Hitler's confidence for so long?

We should only be surprised at our continued ability to feel surprise. Inscription to be printed at the head of all memo pads on which telephone messages from OKW were written down?

But the singleminded Field-Marshal was not the man to seek diversion in the mordant philosophy of a seventeenth-century French aristocrat, even if he was sitting at the man's inlaid Renaissance desk and surrounded by his rather magnificent tapestries. But the historic associations were not lost on his intellectual Chief-of-Staff, General Dr. Hans Speidel, who had become a staunch friend as well as admirer since his appointment to Army Group B at the beginning of April. Speidel was unusual in being a Doctor of Philosophy in addition to having what it took to achieve the rank of lieutenant general in the German Army. For the short tempestuous climax of the war they spent together they made a good team, these two; the sage balance of the intellectual staff officer complementing the impulsive flair of the man of action. Every day they visited different parts of the front inspecting what was done, was being done and had still to be done; criticizing, correcting, suggesting, encouraging. In the evenings they would stroll together through the lovely gardens of La Roche Guyon discussing what they had seen, planning the next day's programme. By accident no Nazi political officer had been attached to the headquarters (something for which Speidel was later blamed when he was interrogated by the Gestapo). In consequence the two men were able to converse freely about the war situation and leadership and their growing conviction that an early peace was the only hope of saving Germany. They were not the only generals thinking along these lines at this time, but most of them had to lower their voices and double-check to whom they were talking, before saying so.

Early in May, Rommel ordered a special effort to strengthen the defences in the Normandy sector. This was not merely in implementation of Hitler's Normandy "hunch" of April—which had been followed by several "watch Normandy" warnings—but also because Army Group B Intelligence had lately reported that the Allies were taking a particular interest in this part of the coast. In addition, Intelligence claims to have identified the American armies in the southwest of England, the British in the southeast, all seemed to point to an American landing in Normandy, followed perhaps by a British in the Pas de Calais. Rommel had accepted the general view that there would be at least two landings, but now he was convinced that Normandy was to be first on the list. And he was determined that the first should be the last—and should last no more than a day.

Accordingly, while his subordinates were ordered to redouble their efforts throughout the Normandy sector, he requested certain specific additions to his forces. In view of what happened later it is worth looking at the map and memorizing the extra forces for which Rommel asked in May. The course of history might have been more than slightly bent if his request had been granted.

The Calvados coast of Normandy extends for sixty miles along the Bay of the Seine between the Cotentin Peninsula and the southern shore of the Seine estuary. A number of rivers flow northwards into the bay of which the Vire and the Orne (thirty miles west of it) are the most important—the city of Caen being ten miles from the mouth of the latter, the town of Saint-Lô twenty from the mouth of the former. Bayeux is about halfway between these two towns. Cherbourg is at the tip of the Cotentin Peninsula; Carentan at its base. Avranches, of which more will be heard, is at the southern end of the west side of this peninsula where Normandy makes a right-angled turn to become Brittany.

What Rommel asked for in May to combat an Allied landing he was now convinced would be launched against this region was a complete antiaircraft corps (twenty-four batteries) in the area between the Orne and Vire Rivers; the 12th SS Panzer Division to the Cotentin Peninsula, a brigade of *Nebelwerfer* (six-barrelled heavy mortars) to the south of Carentan, the elite Panzer Lehr Division to the area of Avranches, and finally he asked for the Navy to start intensively mining the Bay of the Seine.

What happened was this. Antiaircraft units were part of the Luftwaffe under the (remote) control of Goering at OKW or his gangster-style country house Karinhall in Germany.

Goering would not authorize the antiaircraft corps that Rommel requested though one was available.

Hitler refused to authorize the moves of the two panzer divisions requested: he also refused the *Nebelwerfer* brigade for the southern base of the peninsula. Like the Luftwaffe, the Navy was also unwilling to oblige the Army. The contribution of C-in-C West, Admiral Kranke, to the Atlantic Wall was a notable one. To begin with he had advised that the Normandy coast was impossible for a landing as it was too rocky—as a result of which the coast was completely undefended when Rommel arrived there at the turn of the year. He now declined to mine the Bay of the Seine, as requested, and went on with what he was then doing, mining the Bay of Biscay.

And so with time fast running out, the heads of the different armed services continued to obstruct the one man who might have saved them; and all for the sake of false pride, for the German Navy and Air Force had for all practical purposes largely ceased to exist. But this would not stop Reichsmarschall Goering refusing to move a few antiaircraft batteries to where Rommel wanted them, and Admiral Kranke would still refuse to give him the five thousand units of Marines stationed uselessly in Paris instead of on the coast where they could more usefully have manned the defences.

Chapter 25

ROMMEL—UBIQUITOUS
AND TIRELESS

☐ The troops manning the Atlantic Wall knew nothing of the high level arguments whether the Panzer divisions should be right behind them near the coast or in reserve in the forests around Paris. They neither knew nor would they have cared much if they had known. The hypothetical disagreements of remote figures that they scarcely even knew by name were no concern of the men in the mortar and machine-gun crews, the riflemen in the section posts. When it came to officers other than those of their own units one field-marshal or general was little different from another and bore no relation to their personal everyday lives. Except Rommel.

Rommel was the only one that they all knew almost as well as they knew their own battalion officers. His fame was legendary. Since his arrival in the West the Goebbels propaganda machine had been giving him maximum "production." Rommel cooperated fully in this not because he enjoyed the limelight but because he, better than anyone else, knew the true inadequacy of the Atlantic Wall and therefore the need to project by every known means the notion that it was impregnable.

A continuous flow of newspaper pictures ensured that hardly a man or woman in Germany was unfamiliar with Rommel's face and his strenuous efforts to buttress the western defences. To the troops themselves the Field-Marshal was more than a newspaper photograph; he was constantly in their midst; querying, probing, testing, ordering; too often for the peace of mind of some of them. There would be a screech of brakes, then he would appear suddenly from nowhere and immediately get down to business. How many concrete tetrahedra had the Todt people added to the foreshore obstacles since the beginning of the month? Would not that machine-gun nest have a better field of fire if sited twenty yards to the left? How much reserve ammunition was there for this heavy battery? How were the deliveries of iron rail lengths for the beach obstacle programme? Had the position improved? His memory was uncomfortably accurate, he would not be sidetracked with an excuse. His eye missed nothing. No detail of the merest platoon layout was too unimportant to escape his questioning attention. He had never been one to exercise command through written orders dispatched from a desk in a distant headquarters. Many regimental officers on the Atlantic Wall sometimes found themselves wishing that he was. To the incompetent and uncertain his apparent ubiquity, his brisk descents on the front without warning or ceremony, were always disconcerting, often painful. He was exacting to work under and hard to please: but he knew how to praise and encourage as well as how to rebuke. Above all he knew how to talk to soldiers in their own language and enjoyed being at the front with them. He was always happier at the front than in a headquarters mess. In a word he was a soldier's soldier.

There was tragic inevitability as well as perceptive judgment in the casting of this most personal and dedicated of leaders as Siegfried in the twentieth century Götterdämmerung that now darkened Fortress Europe, the fading dream of Hitler and the whole disintegrating Nazi myth itself.

There is nothing in warfare quite like the pregnant suspense that precedes an invasion by sea. The lull before any great offensive is of course imbued with this sensation. The beguiling emptiness and innocence of no man's land, the oppressive straining of the imagination to fathom what lies beyond, the loaded calm; the anxiety of the leaders as to whether they have understood the orders correctly, whether they have thought of everything; the anxiety of the led as to whether it is going to be as bad as the last time, or worse; these fears and pre-battle tensions are common to all offensives. They are timeless and universal and yoke the two contestants in a private shared intimacy from which the rest of mankind is for the time being excluded. In the comradeship of their unspoken fear the two sides temporarily achieve oneness, for neither personally desired nor caused the predicament which now claims them both and in which they must fight one another. The communion of the front line is theirs alone and no one else in the world exists.

These patterns of sensation are to a greater or lesser extent common to every situation in which two armies face one another, one warily defensive, the other preparing to strike. But if no man's land happens to be no man's water (so to say) and the attack is to come across the sea, then all these tensions are heightened and intensified; for the sea adds a formidable extra dimension to the situation, complicating it with its own character and the unpredictability of its moods. To an attacker who proposes to cross the sea to launch his offensive the first hazard is the sea itself which alone may wreck the enterprise. To the defender the sensation of expectancy and fearful apprehension before a seaborne invasion is intensified and complicated to an extent unmatched by any other defensive operation of war.

A rising wind and choppy sea may comfortingly suggest that no immediate invasion is likely. But what if it is not exactly rough, just a little disturbed, and it is hard to tell whether it is more or less disturbed than it was two hours before; then, to the other guessing games of those who have nothing to do but wait and watch, is added this further speculation about the weather. Could tomorrow be the day? Would it be feasible in these conditions? Or can one assume that it is too rough? Or have *they* made allowance for this degree of turbulence? What, anyway, *is* rough in this situation?

The duty of the anonymous sentry in these circumstances is harder than might be supposed. To project the senses with maximum alertness for two hours at a time can be physically as well as mentally exhausting. The painter or musician may stare as intently at the sea and find the experience pleasurable and inspiring because they are sublimating into picture or sound what they feel as well as what they see. But the soldier watches only for danger; the sudden tattooing of the horizon with myriad specks that will grow into hieroglyphics and finally into a line of ships; the dispersal of the habitual early morning mist to disclose an armada much nearer than the horizon and stretching as far as the eye can scan. The sea can hypnotize the sentinel who peers at it for long with fear in his heart. He begins to see what is not there; two green lights, perhaps, or it might have been one red; was that a flashing light—or a shooting star—or was it nothing at all? The eye and the imagination play tricks. And all the time in May 1944 there was the incessant drone of aircraft crossing and recrossing between England and France to strafe and bomb the defence works so carefully constructed, and to fret the nerves of those who must then immediately rebuild and restore them. Peering from a trench or patrolling a few yards of deserted sandhill with only his Schmeisser carbine for company, it became easier, the longer it went on, for a man to see light signals that were not there, to hear night sounds that did not occur.

To a cat alertness is indivisible, an absolute. Either he is fully alert or he is not alert at all. Human sensibility is less dependable. Armies know this. Aware of the parable of the boy who cried "wolf" too often, aware that maximum alertness unduly protracted can exhaust the mind and the body, they make allowance for this by rationalizing alertness and defining degrees of it. They try to control it like electric current, turning the voltage of vigilance up or down as required. So that when a full alert is ordered it can, within the limits of human fallibility, be quite literally maintained.

So on both sides of the Channel, in mounting suspense, the two great armies went about their final preparations for the day of decision that might be tomorrow or the next day, but might not be for weeks: the day when the respective assignments of Eisenhower and von Rundstedt would seem to have been curiously foreshadowed three centuries before by Milton in the last lines of his sonnet on his blindness:

> . . . Thousands at his bidding speed
> And post o'er Land and Ocean without rest:
>   They also serve who only stand and waite.

To "only stand and waite" was the harder lot. In this kind of context to strike is preferable to the long wait to be struck.

One hour before midnight on May 11, some 1600 guns shattered the tranquil, balmy starlit night with a fabricated hurricane that screamed without pause for forty minutes. The skyline shimmered with St. Vitus gun-flashes. The air sighed and whined. The ground trembled and shuddered. But it was not over the English Channel that the tempest broke but in central Italy one thousand miles to the south.

In his Special Order of the Day the Allied Commander-in-Chief, General Sir Harold Alexander, told the Fifth and Eighth Armies that the Allied armed forces were now assembling for the final battles. "From east and west, from north and south" blows were about to fall which would result in the final destruction of the Nazis. "To us in Italy," he said,[1] "has been given the honour to strike the first blow."

When the 1600 guns opened fire, General von Senger, Commander of the XIV Panzer Corps which had held the all-important Cassino sector against repeated attacks for four months, was not on hand to hear them. He was still on leave in Germany enjoying a respite at his home after the investiture and course on the Obersalzburg described in an earlier chapter. Before leaving the Italian front in mid-April he had been assured by Tenth Army Intelligence that the Allied offensive was unlikely to start before May 24. Another Allied deception plan had been successfully misleading. General von Senger had to cut short his leave and hurry back to Italy.

Chapter 26

GRIM STRUGGLE IN ITALY— THE THIRD FRONT

☐ Set against happenings elsewhere that winter and spring —the smoking ruins of German cities, the erosive tide of the Russian advance surging ever westward till its foremost wavelets were lapping the borders of East Europe, the belated haste to repair the deficiencies of the Atlantic Wall—against all this, the winter battles in Italy, of which Monte Cassino was the symbol and the centre-piece, might seem a splendid irrelevance; a kind of epic libretto for an opera for which no one had written the music. Yet it had its place in the over-all pattern, though there is scope for much historical argument about precisely what that place was. It is fair to say, however, that for both sides Cassino in the end had considerable relevance, if only negatively: that is to say a relevance to what might have been. By attracting good German divisions into a battle of attrition and holding them there the Allies fulfilled the first aim of their Italy strategy. By allowing them to be drawn there Hitler unnecessarily wasted good divisions he could not afford to lose, and in March, the tightness of the position was clear when von Rundstedt was reduced to a single panzer division in France because two had had to go urgently to the Eastern Front and two to Italy. A withdrawal to a line in northern Italy[1] would have enabled Hitler to withdraw divisions from Italy for use in the East or the West instead of sending more there. The Allies, having achieved their first aim of containing German divisions in Italy, later failed to exploit the victory they eventually won, this failure being a consequence of the Anglo-American strategic dispute that has already been adumbrated.

It has already been briefly explained that the Gustav Line at Cassino had been constructed by the Germans along a natural defence barrier of quite exceptional strength, halfway between Naples and Rome astride the main inland road that then connected the two cities, and across the Liri Valley through which the road ran. The strength of the defence system was based on the fifteen-mile Garigliano-Rapido river line in conjunction with the mountain mass with which it connects at the small town of Cassino. This river line stretches like a tight cord across the entrance to the Liri Valley as far as the town and the 1700-foot mountain of Monte Cassino which soars steeply behind it. It was here that the then main road from Naples (now rendered obsolete by the Autostrada del Sole) curved round the base of Monte Cassino to enter the valley and continue northward to Rome. Monte Cassino is the first of a continuing series of mountains stretching north and east from Cassino into the country's central mountain range.

It towered therefore like a sentinel above the old main route where it entered the valley, and it completely dominated the entire width of the flat valley entrance. From a military point of view the superb observation from Monte Cassino and the adjacent heights made it possible for defenders holding them to control any attempt to cross the river and enter the valley. In the winter rains the valley is waterlogged and impassable for tanks or wheeled transport. The rocky trackless mountain mass towering above the valley is equally impassable. Mules are the only form of transport with which troops fighting in this country can be supplied. Massively sprawled on the summit of Monte Cassino, like a top-heavy crown, was the sixth-century Benedictine Abbey, cradle not only of the Benedictine Order but of all western Christianity and culture; an immense building two hundred yards long, a hundred wide, and having the characteristics of a fortress with its rows of small cell windows and its great walls ten feet thick at the base. From the moment it came into view it seemed to become for the Allied soldiers the symbol of the defensive system of which it was the central pivot, towering above the junction where river line so suddenly reared up into mountain mass.

Before they made their first attempt to break through at Cassino the Allied armies had received some significant reinforcements. As well as more American and British divisions the new arrivals, mainly from North Africa, included General Alphonse Juin's French Corps of French-officered Algerian and Moroccan mountain troops; the Polish Corps of General Wladislaw Anders consisting of two infantry divisions and one armoured brigade. The Commonwealth addition included New Zealand and South African divisions and two British-Indian divisions.

The Cassino sector of the Gustav line was in the care of XIV Panzer Corps commanded by General von Senger und Etterlin. We have already noted some of the unusual attributes of the scholarly von Senger, partly educated at Oxford, an Anglophile, a glutton for the cultural exploration for which service in Italy provided such agreeable opportunity, a suspect anti-Nazi, one of the "unreliable generals" on whom the political officers kept a sharp eye. To all this was added one further circumstantial improbability. He was an oblate of the Benedictine Order. It was curious that of all the generals in the German Army this particular one chanced to find himself the defender of Monte Cassino, the supreme foundation of the Benedictine Order, against the Allies.

The first Allied attempt to break through at Cassino came in January 1944 (while the Russians were liberating Leningrad). It was a four-phase offensive launched when the gales of an exceptionally severe winter were swelling the rivers and flooding the already water-logged approaches to the Liri Valley and the valley itself. It opened with an advance by Gen-

315

eral Juin's Moroccan and Algerian mountain divisions into the heights north of Monte Cassino against von Senger's left wing. The French advanced several miles to outflank Cassino from the north but the German left held firm.

The second phase was an attack on von Senger's extreme right by a British corps which forced the Garigliano near its mouth and advanced northward into the foothills of the Aurunci mountains which give the Liri Valley its western wall. The German commander judged that this must be the Allied main effort—it was the direction from which he himself would have tried to outflank the Cassino position—and, going over his army commanders' head, he applied directly to Kesselring for the two army group reserve divisions, which he held in readiness to meet a development of the British threat to roll up his right wing.[2] To his surprise the initial British momentum was not reinforced. Instead, a third phase of the offensive was launched—this time by a U.S. corps attacking the German centre with two divisions.

The first of these attempted a crossing of the Rapido five miles south of Cassino with a view to driving straight up the Liri Valley. But the river-crossing operation was mismanaged and von Senger's centre had no difficulty in smashing the attack with heavy losses to the American division. The U.S. Corps immediately renewed the attack with its second division which was more successful. This force managed to ford the Upper Rapido north of Cassino and having done so clawed its way with great bravery and under continuous fire up the rocky slopes to form a mountain bridgehead which it then expanded to within one thousand yards of Monte Cassino on its north side and to the left of the bridgehead already established by the French. The Americans had given von Senger many anxious moments but his front was able to halt their attack, as it had held the first two, because his divisions held all the key high-points and were established in prepared positions, whereas the attackers had to fight their way, under continuous observation, up bare slopes that were too hard for them to dig themselves into when they took up a position: crude stone shelters being the nearest approximation to a foxhole or trench open to them.

In the last week of January the Allies launched the fourth phase of the offensive, the operation intended to clinch it. An Anglo-American task force made an assault landing from the sea on beaches at Anzio, 35 miles south of Rome and 60 miles behind the German line at Cassino. The landing force found the beach undefended and there was a fleeting prospect of racing forward to the main road to cut off the German Tenth Army fighting at Cassino and then to seize Rome with a swift *coup de main*. For a number of reasons this did not happen. The decision of the Combined Chiefs of Staff to give the Pacific Theatre priority of claim on landing craft at the end of the Sicily campaign had left the Mediterranean Theatre short. There were only enough of them to make the Anzio landing with an infantry force of scarcely adequate strength and without the light armour that might have made an ambitious exploitation to Rome possible. In addition the U.S. force commander, Major General John P. Lucas, was unfortunately a man of extreme caution and orthodoxy. His immediate reaction to his good fortune of an unopposed landing was to consolidate his beachhead and build up his strength to meet counterattack. The chance was lost. The Germans, who had long expected the Allies to make more frequent amphibious use of Italy's long coasts, had a standing "fire brigade" scheme whereby divisions permanently had units earmarked to be rushed to meet amphibious landings in coastal areas to which they were readily accessible. Within twenty-four hours they had thrown a defensive perimeter around the beachhead and within forty-eight hours they had enough forces on the spot to contain it. Churchill, whose idea the landing had been, was bitterly reminded of Gallipoli, his similar pet scheme of the First World War.

"I had hoped that we were hurling a wild cat onto the shore," he growled,[3] "But all we had got was a stranded whale."

The Allies had hoped that the new threat to the rear of the German Tenth Army would at least force von Vietinghoff to send divisions back from the Cassino front to meet it. In the event only one division had to move away from Cassino to give temporary help and it was soon back. General von Mackensen's Fourteenth Army, previously in northern Italy, now took over the new Anzio front and within a short time counterattacks with up to four divisions were making successive attempts to drive the Allied beachhead force into the sea. The landing had not worked out as the Allies had hoped, but Hitler (with the cross-Channel invasion increasingly clouding his thoughts) was now engaged in a full-scale two-front campaign in Italy where half-a-dozen divisions of each side would soon be fighting it out at Anzio and double that number at Cassino. What we have described as the "splendid irrelevance" was acquiring its relevance—perhaps sometimes for the wrong reasons—as it went along.

In mid-February the Allies resumed the offensive, now focused on Monte Cassino itself, with a fresh British corps that had relieved the Americans, exhausted and depleted by three weeks of continuous and costly fighting. While New Zealanders attacked the strongpoint of Cassino railroad station in the valley, British and Indians stormed the steep slopes of Monte Cassino itself in an attempt to capture the vast building at its summit. This was the attack preceded by the famous and controversial air bombardment of the Benedictine monastery by heavy bombers.

General von Senger watched the bombing with the commander of the 90 Panzer Grenadier Division. "Both of us," he wrote,[4] "were at a loss to know what this appalling spectacle signified. . . . As a tactical prelude the destruction of the abbey appeared to have no significance. We felt sad at the failure of our efforts to preserve the abbey in the midst of the battlefield."

It would be inappropriate to this narrative to reopen at length the controversy provoked by the bombing; a controversy that from all points of view has been thoroughly discussed elsewhere. It will be enough in the present context to add these brief comments to von Senger's remarks quoted above.

It is pertinent to point out that the Allies had no means of knowing that von Senger had given orders that no German soldier was to set foot in the monastery; that front-line observers sent back constant reports that they were being fired on from its vicinity; that reports from civilian as well as military sources lent weight to the notion that the abbey was being used for military purposes. The Allies' dilemma was summed up by the commander of the New Zealand Division, General Sir Howard K. Kippenberger:[5]

> Opinion . . . as to whether the abbey was occupied was divided. Personally I thought the point immaterial. If not occupied today it might be tomorrow and it did not appear that it would be difficult for the enemy to bring reserves into it during the progress of an attack, or for troops to take shelter there if driven from positions outside.
>
> It was impossible to ask troops to storm a hill surmounted by an intact building such as this, capable of sheltering several hundred infantry in perfect security from shellfire and ready at the critical moment to emerge and counter attack.

One must re-emphasize that Monte Cassino was a vital hill feature dominating the most critical point of a prepared system of fortifications. It was crowned by this vast building more than twice the size of Buckingham Palace. Was it not a little naive of the German general to imagine that it could survive such a situation, right in the middle of the front line, unscathed? Only a few weeks before, another German formation had evacuated the greater part of the movable art treasures and the priceless collection of manuscripts to Rome for safe keeping; the majority of the monks had also been evacuated. The only reason the Abbot and five monks had been allowed to stay behind as a caretaker party was that the Abbott had insisted. This evacuation, highly creditable to the Germans, was surely itself a realistic acceptance of the inevitable: how could such a building come unhurt through one or more hard battles in which it was itself a crucial part of the front line?

More valid is von Senger's comment that the bombing served no useful tactical purpose. What he did not know was that its timing was a bad blunder arising from a failure of liaison between the Allied air and ground commands. When, after long and agonizing consideration, it was finally decided to bomb the monastery—chiefly as a result of the insistence of the divisional commanders who would have to order their infantry up the forbidding mountainside—it became an Air responsibility. The Air Command for reasons of their own decided to carry out the bombing a day earlier than the date agreed, but omitted to tell the Army of the change. There could therefore be no question of the ground attack moving forward immediately the bombing ended. To cap this ludicrous failure to co-ordinate, the first the army knew about the change was when some of the first bombs fell on their forward troops causing a dozen casualties. Others hit a Moroccan field hospital injuring another forty. Another bomb destroyed the command-trailer of the Eighth Army Commander, who was fortunately not in it at the time. The ground attack therefore had to go in that night before it was ready, with out proper reconnaissance, and without the completion of its difficult supply arrangements—everything, including drinking water, having to be brought up to the mountain bridgehead by mule and at night as every inch of the seven-mile route was under German observation and exposed to mortar and artillery fire.

In the event, therefore, the bombing of Monte Cassino was a disaster—but not for the reasons that von Senger and other

German critics have suggested. From von Senger's military point of view—as opposed to his personal regret which was undoubtedly genuine—the bombing made his task easier. In the absence of any significant attack immediately after it was over, the German 1st Parachute Division, now responsible for this sector, were able to move into the monumental ruin and convert the rubble and broken masonry into an immense strongpoint. Attacked on three successive nights by a British-Indian division that included three battalions of Gurkhas, most redoubtable of mountain fighters, 1st Parachute effectively broke up all three attacks with heavy losses to the attackers. (In two nights one British battalion lost twelve out of fifteen officers, 162 out of 313 other ranks—all killed.)

By mid-March (when the Russians were recapturing large tracts of the Ukraine) the Allies were ready to try again at Cassino. In a month of static warfare reminiscent of the First World War—with the two front lines in places only yards apart, and both sides still limited by rain and mountain to the use of mules for all their supplies—the German paratroopers had plenty of time in which to perfect the citadel they had created out of Monte Cassino's rubble and to develop a series of strongpoints connecting it down the mountainside with the long-fortified ruins of Cassino town 1700 feet below. Hitler became excited by the "heroic defence of Cassino" which partly made up for the withdrawals in Russia and the failures of von Mackensen's Fourteenth Army to eliminate what Hitler now called the "abscess" at Anzio where the Allied beachhead had expanded to four divisions with enough tanks and artillery to frustrate the repeated counterattacks that von Mackensen threw against it.

The third attack at Cassino, on March 15, was made by the same two divisions as that in February—the New Zealand and the 4th British-Indian Divisions. This time the attack was preceded by an annihilating area-bombing of Cassino town by relays of the heaviest strategic bombers, the first time heavy bombers were used in this way to support a ground attack. In three hours they were scheduled to drop over one thousand tons of bombs on an area half a mile square. As soon as the bombing ended at noon the New Zealanders were to advance with tanks to the northern end of the town at the foot of Monte Cassino, overrun what was left of it while the surviving defenders (if any) were still stunned, and then hurry on into the Liri Valley. The British and Indians, following close behind, were to strike up Monte Cassino, overcoming in turn the mountainside strongpoints and then continuing uphill to a jumping-off line from which they could make the final assault on the monastery ruin.

Once again the Allied offensive went wrong. The New Zealanders advanced cautiously with platoons instead of battalions, and when they reached the town they found that the bombing, in addition to annihilating the equivalent of a battalion of Germans defending it, had turned it into a chaotic obstacle which their tanks could not penetrate without assistance from engineers. Instead of taking the town "on the run" as had been intended, they had to inch their way into a devastation that now bore no relation to their maps and plans. The heavy bombs had churned the already chaotic ruins into a moonscape of giant craters and mountainous rubble heaps in which the tanks were virtually helpless. It took them all afternoon, instead of an hour, just to fight their way in. The surviving Germans had plenty of time to recover and were soon proving that they had by no means been wiped out by the bombardment, though their losses had been heavy.

In the late afternoon, as if to punish the New Zealanders for their failure to rush the town fast and in strength, the heavens opened on the Germans' behalf and torrential rain drenched the area, turning the huge craters into lakes impassable by tanks and the rubble into a slimy morass in which the infantry slithered helplessly, especially at night, when several fell with their heavy equipment into the flooded craters and were drowned. A Stalingrad-type battle in the mud and rubble, the cellars and sewers of the town ruins now developed and went on night and day for a week and with few positive gains by the New Zealanders.

Simultaneously the British and Indians dragged their way by stages up the steep mountainside, being supplied each night by armies of porters. One Gurkha company fought its way to a ledge only 150 yards from the summit but could not be reinforced sufficiently to make an effective attack on the monastery. After a week General Alexander had to accept that the offensive had failed. In the February and March attacks the New Zealand Division had sustained 1600 casualties, the British and Indians 3000. All they had to show for it was the Cassino station strongpoint, the greater part of the rubble that had once been a town, and a small hill feature at the foot of Monte Cassino. The German 1st Parachute Division, on whom the burden of the defence had fallen, had earned from the Allied army group commander the encomium[6] "the finest division in the German Army." General von Senger's XIV corps front was still intact—but perhaps it was during the appalling agony of the close-quarter fighting in the terrible week that began on the Ides of March 1944 that this reflective general framed the thought that he was later to enshrine in his *Memoirs* in these words:[7]

> What will be the judgment of history on those of us who had the perspicacity and the integrity to recognise that defeat was inescapable, yet continued to fight and shed blood?

His battle headquarters during the offensive was hard by the birthplace of St. Thomas Aquinas and he found comfort, he tells us, in the teaching of the thirteenth-century Christian philosopher "that no man can be held answerable for the misdeeds of those over whom he has no power."

The six divisions of von Senger's corps were understandably elated after the three winter victories in which each had played some part. They were delighted with the attention their efforts had attracted in the German press. Despite the nightmare of daily existence on this front even when things were quiet, the brasher of them began to feel confident that no attack would ever shift them. They had smashed three and their now well-tested positions could only be made even stronger and better. But for the more thoughtful among them there was a nagging thought at the back of their minds to take some of the glow out of their soaring confidence. The atrocious winter, that had been so good an ally, could not last forever. One day soon it would suddenly be spring. The rivers would subside, the valleys and plains would dry out and the Allies would be able to deploy once again their great superiority of machines.

Even before the March offensive had petered out General Alexander was preparing with his staff a comprehensive regrouping of his armies that was to be carried out secretly and would take until the beginning of May to complete. With all movement strictly limited to the hours of darkness the greater part of the Eighth Army, with all its paraphernalia of supporting arms, was to move alongside the Fifth on the Tyrrhenian side of Italy, leaving minimal holding forces to block up the Adriatic front and the mountainous centre.

So secretly was this reshuffle carried out during the next few weeks, so efficiently did the Allied deception arrangements cover it, that when General von Senger left for Berchtesgaden on April 18 for the investiture, course and furlough already noted, he was content to leave behind a general warning order to all forces under his command to be ready for an Allied offensive any time after May 24. So—relaxing with his family and temporarily without a care in the world—he was as surprised as his C-in-C Field-Marshal Kesselring when he learned that on May 11, some 1600 Allied guns—raining shells by the thousand on the Gustav line from Cassino to the coast—had proclaimed to the German Tenth Army that their Intelligence estimate was two weeks out; on the wrong side.

He flew back to Italy at once and before rejoining his corps headquarters at the front learned from Kesselring the broad shape of the latest Allied effort and the progress so far made. Alexander had packed the fifteen-mile front with both his armies and was attacking with the Fifth on the right (as the Germans saw it) and the Eighth on the left. Essentially it was an elaboration of Alexander's four-prong January offensive with the difference that each prong was now three times as powerful and all four thrusts had been made simultaneously instead of successively. The German Tenth Army's right wing was being assaulted by an American Corps advancing up the coast with the French Expeditionary Corps inland on the Americans' right. The German left centre was being attacked by Eighth Army with a British Corps that had forced a crossing of the Rapido five miles south of Cassino and was now advancing north to cut the Rome road beyond, while the Polish Corps, now with the Eighth Army, attacked the extreme left of the German positions in the mountains north of Cassino. From the now familiar mountain bridgehead the Poles were trying to isolate the old enemy Monte Cassino from the north by forcing their way down the gullies past its rear to join hands with the British wheeling round to the road from the opposite side.

The American attack on the coast, the British and Polish attacks to encircle Cassino on the left, were strongly resisted: to begin with progress was costly and slow. Juin's French Corps, however, soon began to make swift progress. The switch of the French from the mountains above Cassino to the Fifth Army front had come as a complete surprise to the Germans, who had been further surprised by the augmenting of this corps since January from two divisions to four plus an additional ten thousand Moroccan *goumiers*. Alexander had exploited the enlargement of the French corps, and its secret transfer to a different part of the front, by assigning to Juin a thrust-line into mountain terrain that only his expert mountain fighters could have handled and which the Germans had regarded as "impossible" and had therefore not heavily defended. As a result, the surprise presence of the French, and their surprise attack from the least probable direction into the mountains south and west of the Liri Valley, proved to be the key factor in the Allies' success. Their advance was as rapid as it had been unexpected and it soon began to ease the resistance to the Americans on their left and the British and Poles in their grim battle to settle the issue at Cassino.

Within six days Kesselring—with Monte Cassino almost encircled, the French well forward in the Liri Valley and the Americans now smoothly moving up the coast—ordered a withdrawal to the prearranged switch line six miles behind the Gustav. The German paratroopers were reluctant to abandon "their" Monte Cassino but did so on May 17, and when the Poles entered it the next day they found only the wounded who had been left behind and the doctors looking after them. The 1st Parachute Division's delay in "consenting" to withdraw is blamed by Kesselring[8] for the fact that the German left wing did not man the switch line behind them in time.

With the disposal, at long last, of the Cassino bastion that had defied them for so long, the Allied armoured divisions now stampeded up the Liri Valley, quickly broke through the switch line acting as backstop to the Gustav line, and for a day or two the traffic congestion they created on the few roads available delayed them more than the rearguards of the retreating Tenth Army.

The big question for Kesselring now was when would Alexander go for the knock-out by ordering the Anzio beachhead force to break out and advance to cut off the escape of the retreating Tenth Army? On May 19, to stiffen the resistance of the now dissolving Tenth he ordered von Mackensen, the Commander of the Fourteenth Army, to place 29th Panzer Grenadiers at Tenth Army's disposal. With the beachhead break-out due any day, the Fourteenth Army Commander was unwilling to part with this valuable reserve. When, the following evening, Kesselring discovered that the division had still not moved he gave von Mackensen a firmer order and pointed out that apart from any other consideration the new position he had ordered for the 29th Panzer Grenadiers would protect von Mackensen's southern flank against the main body of Fifth Army now approaching rapidly from the south and hoping to join up with the rest of the Fifth in the beachhead area. The move was therefore carried out, but still half-heartedly with the result that the division was caught between two fronts before it had taken up proper positions and was badly cut up. Kesselring's attempt to plug the gap between Fourteenth Army and the retreating Tenth had failed. On May 23 Alexander ordered the beachhead element of Fifth Army to break out. They did so without difficulty and in forty-eight hours the American spearhead was driving east to cut the main Rome road and so cut off the Tenth Army's retreat at Valmontone. This was the objective laid down by the Army Group Commander Alexander for the break-out.

As the cut-off spearhead, led by Major General Lucian K. Truscott's crack U.S. 3rd Division was nearing Valmontone on May 25, Truscott was amazed to receive a new order from the Fifth Army Commander, General Mark Clark, ordering him to switch direction to the northwest and make for the capital. The only reason for this curious adaptation of Alexander's explicit order was a somewhat college-boy determination on the part of Clark to be first into Rome. Truscott has written:[9] "I was dumbfounded . . . this was no time to drive to the northwest where the enemy was still strong; we should pour our maximum power into the Valmontone Gap to insure destruction of the retreating German Army . . . such was the order that turned the main effort of the beachhead forces from the Valmontone Gap and prevented the destruction of the German Tenth Army."

Clark lamely justified his action afterwards in these words:[10] "I was determined that the Fifth Army was going to capture Rome, and I was probably oversensitive to indications that practically everybody else was trying to get into the act." For Kesselring and the German Tenth Army this was a lucky escape. The rapidly disintegrating Fourteenth Army took a final battering from the forces now heading for Rome, while the larger and more capable Tenth withdrew east of the capital by the roads leading through the centre to the mountainous north of a country that seems to have been specifically designed by the Almighty for the inspiration of artists and the convenience of generals conducting military withdrawals.

Chapter 27

THE START OF A PLOT

☐ In May while Kesselring's armies in Italy began to give way to the climactic Allied offensive that for a short while was to lift the half-forgotten secondary campaign to a place in the sun, preinvasion tension mounted in France; eased only by a rash forecast by the meteorological experts of German Intelligence that if it had not taken place by May 18 (the day Monte Cassino was captured) weather and tide conditions would probably ensure its deferment to August.

The argument over the positioning of the panzer reserve continued as strenuously as ever, except that von Rundstedt was now content to leave it to his younger subordinates, Rommel and Geyr von Schweppenburg, to fight it out between them. While the Commander of Army Group B was no less determined to have the panzer divisions right forward under his tactical control, the Commander of Panzer Group West, von Schweppenburg, was equally adamant about keeping them concentrated in the interior. The panzer general had an ally in General Heinz Guderian, Inspector General of Panzer Forces, who had visited France and agreed that the notion of a central reserve was "classically" correct; a position from which von Rundstedt himself had never withdrawn; since he could not feel as certain as Hitler and Rommel now felt that Normandy was the Allied choice for the first landing. What if it turned out not to be and the panzers were then caught in the wrong place?

General von Schweppenburg felt so strongly about the position that he went to Berchtesgaden to have it out with Hitler. The outcome was a compromise that pleased nobody. By the middle of May the Führer had allocated three of the six panzer divisions in northern France (the 2nd, 21st and 116th) to Rommel as an Army Group B reserve: the other, and more formidable, trio (the 1st and 12th SS and the elite Panzer Lehr) were designated an OKW reserve and could not therefore be moved except on Hitler's direct orders. Of Rommel's three panzer divisions only the 21st was placed close to the Normandy coast as he had wanted; it was near Caen.

The other two, 2nd and 116th Panzer Divisions, were both east of the Seine behind Fifteenth Army's front. Of the three OKW reserve formations both 12th SS Panzer and Panzer Lehr were well inland from the Normandy coast, while 1st SS was in Belgium.

Thus the final layout of von Rundstedt's western command (from right to left) was Army Group B (88th Netherlands Corps, Fifteenth Army, Seventh Army) with six panzer divisions and extending from the Zuider Zee to the Loire south of the Brittany peninsula. From the Loire southward was held by General Johannes Blaskowitz's Army Group G (First Army on the Atlantic, 19th Army covering the Mediterranean) which had the other three panzer divisions in the west, 11 Panzer inland from Bordeaux, 2nd SS Panzer fifty miles north of Toulouse and 17th SS Panzer Grenadier between Poitiers and the Loire. In all Field-Marshal von Rundstedt had fifty-nine divisions in his two army groups by the beginning of June. In the air and at sea his forces were almost laughable in view of what they would be up against. At any given time he could count on no more than five hundred serviceable aircraft of all types, his naval forces amounted to fifty obsolete submarines and a number of motor torpedo boats, armed trawlers, and other light naval vessels. Over even this handful of aircraft and naval forces he had no direct control but had to apply to the Naval or Air Commands if he wished to employ them.

Not the least of Rommel's problems was the difficulty of conveying to subordinate commanders from the Eastern Front the different kind of battle they would soon be facing. A great many key command positions in the West had by this time been filled by men who had previously known only the Eastern Front. These "Easterners" almost invariably arrived in the West with a superiority complex. After *their* war, the *real* war, the West was going to be child's play. But air forces had played little part in the Eastern campaigns since the early days of German victories. The Russian victories had been achieved in massive land battles in which their air forces played only a minor part. The "Easterners" (Geyr von Schweppenburg was an example) were inclined to assume that it would be just as easy to switch tank forces from one part of the front to another as it had been in Russia. Rommel had the greatest difficulty in penetrating their somewhat patronizing attitudes and convincing them that Anglo-American air supremacy had rendered German mobile warfare obsolete. He was talking about this one day to his old

Africa colleague General Fritz Bayerlein (now command-ing the Panzer Lehr Division) as they walked in the grounds of La Roche Guyon. There was weary exasperation in the Field-Marshal's voice as he blurted out to his subordinate:[1]

> Our friends from the East cannot imagine what they're in for here. It's not a matter of fanatical hordes to be driven forward in masses against our line, with no regard for casualties and little recourse to tactical craft; here we are facing an enemy who applies all his native intelligence to the use of his many technical resources, who spares no expendi-ture of material and whose every operation goes its course as though it had been the subject of repeated rehearsal. Dash and doggedness alone no longer make a soldier, Bayerlein; he must have sufficient intelligence to enable him to get the most out of his fighting machine. And that's something these people can do, we found that out in Africa.

"From the experience I had recently gained in the East," commented Bayerlein, "I could do nothing but agree." In-vasion was not however the only topic discussed on the long walks under the tall trees of La Roche Guyon every evening. It was there that Rommel became involved in a politico-mili-tary conspiracy to unseat Hitler and end the war. The roots of the conspiracy went back to pre-war days when Dr. Karl Goerdeler, a staunchly conservative and successful Mayor of Leipzig laid the political foundations of an anti-Hitler Re-sistance while General Ludwig Beck, the Army Chief of Staff before the war, until he resigned in 1938 at the time of the Munich Pact, took care of its military side. The con-spiracy had been carefully nursed, through the years, but had achieved little; partly because of the effectiveness of Hitler's Gestapo-controlled tyranny and also because in its early days, as later, it was cold-shouldered first by London and later by Washington when it tenuously made contact through devious neutral channels. But nursed along militarily by Beck, politically by Goerdeler, it kept alive bravely but without much effect until the Allies "Unconditional Surren-der" policy introduced early in 1943 seemed to finish off any prospect of an alternative to the Nazi regime making effec-tive contact with the Allied cause. Nevertheless a potential "shadow government" existed on paper, a number of senior soldiers including Field-Marshals von Mannstein and von

Kluge were sympathetic though careful not to commit themselves openly, and in 1943 three unsuccessful attempts to assassinate Hitler were made.

In October of that year the military side of the movement was rejuvenated by the appointment of a young Colonel of the General Staff, Count Claus von Stauffenberg, to take it over and supply the dynamic that was now getting beyond the ageing and now ailing Beck. Count von Stauffenberg was a brilliant young patrician with a cavalryman's dashing leadership and an intellect that had early marked him out as a future Chief of Staff. As with many cavalrymen the cavalier spirit had been directed into tanks, and in 1943 he was a senior staff officer of the 10th Panzer Division in Tunisia. During the battle of Kasserine von Stauffenberg was so badly wounded in a low-flying Allied air attack that he only just survived his multiple injuries. After a long period in hospitals in Tunis and Germany, he eventually emerged with one eye and only his left arm the hand of which had been reduced to three fingers. He refused an artificial right arm and assiduously trained himself to do with a thumb and two left fingers most of the things for which other men need ten. He also dedicated himself to one last mission on behalf of Germany: to kill Hitler.

He was appointed deputy to the Head of the Army Command Office in Berlin, General Friedrich Olbricht, a prominent military member of the Resistance, an appointment helpful to their common purpose. This section of the central war office dealt with reinforcements and postings. In the ordinary way these would have been matters of detail beneath the attention of a Commander-in-Chief. But it was one of Hitler's peculiar weaknesses that he did concern himself with just such matters of trivial detail: which panzer division had been brought up to what strength and to which front it was to be moved: so that von Stauffenberg was doing a job that would necessitate reasonably frequent visits to Supreme Headquarters: for obviously the first qualification of a would-be killer of the Führer was that he should have legitimate access to his closely guarded presence.

Still under the basic leadership of Dr. Goerdeler and General Beck—but with the brilliant von Stauffenberg now enrolled to plan and execute its key operation—the conspiracy gained strength in 1943 and 1944 spreading its ramifications throughout the army through nods and winks and meaning silences.

Although it was not difficult to enlist the sympathy of the

senior generals it was not easy to persuade them to become activists. This was simply because they were the men they were. The whole essence of the soldier's ethos is based on the mystique of obedience and loyalty. The personal oath of loyalty to Hitler that every German soldier had to take was not lightly undertaken. He was not saluting the person inside the ridiculous uniform but the hereditary concept represented by it—that of the Emperor of Prussia. He would not lightly violate that oath however much he might hate and despise the besotted psychopath from a Vienna slum to whom it had been sworn. The German officer corps was conditioned from the beginning of its military education to be above politics. And the military *coup d'état* is not an occupation of civilized nations but of the immature. These points need to be borne in mind before making a blanket condemnation of "the German generals," for failing to get rid of Hitler. It was not an easy thing to do even if they had wanted to do it. It is a more valid criticism to suggest that having done well professionally out of the war some of them may have been reluctant to jeopardize the rewards of their professional success and seniority by aligning themselves with any organized anti-Hitler movement. But there were many who *were* prepared to take the risk and because their efforts were unsuccessful, less than justice has been accorded them by the postwar world at large. One such was Field-Marshal Erwin Rommel.

From the beginning of April, when his somewhat enigmatic intellectual Chief of Staff, the bespectacled General Dr. Hans Speidel, reported for duty at La Roche Guyon, the political situation was discussed by the two men almost as much and as freely as the military problems posed by the coming invasion. It has been mentioned that through an administrative oversight the customary party "political officer" had not been posted to watch over the headquarters of Army Group B and that Rommel and Speidel had taken care to ensure that the error was not brought to the attention of the higher authorities. They were accordingly able to converse freely about what was in their minds without having to keep glancing over their shoulders or lowering their voices. What was in their minds was that the criminal regime of Hitler had brought their country to the brink of total defeat and destruction and that the war must be ended before the Allies invaded. They soon established a complete personal *rapport* and Speidel, already well *au fait* with the anti-Nazi conspiracy, found a ready listener in his new chief when he set about apprising him of what was being plotted.

On April 14 Speidel represented Rommel at a secret meeting at Freudenstadt in Württemberg, with Dr. Karl Strölin, Lord Mayor of Stuttgart, another of the plotters. Strölin was a friend of Goerdeler's and had been asked by him to try to enlist the support of Rommel. So it was in a sense as Goerdeler's agent that Strölin, as a first step, met Speidel secretly on April 14 and gave him (for onward transmission to Rommel) an up-to-the-minute breakdown on the plot. The military arrangements were still under the direction of General Beck assisted by General Wagner, the Quartermaster General of the Army, and with the dazzling Colonel von Stauffenberg as the chosen executant of its key operation, the assassination of Hitler. Other key military members were the Military Governor of Belgium and Northern France, General Alexander von Falkenhausen, whose headquarters was in Brussels; and, in Paris, General Karl Heinrich von Stulpnagel, Military Governor of France. Among others involved were Ernst Junger, author and philosopher, a captain on von Stulpnagel's staff, and Constantin von Neurath, a well-known German diplomat of pre-war days. A coalition government of anti-Nazis drawn from all political parties was lined up to take over under Goerdeler if the conspiracy succeeded.

As it could not have failed to attract the notice of the Gestapo if Rommel had attempted to visit Goerdeler or Strölin, the two men made surreptitious visits to La Roche Guyon instead. Thus the ancestral portraits of the La Rochefoucaulds—including that of the author of the celebrated *Maxims*—gazed quizzically down not only on generals, colonels, and engineer officers coming in at all hours with reports from the front, but also on a smaller stream of other visitors making discreet calls to discuss how the conspiracy was shaping.

Rommel was soon won over by the conspirators and accepted their plan in principle but with certain important reservations as we shall see. Field-Marshal von Rundstedt was fully informed of what was going on by the generals concerned but though fully sympathetic with their aims declined to take an active part in the conspiracy. He was an old man, increasingly feeling his age; and what was proposed, he felt, was work for younger men. Speidel analyzed von Rundstedt's attitude in this way:[2]

Rundstedt was an eminent strategist, a master of the rules of war, but in the last few years he had lost with advancing age the creative impulse and the clear sense of responsibility towards the nation. Symptoms of this lapse were sarcastic comments or indifference. Of course he despised Hitler and referred to him in all private conversations, as Hindenberg did, with the nickname of "the Bohemian Corporal." But he seemed to think that the height of wisdom was to make studied representations and write grave situation reports. He left action to others. When Rommel sought to move him to send joint demands to Hitler, Rundstedt exclaimed:

"You are young. The people know and love you. You do it!"

The support of Germany's most popular and famous Field-Marshal gave the conspiracy just the shot in the arm it needed after the long plodding years of discouragement and the earlier unsuccessful attempts to kill Hitler. Rommel was "box-office"; as much of a hero-figure to the general public as he was idolized within the Army; the ideal figurehead for the Goerdeler-Strölin-Beck enterprise. But on one point Rommel was firmly at variance with the others.

He was strongly opposed to the idea of assassination. To kill Hitler, argued Rommel, would only make him a martyr in the eyes of the people and it would rally the considerable praetorian guard of SS and security forces assiduously built up and multiplied through the years by the execrable Himmler. Hitler, he insisted, must be arrested by the Army—if necessary he would send trusted panzer divisions to assist—and must then be brought to trial before a German court. The German people who had elected him must try him for the crimes committed in their name. The question was the subject of much argument at the secret meetings at La Roche Guyon. Goerdeler's view was that keeping Hitler in captivity would probably lead to civil war. Rommel, expanding his own ideas, suggested that as soon as Hitler was under arrest, he himself and von Rundstedt should make direct contact with the Allied Command asking for an armistice on the following terms: the Germans immediately to evacuate all occupied territory after completing an orderly administrative handover to the Allies, and then to withdraw behind the 1939 boundaries of Germany. In return, the Allies to cease the bombing of Germany. Rommel further hoped to contact the Allied Command and pave the way for such an armistice before the invasion.

Although Rommel and the others reached fairly general agreement, the assassination issue remained deadlocked and had to be left in abeyance for the time being.

With regard to Rommel's opposition to assassination, it was decided that von Stauffenberg, who was not present at the meetings at La Roche Guyon, should visit Rommel as soon as possible and go to work on him with his considerable and persuasive personality which his injuries had done nothing to impair. Indeed, his black eyepatch, armless right sleeve and his invariable debonair refusal of help in performing tasks for which the thumb and two fingers of his left hand were obviously insufficient had added an extra dash of heroic style and panache to his youthful good looks and presence. But it was not possible to arrange a meeting before the invasion took place.

In addition, the practicalities of making contact with the Allied Command before the invasion proved insuperable. There was, after all, no "hot line" between the headquarters of von Rundstedt and Eisenhower. Nor did the efforts of Goerdeler and company to put out feelers through Allied Embassies in Spain, Portugal, and Switzerland lead to any useful arrangement. It was appreciated that Unconditional Surrender was a stumbling-block but it was felt that the Allies could not indefinitely play hard-to-get if the cost of this would be thousands more lives lost and a prolonging of the war.

Then came the misleading meteorological forecast that if the invasion had not been launched by May 18 it was unlikely to occur before August. When this date had been passed the conspirators felt that the time factor had now eased and there was still time in which to resolve their various differences.

Chapter 28

INVASION, THE CLIMAX

☐ In the early morning sunshine of Sunday, June 4, 1944, a tidal wave of Fifth Army tanks, armoured cars, jeeps, trucks, and artillery pieces of all shapes and sizes clattered, roared, squealed, and clanked up the last few miles of the torn dusty Appian Way to occupy Rome, and thus facilitate Kesselring's withdrawal northwards of his broken Tenth and Fourteenth Armies, whose escape the Fifth Army could more usefully have been preventing, had their commander done what he was supposed to do.

At four o'clock on this same Sunday morning, in the early morning chill of a tent near Portsmouth, England's foremost naval base, General Dwight D. Eisenhower braced himself to make one of the most momentous military decisions in history. The invasion of Fortress Europe, the grand climax to all the dark years of Hitler's domination, was scheduled to strike the coast of France early the following morning of Monday, June 5.

At this four A.M. meeting on Sunday, Eisenhower and his chief Navy, Army, and Air subordinates were assembled in the damp and chilly tent to receive the all-important meteorological forecast on which Eisenhower alone would have to decide whether or not to order the invasion to go forward as planned. The report was discouraging.[1] "Low clouds, high winds, and formidable wave action were predicted to make a landing a most hazardous affair. The meteorologists said that air support would be impossible, naval gunfire would be inefficient, and even the handling of small boats would be rendered difficult." Eisenhower felt that he had no alternative but to postpone the operation for twenty-four hours, that is until the early morning of Tuesday June 6.

On Monday, Rome, unlike the English Channel, was ablaze with June sunshine as General Mark Clark celebrated his short-lived Roman triumph with a flamboyant press conference on the Capitoline Hill. That day the press of the free world accorded their headlines and most of their column-inches to the capture of Rome. But at 3:30 A.M. of this same

Monday, June 5, Eisenhower and his three principal subordinates were again assembled in the cold little camp, this time everyone even more tense and fretful, to hear from the weather men. The distant Roman holiday in the hot sunshine was something which seemed to have no significance whatever unless to mock them. They prayed that a second postponement would not be necessary. It would involve all sorts of complications in an enterprise of this magnitude. For example ships from the more distant British ports were already at sea and would have to return to port to refuel. The signs, as the commanders gathered for the Monday meeting, were if anything less hopeful. At this desolate 3:30 A.M. conference "Our little camp"—in Eisenhower's words[2]—"was shaking and shuddering under a wind of almost hurricane proportions and the accompanying rain seemed to be travelling in horizontal streaks."

The Royal Air Force officer in charge of the meteorologists, a shrewd psychologist as well as a man with the courage of his professional convictions, began by authenticating his section's reliability. His forecast of yesterday, he said, had worked out exactly as he had predicted: had the landing been attempted today, as originally intended, it would undoubtedly have been a disaster. Having made this point he went on to astonish his eminent and increasingly gloomy audience by forecasting a break in the weather from early the following morning, Tuesday, June 6. The good weather should last thirty-six hours. There might be a deterioration after the first landings and before the administrative build-up could get properly started—but he could guarantee them thirty-six hours of good weather. Watching the horizontal rain and listening to the hurricane-like wind, Eisenhower had still to make the decision by himself. The loneliness of supreme command can seldom have weighed more heavily on a man called to a high destiny. In the wind and the rain he decided that the next day, Tuesday, June 6, should irrevocably be the day. And he no doubt prayed, as he had never prayed before, that the quiet Scot, who felt confident enough to commit himself to a promise of thirty-six hours of fine weather so soon and against all the apparent evidence, was right.

On the German side of the Channel the terrible weather of Sunday and Monday was a comfort to everyone. An imminent invasion, for those who await it, is undoubtedly the occasion of occasions that supremely vindicates the proverb about an ill wind.

335

Among those who derived comfort from the capricious weather in the English Channel was Field-Marshal Erwin Rommel. The diary kept by his aide-de-camp has this entry covering the days of Eisenhower's ordeal-by-meteorologist at Portsmouth:

> "5th-8th June 1944.[3] Fears of an invasion during this period were rendered all the less by the fact that tides were very unfavourable for the days following, and the fact that no amount of air reconnaissance had given the slightest indication that a landing was imminent. The most urgent need was to speak to the Führer on the Obersalzberg, convey to him the extent of the man-power and material inferiority we would suffer in the event of a landing, and request the dispatch of two further panzer divisions, an AA corps and a Nebelwerfer brigade to Normandy."

Having obtained von Rundstedt's permission to make the trip and having telephoned Hitler's chief adjutant, Schmundt, for an appointment, Rommel left La Roche Guyon by car early on the morning of June 5 leaving General Speidel in charge. He headed first for his home at Herrlungen near Ulm where he proposed to spend the night with his wife and to drive on to Berchtesgaden next day. As Rommel relaxed in easy clothes, enjoying the last simple domestic evening he was to spend for some time to come, the greatest armada in history was moving to its marshalling points in the English Channel from every port in the southern half of Great Britain. Soon after dark, and to a strict timetable worked out in relation to their different speeds and the varying distances each had to travel, they gently rolled, pitched and tossed into position and began the journey across the Channel where it is some eighty miles wide. According to the British official historian there were in all 6939 of them made up of 1213 warships, 4126 landing ships and craft, 736 ancillary ships and craft, and 864 merchant ships. The warships were 79 percent British and Canadian, 16½ percent American, and the other 4½ percent were naval units of other Allies. The naval vessels included six battleships, two monitors with fifteen-inch guns, two cruisers, 119 destroyers, 113 sloops, corvettes, and frigates.[4] It was a manifestation of seaborne power beyond the wildest dreams of the most megalomaniac film producer, a visual *tour de force* of beauty and terror the like of which had never been seen before and would never be seen again.

The descendants of William the Conqueror, who had crossed these waters in the reverse direction to conquer England nearly nine centuries before, were on their way back to what they could fairly call the land of their fathers. Among their first objectives would be the small Gothic-Norman town of Bayeux, home of the most famous of all tapestries, which chronicles in detail that earlier conquest of 1066, and is therefore a unique medieval historical document as well as a masterpiece of world art. The Bishop of Bayeux who accompanied the Conqueror is thought to have commissioned the tapestry from a workshop of Saxon weavers. Had his successor in 1944 been like-minded no weavers on earth could have been found to encompass the scope and scale of events that were to link England and Normandy in this new conquest. This time Bayeux would have to guard well the tapestry of the earlier conquest that was its great pride, letting history and the motion picture weave for posterity the story of the twentieth-century Norman Conquest now about to unfold.

From dusk the sky throbbed with the continuing roar of aircraft, a roar familiar yet this time seemingly more purposeful and more continuous: from midnight soaring in a crescendo of sound that seemed always to have reached its peak yet always becoming greater; an infinite crescendo without end, dreadful and awe-inspiring, a sound that might have portended Judgment Day itself. The crash of bombs reverberated up and down the coast and far inland. Soon after midnight the aircraft began to drop not only bombs but men. Twenty-three thousand paratroopers dropped from the sky that night: two U.S. Airborne Divisions, Major General Maxwell D. Taylor's 101st and Major General Matthew B. Ridgway's 82nd, in the Cotentin Peninsula to cut it off south of Cherbourg; one British, the 6th, to the east to seize the crossings of the Vire and the Caen Canal and secure the East flank of the invasion area. Then at 0530 the naval bombardment unloosed its fury and the coast of France seemed to dissolve in dust and smoke, and the small boats moved in and men began to splash through the water, to be blown up in it, or to sink in assault craft ripped open on the submerged obstacles, or to be shot down—but some of them to scramble ashore.

It had started.

Hitler's intuition, subsequently supported by Rommel's reasoning, had been right. The chosen invasion objective was a sixty-mile stretch of the Normandy coast from the River Orne and the Caen Canal in the east to the Cotentin

Peninsula in the west. The initial landing force, much smaller than the Germans expected, consisted of two British and one Canadian Division assaulting three beaches Sword, Juno, and Gold on the German right; on the left three U.S. Divisions assaulting two beaches Omaha and Utah forming an angle where the east-west Calvados coast turns north towards Cherbourg up the east side of the Cotentin peninsula. The Anglo-Canadian divisions were the vanguard of General Sir Bernard Montgomery's 21st Army Group. The American landing forces (from the U.S. First Army of General Courtney H. Hodges) was the vanguard of General Omar N. Bradley's 12th Army Group which would in due course comprise Hodges' First and General George S. Patton's Third Armies. The three airborne divisions preceded by a few hours the main landings with the object of securing vital supporting objectives inland before joining up with the main landing force.

The Germans had become so imbued psychologically with the notion that American power was limitless, that they had assumed that some sixty or seventy Allied divisions were standing by for the invasion. In fact there were but thirty-five, and shipping resources were such that it would not be possible to land the last of them in France until seven weeks after D-day. Although overwhelmingly strong in the air (11,500 aircraft) and at sea, the Allied ground forces would for some time be numerically below parity.

In all areas of human experience a climactic confrontation, too long prepared, studied, brooded over and anticipated often proves in the event to be something of an anticlimax. To an extent they did not dare to believe possible the Allies obtained surprise. Not merely through their deception plans but because of the bad weather in the first days of June. Yet the odd thing is that German Intelligence correctly identified the code signals by which the Allied Command proposed to issue a warning order to the French Resistance followed by a second that would mean the invasion was scheduled within forty-eight hours. The method chosen was to drop a couplet by the Poet Paul Verlaine into the daily BBC broadcast in French, one line at a time. The first line would signify a general alert. The second line would indicate the opening of the invasion within forty-eight hours. A Fifteenth Army monitor duly picked up the first line of the couplet on June 1 and the second at 9:15 P.M. on June 5. Fifteenth Army was accordingly fully alerted, but neither von Rundstedt, nor Seventh Army nor Army Group B took any action. The weather during the day had been too bad for air reconnaissance and von Rundstedt and his senior commanders in the West preferred the evidence of their eyes to that of their radio monitors in deciding that an immediate invasion was out of the question in the prevailing weather conditions. This is clear from the number of senior men away from their posts on June 6. Rommel, as we have seen, had spent the night at his home in Germany and was intending to move on to Berchtesgaden for his interview with Hitler during the day. General Dollmann, the Commander of Seventh Army, was away in Rennes running an anti-invasion exercise to deal with a possible landing in Brittany: several of his divisional commanders were taking part in it and one, the Commander of the 91st Parachute Division, was killed in an air attack on his way back to the front. General Sepp Dietrich, Commander of the two divisions of the 1st SS Panzer Corps, the most powerful of the OKW reserve formations behind Army Group B, was away in Brussels. In fact the only top men on hand were von Rundstedt himself, von Salmuth, Commander of Fifteenth Army, whose front was not being attacked, and von Schweppenburg, who was in charge of Panzer Group West but as yet had no power to do anything with them except on orders from above.

At 0300 when the Allied paratroopers were dropping, von Rundstedt informed OKW (then in Berchtesgaden) that this looked like the invasion, that Normandy seemed to be the chosen place and could the three OKW reserve panzer divisions be released for his use as the situation demanded? Jodl, without reference to Hitler, said that they already knew about the air drop; that it was too soon to tell whether or not this was the main landing; that until they knew more definitely, the OKW reserve divisions must not be touched without his permission; and that Army Group B must deal with the landing with their own forces.[5]

At 0630 General Speidel, holding the fort at Army Group B, telephoned Rommel at his home with the bad news. Rommel said he would cancel the visit to Hitler and return at once, though it would take him most of the day to get back. In the meantime Speidel was to pass on an order to 21st Panzer Division (the only armoured division right on the spot) to counterattack as soon as possible. What Rommel had feared had happened. He had been caught with one instead of three panzer divisions near the invasion coast.

The Seventh Army defenders stood up well under their cataclysmic ordeal by naval and air bombardment. But the invaders continued to come ashore on the five landing beaches aided by such technical devices as flail tanks (to thresh a path through the minefields with whirling lengths of chain from a revolving drum on the front of the tank), partly amphibious tanks to lead the way on to the beaches, track-laying tanks that unfolded behind them a pathway for wheeled vehicles, and that most remarkable of all technical devices the courageous infantryman, heavily laden with weapons and equipment who, after a night of seasickness, could still wade doggedly through chest-high water now filling with corpses and reddened by the manner of their going, picking their way through submerged obstacles—many of them exploding all around them—to stagger onto a beach raked with fire and still push on into the sandhills or fields beyond. Hundreds of them were cut down or blown to bits in the sea or just out of it; thousands of them got through to form those first chaotic and precarious little posts which eventually add up to a blob on the map called a beachhead.

By 1000 the 21st Panzer Division, in accordance with the telephoned orders of Field-Marshal Rommel, was ready to counter-attack west of the Orne on the German right of the invaded front where the British had landed: their objective to destroy the British airborne lodgements along the river and to cut through to the sea to roll up the eastern flank of the Allied beachhead. Then Seventh Army changed the orders to an attack west of the Orne. As a result of the consequent delay the Division did not get on the move till afternoon and then with only a battle group.

The hardest ordeal in the early stages of the invasion was that of the Americans on Omaha beach. There were two reasons for this. First, it was the most strongly defended of the chosen landing places; the powerful and experienced German 352nd Division had been in position there for three months undetected by Allied Intelligence and was ideally placed to oppose the landing. Secondly, the Americans in the early stages had little armoured support having rejected the partly amphibious tanks, flail tanks, and path-laying tanks (colloquially known as the "funnies") specially developed for the occasion by the British and offered to General Bradley but regarded by his staff with some scepticism. These "Funnies" helped the British and Canadian landings and might have helped to make Omaha less of a day-long agony. While the Americans on neighbouring Utah established their beachhead comparatively easily, Omaha was the one landing out of the five that was a "close-run thing" until the end of the day and even on the second day.

During the day Army Group B and Seventh Army made desperate pleas by telephone for the release for counterattack of the 1st SS Panzer Corps from OKW reserve but this was not authorized until four o'clock in the afternoon by which time it was too late for the two divisions to move until evening, for use the next day. During the late afternoon the counterattack by 21st Panzer against the British flank made headway but as its spearhead came within reach of the coast a cloud of 250 glider-towing aircraft with fighter escort, came in low out of the setting sun and cut off the spearhead from the rest of the division, which had to withdraw. The Germans later credited the Allied command with having swiftly launched this airdrop to frustrate the armoured counterattack.[6] In fact, it was coincidental that its timing worked out so conveniently for the Allies. This was the second half of the British 6th Airborne Division, the gliderborne part, landing according to its original schedule to join the parachutists who had dropped during the night. Its timely descent through the German antiaircraft fire with the loss of only one aircraft not only frustrated the Germans' first dangerous counterattack but doubled the strength of the 6th Airborne Division which had been fighting since the early hours of the morning and brought them equipment and supplies. It had been a day without precedent in the annals of warfare, but by the end of it the vital first breach of the Atlantic Wall had been effected: 57,500 Americans[7] and 75,215 British and Canadians had established themselves on the coast of Normandy. In addition 15,500 American and 7900 British airborne troops had dropped from the sky and were now helping the others to secure and widen their bridgeheads. By the time he arrived back at his headquarters in La Roche Guyon none knew better than Field-Marshal Rommel that the war was finally lost. The invasion had *not* been smashed on the vital first day as he had intended. The Allies had cracked the wall of Fortress Europe and now nothing could stop them pouring through the breach.

As Rommel had anticipated, and as he had repeatedly tried to warn his colleagues and superiors, Allied air and seapower had made the landings possible. The impotence of the German Navy and Air Force on that terrible first day had been almost pathetic. There had been nothing to prevent the allied battleships and cruisers coming in close to deliver their pulverizing broadsides. Since the earliest hours of D-day the Allied air forces had flown no fewer than 14,000 sorties at a cost of only 127 aircraft lost and 63 damaged. Not until late afternoon did four forlorn Heinkels make a suicidal bombing attack on the tempting clutter of men and machines on the landing beaches. Out of the sky swooped Allied fighters and none of the Heinkels made the return journey. Europe was no longer a fortress. The Allied armies were ineluctably through its outer wall: right there: on the inside.

One thing seemed clear to von Rundstedt and the German Supreme Command that first night. They knew by then, from identifications of prisoners, the extent of the forces that had landed in Normandy. The comparative smallness of the force fitted their preconceived conviction that there would be more than one landing. Clearly Normandy was only the beginning. They had been taken in by the fictitious American Army Group allegedly standing by in southeast England. It was not difficult for the Allies to reinforce the large falsehood with the fragment of solid truth that General George S. Patton had not yet arrived in France. What more natural than that the dynamic Patton, the Allies' most thrustful tank general—the "American Guderian"—was to command the new Army Group, land with it in the Pas de Calais and head for Germany? So the one firm decision at the end of the chaotic first day of Normandy was that Fifteenth Army must stand by for a second landing, its ample reserves—five infantry, two panzer divisions—must not be touched. Seventh Army must handle Normandy on its own. Needless to say Rommel vigorously opposed this idea. As soon as he reached the front late on D-day he asked for reserve divisions of Fifteenth Army to be sent across the Seine to the Seventh; he also asked for the substantial garrison of 35,000 (including an infantry division), uselessly tied up in the Channel Islands; and for the four panzer divisions in the southern half of France. All these requests[8] were refused with the exception of a single infantry division of Fifteenth Army which was sent across the Seine to Seventh Army.

Admittedly OKW had now released Dietrich's 1st SS Panzer Corps (Panzer Lehr and 12th SS Panzer divisions). It will be remembered that Rommel had earlier asked for both these divisions to be moved near the coast, where their presence on D-day would have been invaluable and might have been decisive. Now both would have to travel some distance to the front, running the gauntlet of the Allied air umbrella. Nevertheless he ordered Dietrich to repeat on June 7 the counterattack unsuccessfully launched by 21st Panzer on D-day. His mission was to drive the British into the sea, while the American beachheads were contained. Then he learned that Panzer Lehr, who would have to move 130 miles by road, could not arrive until at least June 8, so he told Dietrich to make the attack with 12th SS and 21st Panzer only, without waiting for Panzer Lehr. At midnight on June 6 the two divisions, with between them 150 tanks and five infantry battalions, were in the Caen area. But Dietrich's hope of launching a concerted counterattack at dawn was frustrated by delay in replenishing his fuel supply. With the arrival of daylight both divisions were heavily attacked from the air and then became involved in defensive battles against Allied attacks. Their strength being thus dissipated, it was afternoon before they could concentrate for their own attack which was then made weakly and was easily held. Throughout the day the third division of the corps Panzer Lehr, ordered to move up to the battlefield in daylight, was experiencing the nightmare journey that Rommel had predicted for any armoured division that exposed itself to Allied air supremeacy by day. Though heavily camouflaged and trying to confine its movement to the fringes of woods away from the roads, it still lost (in addition to five tanks) forty gasoline trucks, ninety other trucks, and eighty-four half-tracks and mobile guns. Dietrich was ordered to attack again on June 8 using all three divisions, thus the Panzer Lehr were thrown into the battle piecemeal as they straggled on to the scene depleted and disorganized. By June 9 the counterattacking panzers were firmly held and forced on to the defensive, having suffered crippling losses not only from air attack but through the heavy use of naval bombardment that the Allies were still able to exploit. By June 10, the fifth day of the invasion the British and American beachheads had joined up to form a continuous bridgehead and while the British engaged the panzer counterattacks near Caen, the Americans linked up their Utah and Omaha forces and captured Carentan, where the Germans were trying to drive a wedge between the two American beachheads. Bradley could now proceed to the clearing of the Cotentin Peninsula and the capture of Cherbourg with his right, while his left struck southward towards Saint-Lô in parallel with Montgomery's advance on Caen farther east.

The Allies were methodically and quickly building up their strength to a point where they had numerical superiority over the defenders and the German counterattacks were failing because they could not organize themselves and move to where they were wanted in the face of the continuous Allied air effort. Still Rommel had one more try. He ordered Geyr von Schweppenburg forward from Paris with his Panzer Group West Headquarters to prepare a major attack on the Bayeux-Caen sector with the three panzer divisions that were already there: to which would be added a parachute corps coming up from Brittany and the forces respectively on the right of the Seventh Army and the left of the Fifteenth. General von Schweppenburg was one of the "Eastern" generals who had been sceptical about Rommel's warnings that Allied air strength would paralyze movement of the panzer divisions. He was to learn the hard way how right Rommel had been. On June 10, von Schweppenburg's headquarters was located in an orchard twelve miles south of Caen while the Commander of Panzer Group West made his final plans for the set-piece counterattack that Rommel had ordered, an attack designed to split the Allied bridgehead in two. In his Russian experience von Schweppenburg had never come up against an enemy with command of the sky so he was casual about camouflage, his radio trucks and command trailers were parked without any particular regard to concealment, and his staff officers carelessly wandered about the Command Post area displaying on their trousers the bold red stripe of the General Staff. It would have been difficult indeed for Allied observers in spotter planes or on routine air reconnaissance patrol not to identify this caravanserai as a headquarters of some importance. Surely enough it was spotted and duly scheduled as a target. On the evening of June 10 the Royal Air Force accurately bombed the headquarters killing or wounding all seventeen of its staff officers including von Schweppenburg, and his Chief of Staff, and destroying all its radio trucks and most of its other transport. So complete was the stroke that it was twelve hours before Seventh Army heard about it. The slightly wounded von Schweppenburg was evacuated to Paris and General Dietrich of 1st SS Panzer Corps was ordered to resume command of the counterattack force he had barely relinquished. As the three panzer divisions were now fully engaged in a defensive battle with the British and Canadians there was little that Dietrich could do except to cancel von Schweppenburg's ambitious plan and peg away with local counterattacks as before. Rommel's grand plan for a supreme effort to split the Allied bridgehead in half had blown up in a shower of bomb fragments. From now on it would have to be a merciless battle of attrition in the difficult Norman countryside with the Allies using their huge air power to isolate the battlefield, to wear out the German strength already engaged, and to prevent supplies or reinforcements from reaching the scene except at appalling cost.

Chapter 29

"MAKE PEACE, YOU FOOLS!"

☐ From the German point of view the organized chaos of the battle of Normandy, where the fate of Fortress Europe was finally settled, can be simplified into a succession of crisis points.

The first was the evening of D-day by which time the Allies had landed 150,000 soldiers at five points and it was clear that they had the air and naval power to keep them there. (Seven weeks later the number landed was 1,500,000.)

The second was five days later by which time the failure of the first German counterattacks had shown—as Rommel had predicted—that the overwhelming air power of the Allies was irresistible and had the capability to paralyze road and rail movement and so prevent counteroffensive forces from reaching the battlefield in time or in any shape to fight. Thus it was possible for the Allies to consolidate their footholds, even the most precarious of them, and steadily expand and extend them from five beachheads into one continuous bridgehead. Complete control of the air and the water enabled General Eisenhower to pour supplies and reinforcements into this bridgehead faster than the Germans could replace the losses of men and equipment they incurred trying to thwart him.

The third crisis point was a meeting between von Rundstedt, Rommel, and Hitler at Margival near Soissons on June 17. The meeting had two motivations. First the two Field-Marshals wished to tell the Führer bluntly how hopeless they considered the situation to be. Secondly, they wanted to convey to him that it would mean a great deal to the troops if he were to put in an appearance at the front. Hitler was fond of referring to his experience as a front-line soldier in the First World War, especially when he wished to be insulting about the General Staff. But despite his boasts that he knew more about the real meaning of war than any of them, he took good care never to visit the front either in the East or the West. It was known to the German troops in Normandy that Churchill had taken the first opportunity to visit the Allied soldiers, and the German commanders were pressing for a similar visit to their side of the fence by Hitler. This was another matter the Field-Marshals hoped to raise. There was irony in the choice of rendezvous for the June 17 meeting. It took place in the complex of luxurious bombproof bunkers built there in 1940 as the headquarters from which Hitler and OKW intended to direct the invasion of England.

The headquarters was in a deep railway cutting near the mouth of a tunnel in which Hitler's special train could conveniently be halted. A telephone call on June 16 summoned the two Field-Marshals and their Chiefs of Staff, Speidel and Blumentritt to meet Hitler at nine the following morning to report on the situation. This meant that Rommel had to drive 140 miles immediately after returning to La Roche Guyon at three A.M. from a tour of the front that had lasted twenty-one hours. He was therefore tired and testy and in the mood to be blunt and critical. Hitler came by plane and car from Berchtesgaden with Jodl, his chief adjutant Schmundt, and others of the OKW entourage. According to Speidel "he looked worn and sleepless, playing nervously with his spectacles and an array of coloured pencils, which he held between his fingers. He was the only one who sat, hunched upon a stool, while the Field-Marshals stood. There was a curt and frosty greeting from Hitler, who then raised his voice and spoke bitterly of his displeasure that the Allied landings should have succeeded. He held the field commanders to be guilty of incompetence. 'The fortress of Cherbourg is to be held at all costs,' he exclaimed." [1] (The Americans captured it without much difficulty one week later.)

Field-Marshal von Rundstedt made a short formal introductory statement in which he emphasized that no effective counter-offensive could be mounted in the face of the Allies' air supremacy and their naval artillery which had so far exerted a crucial influence on the land battle. He then handed over to Rommel who went further. Rommel doubted whether they could even contain the bridgehead unless the Luftwaffe could be persuaded to emerge from its eclipse and protect his supply lines and unless he could be given a free hand to run the battle in his own way. He no longer thought there was any likelihood of a second landing in the Pas de Calais and he therefore wanted permission to use the whole of his army group as he thought fit. He guessed that the allied plan was to break out southward towards Paris from Caen and the Cotentin Peninsula, while a second thrust was made towards Avranches to cut off the Brittany peninsula. The first thing he wanted to do was to withdraw the Caen front and establish a new line southward along the river Orne and then westward along the line of hills from Mount Pincon. This would bring the front out of range of the Allies' naval artillery which had proved so devastating in the earlier fighting: and it would enable him to disengage his hard-pressed panzer divisions and reorganize them for new counterattacks.[2]

Rommel stressed that officers and men had done all that could be expected of them and more: that they had simply been overwhelmed by the fury of the Allied air supremacy and naval bombardments on top of a vast superiority of ordinary artillery. He hotly disputed an Allied communiqué which said that units defending the Atlantic Wall had been surprised in their sleep, a statement that Hitler had been only too ready to believe. Rommel said that Cherbourg would fall within a week and it would be sensible to withdraw its sizeable garrison to a more tenable position immediately. Hitler rejected this last suggestion and also the proposal to pull the Caen front back. Withdrawal of any kind in any circumstances was still the dirtiest word in his vocabulary.

Rommel's vivid description of the destructive power of Allied army, air, and naval equipment was greeted with scepticism by the Führer. It gave him an excuse to digress into one of the familiar monologues in which he could hold forth on the secret new wonder weapons that his own experts would soon have ready. The V-1 (flying bomb) offensive against London had opened only two nights before. Londoners could look forwad to not less than a thousand a week of them in the next three months. Rommel suggested that the flying bombs would be more usefully directed against the south of England ports, jammed with troops and military equipment, or even against the Normandy beaches. Hitler called in an expert to explain that the V-1 was not accurate enough to hit anything smaller than London. Other secret marvels were on the way, continued Hitler. The V-2 rocket, a high-speed submarine capable of thirty knots under water and also capable of remaining submerged for days on end. He conceded that the Luftwaffe had failed recently. He blamed its High Command for indecision in experimenting with too many different types of new aircraft instead of settling for one or two and mass producing them. But soon, he said, the position was going to change. The first thousand of the new jet fighters would be ready and they would quickly break the domination of the Allies in the sky. When Rommel asked if a few squadrons of these jets could be put into service in the West immediately the answer was that they were not yet quite ready; there were teething troubles that would have to be put right. But before long there would be "masses of jet fighters" to shatter the air supremacy of the Allies. There would also be four times as many V-bombs and he could visualize "the imminent collapse of Britain under V-bombs and jet-fighter attack."

At one stage of the conference Allied aircraft were heard approaching and the conference had to adjourn to the Führer's air-raid shelter where there was only enough room for six—Hitler and his adjutant, the two Field-Marshals and their Chiefs of Staff. With Jodl and the others out of the way Rommel took the opportunity to confront Hitler with what was in effect the sixty-four-dollar question. Choosing his words without equivocation he bluntly prophesied that the German front in the West would collapse and that nothing could then stop the Allies sweeping on into Germany. He said that the Italian front would "crumble away" and "he doubted whether the Russian front could be held." He said that "Germany was politically isolated, which was a fatal weakness, no matter what propaganda might say." Then he told the Führer that "it was urgently necessary to end the war."

"Don't you worry about the future course of the war," Hitler retorted. "Look to your own invasion front." The fate of the soldier who had once been Hitler's favourite general was probably sealed in those few moments. .

The conference in Margival had lasted from 9 a.m. to 4 p.m. with an adjournment for lunch, a one-course meal at which Hitler bolted a heaped plate of rice and vegetables after it had been previously tasted for him. Pills and liqueur glasses of various medicines were ranged round the place and he sampled them in turn. Two SS men stood behind his chair.[3]

During the day Rommel periodically reminded Hitler that the Supreme Command had not troubled to obtain any first-hand impressions of the front. "These orders are worked out round the table and there's no front-line knowledge behind them. You demand our confidence, but you do not trust us yourself," he said heatedly. Hitler did not like this kind of talk but Rommel's point was taken and before the conference broke up Speidel was instructed to prepare a programme for an early visit of the Führer to La Roche Guyon and selected headquarters at the front where he could talk to commanders of all levels. Something, it seemed, had been achieved during this third crisis day of Normandy—though neither Rommel nor von Rundstedt had any confidence in the vague promises of reinforcements and new equipment that Hitler could so easily dispense. But at least he had been shamed into agreeing to show his face in Normandy to a few of the fifteen and sixteen-year-old boys who were dying for his lost cause, some of whom (God help them) still thought he was marvellous. But even this tiny dubious treat was to be denied the German soldiers. Next day Speidel telephoned his opposite number at Saint-Germain to ask if the von Rundstedt headquarters knew yet on which day and at what time The Führer was expected to arrive from Margival for the proposed grand tour. Speidel was informed that there would be no grand tour. Margival, he learned, unoccupied since its construction in 1940 until the previous day's conference, was once more a vacant property. After the Field-Marshals had left, it seemed, the Margival conference had dispersed on a note of farce.

As Hitler's expert had pointed out at the conference, the V-1 flying bomb was a self-steering mechanism which could not hit a target smaller than London. Sometimes, it was now apparent, it could not even manage that. Shortly after the departure of the disillusioned Field-Marshals to their headquarters, a V-1—heading for the French coast and England on a course that would cause its still unfamiliar sight and sound to strike fear into the hearts of those cockneys above whose heads and homes it would soon be sputtering on its pilotless way—executed an unscheduled U-turn and flew back over, of all places, Margival; where, with an uncanny automative discernment that shamed its piloted kin, the tiny engine cut out—the sign, as Londoners were rapidly learning, that the big bang would come in a matter of seconds. The bunkers of Margival were far to massive to be hurt by the explosion, and no one minded except Hitler.

For the Führer it had been a terrible day. The Normandy front, he had been told, was bound to collapse. His Luftwaffe, he had been told, had ceased to exist. To cap it all his favourite

349

Field-Marshal had looked him in the eye and told him to end the war. And now he had been nearly blown to bits by his own secret weapon. It was too much!

He jumped into his car and fled to Metz where his plane was ready to take him to Berchtesgaden—where he could keep clear of recalcitrant Field-Marshals and flying bombs for a while.

On the Caen front the teenage boys of the 12th SS Panzer Division "Hitler Youth" fanatically resisted the efforts of the British and Canadians to break through them. Blond-haired, pink-faced, hate-filled babies, they endured like men the thousand-bomber attacks, the great shells of three hundred warships, the tide of tanks that were always replaced no matter how many they destroyed. They were almost the last category of German male to whom a glimpse of, or perhaps a handshake from, the Führer would still mean anything and now they were to be denied even this. In their innocence they had been apprenticed to evil and now like an incurable disease were fated to die unthanked and unloved. Their Führer had forsaken them but still they fought till they dropped in the disintegrating European fortress the Führer had built.

The fourth crisis day of Normandy was June 23 when the Russians opened their summer offensive. Contrary to German expectations that they would launch it in the south between the Pripet Marshes and the Black Sea, they attacked in the centre with four armies under Marshals Zhukov and Vassilevsky. In six days they had broken through Field-Marshal Ernst von Busch's Army Group Centre in six places and in ten they had captured Minsk, the capital of Byelorussia, which they celebrated by parading 57,000 German prisoners through the streets of Moscow: partly to disprove German claims that they had executed a planned withdrawal from Byelorussia, partly as a snub to the Western Allies implying that the Normandy landing had not had the slightest influence on the proceedings in Russia.[4] (Stalin's approach to the concept of alliance and teamwork was less altruistic and generous than that of General Eisenhower!) One positive link between the two offensives, however, was that shortly before the Russians attacked, Hitler had authorized the move of the crack 2nd SS Panzer Corps from the East to Normandy. It was in transit at the time it was most urgently needed, and its loss to the Russian front was certainly felt. It was an unhappy time for Hitler which the inevitable sacking of Field-Marshal von Busch, commander of the beaten Army Group

Centre, and his replacement by Field-Marshal Walther Model did little to relieve. The stark and inescapable fact was that the German Army, the arch-exponent of the giant pincer movement was itself now trapped, between East and West, in the pincer to end all pincers. Fortress Europe was not merely crumbling and disintegrating, nothing could now prevent its being systematically razed to the ground in dust and ashes, and bulldozed into final extinction.

On June 26, three days after the opening of the offensive on the Eastern front, General Bradley took "fortress Cherbourg" and this was the fifth crisis point of Normandy. With the Cotentin Peninsula now mopped up, the Americans could concentrate fully on the southward thrust alongside the British to break out of the bridgehead through Saint-Lô and Caen. When Hitler heard about Cherbourg he flew into a rage and ordered von Rundstedt to court-martial General Dollmann the C-in-C of Seventh Army whom he held responsible. This von Rundstedt refused to do stating flatly that he would agree to no more than a straightforward factual inquiry into the loss of the port. The arranging of this inquiry was deputed to Rommel as the Army Group Commander. Meanwhile Hitler ordered a massive counterattack with all available armour to be directed against the American and British sectors of the front in turn. But as "all available armour" was heavily engaged in the intensifying battle of attrition on the Saint Lô–Caen sector, the new counterattack could not be carried out until 2nd SS Panzer Corps completed its journey from the Eastern Front. Meanwhile, Hitler, convinced that Normandy was getting out of hand, ordered all his top commanders in the West to attend a conference at Berchtesgaden on June 29. Rommel and von Rundstedt were given so little notice that they had to drive all night to get there by morning. (Because of the Allies' air supremacy, senior commanders were forbidden to fly.) Then Hitler kept them waiting till evening before he saw them. The entire OKW entourage was present and also the air and naval commanders in the West.

The Field-Marshals wasted no time and minced no words. They told Hitler that the situation was deteriorating rapidly and with the Russians now on the move the only proper course was to end hostilities in the West as soon as possible.[5] As at Margival Hitler made no direct reply but simply repeated the familiar dissertation on the new miracle weapons that would soon be available to give an entirely new look to the war. Jet aircraft, V-weapons and high-speed submarines would bring about "the miraculous turning-point of the war." Relentlessly the Field-Marshals asked the Führer if they might talk to him alone. He refused, curtly indicated that they need not prolong their stay, and did not even ask them to stay to a meal. The Field-Marshals drove back to their respective Command Posts angry, frustrated and convinced that they would be relieved of their commands. On arrival they learned that General Dollmann, C-in-C of Seventh Army, worried by the court of inquiry into the loss of Cherbourg that was hanging over his head, had saved himself and everyone else concerned much trouble by dying of a heart attack that morning.

On July 1, bad weather having for once kept the sky clear of Allied aircraft, 2nd Panzer Corps, using battle groups from four divisions, made a new attempt to break into the British front at Caen. But even without his usual air support Montgomery comfortably held the attack. That night when he telephoned OKW von Rundstedt told Keitel that this latest failure was "the writing on the wall." Chester Wilmot has recorded what followed:

"What shall we do?" cried the despairing Keitel. "What shall we do?"

"Make peace, you fools," said von Rundstedt.[6] "What else can you do?"

Keitel, the faithful sycophant and lackey-in-chief at OKW, promptly reported this conversation to the Führer who promptly sent von Rundstedt a letter informing him that his place as Commander-in-Chief West would be taken over forthwith by Field-Marshal Gunther von Kluge. Enclosed with the letter—delivered by one of Hitler's adjutants—was the customary parting present, the Oak Leaves to the Knight's Cross of the Iron Cross. On July 4 von Rundstedt visited La Roche Guyon to say goodbye to Rommel. There is no need to doubt that he was sincere when he told Rommel that he was "thankful that he would not be in command during the catastrophe that lay ahead." [7] The same day Geyr von Schweppenburg, almost recovered from his slight wound, sustained during the bombing of his headquarters on June 10, was told that he too had been relieved of the command of Panzer Group West. The Panzer Group was to receive not only a new commander (General Heinrich Hans Eberbach) but a new name. Henceforth it would be known as Fifth Panzer Army. He was blamed for the failure of the 2nd SS Panzer Corps' counterattack to crack Montgomery's front. He had unwisely ended his report:

The choice is now between tactical botching combined with a rigid defence, which leaves all the initiative to the enemy, and an elastic strategy that would at least seize the initiative. The Panzer troops believe that an elastic strategy is the better and firmer decision to take.[8]

Berchtesgaden clearly did not share the Panzer troops' enthusiasm for an elastic strategy. For von Schweppenburg there were no Oak Leaves.

So ended the Berchtesgaden conference and its aftermath —the sixth crisis of Normandy.

Field-Marshal von Kluge had commanded Army Group Centre in Russia until a road accident had rescued him from this arduous burden a few months before. He was an artilleryman with a good military record but a certain emotional imbalance, as instanced by the ridiculous episode of challenging General Guderian to a duel the year before. He arrived in the West on July 5 with the usual contemptuous superiority complex of the "Eastern" generals, and glowing with aggressive righteousness after two weeks of brainwashing by Hitler, Keitel, and Jodl at Berchtesgaden, where he had been told that the difficulties in the West were entirely due to bad leadership. He paid his first visit to Rommel at La Roche Guyon in the gauche mood of a sergeant who has been told to grip hold of a bad platoon and show them that he is the boss. He picked a quarrel right away. He said that von Rundstedt's dismissal indicated Hitler's dissatisfaction with the leadership in the West and added that "Rommel, too, does not enjoy the absolute confidence of the Führer." He said that the feeling at Supreme Headquarters was that "Rommel allows himself to be too easily impressed by the allegedly overpowering effect of enemy weapons and is too inclined to pessimism." It was also thought that Rommel was obstinate and self-willed and was not whole-hearted in carrying out the Führer's wishes. He ended with a solemn warning:[9]

"Field-Marshal Rommel, you must obey unconditionally from now on. It is good advice that I am giving you."

A furious argument now developed and the Chiefs of Staff were asked to leave the room so that the Field-Marshals could continue their slanging-match with voices uninhibitedly raised. Rommel angrily rejected the strictures of OKW and demanded that von Kluge withdraw his insulting allegations and confirm in writing that he had withdrawn them. He suggested icily that it might be a good idea if von Kluge reserved his conclusions until he had visited the front and had heard what the fighting commanders and troops had to say. What particularly upset Rommel was that von Kluge made no reference to the more important political problem of how to save Germany—although he happened to know that von Kluge had been sympathetically in touch with the anti-Hitler Plot. And yet in two short weeks the brain-washers of Berchtesgaden appeared to have taken complete possession of his uncertain mind. It was clear that von Kluge was one of the few commanders left on whom Hitler could still work his "spell." It was an unhappy augury.

On the following day the new Commander-in-Chief West set off on a two-day tour of the Seventh Army front visiting all the main headquarters and getting the impressions of senior and junior commanders as well as talking to many non-commissioned officers and men. To give him his due (but also as further evidence of his emotional impressionability) von Kluge came back completely "converted," and apologized profusely to Rommel for criticisms he now saw to be completely unjustified, and which he blamed on the false information he had been given at Berchtesgaden. Then, with the vehemence of the converted, he began to tell Rommel that the trouble with Hitler was that he refused to face the truth despite all reports and interviews; that he "lived in a world of dreams, and when the dreams faded looked around for scapegoats." [10]

The Field-Marshals were reconciled. But von Kluge had learned that there were now factors—like the huge Allied air forces—undreamed of in his Eastern Front philosophy.

Chapter 30

THE BOCAGE AND THE BREAK-OUT: ROMMEL WOUNDED

□ The factor (it cannot too often be reiterated) which more than any other determines the nature and character of a battle is the terrain over which it is fought. The vast and roadless steppes of Russia—a snowbound wasteland in winter, a Sahara-hot prairie turning into a dust bowl in high summer; the razor-backed crests and ridges of the Tunisian hills; the alternating river and mountain barriers up the length of Italy; the blistering sands of Libya and Egypt; these had each in turn set their unique conditioning stamp on a campaign or battle quite different from any other. In Normandy it was what the inhabitants call the *bocage*.

The essence of the *bocage* is the system of hedgerows surrounding the small fields, orchards, and farmsteads of this rich dairy country of peasant small holders. The hedgerows, the distinctive feature of the countryside, are banks three or four feet high, with a ditch on either side, and stiff thorny bushes sprouting from them. The roots of the bushes bind the banks into solid barriers and around the orchards there are generally walls. This close country is broken and hilly and in summer thickly clad in trees and bushes. Between the small fields are many sunken lanes and cattle tracks, so closely hidden by the hedgerows arching above them, that to stand at one end and peer up one of these lanes gives the impression that one is looking into a green tunnel.

It scarcely needs to be pointed out that if this *bocage*, luscious to look at and delightful for those who like quiet country walks, happens to lie in the way of a mechanized war, it will lend its favours to the defender rather than the attacker. The close network of ditches, banks, walls, hedgerows, and sunken lanes might have been custom-built to conceal anti-tank guns, defending tanks, machine guns, mortars, and grenadiers until an attacker is within point-blank range. Conversely it is appalling country for tanks and mobile guns trying to advance: for it is intersected by few metalled roads, it is frequently broken by steep valleys and thickly wooded hills, the fields are seldom more than between a hundred and two hundred yards long, and most of the hedgerows as well as the frequent walls are effective obstacles. Finally the luxuriant verdant tangle of the *bocage* is perfectly suited to the deadly craft of the sniper. American and British tank commanders soon round this out when they risked the customary *bravura* of riding into action with their turrets open.

After the failure of his first aim—to crush the invasion on the beaches—Field-Marshal Rommel, privately convinced that the war was now lost, had only one course open to him: to fight a delaying action in the *bocage* belt, which extends for some twenty miles inland from the coast. By making a hard fight of it in this highly defensible terrain, he hoped to gain time in which Hitler might be persuaded by the realities of the situation to see reason, and personal contact might somehow be established between himself and the Allied

Command. He was not unaware of the respect he commanded on the Allied side and the compliments that had been paid at various times to his generalship throughout the world by, among others, Winston Churchill himself. As a fundamentally simple, honest, and direct soldier Rommel's instinct told him that he could talk business with his fellow soldiers Eisenhower and Montgomery if only Hitler and his cronies could be kept out of it. Through the secret link between La Roche Guyon and the anti-Hitler plotters he kept in touch with developments but was still adamant that assassination was not the proper way: Hitler must be arrested. So he addressed himself with his customary zeal to the battle of the *bocage* with a dichotomy of feeling that is perhaps the hardest of all for a general to bear: tautologically trying his best to win a battle he wanted, for deeper reasons, to lose. So there developed in the unyielding Normandy *bocage*, as close and secretive as the Normandy peasant whom it had bred, that hard attritional second phase of any critical battle between first-class opponents which American soldiers call a "slugging match," British troops a "dog-fight": the stage when nobody seems to be winning, casualties mount up, and an interminable stalemate seems to have been reached. It is the supreme testing time for commanders for it is then that press and public and even the troops themselves become querulous and critics begin to ask why progress is so slow. In the Second World War it became a facile habit of war correspondents and armchair critics to measure success in terms of mileages gained and place names captured. An added complication in Normandy was that this vast Allied enterprise was being closely attended by an Allied corps of reporters almost as numerous as the soldiers. Unfortunately, war does not work out primarily to fit in with newspaper deadlines and success stories. With all the goodwill in the world, generals cannot disclose to newspaperman in advance the fullest details of their plans. And although the great majority of the war correspondents performed their difficult task with tact, forebearance, and responsibility, there was a minority not above stirring up trouble by partisan attacks on particular generals and mischievous innuendo that one Allied army was being expended more ruthlessly than another. The battle of the *bocage* reached this fretful, will-it-never-end stage a month after the invasion when the British were still trying to complete the capture of Caen on the Allied left and the Americans were still making costly attacks to take Saint-Lô, the other key intersection point of main roads thirty-five miles to the west.

With the capture of the greater part of Caen on July 10, General Montgomery prepared to launch the offensive on the Saint-Lô–Caen front that was to blast the Allied armies out of the green maze of the *bocage* into the open tanking country to Paris and beyond.

For this crucial break-out offensive, Montgomery was still in command of the whole Allied front, both his own 21st Army Group as well as General Hodges' First Army which would later be joined by General Patton's Third Army to form the U.S. 12th Army Group under General Bradley—whereupon General Eisenhower would move Supreme Headquarters from England to France and take personal charge of all Anglo-American forces. By mid-July Patton and his Third Army had moved secretly over to France and were lying low in the orchards and woods of the Cotentin in readiness for the climax of the Anglo-American offensive that Montgomery was now preparing.

Montgomery's Caen offensive was criticized at the time and has been criticized since, mainly because its intention and purpose were misunderstood—even by some of his colleagues at Supreme Headquarters who should have known better. This misunderstanding was admittedly aggravated by the idiosyncratic Montgomery's mistake, on this occasion as on others, of making a premature and overconfident progress report. From the beginning Montgomery's strategy was clear and consistent and as explained by him to all concerned in April in London. It was to attract and engage as much of the German armoured reserve as possible on the British-Canadian left of the Allied front, so that General Bradley's Americans could break out more easily on the right, where the German defences had been systematically reduced by the British action. To give effect to this strategy meant that the British and Canadians had to make repeated attacks in the Caen area (first to take the town and then to advance beyond it) fighting thankless battles of attrition so as to draw to their front the German panzers that would otherwise have been opposing the Americans in the Saint-Lô sector. To the uninstructed among the press, the public, and even at Supreme Headquarters, these repeated and seemingly unsuccessful attacks to wear out German strength and draw in more reserves, began to look like failure. Why was the advance so slow? What had gone wrong?

The break-out offensive which Montgomery planned to open on July 18 was to bring his strategic design to a climax. He would strike first with the British on the left and in sufficient strength to make the Germans think that this was the main effort so that they would throw in every last reserve against it. Then, on the following day, General Bradley would launch the U.S. First Army on the less heavily defended right in what was really going to be the main effort. The only difficulty was that the Americans could not take Saint-Lô until July 18 so that it was not possible for Bradley to attack on the right the day after Montgomery attacked on the left. Then heavy rain delayed Bradley further. So, in the event, the American offensive did not open until a week after the British. The delay was unfortunate but entirely due to the weather, and its curtailment of air activity. How successfully Montgomery's strategic plan had worked out is shown by the relative German strength opposite the British and American fronts by the time the Americans were ready for their break-out. Engaging the British front were seven panzer divisions and four heavy (Tiger) tank battalions. On the American front there were but two panzer divisions, one panzer grenadier division (with assault guns but no tanks).[1] This line-up speaks for itself.

Correctly appreciating from the signs that a major offensive was being prepared on the British front at Caen, and wrongly supposing (as he was meant to suppose) that this was *the* big push to burst out of the bridgehead and drive towards Paris, Rommel fell into Montgomery's trap by continually reinforcing the Caen front with still more armour in depth to hold the expected onslaught. On July 17 he made his daily visit to the front to check that all was in readiness and visiting all the key command posts. At 1600 hours he left the headquarters of 1st SS Panzer Corps to return to La Roche Guyon. In the car, in addition to Daniel, his driver from Africa days, were Captain Lang and Sergeant Holke. Daniel drove fast along the main road south from Lisieux. This route runs through the heart of the Pays d'Auge which produces some of the most famous cheeses in the world. Camembert and Pont-l'Eveque are two of its villages. But the four occupants of the staff car are unlikely to have been thinking of cheese, they were keeping a wary eye on the sky. Wrecks along the sides of all roads, some still burning, testified to the relentless vigilance of the Allied fighters and fighter-bombers which ceaselessly patrolled the sky, to make the shortest routine road journey in daylight an act of considerable daring. Between Livarot and Vimoutiers, Sergeant Holke, who was acting as air "spotter," suddenly shouted a warning that aircraft were approaching. Daniel was told to make as fast as possible for a side turning three

358

hundred yards ahead. Before he could reach it the fighter dived to a few feet above the road, its cannon and machine guns blazing. A cannon shell tore into the side of the speeding staff car, shattering the left shoulder and arm of the driver; Rommel was hit in the temple and cheekbone and knocked unconscious by a triple fracture of the skull. The speeding car, out of control, crashed into a tree, bounced off, then overturned in a ditch. Daniel, the driver, was virtually dead (he died in the night); Rommel sprawled unconscious in the middle of the road. The captain and the sergeant, badly shaken but uninjured, carried the unconscious Field-Marshal to a nearby farm where they could leave him while they went to look for an Army unit that could organize an ambulance.

By a strange chance almost too macabre in its improbability the Normandy farm, where the unconscious Rommel lay until the ambulance arrived, was named Saint-Foy-de-Montgommery.

In the early morning of July 18 surgeons at the Luftwaffe hospital at Bernay, twenty-five miles from the scene of the crash, continued their night-long battle to save the life of Field-Marshal Rommel. They had diagnosed his injuries as a fracture at the base of the skull, two fractures of the temple, a shattered cheekbone, a wound in the left eye, severe face cuts from flying glass and concussion.[2] While they persevered with a task that they feared was hopeless, two thousand Allied bombers saturated an area five miles deep south of Caen, dropping eight thousand tons of bombs in two hours on a front where the Germans had concentrated seven panzer divisions and four Tiger tank battalions. When the bombardment ceased the British Second Army, led by the seven hundred tanks of three armoured divisions, rolled forward through the cratered desolation to seize the Bourquebus ridge five miles south of the city and overlooking a plain where Supreme Headquarters wished to establish airfields. This was the start of Montgomery's gigantic feint designed to retain and bleed on this front the German panzer strength in order to give a clearer run to Bradley's forthcoming break-out forty miles to the west. The British divisions had orders to break through to their objective regardless of losses and during the day one division lost more than a hundred tanks. But the Field-Marshal, now fighting for his life in the Luftwaffe hospital at Bernay, had done his work well. Anticipating this attack, and assuming that it was to be the Allies' supreme effort to achieve a break-out from the confinement of the bridgehead into the open country to the south, Rommel had concentrated almost his entire panzer strength here and had disposed it in such depth that the British tanks found that, despite the bombardment and the barrage that followed, they were soon encountering successive screens of heavy tanks and antitank guns, so that no sooner was one penetrated or eliminated than another was waiting for them. By the third day July 20 they were fighting hard for the Bourquebus ridge by which time they had discovered the extreme depth in which Rommel had sited his successive antitank barriers. Then to the rescue of the Germans came a deluge of rain—still the most effective *deus ex machina* to a hard-pressed army—and in a few hours the stricken moonscape of the Caen battlefield was emulating the glutinous impassability of the legendary mud of Ypres and Passchendaele in the First World War. The same rain which finally halted Montgomery's push at Caen forced Bradley to postpone his effort at Saint-Lô; as, apart from its effect on the ground, the weather deterioration had temporarily rendered adequate air support impossible. The American soldiers were to remember as the most miserable of the Normandy campaign the five days they spent in waterlogged foxholes waiting to attack, while the soaking rain drenched them through the *bocage*.

It was now that Montgomery came under heavy criticism from the uninformed—who could not know the whole picture nor the state of the ground—as well as from those who should have known better: for example, General Eisenhower's British Deputy Supreme Commander, Air Marshal Sir Arthur W. Tedder. Tedder complained strongly to Eisenhower about Montgomery's pulling out his tanks when the mud made further advance impossible. The Air Marshal's impatience recalls that of another air commander in not dissimilar circumstances, the German Air General Wolfram von Richthofen at Stalingrad when he complained that Paulus's Sixth Army had failed to exploit the openings blasted for them by the Luftwaffe. It was perhaps inevitable that airmen, whose battles were fought at four hundred miles an hour, found it difficult at times to adjust to the pace of infantry and tanks fighting in mud. Something else that the airmen—exulting in their bombing power were apt to forget—was that the truly surprising thing about massive concentrated bombardment in 1944 was not how much it annihilated but how much it left standing. Despite the eight thousand tons of bombs dropped in advance of Montgomery's attack, there were still large numbers of heavy tanks and well-sited antitank guns still there at the end of it; and enough shaken, but brave and determined, survivors to use them. Part of the trouble was an overconfident statement by Montgomery early in the battle which overeager headline writers transmuted into an impression that a complete breakthrough was imminent, when it had not even been intended. The plan was still the same: Montgomery on the Allied left to make the running and draw the fire, Bradley to make the breakthrough on the right—when the weather of this record terrible Normandy summer permitted.[3]

But on the German side on July 20 even the heaven-sent rains of northern Normandy were dwarfed by an event many hundreds of miles away at Rastenburg, the Wolf's Lair, in East Prussia to which OKW had recently returned from Berchtesgaden. At this supreme moment of the battle of Normandy, the first stage of the final battle for Europe, Hitler's Fortress Europe nearly blew up from within.

Chapter 31

JULY 20: THE PLOT THAT FAILED

☐ The wounding of Rommel on June 17, the eve of the great Allied offensive, was a deeply felt personal loss to the German armies in Normandy to whom he was so much more than a figurehead. To those on the eve of another battle, the anti-Hitler plotters, it was a grievous blow of a different kind. Though Rommel had refused to go all the way with them and agree to an assassination he had offered his great authority, prestige, and popularity in every way short of that extreme. He was the centrepiece of their endeavours, its firm base, almost its badge of respectability: the indispensable strong man for the situation that would follow the coup if successful. Its chief military organizers in Berlin, General Olbricht, head of the General Army Office, and his Chief of Staff Colonel von Stauffenberg, were as determined as ever to go through with their long prepared plan even though there were doubters who were thinking that they had left it too late, that the time had passed. So on the morning of July 20—with Montgomery's wing of the Allied offensive bogging down in the mud of Caen, and Bradley's drenched and miserable in the mud of Saint-Lô waiting to get started—the scene of this narrative switches briefly to Berlin, where it was a pleasant sunny morning, and to Rastenburg in East Prussia where the day was warming fast and would become stiflingly hot by noon.

At six that morning a staff car called at the house of Colonel Count Claus Schenk von Stauffenberg in the Berlin suburb of Wannsee. In his new official capacity, since July 1, of Chief of Staff to General Fritz Fromm commanding the Home Army he had to attend the midday conference at OKW and report to Hitler on the progress made with the formation of a new reserve to be called the People's Grenadiers. On the way to the airfield at Rangsdorf, forty-five minutes away, he picked up his adjutant and friend, Lieutenant Werner von Haeften, a good-looking man of thirty-five, two years younger than himself. At seven they took off in a military plane provided by General Wagner, the Quartermaster General of the Army, who was a leading member of the conspiracy. The flight to Rastenburg would take about three hours. At the side of von Stauffenberg was a thick black briefcase bulging not only with the papers from which he would make his report to Hitler on the Home Army, but with something else: wrapped in a shirt was a kilogram of plastic explosive.

The thirty-seven-year-old colonel, with the empty right sleeve and the black patch where his left eye should have been, was on his way to carry out what he had increasingly come to regard as a divine mission: to perform an act that would cause rejoicing throughout the world not least to many people in Germany itself. He was on his way to kill Hitler.

Stauffenberg had been singlemindedly convinced that he must perform this deed ever since the day in 1943 when, convalescing from the wounds he had sustained in the North Africa fighting, he had remarked to his wife:

"You know I feel I must do something now, to save Germany. We General Staff Officers must all accept our share of the responsibility." [1]

Like many of those who by this time filled key places in the conspiracy von Stauffenberg was a religious man, a devout Catholic; and devout Catholics do not lightly undertake to commit murder. Nor (according to those who knew him and have made a study of his life and motives) was he the type to look for a martyr's crown. He was, as we have seen, a debonair patrician with a cavalryman's gay flair for soldiering laced with a born staff officer's intellectual clarity. He was a true patriot who had given a great deal for his country and felt more than most the cancer on its honour represented by Hitler and Nazism. Fully aware of the risks involved to himself, his wife, and their four children—the consequences of failure did not bear thinking about—he nevertheless saw it as his duty to place on record for posterity a clear statement that there had been a large number of Germans who rejected Hitler and all he stood for long before he was defeated, and had been prevented from saying so before only by the devilish efficiency of the police state the Führer had created.

It must be said that the Allied leadership had never given either help or encouragement to this anti-Nazi element. Only a week before, Allen Dulles, chief of the American Secret Service, who was in contact with the conspiracy, informed Washington that an attempt on Hitler's life was imminent. The warning was received with the same cool indifference that the British Foreign Office had shown to previous hints and feelers put out through neutral embassies. It was as though the puritanism in the Anglo-American character had now fully taken charge with Unconditional Surrender as its monotonously reiterated battle cry. Puritanism is always punitive and there seems little doubt that the Allied attitude had an unhealthy punitive motivation. The fear of a new "stab in the back" legend (the legend after the First World War that the German Army had never been beaten in the field; but had been let down by the leadership at home) dominated all other considerations and the notion that "this time Germany must be taught a lesson" was rooted and inflexible. And because time was running out, von Stauffenberg was more than ever convinced that the long-planned gesture must somehow be made.

The plot of July 20 fell into two distinct phases. First the killing at Rastenburg followed by the escape and flight back to Berlin of von Stauffenberg. Secondly, the take-over of Berlin, Vienna, Munich, Cologne, and other key centres by the Home Army of which von Stauffenberg had become Chief of Staff on July 1, but whose Commander, General Fromm, was not in the conspiracy. The second part of the operation, the take-over, was codenamed Valkyrie and its planning through the months had been ingenious. It had been represented to Hitler that the millions of foreign workers in Germany constituted a potential menace and that an operation to take over key centres should be prepared in case of an organized insurrection of the foreign workers. Hitler had readily agreed and Valkyrie had been possible to plan in detail with the Home Army, the Berlin police, and the forces of the Military Governors of France and Belgium. As soon as Hitler was confirmed dead, Valkyrie would be launched and the German Command in the West, von Kluge, would ask the Western Allies for an armistice, while all German mobile units would rush east to bolster the armies withdrawing from the Russians.

The weakness in the plan was that von Stauffenberg would have to play the leading role in both phases of it. As Chief of Staff Home Army he was (a) the only man certain to have opportunities to visit Hitler on business and was still therefore the ideal killer: and (b) the only man who could activate Valkyrie by issuing orders to the Home Army in Berlin in the name of its commander, the doubtful Fromm, before the latter knew exactly what was happening. But a three-hour plane journey separated Rastenburg from Berlin. It was awkward to say the least and an appalling double strain for von Stauffenberg to bear. But he insisted that he could do it.

The plastic bomb with which he proposed to blow up the Wolfs Lair was of British manufacture, a malleable putty-like substance that the British had distributed to Resistance forces in France and Poland for sabotage. It was detonated by a simple smokeless noiseless detonator which was activated by pinching the neck to break an acid-containing phial which then eroded the wire holding back the firing pin so as to give an explosion within ten minutes. An engineer officer had confirmed that one kilogram of the plastic would be sufficient for the present purpose. As he had no right arm and but the thumb and two fingers of his left hand, von Stauffenberg carried in his pocket a tiny pair of pliers with which to pinch the detonator when the time came.

Carrying his lethal hand baggage between Berlin and Supreme Headquarters was something that von Stauffenberg was becoming used to. It was fortunate that his nerves were strong and his brain cool. This was the third time in ten days that he and his loaded briefcase had journeyed by air and this time he hoped it would not be necessary to bring the thing back again. On July 11, before OKW left Berchtesgaden, there had been a chance for what von Stauffenberg had in mind, when he was summoned to the presence. At that time the plotters were too ambitiously aiming at three birds with one stone. The bomb was not to be exploded unless Himmler and Goering were also present. At Berchtesgaden von Stauffenberg found that Himmler was absent. He telephoned General Olbricht in Berlin for instructions. Olbricht told him to cancel the operation and return to Berlin with the bomb.

Four days later, on July 15, von Stauffenberg had to attend a meeting with Hitler at Rastenburg (to which OKW had just returned). His new chief, Fromm, Commander of the Home Army was also to be present. At 1:30 he slipped out to telephone Olbricht and confirm that this time everything seemed to be in order. Olbricht told him to go ahead and then himself set in motion the follow-up operation, Valkyrie. But by the time he had returned to the conference Hitler had left. Von Stauffenberg had to telephone Olbricht again telling him to cancel Valkyrie, the take-over operation, and as it was too late to do this, Olbricht had to get out of his difficulty by pretending that the whole thing had been an internal security exercise. Once again von Stauffenberg had to make the three-hour flight back to Berlin with the ill-fated briefcase.

By July 20 the conspirators had agreed to be satisfied with the death of Hitler alone, regardless of whether Himmler and Goering were also on hand. There was accordingly just a touch of desperation about the venture now. The star performer still managed to present his customary air of casual charm and cool professionalism but there was a growing sense of fatality among the others involved. This, they all seemed to be feeling, was the last chance. This time the bomb was travelling with a one-way ticket.

The aircraft touched down shortly after ten. A staff car was waiting to take von Stauffenberg and his adjutant and two other staff officers who had also been on the plane, the ten miles to the Wolf's Lair. Before leaving the airstrip von Stauffenberg's adjutant, Lieutenant von Haeften, told the pilot that from twelve o'clock he must be ready for an immediate take-off. The ten-mile journey took half an hour because of the close scrutiny of the staff car and its occupants at each of three check points. The first was the entrance to the main compound a circle of pillboxes, minefields, and barbed-wire fencing. It was two miles from this first ring to the second compound, the perimeter of which was also heavily mined and in addition was thickly surrounded by electrified barbed wire. At the entrance to both these compounds all cars were carefully checked and guards telephoned the other check points to tell them who was arriving or leaving. Half a mile beyond the second check point was the third known as the Officers' Guardpost. This was the entrance to the compound where the various offices were located and most of the work of OKW was done. Two hundred yards farther on was the smaller Compound One, the holy of holies, surrounded by a thick tangle of high barbed-wire fencing and patrolled day and night by relays of SS guards. There were three buildings in this compound, the Operations Hut, Hitler's heavily concreted personal bunker, and near it the kennel of his Alsatian bitch Blondi. The daily situation conferences were usually held in the Operations Hut unless enemy bombers were known to be active when they were held instead in a reinforced operations bunker just outside Compound One.

At the Officers' Guard check point von Stauffenberg and his adjutant reported to the camp commandant and then went into the mess for breakfast. From there von Stauffenberg went alone to the office of General Fellgiebel, Chief Signals Officer of the German Army. Fellgiebel was in the conspiracy and as Signals chief had an important part to play. As soon as Hitler was dead, it was Fellgiebel's job to give such orders as would ensure that Rastenburg's communications with the rest of the world were cut for at least an hour and if possible two to give the conspirators in Berlin time to carry out Valkyrie, set up the new government and transmit the necessary orders to other German cities and to Paris, Vienna, Prague, Brussels, and Oslo. After finalizing arrangements with Fellgiebel, von Stauffenberg went on to the office of General Buhle. Buhle was the OKH senior permanent representative at OKW and as such was concerned with the official business that had brought von Stauffenberg to Rastenburg that day, namely, the formation of the new "People's Grenadier" division of the Reserve Army. It was to report on this latest pet fad of Hitler's that von Stauffenberg had been summoned to the Wolf's Lair at all that day. After the tensions and false alarms of the previous ten days and the extreme suspense of that morning since leaving his home at six, von Stauffenberg must have worked hard to put any heart into this long tedious staff discussion of routine administrative matters that, anyway, would not matter in a couple of hours' time. Shortly after twelve, von Stauffenberg and Buhle walked over to the office of Field-Marshal Keitel—officially the Chief of Staff at OKW, unofficially lackey-in-chief and senior commissioned sycophant to the Führer. It was part of Keitel's job to act as Court Chamberlain, chivvying the more junior visitors conciliating the more senior, in a constant fret that everyone was going to arrive late and displease the Führer by talking for too long, and generally flapping around (to borrow a favourite expression of Field Marshal Montgomery's) "like a wet hen." Stauffenberg told Keitel the drift of what he was going to report to Hitler, and Keitel told him to keep it short.

Shortly before 12:30 the four men—Keitel, and his adjutant, von Stauffenberg and Buhle—left Keitel's office to walk over to the Operations Hut in Compound One. On the way out von Stauffenberg excused himself, saying that he wished to pick up his cap and belt in the anteroom but in reality to activate the detonator of the bomb inside his briefcase by nipping it with the small pliers he had brought. But von Stauffenberg had only three fingers of his left hand with which to do this and he did not reappear immediately. Keitel, as ever terrified that they would be late, shouted to him to hurry up. He emerged at that moment and they all started walking to the Operations Hut. It took them three minutes to get there which meant that the bomb would be detonated in exactly seven minutes.

The Operations Hut was a typical large wooden Army building of standard design except that it had been reinforced by an inner lining of concrete two inches thick. It consisted of an entrance hall with lavatories on one side and a telephone exchange in charge of a Sergeant Major of Signals on the other. Entry to the conference room was through double doors on the far side of the entrance hall. The conference room, a rectangle extending to the far end of the hut, was 30 feet by 15 and almost bare except for a single heavy table 18 feet long, 5 wide. Ten windows on the three outside walls flooded the room with light and Hitler's place was in the centre of the long side of the table nearest the entrance door so that he faced the three window walls and sat with his back to the door. The long table rested not on legs but on thick wooden supports that extended across its full width.

On the way through the entrance hall von Stauffenberg told the Signals Sergeant Major that he was expecting an important call from Berlin and that if it came through he was to be informed at once as it related to the report he had to make to the Führer. The four men, led by Keitel, then tiptoed through the double door into the conference hall. As Keitel had feared they were late. The conference had started. The Deputy Chief-of-Staff of OKH was reading out the daily situation report from the Eastern Front. Hitler, sitting with his back to the door, looked round as they entered and saluted. Keitel explained von Stauffenberg's presence and the subject on which he would be reporting, then took up his usual place on Hitler's left. There were some twenty officers standing round the table. Bending quickly von Stauffenberg thrust the briefcase under the table leaning it against the wooden table support nearest to Hitler. The time was 12:37. The officer from Army High Command went on drily reading his report from the Eastern Front. Von Stauffenberg slipped out of the room, left the hut and joined General of Signals Fellgiebel in his office to smoke a necessary cigarette and keep an eye on the Operations Hut. The staff car was nearby with his adjutant, von Haeften, inside it.

Meanwhile, Keitel, noticing his absence and fearing he might not be ready to speak as soon as the OKH man had finished, went outside to look for him thinking he might be receiving that telephone call he had mentioned to the Signals exchange on the way in. But the Sergeant Major said that the one-armed colonel with the black eyepatch had left the building. Keitel returned distractedly to the conference hall wondering what on earth he could say to Hitler if the colonel had not returned by the time he had to make his report. He need not have worried. As he stepped inside the hall to resume his place the hut blew up in his face. . . .

What von Stauffenberg and Fellgiebel saw and heard from outside the latter's office at 12:42 was a tremendous explosion. Windows were shattered and blown out, dust and debris flew, the roof partly caved in and men could be heard screaming. This time the plot appeared to have succeeded. Fellgiebel now had two tasks. The first was to let the plotters in Berlin know that the bomb had been successfully exploded; the second was to take steps to keep the Wolf's Lair cut off from inward or outward communication for the next hour or two.

Von Stauffenberg joined von Haeften in the staff car and they drove off for the airstrip at high speed. He still had to make his way out through the three check points before a general alarm was raised. His successful negotiation of this triple hazard by a mixture of bluff, bravado, quicksilver opportunist thinking and his inbred sense of authority was in many ways the most brilliant part of his daring coup. The speeding car reached the airstrip less than thirty minutes after the explosion and before anyone had thought of getting word to the airstrip guard. The pilot was ready as he had been warned to be and within a few minutes the two officers were flying over the Prussian plain headed for Berlin—a journey that would seem the longest three hours either of them had ever passed. But at least they could now smoke and think and give their nerves a rest after the tense ordeal of the morning.

From what he had seen and heard of the explosion from near at hand, it seemed to von Stauffenberg (who, after all, had had plenty of experience of the more violent manifestations of war) that everyone who had been in the conference hall must now be dead or very gravely, if not mortally, wounded. But there was one factor of which he had not appreciated the significance that morning and two other things which he did not and could not know. The factor that had not been allowed for was the extreme sultry heat of the day which made it necessary to open all ten windows of the conference hall to their fullest extent. As a result the effect of an explosive charge relying wholly on blast and not on the fragmentation of a bombcase was bound to be reduced. But even more important were the two things that von Stauffenberg was not in a position to know. The first was that shortly after he had slipped out of the conference hall one of the officers present, moving close to the table, caught his foot against the briefcase. Reaching down he picked it up and moved it out of the way to the other side of the table support against which its owner had rested it—so that now the heavy support was between Hitler and the bomb. The second was that immediately before the explosion occurred Hitler had risen from his chair to peer through his magnifying glass at one of the more distant maps arrayed on the table before him. At the moment of detonation, therefore, he happened to be half-sprawled across the table in the posture of a billiard-player cueing a shot from an inaccessible position across the table. He had both the thick oak table support and the heavy table-top itself between the blast and the greater part of his person. Calamitously, therefore, the bomb, which killed four of those present and injured most of the others, did not kill Hitler. He was blown, appropriately, into Keitel's arms. His right arm was paralyzed, his eardrums were damaged and his right ear was to remain permanently deaf, his hair and both legs were burned and the blast took off half his trousers. For lackey-in-chief Keitel there was a brief opportunity to implant in actuality that ritual kiss on the Führer's rear which, metaphorically, is generally held to be the sycophant's ultimate obeisance. But he merely put a helping arm round his Führer's shoulder and helped him tenderly out of the shattered building. Trauma took its time and Hitler remained calm for some time joining in the speculation whether the bomb had been delivered by a single Allied plane or had been planted by civilian workers employed in the camp. At four he met the train bringing his old crony Mussolini, who was paying a social call, and showed his visitor over the wrecked building. It was not until they were having tea together that the reaction set in. Then came the outburst; the screaming frenzy, the howl of hate and the sobbing hysterical threat of such a vengeance as had never been.[2]

The complicated details of how and why the Berlin end of the plot went hopelessly wrong need not concern this narrative. The point that matters is that the plot had failed when the bomb failed to kill Hitler. Had the leaders in Berlin acted with the same speed and cool nerve of von Stauffenberg the military coup in Berlin and the other main centres might still have succeeded in its object. The fatal obstacle to its energetic launching was the fact that von Stauffenberg, who had emerged as the enterprise's most determined driving force, was unfortunately immobilized in an aircraft during the vital three hours after the bomb exploded. Fellgiebel did his work well, blocking Rastenburg's communications for two-and-a-half hours. But instead of setting Valkyrie in motion immediately, the men in Berlin waited for confirmation that Hitler really was dead. Time was lost in feverish telephoning of key men not immediately on the spot. The false alarm of five days before, when Valkyrie had had to be cancelled when it was already in operation, seemed to cast a blight of caution and wariness over its initiation on July 20. Men who might have accepted a *fait accompli* if quickly and firmly effected had time to hesitate to see which way the cat jumped. Fromm, for instance, Commander of the Home Army, would not allow his deputy Olbricht, one of the leading plotters, to authorize Valkyrie until he had succeeded in contacting Keitel (despite the OKW Signals block) who assured him that Hitler had survived the bomb. By four von Stauffenberg was back assuring everyone that he had seen the bomb explode, and desperately trying to galvanize everyone into action.

The most important military unit in Berlin was the Guard Battalion of the crack *Grossdeutschland* Division and during the afternoon its twenty-seven-year-old commander, Major Remer, was sent to arrest the Minister of Propaganda Dr. Goebbels. Goebbels had no difficulty in outwitting the young officer. He put a call through to Rastenburg and produced Hitler on the telephone so that the Major could satisfy himself that the Führer was very much alive. On the telephone Hitler now promoted Major Remer to Colonel and ordered him to crush the rebellion in Berlin and to take orders only from Himmler, Goebbels, or General Reineke, a Nazi officer who happened to be in the city. It is one of the mysteries of the *putsch* why a move as important as the arrest of Goebbels was entrusted to a junior officer not even in the conspiracy and unknown to its leaders. This was no occasion for sending a boy to do a man's work.

Another key figure whose potentially powerful participation was petrified by fatal indecision was the Commander-in-Chief West, Field-Marshal von Kluge who, without Rommel's fortifying presence, declined to approach the Allied Command to seek an armistice until Hitler's demise was beyond doubt.

By early evening Hitler had telephoned instructions to Goebbels to broadcast a communiqué on his miraculous escape and Himmler, the new Commander of the Home Army, was on his way to Berlin to take over a task after his own sadistic heart. The conspiracy now went to pieces and it was a company of the newly promoted Colonel Remer's Guard Battalion that provided the firing squad which executed von Stauffenberg, his adjutant von Haeften, and two others in the glare of car headlights, after the ambivalent General Fromm had finally opted for Hitler and pronounced a summary death sentence. One of the two original architects of the plot, General Beck, was told to shoot himself; had two unsuccessful attempts to do so before being finished off by a non-commissioned officer who was told to "help the old man." The end of these officers was quick and clean compared with what was to happen later.

Some progress had been made with Valkyrie but in the end too many of the key figures became petrified with indecision as it became increasingly clear that Saint George had palpably failed to kill the dragon. By the end of the day the retributive forces of the most efficient police state in history were ready to go into action under Heinrich Himmler and take Hitler's revenge for him.

What followed was appalling even by Nazi standards. Not only was Nazi justice done and seen to be done but done bestially as a mob entertainment and with maximum regard for *schadenfreude*. It is estimated that some five thousand, some of them not even implicated in the plot, were extensively tortured before undergoing a grisly mock trial before the People's Court and then being executed. Another twenty thousand at least went to concentration camps from which they did not return. The tone of the People's Court proceedings may be gathered from the experience of the elderly Field-

Marshal Erwin von Witzleben who was deprived of his false teeth, belt, and braces so that he had to stand throughout his trial holding up his trousers. When the time came to execute the chief leaders of the conspiracy the method chosen was to hang them from butchers' hooks with piano wire so that they took a long time to die. The hangings, with drunken guards jeering and yelling insults, were filmed by the government film unit and prints were flown to Rastenburg for the entertainment of Hitler and his entourage.

The unsuccessful plot was the last of the many battles of the Second World War which invite the verdict "too little and too late."

Among the eventual victims were Field-Marshals von Kluge and Rommel who preferred suicide to a trial before the People's Court in Berlin. Rommel's private comment to his family and friends was brief and soldierly:

> "Stauffenberg had bungled it and a front-line soldier would have finished Hitler off."

To his son Manfred he remarked later:

> "The attempt on Hitler was stupid. What we had to fear with this man was not his deeds, but the aura which surrounded him in the eyes of the German people. The revolt should not have started in Berlin but in the West."

It was some time before Himmler's men caught up with the other principal architect of the conspiracy, the former Mayor of Leipzig, Dr. Goerdeler. He went into hiding where he remained until a woman betrayed him for the reward placed on his head. As he lay in prison awaiting his hideous execution, Dr. Karl Goerdeler wrote a simple moving sentence which is sure of its place in the pages of German history:

> "I beg the world to accept our martyr's fate as penance for the German people."

So ended the third expiation of the German nation for accepting Hitler. The first was that of the people in the blazing cities of the Third Reich, the second was that of the soldiers in the field from Stalingrad to the pitiless air castigation of Normandy. The third was July 20, when the nearest approximation to a liberal opposition to Hitler paid the penalty of failure.

For Hitler the plot had cleared the air. It gave him an excuse to break the power of the generals he despised and distrusted and to transfer it to Himmler's SS policemen. He emerged more autocratically powerful than ever, secure now on the pinnacle of his neuroses that had reached the far side of insanity. Nothing now could restrain the psychopathic Samson from tearing down the temple about his countrymen's ears. Nothing, paradoxically, could save the German people any more except the crushing advance from east and west and south of their military opponents. Ironically, the razing of the German citadel of Fortress Europe was to be the greatest liberation of them all.

Chapter 32

END OF A FORTRESS: VICTORY STAMPEDE OF THE AMERICAN TANKS

☐ Two days after July 20 throughout which, to the annoyance of his more activist brother officers, he had remained poker-faced, von Kluge forwarded to Supreme Headquarters Rommel's last report written just before he was wounded. It repeated in stronger terms the realistic view of the situation he had put forward without success at Margival and at Berchtesgaden. It said in effect that nothing could prevent an Allied breakthrough in the very near future and demanded that the Führer "draw the appropriate conclusion." [1] Since the invasion, Army Group B had lost 3000 officers and 110,000 other ranks: but had received only 10,000 replacements. [2] Allied casualties had been slightly higher (as the attackers' usually are) but they had been fully replaced. There were now one million Allied soldiers on French soil.

Field-Marshal von Kluge could have sat on the Rommel report, which read more like an ultimatum. To his credit he sent it on with a covering letter endorsing what it said. Nothing could stop the German front cracking in the near future. Only the exceptional July rains had given it a brief respite. The "appropriate conclusion" was obvious and von Kluge asked for freedom of action to make such tactical withdrawals as might be necessary to save the Seventh, Fifteenth, and Fifth Panzer Armies from destruction.

From the deep security of the eighteen feet of concrete protecting his distant bunker at Rastenburg, the Führer of the Third Reich—his split right eardrum still hurting, but his leg twitch strangely cured since the bomb—condemned yet another German military host to death. There would be no freedom of action. There would be no withdrawal. Not a yard of ground must be given up. Even the spirit of Thermopylae would be mocked into final absurdity. The OKW directive wrote itself. And the days of von Kluge and Rommel were definitely numbered, always supposing that Rommel recovered from his wounds, which, thanks to his exceptional toughness and fitness, he now showed the first signs of doing.

From July 19, when they captured Saint-Lô, until July 25, the U.S. First Army sat miserably in the rain awaiting the weather improvement that would enable General Bradley to launch the offensive that should have started the day after Montgomery's at Caen on the 18th. It could not start until the weather had improved sufficiently for the Allied air forces to provide the preliminary bombardment that was to precede it. Bradley, as frustrated as his men, had to postpone the offensive from day to day hoping that next day the weather would improve. By July 25 there had been a sufficient drying out for the attack to be definitely scheduled for the following day. On July 26, therefore, between 9:40 A.M. and midday there was unloosed on the Saint-Lô sector of the German line the most devastating bombardment that had yet been seen in Normandy. Some 2500 aircraft were in action that morning including 1600 Fortresses. The brunt of this annihilating bomb carpet four miles deep was borne by General Bayerlein's Panzer Lehr Division (a once crack formation made up of the demonstration battalions of some of the main panzer schools and therefore superbly equipped, but by now reduced by a month's non-stop combat to half its strength). This was how the American bombardment was described by General Bayerlein:[3]

> Units holding the front were almost completely wiped out, despite, in many cases, the best possible equipment of tanks, anti-tank guns and self-propelled guns. Back and forth the bomb carpets were laid, artillery positions were wiped out, tanks overturned and buried, infantry positions flattened and all roads and

tracks destroyed. By midday the entire area resembled a moon landscape, with the bomb craters touching rim to rim, and there was no longer any hope of getting out any of our weapons. All signal communications had been cut and no command was possible. The shock effect on the troops was indescribable. Several of the men went mad and rushed dementedly round in the open until they were cut down by splinters.

Then the Americans advanced through the hideous chaos their own airmen had made—so close was the bombing that it had killed a hundred of the soldiers it was supposed to be helping—and it was now that an hitherto unknown non-commissioned officer of Major General Edward H. Brooks' 2nd Armored Division added his modest sentence to the pages of American military history.

To all the Allied soldiers the Normandy *bocage* or hedge-row country had come as an unpleasant and baffling surprise. To the Americans particularly the crisscross of hedgerows, banks, ditches, and sunken lanes had become intolerable because they had never experienced anything like it in their own country. It was a texture and form of landscape that they had not previously known existed. Tanks that tried to force their way through the hedgerows usually ended with the front half of their unarmoured bellies projecting upwards for the German gunners, lurking in the adjacent ditches, to pick off at their leisure; while the tank's own guns, sticking helplessly up in the air, could engage nothing and nobody. Nor could the four-foot banks be easily crumbled because the age-toughened roots of the ancient hedges bound them with iron sinews. The Americans had developed a terrible hatred of the hedgerows and never more so than during the seven miserable days that had just passed. If there is one thing for the combat soldier worse than waiting day after day for a big attack to begin, it is to be cold and soaked to the skin while doing so.

One of the outstanding military virtues of the American soldier is a natural gift for improvisation, especially where machinery is concerned. Among those who brooded on the obstructive nature of the hedgerow country was Sergeant Curtis J. Culin of 2nd Armored who, after a certain amount of experiment, came up with an idea which was brought to the notice of his commanding general, and then of General Bradley himself who called for a demonstration and was delighted by it. Sergeant Culin's idea was to weld eight sharpened steel "tusks" to the lower front of a Sherman tank two feet above the ground. A rhinoceros (as these modified Shermans were inevitably called) could charge a hedgerow at 10-15 miles an hour and hack, slash, and batter its way through the severed roots and loosened earth with little loss of speed, while the following tanks could then enlarge the gaps. In the process a "rhino" festooned itself with enough Norman foliage to give it an unrivalled suit of camouflage for its next halt.

Quartermasters do not of course carry large stores of steel blades to cater for the whims of imaginative sergeants. But, by the grace of Rommel, the Normandy beaches were still sprouting thousands of lengths of railroad track that had been planted there as obstacles to cut up Allied landing craft but could now be adapted to cutting up the configuration of the Norman countryside instead. The delighted Bradley ordered his tank workshops to modify as many Shermans as possible.

The rhino would be his "secret weapon" for the break-out. The maddening, tantalizing, heart-breaking Normandy *bocage* had turned out to be an unexpectedly strong inner wall of Fortress Europe. It would not remain intact much longer. The outer wall had been shattered and penetrated. Now it was the turn of the inner. This was the climax. The tall, taciturn professional soldier, Bradley, a general who eschewed showmanship and superfluous talk, was now going to break the last crust of the German defences in Normandy. The First Army began to advance south through the rubble of obliterated Saint-Lô and through the four-mile zone saturated by the air forces, only to find, as always, that the defenders had not been completely wiped out; that there were still enough stubborn survivors to fight back. The rhino-Shermans were soon tearing their way through the hedgerows to give the American armour a mobility it had not yet experienced in this country. Too late von Kluge ordered two panzer divisions from the Caen sector to make a forced march west to meet the new American thrust. They were to seize at all costs the key road junction and coastal bottleneck of Avranches in the elbow of the Bay of Mont-Saint-Michel near the Normandy-Brittany boundary. For three days it was hard fighting. Then the German front collapsed. Bradley had broken through. Blaming LXXXIV Corps for the collapse of the German left wing, von Kluge sacked its commander and the Army Chief of Staff and took command of Seventh Army himself. Disintegration was now setting in. The exhausted Seventh Army could hold out no longer no matter how much Hitler exhorted them to do so. Bradley had broken out of the bridgehead and soon the trickle through the gap would become a flood. The climax was near. The two panzer divisions on their way from the Caen front were being attacked from the air all the way. It was a desperate race to reach Avranches before the Americans.

Hundreds of utterly demoralized prisoners were now being picked up by the Americans. On July 30 the U.S. VIII Corps (under command of General George S. Patton's Third Army) sent its 4th Armored Division tanks racing through the gap on the coast where the German left wing had collapsed and by dusk on that evening they were in Avranches. The panzers on their way to prevent just this had not yet arrived. In a near-hysterical state of nervous excitement the unfortunate von Kluge (now acting as Seventh Army Commander as well as C-in-C Army Group B and C-in-C West) told his Chief of Staff at Western Command:[4] "The situation here is completely farcical . . . yesterday I took charge of the corps and the army . . . Things are in a gigantic mess here . . . the infantry have completely disintegrated and the troops are no longer fighting properly. They are putting up a wretched show." Far away at OKW Jodl, at last facing the inevitable, was ordering plans for a withdrawal to be prepared, though Hitler still fatuously raved about no withdrawal in any circumstances.

So Bradley, playing the "straight" part, created the opening at the end of July. The scene was set for Patton, the temperamental prima donna, to race through it and for a time take over the centre of the stage with his brilliant exploitation of the opportunity that Bradley had provided.

Patton was the most colourful as well as, within limits, the most dynamic American battle commander who served in the European and Mediterranean Theatres. Like Montgomery in the British Army he was brusque, opinionated, idiosyncratic, and flamboyant, with little talent for being an ally and a considerable talent for upsetting people and provoking controversy. There the similarity between these two lively personalities—otherwise totally dissimilar—ended. Patton had gone to Sicily as commander of the U.S. Seventh Army with Bradley as one of his corps commanders. At the end of that campaign he had been involved in two notorious incidents in which he had slapped unwounded soldiers in hospital, accusing them of malingering, and had been disciplined for this action by General Eisenhower as well as by the American press. Now their roles were reversed. It was Patton who was Bradley's subordinate—as Commanding General of the Third Army which from August 1 joined General Courtney H. Hodges' First Army to form Bradley's 12 Army Group. Bradley, the steadier, maturer and more balanced character had graduated naturally and without fuss to the Army Group level, while Patton (whose faults were as pronounced as his military virtues) had been accurately assessed by his superiors for what he was, a superb battle commander of a tank army; the nearest approach to an Allied Guderian; but lacking the balanced character and military intellect for the higher direction of a group of armies.

Patton, who sported a pearl-handled pistol on either hip, was a product of the U.S. Cavalry tradition which derives from American frontier days, the opening up of the West, and the crucible of the Civil War. Like the German panzer generals—notably Guderian and von Kleist, who had outclassed and utterly bewildered the untrained Russian hordes in the early months of the Eastern campaign and again in the summer of 1942 before they were stopped on the Don and the Volga—Patton had the same panache and swashbuckling disregard of such basic military pedantry as securing his flanks and pausing for his administration to catch up. He believed in going like a thunderbolt for his objective without pausing for anyone or anything until it was reached. The superabundance of Allied material on this occasion and the American aptitude for servicing as well as getting the utmost use out of gasoline-driven machinery made it easier for Patton to subordinate all considerations to bold action, leaving the administration to look after itself.

As Patton and his fresh Third Army made their spectacular first appearance on the scene by seizing the Avranches bottleneck before von Kluge could stop them, the grand design approached its grand dénouement. Montgomery's British and Canadian armies had drawn the greater part of the German armoured strength to the Caen front and kept it there by engaging it in repeated attritional battles intended to bleed and weaken it. Simultaneously General Hodges' First Army on the western sector of the line had fought its equally constant battles of attrition in the Saint-Lô area to achieve a breakthrough. The breakthrough had now been achieved and Patton and his Third Army had emerged from hiding fresh and eager to charge through the opening. The last stage of Montgomery's design had been reached. Caen, which he called the eastern bastion, would now become the hinge of a great turning movement. The whole front would now start swinging south and then east with the Americans making the turn from the west of the line and the British and Canadians holding firm at the hinge and then conforming with the American move as it developed. It had not gone entirely according to schedule; war seldom does except in the unrealistic dreams of armchair strategists whose calculations always presuppose superb weather, predictable terrain, and soldiers uniformly fresh and brave; but it had gone according to plan. The hard, unrewarding task of setting up the last phase had been completed by Montgomery and Bradley and their armies working closely together. It was now for Patton to score the goals and carry off the prize. In war, as in many games, this is often the way.

A single road runs south along the coast from Avranches to Pontaubault, five miles away, from which three roads fan out into Brittany and southern Normandy. Patton did not stop in Avranches to visit the botanical gardens or admire the scenery—Mont-Saint-Michel in the bay is a favourite attraction for tourists—he sent the Third Army troops through the five-mile bottleneck into Brittany as fast as they could go. In a desperate attempt to frustrate the breakthrough, the German Third Air Fleet used its entire remaining bomber force in suicidal but unavailing efforts to destroy the bridges which carry the single road over two rivers. The American tank and infantry divisions poured through in an endless stream all day and all night; no one, from Patton downwards, giving a thought to anything but to keep the stream moving and moving fast. Flanks were disregarded, air attacks ignored; vehicle dispersion was forgotten, traffic control was concerned only to keep the columns moving. In three days and nights Patton moved seven divisions through the bottleneck to Pontaubault where they fanned out and began to overrun Brittany.

The German left wing from Saint-Lô to Saint-Malo had given way and was now reduced to disconnected pockets of defenders holding out on their own or waiting to give themselves up. In a telephone call to OKW von Kluge described to Jodl the chaotic situation, strongly urging the formation of a new line of defence along the Seine. He asked for an appointment with Hitler so that he could try to convince him that this was now the only hope.

Hitler replied with a written order that the Americans were on no account to be allowed to break out. Army Group B was to withdraw all its panzer divisions from the line to form a counterattack force which would then attack and retake Avranches and block the American exit. Von Kluge protested that the withdrawal of the panzers would result in a collapse of the whole line. He was overruled and while Patton was already streaming south from Avranches into Brittany, the panzer divisions were disengaged from the front with difficulty; and with even greater difficulty moved across to the area east of Mortain twenty miles southeast of Avranches. It took six days to assemble the counterattack force east of Mortain. Not only did the front have to be adjusted to fill the gaps that the departing panzers would leave, but the divisions were delayed and depleted by constant air attacks while on the move.

Even so, if fresh divisions at full strength had been available to make the attack against what was by now an extended and vulnerable American flank, the Mortain counterattack on Avranches might have made sense. But these German divisions had been systematically mauled out of all recognition by weeks of hard fighting on the Caen front. Either in tanks or men none was up to more than half strength. Against the unequal odds they had fought as hard and as bravely as could be expected of any men. But they were exhausted, short of equipment, and in no state to make what was to be the last do-or-die counterattack of the Normandy battle.

The counterattack force was under the command of General Eberhart, now commanding Fifth Panzer Army. It was not ready to attack until August 7, by which time Patton's tanks were rampaging with little opposition through Brittany, and all that was showing of them was their long line of communications through the Avranches bottleneck to their rear echelons and General Hodges' First Army. Hodges was making a short wheel east to protect Third Army's rear and begin to squeeze the remainder of Army Group B eastward inside a pocket rapidly forming between Bradley's 12th and Montgomery's 21st Army Group now starting to push southward towards Falaise.

The German counterattack, forcefully led by 2nd Panzer Division followed by what was left of three other armoured divisions, opened early in the morning of August 7 under cover of a thick mist. Eberhart took Mortain and was halfway to Avranches and moving well when the mist cleared, leaving his tanks exposed to the Allied air forces which arrived overhead within a few minutes. Relays of fighters and bombers began a systematic destruction of the counterattacking force which was soon stopped; not the least of its over-whelming difficulties being a new Royal Air Force fighter called the Typhoon which carried an armament of eight sixty-pound rockets and was the most devastating tank-destroyer that had yet been produced by either side. Eberhart could make no further progress but he was ordered by Hitler to renew the attack on the following day. To give him protection three hundred fighters were ordered to cover the second day's operations. It made no difference. They were driven off or destroyed before they could reach the battle zone. The counterattack fared no better on the second day than it had done on the first. The First Army had adjusted its positions to protect the flank of the southward-speeding Third and, with the support of another maximum effort by the air forces, had no great difficulty in holding and finally stopping Eberhart's resumed advance. The odds were too great. The last German counterattack in Normandy had failed.

Having overrun most of a virtually defenceless Brittany at the double, Patton was ordered by Bradley to turn the Third Army east and drive towards Alençon and Le Mans while the American and Anglo-Canadian pincers began their methodical annihilation of the broken remnants of the German Seventh, Fifteenth, and Fifth Panzer Armies in the pocket where they were now trapped near Falaise. Fortress Europe had been broken wide open and through the gap tanks and trucks and guns without end were racing in a demented flood to the kill.

Patton was moving faster now, heedless of flanks, heedless of administration, heedless of groups that tried to resist, heedless of strongpoints that could be sped past and left for others to clean up, heedless of gasoline so long as it arrived, heedless of Allies to right or to left so long as they did not get in his way; concerned only with his precious Third Army (to whom all roads now belonged by divine right) and the way ahead to the heart of France. Patton was following the dictum of Guderian that "the objective of the armoured division is the enemy capital."

The *bocage* of Normandy was far to the rear and already forgotten. Bradley's rhinoceros-Shermans, so important a few days before, were already as obsolete as the scythes on Boadicea's chariot wheels. Nothing could stop Patton now. The Third Army was in overdrive and the gasoline was there.

For Hitler August was proving a terrible month and there was worse to come. On the 20th the Russians made a major breakthrough in the South Ukraine, crippling two German and two Rumanian armies. Bulgaria had had enough and on August 24 sought an armistice with the U.S.S.R. Rumania had had enough and on the following day the people deposed their dictator, Ion Antonescu—Hitler losing not only an ally but, a more grievous loss at this critical time, the great Ploesti oilfields. There was insurrection in occupied Czechoslovakia; Finland was about to defect and seek a separate peace with Russia. The Germans were retreating on the Italian front. The Soviet armies were fast approaching East Prussia and the Wolf's Lair itself; the Wolf would shortly require a new lair.

In the East, in the West, in the South the monstrous myth of Fortress Europe was disintegrating in the ashes and rubble of its own arrogant presumption.

This was the end of Hitler's Fortress Europe, though it was not the end of the war. That was to be deferred for another nine months. The fortress was disintegrating everywhere and Paris was French again before the end of the month. But Germany, the citadel, and Berlin, the last keep, had still to be taken. The agony and the death throes would have to go on for three-quarters of a year longer before the bombing of the people and the killing of the soldiers stopped; before Hitler and Goebbels shot themselves in the flames of a stricken, burning Berlin; before his criminal accomplices Himmler and Goering, cut down at last to size in Allied custody, cheated the hangman's rope by taking poison. Trapped between the Allied folly of Unconditional Surrender on the one hand, and, on the other, the callous vindictive sentence of death imposed on them by their Führer for losing his war, the German soldiers fought on to the last hopeless days with a desperate bravery that can only be described as astonishing: achieving in defeat a manifestation of courage that in the long run may seem more memorable than the military virtuosity of the early blitzkrieg victories against enemies still untrained. The soldiers, too, were Hitler's victims and it was they who in the end paid the heaviest price; and in the process restored to German arms some of the pride and honour that their manic Führer had so debased and tarnished.

Not only the soldiers but the people in the burning devastated cities endured bravely to the last the final and terrible nine-months' expiation of whatever share of the Nazi guilt was theirs. "Only on the firm foundation of unyielding despair can the soul's habitation henceforth be safely built." The philosopher Bertrand Russell wrote these words when he was a young man of thirty-one. They may be thought to have some relevance to how these same German people were to undergo a rebirth and renascence within only ten years of the war's end: a recovery beyond the capacity of most of the victors.

Patton's tanks, swirling through France like a tidal wave—Nemesis in olive drab armour—were sounding the first strident bars of this agonizing, elegiac finale. But they were something more than that.

They were the outriders for America's return to the council chambers of Europe.

They were the pulsing plasma of the New World injecting new vitality into the tired bloodstream of the Old.

They were the symbol of a new American military tradition tempered in battle and an essential adjunct to the new world responsibilities that America was now destined to assume. They were the free world's hope that the Pax Britannica, now due for retirement, would be replaced by a Pax Americana and not by a Pax Slavonica.

Patton's tanks were grinding into the dust of a torn and bleeding Europe the tablets of the long outdated Monroe Doctrine.

Patton's speeding, exultant, unstoppable tanks were hustling America back into Europe in an intimate association that would have been unthinkable a generation earlier; a new and different Europe that, looking ahead, was for the first time beginning to think of itself as an entity and not as a collection of quarrelsome states.

"This noble continent . . . is the origin of most of the culture, arts, philosophy and science of both ancient and modern times. If Europe were once united in the sharing of its common inheritance there would be no limit to the happiness, to the prosperity and glory which its three to four hundred million people would enjoy."

These words were addressed by Winston Churchill to a European audience at Zurich in 1946 in the course of one of the most celebrated of his postwar speeches, when the great war leader was looking ahead to new horizons of peace and hope. "If Europe were once united . . ."

It is perhaps the final and supreme irony of these times that it took Adolf Hitler to convince the Europeans that there might, after all, be something in this idea.

NOTES

Part One

CHAPTER ONE
1. Walter Warlimont, *Inside Hitler's Headquarters*.
2. Ibid.
3. Alan Bullock, *Hitler*.
4. Robert E. Sherwood, *Roosevelt and Hopkins: An Intimate History*.
5. Bullock, *op. cit.*, quoting Tippelskirch.

CHAPTER TWO
1. Halder's *Diary*.
2. Warlimont, *op. cit.*
3. Ciano's *Diary*.
4. Warlimont, *op. cit.*
5. The Goebbels Diaries.

CHAPTER THREE
1. B. H. Liddell Hart, *The Other Side of the Hill*.
2. Ibid.
3. General Heinz Guderian, *Panzer Leader*.
4. Liddell Hart, *op. cit.*
5. Guderian, *op. cit.*
6. Alan Clark, *Barbarossa*.
7. Guderian, *op. cit.*
8. Halder's *Diary*.
9. Liddell Hart, *op. cit.*

CHAPTER FOUR
1. General Guenther Blumentritt, *Von Rundstedt: The Soldier and the Man*.
2. *Hitler's War Directives,* ed. H. R. Trevor-Roper.
3. Blumentritt, *op. cit.*

CHAPTER FIVE
1. The Goebbels Diaries.
2. Warlimont, *op. cit.*

3. Sir Arthur Bryant, *The Turn of the Tide* (quoting the *Alanbrook Diaries*.)
4. Ciano's *Diary*.

CHAPTER SIX
1. The Goebbels Diaries.
2. Warlimont, *op. cit.*
3. The American for an earlier Second Front in Europe is skillfully, if unconvincingly, argued by Trumbull Higgins in *Winston Churchill and the Second Front.*
4. Churchill, *Second World War,* Vol. IV.

CHAPTER SEVEN
1. Ross Munro, *Gauntlet to Overlord.*
2. Narrative of Dieppe Raid based mainly on Canadian Official History, *The Canadian Army at War 1939-45* by C. P. Stacey; *Dieppe: The Dawn of Decision* by Jacques Mordal; *Dieppe: The Shame and the Glory* by Terence Robertson.

Part Two

CHAPTER EIGHT
1. *Rommel Papers,* ed. B. H. Liddell Hart.
2. Rommel, *op. cit.*
3. Ibid.
4. Ibid.
5. Ibid.
6. Ibid.
7. Ibid.
8. Narrative and statistics from Rommel, *op. cit.*; British official figures; *The Battle of El Alamein,* by Fred Majdalany.

CHAPTER NINE
1. Statement to Liddell Hart after the war, *The Other Side of the Hill, op. cit.*
2. Alexander Werth, *Russia at War 1941-45.*
3. Walter Goerlitz, *Paulus and Stalingrad.*
4. Ibid.
5. Personal details Paul Carell, *Hitler Moves East 1941-43.*

CHAPTER TEN
1. Halder's *Diary* quoted by Goerlitz, *op. cit.*
2. Goerlitz, *op. cit.*
3. Ibid.
4. Ibid.
5. V. I. Chuikov, *The Battle for Stalingrad.*
6. Goerlitz, *op. cit.*
7. Ibid.
8. Werth, *op. cit.*
9. Chuikov, *op. cit.*

CHAPTER ELEVEN
1. Rommel, *op. cit.*
2. Ciano, *op. cit.*
3. Rommel, *op. cit.*
4. Ibid.
5. Ibid.

CHAPTER TWELVE
1. Rommel, *op. cit.*
2. Ibid.
3. Ibid.
4. Ibid.
5. Ibid.
6. Ibid.

Part Three

CHAPTER THIRTEEN
1. Ciano's *Diary.*
2. Official British *History of the Second World War: Mediterranean & Middle East, Vol. IV,* I. S. O. Playfair & C. J. C. Molony.
3. Walter Warlimont, *The Decision in the Mediterranean 1942* in *Decisive Battles of World War II: The German View,* ed. Hans-Adolf Jacobsen & Jurgen Rohwer.
4. Playfair & Molony, *op. cit.*
5. Ibid.
6. Ibid.
7. Details of Tiger and Focke-Wolfe from Playfair & Molony, *op. cit.*
8. Rommel, *op. cit.*

CHAPTER FOURTEEN
1. Hans Rumpf, *The Bombing of Germany*.
2. Ibid.
3. B. H. Liddell Hart, *The Revolution in Warfare*.

CHAPTER FIFTEEN
1. Trans. Franz Schneider & Charles Gullans, *Last Letters From Stalingrad*, first published in Germany under title *Letzte Briefe Aus Stalingrad*.
2. Goerlitz, *op. cit.*
3. Fragment No. 47 Führer Conferences, shorthand notes.

CHAPTER SIXTEEN
1. Churchill, *op. cit.*
2. Ibid.
3. Warlimont, *Inside Hitler's Headquarters*.
4. Rommel, *op. cit.*
5. Ibid.
6. Ibid.
7. Ibid.
8. Ibid.
9. Ibid.
10. Ibid.

CHAPTER SEVENTEEN
1. Field-Marshal Albert Kesselring, *Memoirs*.
2. Playfair & Molony, *op. cit.*

Part Four

CHAPTER EIGHTEEN
1. Warlimont, *op. cit.*
2. Jürgen Rohwer, *The U-Boat War against the Allied Supply Lines* in *Decisive Battles of World War II: The German View*. ed. Hans-Adolf Jacobsen & Jurgen Rohwer.
3. Marshal of the Royal Air Force Sir Arthur Harris, *Bomber Offensive*.
4. Rohwer, *op. cit.*
5. General von Senger und Etterlin, *Neither Hope Nor Fear*.
6. Senger und Etterlin, *op. cit.*
7. Kesselring, *op. cit.*

8. Factual basis of origins and evolution of Operation Citadel, Alan Clark, *Barbarossa*.
9. Guderian, *op. cit.*
10. Ibid.
11. Ibid.

CHAPTER NINETEEN
1. Kesselring, *op. cit.*
2. Ibid.
3. L. F. Ellis (official British) *History of the Second World War, Victory in the West, Vol. I.*
4. Churchill, *op. cit.*
5. Hamburg facts and figures Rumpf, *op. cit.*
6. Harris, *op. cit.*
7. Ibid.
8. Ibid.
9. Hamburg figures Rumpf, *op. cit.*
10. Harris, *op. cit.*

CHAPTER TWENTY
1. Rudolf Bohmler, *Monte Cassino.*
2. Fully described in Christopher Hibbert's *Mussolini.*
3. Hibbert, *op. cit.*
4. Ibid.
5. Ibid.
6. Kesselring *Memoirs, op. cit.*
7. Ibid.
8. Ibid., and Bohmler, *op. cit.*
9. Churchill, *op. cit. Vol. V.*
10. Ibid.
11. Bohmler, *op. cit.;* Kesselring, *op. cit.*
12. Bohmler, *op. cit.*
13. Churchill, *op. cit.*
14. General Dwight D. Eisenhower, *Crusade in Europe.*
15. Churchill, *op. cit.*
16. Eisenhower, *op. cit.*
17. Kesselring, *op. cit.;* General Siegfried Westphal, *The German Army in the West.*

CHAPTER TWENTY-ONE
1. Chester Wilmot, *The Struggle for Europe.*
2. Major General J. F. C. Fuller, *The Second World War.*
3. Churchill, *op. cit.*
4. Ibid.

5. The Goebbels Diaries.
6. Wilmot, *op. cit.*
7. Trevor-Roper, *op. cit.*
8. Basil Collier, *The Battle of the V-Weapons.*
9. Harris, *op. cit.*
10. Rumpf, *op. cit.*
11. Harris, *op. cit.*, but N.B. with losses during same period in night attacks other than against Berlin the total was nearly double Harris's figure of three hundred.
12. Noble Frankland, *The Bombing Offensive against Germany.*
13. Facts relating to development of Mustang; Frankland, *op. cit.*

Part Five

CHAPTER TWENTY-TWO

1. Wilmot, *op. cit.*
2. Rommel Papers, *op. cit.*
3. Blumentritt, *op. cit.*

CHAPTER TWENTY-THREE

1. Rommel, *op. cit.*
2. Ibid.
3. Blumentritt, *op. cit.*
4. Ibid.
5. Rommel, *op. cit.*
6. Geyr von Schweppenburg, *The Critical Years.*
7. Rommel, *op. cit.*
8. Warlimont, *Inside Hitler's Headquarters.*

CHAPTER TWENTY-FOUR

1. *Rommel Papers.*
2. Ibid.
3. Senger und Etterlin, *op. cit.*
4. Ibid.

CHAPTER TWENTY-FIVE

1. General Sir Harold Alexander, *Special Order of the Day.*

CHAPTER TWENTY-SIX

1. Continually advocated by, among others, Rommel and Jodl.
2. General von Senger in a conversation with the author.
3. Churchill, *op. cit.*
4. Senger und Etterlin, *op. cit.*
5. Major General Sir Howard Kippenberger, *Infantry Brigadier.*
6. Field Marshal Lord Alexander in his C-in-C Report on the campaign submitted in 1947.
7. Senger und Etterlin, *op. cit.*
8. Ibid.
9. Lieutenant General L. K. Truscott, Jr., *Command Missions.*
10. General Mark W. Clark, *Calculated Risk.*

CHAPTER TWENTY-SEVEN

1. Lieutenant General Fritz Bayerlein, editorial contrib. *Rommel Papers.*
2. Lieutenant General Dr. Hans Speidel, *We Defended Normandy.*

CHAPTER TWENTY-EIGHT

1. Eisenhower, *op. cit.*
2. Ibid.
3. Rommel Papers, *op. cit.*
4. L. F. Ellis, *op. cit.*
5. Warlimont, *op. cit.*
6. Rommel Papers, *op. cit.*
7. Figures given by Ellis in Official History, *op. cit.*
8. Rommel Papers, *op. cit.*

CHAPTER TWENTY-NINE

1. Speidel, *op. cit.*
2. Ibid. and Rommel Papers, *op. cit.*
3. Speidel, *op. cit.:* Wilmot, *op. cit.*
4. Werth, *op. cit.*
5. Speidel, *op. cit.:* Wilmot, *op. cit.*
6. Wilmot, *op. cit.:* corroborated by General Blumentritt in statement to Wilmot and Liddell Hart.
7. Speidel, *op. cit.*
8. Ibid.
9. Ibid.
10. Ibid.

CHAPTER THIRTY
1. Wilmot, *op. cit.*
2. Details from Desmond Young, *Rommel.*
3. Wilmot, *op. cit.:* Ellis, *op. cit.*

CHAPTER THIRTY-ONE
1. Constantine Fitzgibbon, *The Shirt of Nessus.*
2. Narrative of July 20 based on Fitzgibbon's account in
   The Shirt of Nessus.

CHAPTER THIRTY-TWO
1. Wilmot, *op. cit.*
2. Admiral Friedrich Ruge, *The Invasion of Normandy*
   in *Decisive Battles of World War II* (ed. Jacobsen
   & Rohwer).
3. Bayerlein in Rommel Papers, *op. cit.*
4. Ellis, *op. cit.*

A NOTE ON SOURCES

☐ The wages of victory and defeat are various. At the end of
the Second World War they included the removal to Washington of the greater part of the relevant German archives
and records: an action of the victors perhaps more justifiable in terms of protective custody than of historiographic
ethics. As a result Germany is alone among the leading
participants in the war in not having yet produced her official history of it. Conversely Allied historians, having had
the benefit of access to these documents, have by this time
been able to produce nearly all their scheduled official histories giving full and mostly objective weight to the German
side of events. To speak of those with which I am most
familiar, the British official histories have made excellent
and unbiassed use of the German papers and have conse-
quently been able to give a picture of events that is rounded
and impartial. These sound and well-written histories contrast markedly with the unreadable chronicles laboriously
compiled by the official historians of the First World War,
who laboured interminably at their task for years afterwards
and, indeed, had not completed it by the time the Second
World War had started.

Despite the difficulty of being deprived of so many of
their records, the Germans have nevertheless succeeded in
producing a large volume of valuable contributions to the
history of Hitler's war, ranging from the balanced and scholarly writings of Walter Goerlitz, Hans-Adolf Jacobsen, Jürgen Rohwer, and other historians, to the best of the generals'
reports and memoirs and to such works as General Walter
Warlimont's invaluable journal of day-to-day life at Hitler's
Supreme Headquarters written from his privileged vantage
point as Assistant Chief of Operations to General Alfred
Jodl.

Despite the conflicting emotional pressures and torn loyal-
ties under which they must have been written, the personal
accounts of Field-Marshals von Mannstein and Rommel and
General Guderian (to name the three outstanding ones) are

all notable and balanced additions to a genre of which I suppose Xenophon and Julius Caesar can be called the founders.

Italian sources are not numerous but the Diary of Mussolini's son-in-law and Foreign Minister Count Ciano, with its tart and faintly ribald commentary on the personalities and events of the Fascist-Nazi era up to 1943 (when he fell from grace and was eventually executed), is not only an indispensable source book but entertainingly manifests a strong vein of humour as refreshing as it is unusual to find in the prominent figures of these times.

Russian sources are unsatisfactory mainly because of the Soviet predilection for adapting the facts of history to suit whatever regime happens to be in power at the time. This trendy approach to history reached its ultimate and epitomizing absurdity when, after Stalin's death and discrediting, the name of Russia's most unforgettable battle honour was changed by the new regime to the utterly forgettable Volvograd. For the purpose of this volume I have relied where it is relevant on Marshal Chuikov's account of the Stalingrad battle which impresses one as a soldierly report by a plain front-line soldier, a report without frills and with minimal propagandist heroics. No one in or out of Russia is likely to see in Chuikov a potential Dostoievsky. His plain account of a stirring occasion is the more convincing because of it.

The other valuable Russian source for the Western reader is Alexander Werth's monumental journalistic work *Russia at War 1941-45*. Werth, a Russian-born journalist who emigrated to England after the Revolution and became a regular contributor to British and American journals, spent the war years in Moscow as the accredited correspondent of the London *Sunday Times* and the British Broadcasting Corporation. His *Russia at War* (and, to a lesser extent, his *The Year of Stalingrad*) may be journalism rather than academic history, but it is about as good an account as the Western reader is likely to find of what the war was like from the Russian point of view.

SHORT BIBLIOGRAPHY

German Sources

BLUMENTRITT, General Guenther. *Von Rundstedt: The Soldier and the Man.* London: Odham's 1952.

BÖHMLER, Colonel Rudolf. *Monte Cassino.* (Trans. R. H. Stevens.) London: Cassell 1964.

CARELL, Paul. *Hitler Moves East 1941-43.* Boston: Little, Brown 1964.

GALLAND, General Adolf. *The First and the Last: The Rise and Fall of the German Fighter Forces 1938-45.* New York: Holt 1954.

GEYR VON SCHWEPPENBURG, General Baron. *The Critical Years.* London: Wingate 1952.

GOEBBELS, Dr. Joseph Paul. *The Goebbels Diaries 1942-43.* (Trans. and ed. Louis P. Lochner.) New York: Doubleday 1948.

GOERLITZ, Walter. *Paulus and Stalingrad.* New York: Citadel 1963, London: Methuen 1963.

GUDERIAN, General Heinz. *Panzer Leader.* (Trans. Constantine Fitzgibbon) London: Michael Joseph 1952.

HALDER, General Franz. *Diary.*

HART, B. H. Liddell. *The Other Side of the Hill* (3rd edition revised and enlarged) London: Cassell 1951. Pub. in U.S.A. as *The German Generals Talk.*

————. *The Rommel Papers.* (Incl. contribs. by Frau Lucie-Maria Rommel, Manfred Rommel, General Fritz Bayerlein) London: Collins 1953.

HITLER, Adolf. *Table Talk 1941-44.* London: Oxford 1953.

JACOBSEN, H. A. & ROHWER, J. (Ed.) *Decisive Battles of World War II: The German View.* London: Deutsch 1965, including: *The U-Boat War against Allied Supply Lines,* by Dr. Jürgen Rohwer. *The Decision in the Mediterranean 1942* by General Walter Warlimont. *The Battle for Stalingrad* by Walter Goerlitz. *The Invasion of Normandy* by Admiral Friedrich Ruge.

KESSELRING, Field-Marshal Albert. *Memoirs.* London: William Kimber 1953.

MANNSTEIN, Field-Marshal Erich von. *Lost Victories*. Chicago: Henry Regnery 1950.

MELLENTHIN, General F. W. von. *Panzer Battles 1939-45*. London: Cassell 1955.

RUMPF, Hans. *The Bombing of Germany*. London: Muller 1963.

SCHMIDT, H. W. *With Rommel in the Desert*. London: Harrap 1951. New York: Dutton 1964.

SCHNEIDER, Franz and Gullans Charles (trans.) *Last Letters from Stalingrad*. New York: Morrow 1962; London: Methuen 1962; originally pub. in Germany by C. Bertelsmann Verlag (now Sigbert Mohn Verlag), Guetersloh: 1954.

SENGER UND ETTERLIN, General Frido von. *Neither Fear, Nor Hope*. (Memoirs). London: Macdonald 1963.

SHULMAN, Milton. *Defeat in the West*. London: Secker & Warburg 1947.

SPEIDEL, Lieutenant General Dr. Hans. *Invasion 1944*. Chicago: Henry Regnery 1950. Pub. in England (trans. Ian Colvin) as *We Defended Normandy*. London: Herbert Jenkins 1951.

TREVOR-ROPER, Professor H. R. (ed.) *Blitzkrieg to Defeat: Hitler's War Directives 1939-45*. New York: Holt, Rinehart & Winston 1965. London: Sidgwick & Jackson 1964. Texts of both above editions from Walter Hubatsch, *Hitlers Weisungen für die Kriegführung 1939-45*.

WARLIMONT, General Walter. *Inside Hitler's Headquarters 1939-45*. New York: Praeger 1964. London: Weidenfeld & Nicolson 1964.

WESTPHAL, General Siegfried. *The German Army in the West*. London: Cassell 1951.

B. H. Liddell Hart's *The Other Side of the Hill* and Milton Shulman's *Defeat in the West* are included as German sources because both works consist entirely of statements made by German generals at the end of the war under interrogation by these two authors.

Italian Sources

BADOGLIO, Marshal Pietro. *Italy and the Second World War*. London: Oxford University Press 1948.

CAVALLERO, Marshal Ugo. *Comando Supremo, Diario*. Bologna: 1948. Capelli Editore.

CIANO, Count Galeazzo. *Diary*. (Ed. Malcolm Muggeridge.) London: Heinemann 1947. (Ed. Hugh Gibson) New York: Doubleday 1946.

LECCISOTTI, Tommaso. *Montecassino: La Vita L'Irradiazione*. Florence: Vallecchi Editore 1947.

The Italian Official History of the Second World War.

Russian Sources

CHUIKOV, Marshal V. I. *The Battle for Stalingrad*. New York: Holt, Rinehart and Winston 1964. (Published in England as *The Beginning of the Road*. London: Macgibbon & Kee 1963.)

WERTH, Alexander. *The Year of Stalingrad*. London: Hamish Hamilton 1946. New York: Knopf 1947.

———. *Russia at War 1941–45*. London: Barrie & Rockliff 1964. New York: Dutton 1964.

American, British and Commonwealth Sources (Official)

Six Years of War: The Canadian Army 1939-45 (Colonel C. P. Stacey), Ottawa 1948.

Official History of New Zealand in Second World War, Wellington, New Zealand.

Report by Supreme Commander (General Dwight D. Eisenhower) to Combined Chiefs of Staff on Operations in Europe of Allied Expeditionary Force 6 June 1944-8 May 1945. London 1946.

Official History of the U.S. Army in World War II. Cross Channel Attack by Gordon Harrison. U.S. Govt. Printing Office.

U.S. Army Air Forces in World War II.

United States Strategic Bombing Survey. Over-all Report 1945.

History of the Second World War. United Kingdom Military Series.

Grand Strategy.

Vol. V (August 1943-September 1944) by John Ehrman.

Campaigns

> *The Mediterranean and Middle East. Vol. IV* by Major General I. S. O. Playfair (With Captain F. C. Flynn RN, Brigadier C. J. C. Molony, Group Captain T. P. Gleave.)
> *Victory in the West. Vol. I* by Major L. F. Ellis (with Captain G. R. G. Allen RN, Air Chief Marshal Sir James Robb, Lieutenant Colonel A. E. Warhurst.)
> *The War at Sea. Vols. I-III* by Captain S. W. Roskill RN.
> *The Strategic Air Offensive Vols. I-III* by Sir Charles Webster and Noble Frankland.

All published by Her Majesty's Station Office, London.

American, British and Commonwealth Sources (General)

BRADLEY, General Omar. *A Soldier's Story*. New York: Holt 1951.

BRYANT, Sir Arthur. *The Turn of the Tide* (London: Collins 1957) and *Triumph in the West* (Collins 1959) both based on the Diaries of Field Marshal Viscount Alanbrook.

BULLOCK, Alan. *Hitler: A Study in Tyranny*. London: Odhams 1952.

BUTCHER, Captain Harry C., USNR. *My Three Years with Eisenhower*. New York: Simon & Schuster 1946.

CHURCHILL, Winston S. *The Second World War Vols. IV, V, VI*. Boston: Houghton Mifflin 1951-53.

CLARK, Alan. *Barbarossa: The Russian-German Conflict 1941-45*. New York: Morrow 1965.

CLARK, General Mark W. *Calculated Risk*. New York: Harper 1950.

COLLIER, Basil. *The Battle of the V-Weapons 1944-45*. London: Hodder & Stoughton 1964.

CUNNINGHAM, Admiral of the Fleet Viscount. *A Sailor's Odyssey*. New York: Dutton 1951.

EISENHOWER, General Dwight D. *Crusade in Europe*. New York: Doubleday 1948.

FITZGIBBON, Constantine. *The Shirt of Nessus*. London: Cassell 1956.

FRANKLAND, Noble. *The Bombing Offensive against Germany*. London: Faber & Faber.

FULLER, Major General J. F. C. *The Second World War 1939-45*. London: Eyre & Spottiswoode 1948.

GOURE, Leon. *The Siege of Leningrad*. Stanford University Press 1962.

GUINGAND, Major General Sir Francis de. *Operation Victory*. New York: Scribner's 1947.

HARRIS, Marshal of the Royal Air Force Sir Arthur. *Bomber Offensive*. London: Collins 1947.

HART, B. H. Liddell. *The Revolution in Warfare*. London: Faber & Faber 1946.

HIBBERT, Christopher. *Mussolini*. London: Longmans 1962.

HIGGINS, Trumbull. *Winston Churchill and the Second Front*. New York: O.U.P.

ISMAY, General Lord. *Memoirs*. New York: Viking 1960.

KIPPENBERGER, Major General Sir Howard. *Infantry Brigadier*. London: O.U.P. 1949.

MAJDALANY, Fred. *The Battle of Cassino*. Boston: Houghton Mifflin 1958.

————. *The Battle of El Alamein*. Philadelphia: Lippincott 1965.

MONTGOMERY, Field Marshal Viscount. *Memoirs*. Cleveland, New York: World 1958.

MORDAL, Jacques. *Dieppe: The Dawn of Decision*. (Trans.) London: Souvenir Press 1963.

MORISON, Samuel Eliot. *History of U. S. Naval Operations in World War II*. Boston: Little, Brown 1954.

NORTH, John. *North-west Europe 1944-45*. London: H. M. Stationery Office 1953.

PATTON, General George S., Jr. *War As I Knew It*. Boston: Houghton Mifflin 1947.

ROBERTSON, Terence. *Dieppe: The Shame and the Glory*. London: Hutchinson 1963.

SHERWOOD, Robert E. *Roosevelt and Hopkins: An Intimate History*. New York: Harper 1948.

SHIRER, William L. *The Rise and Fall of the Third Reich*. New York: Simon and Schuster 1960.

TRUSCOTT, Lieutenant General L. K., Jr. *Command Missions*. New York: Dutton 1954.

WHEELER-BENNETT, Sir J. W. *Nemesis of Power: The German Army in Politics 1918-1945*. London: 1953.

WILMOT, Chester. *The Struggle for Europe*. New York: Harper 1952.

YOUNG, Desmond. *Rommel*. London: Collins 1950.

INDEX

INDEX

Abruzzi Mountains, 270

Acquarone, Pietro d', 246, 247, 248

Airplanes (See also Air Forces under specific countries; specific targets): B-17 Flying Fortresses, 237, 238, 278, 279; B-24 Liberators, 237, 238, 278, 279; Focke-Wolfes, 158, 159; Lancaster bombers, 237; P-51B Mustangs, 279; Typhoons, 381

Alam Halfa, 91-94, 122

Alençon, 381

Alexander, Sir Harold: in Italy, 233, 234, 236, 266, 267, 273, 282, 313, 321-25 passim; in Middle East, 85, 206, 208, 209

Alexandria, 56, 82, 84, 89

Algeria and Algerians, 148 ff., 315

Algiers, 149, 205

Allies (See also specific battles, commanders, countries, etc.): Strategic Air Force, 268 (See also specific targets); 12th Army Group, 338 (See also Bradley, Omar); 15th Army Group, 233 ff., 266 ff. (See also Alexander, Sir Harold); 18th Army Group, 206 ff. (See also Alexander, Sir Harold); 21st Army Group, 338 (See also Montgomery, Bernard Law, Viscount)

Alps, 269

Ambrosio, Vittorio, 203, 246, 247, 248, 251, 252

Antisubmarine Warfare Committee, 214-15

Antonescu, Ion, 192, 332

Anzio, 316, 320, 324

Apennines, 264, 272, 284

Arnim, Dietloff von, 196, 198 ff., 205 ff.

Arnold, Henry H., 279

Atlantic, Battle of the, 79, 215-17

Atlantic (West) Wall, 15-16, 18, 282-89, 299 ff., 310, 341, 347

Auchinleck, Sir Claude, 25, 58, 83, 88

Augusta, 233

Aurunci Mountains, 316

Australians, 70

Avranches, 308, 347, 376, 402 ff.

Axis (See also specific battles, countries, leaders): Panzer Army Afrika (German-Italian), 82-95, 124-25, 144-46, 198 ff. (See also Afrika Korps; Rommel, Erwin; specific battles)

Ayeta, Marchese, 251

B-17s. See under Airplanes

B-24s. See under Airplanes

Baade, General, 305-6

Badoglio, Pietro, 218, 245, 249 ff., 264; escapes, resigns, 261

Baedeker raids, 167-68

Balkans, 35, 40, 218, 272, 289

Baltic area, 15, 27, 28, 40

Barricades Artillery factory, 112-13

Bath, England, 167

Bayerlein, Fritz, 91, 93, 286, 302, 328, 374